The Self as Symbolic Space

Studies on the Texts of the Desert of Judah

VOLUME LII

EDITED BY
Florentino García Martínez

ASSOCIATE EDITORS
Peter W. Flint
Eibert J. C. Tigchelaar

THE SELF AS SYMBOLIC SPACE
Constructing Identity and Community at Qumran

The Self as Symbolic Space
Constructing Identity and Community at Qumran

Carol A. Newsom

Society of Biblical Literature
Atlanta

THE SELF AS SYMBOLIC SPACE

Library of Congress Cataloging-in-Publication Data

Newsom, Carol A. (Carol Ann), 1950–
  The self as symbolic space : constructing identity and community at Qumran
/ by Carol A. Newsom.
      p. cm.
  Originally published: Leiden ; Boston : Brill, 2004.
  Includes bibliographical references and index.
  ISBN 978-1-58983-298-5 (paper binding : alk. paper)
  1. Qumran community. 2. Hebrew language–Discourse analysis. 3. Hebrew
language–Religious aspects–Judaism. 4. Thanksgiving Psalms. 5. Manual of
discipline. I. Title.

BM175.Q6N49 2007
296.1'55–dc22   2007043702

Printed in the United States of America
on acid-free paper

For John Strugnell,

generous teacher and gracious mentor

CONTENTS

ACKNOWLEDGEMENTS

This book has had a rather long gestation. I began to pursue my interest in the rhetoric of the sectarian literature of Qumran in a series of articles published between 1990 and 1993. Other obligations required that I put the project on hold for several years, a delay that turned out to be fortuitous. Several works published in the 1990s, both in Qumran studies and in the socio-rhetorical analysis of cultures, helped me to refine my own understanding of what I sought to explore and the methods appropriate to it. My work has been supported throughout this period by a series of grants from the American Council of Learned Societies, the National Endowment for the Humanities, the Emory University Research Council, and by sabbatical leave from the Emory University School of Theology. For this support I am most grateful.

Portions of the arguments presented here have been published in different form in several books and journals: "Apocalyptic and the Discourse of a Sectarian Community," *Journal of Near Eastern Studies* 49 (1990): 135–44; "Kenneth Burke Meets the Teacher of Righteousness: Rhetorical Strategies in the Hodayot and the Serek ha-Yahad," pages 121–31 in *Of Scribes and Scrolls: Studies on the Hebrew Bible, Intertestamental Judaism, and Christian Origins* (1990; edited by H. Attridge, J. Collins, T. Tobin); "The Case of the Blinking I: Discourse of the Self at Qumran," pages 13–23 in *Semeia 57: Discursive Formations, Ascetic Piety and the Interpretation of Early Christian Literature*, Part 1 (1992; edited by V. Wimbush); "Knowing as Doing: the Social Symbolics of Knowledge at Qumran," pages 139–53 in *Semeia 59: Ideological Criticism of Biblical Texts* (1993; edited by D. Jobling and T. Pippin); "Apocalyptic Subjects: The Social Construction of the Self at Qumran," *Journal for the Study of the Pseudepigrapha* 12 (2001): 3–25. I thank the publishers for their permission to incorporate material from those articles in this volume.

I am also indebted to several people who aided and encouraged me during this long process, among them John Collins, Jean Duhaime, Eileen Schuller, and Larry Wills. Also deserving of thanks are the students in the graduate seminar that I taught as the ideas for this book were first developed. Their intellectual adventurousness and keen insight were a great stimulus to my own work. My research assistant, Amy Robertson, provided invaluable help in preparing the manuscript for publication. In this project, as in every other that I have undertaken, a special debt of gratitude is owed to my husband, Rex Matthews. Not only did he encourage me to bring this work to completion but he also shared generously of his own editorial expertise and computer savvy. One final person remains to be thanked—John Strugnell, who first introduced me to Qumran studies and who was generous beyond imagining as a teacher and mentor. To him I dedicate this book.

CHAPTER ONE

COMMUNITIES OF DISCOURSE

QUMRAN AS A COMMUNITY OF DISCOURSE

"I have something to say to the congregation" (1QS 6:13). With those words a member of the Qumran community would seek permission to speak, even though it was not his designated turn to address the assembly. Only if he received their agreement might he say what was on his mind. This moment, poised between speech and silence, permission and prohibition, focuses the crucial but problematic role of speech in this intensely verbal community. The description of the assembly in the Serek ha-Yahad (6:8–13) presents speech as an activity required of every member. It is an object of value to which the community has a right and which it needs to accomplish its common purpose. But speech is also subject to regulation, since it is implicated not only in truth but also in falsehood, deception, and hypocrisy. What is produced and refined in this process is not only the speech of an individual but more importantly the discourse of the community as a whole.

The essential activities that gave the Qumran community its identity are almost all associated with language. Its *raison d'être*, of course, was to do the will of God but the privileged repository of that will was a text that had to be copied, read, studied, and interpreted. This task was not conceived of as an individual one but as one that required the constitution of a community for its accomplishment. Because the Qumran community reflected self-consciously on the nature of its life together and embodied those reflections in texts, we know a significant amount about that life and the way in which it formed a community of discourse.

In a basic sense the community was constituted and maintained through speech acts. Members swore solemn oaths (1QS 5:8) and were separated from the larger society through a series of curses and blessings (2:1–10). The internal structure of the community was shaped in large measure by periodic examinations in which the ability to articulate the fundamental language of the community played a great

part (5:20–25). Prayer and blessing, mutual reproof, and delibera-
tion were all highly self-conscious parts of life together (5:25–6:8).
Even time itself was articulated through acts of praise (10:1–8). The
rich verbal culture of the Qumran community is evident not only
in the abundance of texts collected, copied, and preserved, but above
all in the creation of numerous compositions in familiar and in novel
genres: *serakim, hodayot, pesharim, shirot, berakot,* and so forth. Not
surprisingly, through all this intensive verbal activity the Qumran
community created for itself a distinctive mode of speech, one that
readers tend to recognize in the texts even when its precise definition
remains elusive.

Various sorts of questions could be pursued about the discourse
of the Qumran community. One is the role of speech in the community: why it was important, how it was regulated, what it accomplished in terms of the social life of the community, and so forth.
It is possible to ask this question because the texts, especially the
Serek ha-Yahad, talk explicitly about these things. To inquire into
how the members of the community talked with one another is to
ask a reconstructive question. It involves using the text as a lens to
look at something that lies behind the text, namely, the speech practices of the community. Of course, since one cannot check what the
text claims against one's own observations of the community as it
went about its business, what one may be reconstructing is not what
they actually did but what they thought they did, or intended to do,
or at the very least, what they said they ought to do. A second sort
of question involves looking not through the texts but at them. The
Qumran texts are themselves examples of speech practices. This is
obviously true for those texts that appear to contain scripts for speech
performances, such as prayers or liturgies. But if one construes speech
more generally as verbal utterances, whether written or oral, then
one may ask not only what the texts say about speech but what
kind of speech they are. This approach does not look at texts as
repositories of information only but also as an action performed with
words. It asks of the text "What does it do?" as well as "What does
it say?" Both sorts of inquiry—concerning the nature and function
of speech practices and concerning the rhetorical purposes of particular textual utterances—are essential for understanding the way in
which the Qumran community used language to constitute a world
of meaning, a distinctive identity, a community of values, and a
structure of selfhood.

Although all communities and sub-communities construct themselves in large measure through their discourse, the discourse of a sectarian community that draws its membership at least in part from adult converts tends to have distinctive features. The discourse of the Qumran community was not simply produced to maintain an established society but to create one that distinguished itself from other discursive communities within Second Temple Judaism. The need to create the sentiments of affinity and estrangement required for social boundaries and the need to offer a new identity to persons who had been previously formed in other communities set special conditions for discourse. The practices, verbal and otherwise, that serve to produce and reproduce social relations and identities in an established and dominant culture may be so thoroughly worked into the background hum of discourse as to be virtually inaudible; but for a sectarian community they will tend to be much more explicit. Nevertheless, though the Qumran community was a sectarian group, its discourse cannot be thought of as a sort of mumbling to itself. Nothing that was said at Qumran can be understood without reference to the larger discursive context of Second Temple Judaism. This is true not only for the obviously polemical statements in Qumran texts but also for every utterance. The words they used, the forms of speech, the content of their prayers, and the claims they made about themselves were always in part replies, responses, and counter-claims to utterances made by others within a broader cultural context. To understand the speech of Qumran one must also be alert to the currents of "cross-talk" in which it occurred.

CULTURE AS CONVERSATION

To analyze discourse is to investigate culture through the metaphor of conversation. It is an appealing metaphor, one that has cropped up frequently in cultural analysis.[1] It draws attention to the dialogical quality of social discourse. Each participant tries out ideas on others. But the conversation itself, what passes between persons, belongs neither to one nor the other but is a product of their

---

[1] See, e.g., Burke, *Philosophy of Literary Form*, 110–11; Oakeshott, *Voice of Poetry*, 10–14; Bakhtin, *Dialogic Imagination*, 278–85. See also the critical discussions in Lentricchia, *Criticism and Social Change*, 12–20; and Gunn, *Culture of Criticism*, 63–75.

interaction. The metaphor also stresses the dynamic, temporal element of culture and implies an open-ended quality. There is always some difference of opinion or perspective that moves things along. Conversations are not like Euclidian proofs; there is no theoretical point at which there is nothing more to say. The model of conversation also suggests creativity and even a degree of playfulness. Someone leaves, someone else comes up, and the conversation lurches off in an entirely new direction. It is a good model for culture in that it manages to indicate both its concrete and diffuse qualities. Culture consists of particular utterances yet the whole of the thing is never finished but is continuously in motion and divided among an indefinite number of participants.

The image of culture as conversation is heuristically valuable for thinking about Second Temple Judaism. One can treat the diverse cultural phenomena of Second Temple Judaism as a protracted discussion of the question, "What is it that really constitutes Israel?" Not every society is so preoccupied with a discourse of identity, but the peculiar historical circumstances of Second Temple Judaism brought that issue to the fore. Even when not explicitly engaged in responding to one another, the literary works, religious movements, new social institutions, emerging symbols, and so forth, ceaselessly suggested alternative ways of answering that question. Some, like the Qumran community and the early Jesus movement, even engaged in a kind of social theater, enacting communities of a reconstituted Israel.

Like all metaphors, the image of cultural discourse as conversation has its limitations. It can be misleadingly genteel. Discourse is about the formation of human communities through symbolic interchange, but it is also about the exercise of power within those communities. The image of conversation may obscure the element of struggle that is present in discursive practices. Moreover, the metaphor suggests an exchange among relative equals who all have a certain access to the attention of others. But the discourse of particular cultures is formed in significant ways by the exclusion and silencing of some groups within the society. One thinks of the position of the very poor, of women, of ethnic minorities, of the various categories of outsiders. The relationship is a complex one. Although the silenced may not be direct participants in the shaping of the topics, values, concepts, and symbols that are exchanged through the dominant media, they carry on their own discourse in the margins and interstices of a culture. In addition, these marginal discourses may also function to provide the necessary definitional other that makes a dominant discourse possible. The medieval aristocrat who lived in a world articulated by the discourse of feudalism might have been quite ignorant of the specific cultural world of the villein, but the highly self-conscious elaboration of aristocratic values was formed on the basis of a necessary symbolic distinction between what was base and what was noble. Although the marginalized social groups of brigands in early Roman Palestine had little direct access to the public media of discourse, they became an important definitional other in Josephus' own speech as he attempted to articulate an identity for Jewish society to a post-70 CE audience of gentiles and diaspora Jews.

The metaphor of conversation is also misleading in its suggestion of unproblematic fluency. Times do occur in which the inherited language of a culture can no longer be used with automatic ease and unself-consciousness. Where a language no longer suffices for the discursive situation, it has to be remade; with the remaking of the language comes the remaking of the world itself and those who live in it. This point is argued in the collection of essays by James Boyd White, *When Words Lose Their Meaning*. The title is taken from Thucydides, who assessed the meaning of the chaotic disruption of the Peloponnesian War by asserting that words themselves lost their meaning.[2] Thucydides' history is, at least in part, an examination of the failure of one language and the search for an alternative rhetoric adequate to provide a set of shared meanings for the Greek cities.

At first it might appear difficult to find clear instances of a troubled relationship with language in Second Temple Judaism. There are no self-conscious reflections on the failure of language as explicit as one finds in Thucydides. The problem does emerge in less direct ways, however. The multi-lingual context of Judaism certainly raised the issue, as one can see when one compares the defensive claims made about the adequacy of the Septuagint in a text like Pseudo-Aristeas with the apologetic disclaimers of Ben Sira's grandson for the inadequacies of all translation in the prologue to Sirach. Can the Jewish community articulate its traditions adequately in a nontraditional language? Anxiety about the susceptibility of speech to corruption is also an indicator of an uneasy relationship to language. Although

---

[2] White, *When Words Lose Their Meaning*, 59–92.

the issue of false speech is an ancient topic in wisdom literature,
texts of the Second Temple period develop the theme significantly.
The seductive and misleading speech of the strange woman and the
crooked man in the text of Proverbs 1–9, the self-deceiving reasoning
of the ungodly in Wisdom of Solomon 2, as well as the seductions
of the lying interpreters in the Hodayot are all examples. Moreover,
the opacity of language, at least of divinely inspired language, emerges
as a theme in such texts as Daniel 9. The major index of an anx-
ious relation to language, however, is simply the ubiquity of bibli-
cizing language and genres in late Second Temple literature. Echoes
of the biblical text haunt virtually all of the new literary compositions of this period. It is the "super adequacy" of the biblical idiom
that authors of this period have to confront, a traditional language
that both facilitates and authorizes their speech but at the same time
dominates it. This is not to say that the literary production of Second
Temple Judaism was not creative but to note that authors were
always glancing over their shoulders at the speech of scripture.
Although seldom made explicit, there is an element of the agonistic
in the relation of new texts (rewritten Bible, pseudonymous compositions, commentaries, etc.) to scripture. The new compositions
seek to share in the cultural authority of scripture but also in
some measure to co-opt it.

So long as one keeps in mind these and other limitations of the
metaphor of culture as conversation, it provides a helpful way of
looking at Second Temple Judaism as a community of discourse.
Along with the correctives mentioned above, one should also remember that there is never just a single conversation in a culture or a
single community formed by discourse, as the following section argues.

SPEAKING THE SAME LANGUAGE: DISCOURSE AND COMMUNITY

My understanding of the social dimensions of language has been
significantly shaped by the Bakhtin circle. Although much of the
work of these Russian thinkers was originally composed in the 1920s
and 1930s, the publication of their works in English during the
1980s and 1990s has made them influential in recent Anglo-American
literary and cultural criticism.[3] One of the ideas pursued both by

---

[3] Particularly important for my purposes are Bakhtin, *Dialogic Imagination*, and
Voloshinov, *Marxism and the Philosophy of Language*.

Voloshinov and Bakhtin is that language is always socially stratified and socially stratifying. Its variations serve to map a community in exquisite detail, and not just as a matter of traditional dialect geography. The mapping may be traced along any number of lines— economic class, region, relative urbanization, religion, occupation, gender, age cohort, advocacy group, and so forth. The dialect groups that can be identified within any of these categories will talk about a different range of topics, use a different but overlapping stock of words, and mean something different by some of the same words. The stylistic features of their speech and even some of their grammatical forms will be different. Other aspects of language will vary, too—the speech genres used, the tone, the degree of formality or casualness, the measure of distance or intimacy. All of these features interact to make language use into a highly sensitive marker of social boundaries. Where enough information is available one can even trace highly transient speech communities, those formed by a passing fashion or the influence of a charismatic individual.[4]

Language plays a particularly important role in the coherency of more stable and long-lived groups. The deep affective bonds created by "speaking the same language" are known to anyone who has ever left a linguistic community. The black student in a largely white university knows the sense of well-being that comes from being able to speak Black English with fellow blacks. Women and men who work in contexts dominated by the other gender know the relaxation that comes from being able to talk a gender-inflected speech with members of the same sex. Topics and even speech patterns that would be off limits in the work context are now part of the social bonding of the group. As Richard Terdiman puts it, these social dialects "give differential substance to membership in a social group . . . mediate an internal sense of belonging, an outward sense of otherness."[5] In a significant way they propose an answer to the questions "Who is my neighbor?" and "Who am I?"

Of course, the mapping performed by social dialects is complicated by the fact that people always speak a variety of such dialects. Bakhtin gives the example of the "illiterate peasant, miles away from any urban center . . . [who] nevertheless lived in several language systems: he prayed to God in one language (Church Slavonic), sang

---

[4] Bakhtin, *Dialogic Imagination*, 262–63, 290–91; Voloshinov, 93.
[5] Terdiman, *Discourse/Counter-Discourse*, 54.

songs in another, spoke to his family in a third and, when he began
to dictate petitions to the local authorities through a scribe, he tried
speaking yet a fourth language (the official-literate language, 'paper'
language)."[6] Each language gave the peasant a different identity in
a differently constituted community of widely differing moral significance. He was a suppliant before God, a member of the folk, the
paterfamilias, and a legal claimant with rights and obligations. For
Bakhtin, the peasant serves as an example of someone whose different
languages coexist in relative self-containment. "He passed from one
to the other without thinking, automatically: each was indisputably
in its own place, and the place of each was indisputable. He was
not yet able to regard one language (and the verbal world corresponding to it) through the eyes of another language (that is, the
language of everyday life and the everyday world with the language
of prayer or song, or vice versa)."[7]

This phenomenon is clearly recognizable to biblical scholars who
have studied it under the rubric of form criticism. Each set of speech
forms has its *Sitz im Leben*. In biblical scholarship, however, the investigation has usually focused on the isolation of particular speech
genres and the social location of their origin rather than on the situation of the individual who moved among them. After all, the
scribe, the prophet, and the sage all went to the priest for determi-
nations of clean and unclean. The priest, the scribe, and the prophet
all recited proverbs to their children. The prophet, the sage, and the
priest were all addressed by the Deuteronomic preacher. And all of
them prayed in a language shaped by the Psalms. Their relationships to these various language systems were obviously different. But
all of these language systems, plus many others, were part of the
dense linguistic texture of their world of discourse. They were available—sometimes in a compartmentalized way, sometimes in more
complex interanimation—as structures of social meaning.

One tends not to notice the divergent moral worlds that are embedded in the various discourses one uses. Their very existence in the
repertoire of a person's speech, however, sets up the possibility that
an individual could be called into a more active identification with
one of them. One discourse may emerge as the master discourse

---

[6] Bakhtin, *Dialogical Imagination*, 295–96.
[7] Bakhtin, *Dialogical Imagination*, 296.

through which others are regarded. Such a process would be a kind of ideological awakening. If Bakhtin's peasant begins to orient himself around the legal-official language, to regard it as definitive, he does not cease to speak the other languages but his relationship to them undergoes subtle changes. They may be interpreted in light of the legal language (e.g., the words and metaphors of the prayers might be reaccented)[8] or they may simply become less meaningful and more opaque. As Bakhtin puts it, the various languages become dialogically coordinated rather than compartmentalized.[9]

In Second Temple Judaism, of course, one can note the spread of several discourses that offer a perspective from which others might be dialogically engaged. The language of the Deuteronomic movement becomes broadly influential, as does sapiential discourse. In a somewhat different way the highly technical language of the priesthood also becomes a moral language of extended scope. An apocalyptic way of talking is encountered in a wide variety of texts. These do not remain radically separate discourses, of course, although their distinctiveness is often sufficient to allow one to identify them. But such questions as whether Qumran was an apocalyptic community or a priestly community or a sapiential community might be more fruitfully addressed by examining how the various discourses are dialogically related in Qumran literature. These would not be questions about whether the members were themselves priests or sages or seers but questions about the relationship of various discursive traditions within the speech community of Qumran.[10]

The fact that individuals participate in such a variety of intersecting languages is what facilitates the rhetorical use of language and the intentional creation of communities of persuasion. Every culture has a complex repertoire of identifying signs that are located in various parts of its collective discourse and that will articulate that culture differently. A text or speaker who invokes one or another of them will evoke communities of correspondingly different dimensions and

---

[8] For example, in the book of Job, Job begins to use legal language to examine the assumptions and limitations of received languages of piety. See Newsom, *Book of Job*, 137–38, 155–61.

[9] Bakhtin, *Dialogical Imagination*, 296.

[10] See, for example, the essay by Grossman, "Priesthood as Authority," in which she examines how different Second Temple communities "thought with priests"; that is, used discourse about priests and priestly matters to establish various claims concerning "authority, authenticity, and identity" (117).

orientations.[11] Ancestral terms are a prime example. Whether one invokes Abraham or Jacob evokes an Israel whose relationship to gentiles is differently oriented. But all terms of value, not just ancestral terms, perform this function. An Israel evoked in terms of the symbol of Zion is a somewhat different Israel from one evoked by reference to "the children of Israel." Or again, an appeal to "all who repent of transgression" evokes an Israel internally differentiated on moral grounds rather than one unified as descendants of a common father. Oftentimes the evocation of a particular latent community is a temporary matter, a response to specific and limited circumstances. It may also happen, especially in times of social instability, that slogans and the discourses that they imply can play a significant role in the creation and consolidation of new social formations.[12] The Maccabean slogan, "zeal for the torah," is an obvious example. Its competition and eventual collision with other alternative slogans and designations, such as "the pious ones" or "the repentant of Israel," is a measure of the intense rhetorical attempt to create new communities of discourse that could provide the basis for new social formations.

It is not just the selection of alternative words and competing social dialects that articulate sub-communities within a culture. The rhetorical competition among the social dialects of a society is also generated by the fact that those who compete *do* speak the same language—or at least the same words. In fact what they struggle over is precisely that common language. Obviously not every "a, an, and the" is the object of conflict. Rather, as Voloshinov put it in a well-known formulation, "every stage in the development of a society has its own special and restricted circle of items which alone have access to that society's attention and which are endowed with evaluative accentuation by that attention. Only items within that circle will achieve sign formation and become objects in semiotic communication."[13] In second century Judaism terms such as "torah," "Israel," "covenant," "righteousness," "what is good in his eyes," and many others were precisely the sort of terms that became ideological signs. But as each group used those terms they did so with a

---

[11] Lincoln, *Discourse and the Construction of Society*, 19.
[12] Lincoln, 18.
[13] Voloshinov, 21–22.

different "accentuation." "Torah" has a different flavor in the Maccabean slogan than it does when the Qumran community speaks of "those who do torah" (1QpHab 7:11; 8:1). More subtly, but not less significantly, that term has a different quality in Qumran speech than in the speech of their rivals, "the speakers of smooth things." Simply put, every ideological sign is the site of intersecting accents. It is "socially multiaccentual."

This social accent of the sign is not something that exists as a scholarly abstraction. It exists in the word itself. Only Adam had fresh words to use. The rest of us have to make do with used ones. The characteristic of used words is that they bear the traces of their previous use within them. As Bakhtin says, "each word tastes of the context and contexts in which it has lived its socially charged life; all words and forms are populated by intentions."[14] Individual speakers and listeners may or may not be able to articulate those social contexts but they can recognize them with an accomplished ease—as anyone knows who has attempted to speak to an ideologically mixed group about a controversial topic. You "give yourself away" as soon as you open your mouth. Though there are some words that virtually belong to one social group or another, there are other words that appear at first glance to be common property, words such as "freedom" in modern Western discourse or "covenant" in Second Temple Judaism.[15] Words such as these are not so much common property as they are a common space within which many different intentions and socially charged meanings meet together. This is in part what Bakhtin means when he locates "dialogism" within the word. To use a word, but especially a word that is particularly weighted with past usage, is implicitly to respond to other utterances of the word.[16] In that sense all speech is a response to what has been said before.

Other dimensions of dialogism exist beyond that which is located within the word itself. On the level of the utterance, one never speaks except to someone. Even texts have implied readers. This audience,

---

[14] Bakhtin, *Dialogic Imagination*, 293.

[15] See, for example, the study of Christiansen, *Covenant in Judaism and Paul*, which examines how different ways of construing and articulating the concept of "covenant" served to differentiate various sub-communities within Judaism and in emerging Christianity.

[16] Bakhtin, *Dialogic Imagination*, 275–85.

whether physically present or present in the mind of the speaker or
writer, is no passive figure. Because utterances are always addressed,
the audience participates in the shaping of the utterance. The audience's conceptual horizons do not completely coincide with those of
the speaker, or else there would be nothing to say and no need to
say it. A speaker must orient himself or herself toward the listener
in speaking, anticipating how the listener might hear and respond.
The words of a speaker are not only response but also are formed
by the anticipation of a reply.[17]

With respect to Qumran, for example, along with debating the
question of the authorship of the so-called Hodayot of the Teacher,
one needs to consider the way in which those words are addressed,
not only to God, but indirectly to the community of the sect which
hears them, and to consider how they anticipate a response. One
might also read the Serek ha-Yahad with a view to discerning the
addressee whose imaginative presence inhabits the text. As a community formed in significant measure by adult converts, the Qumran
sect was not a closed community of discourse, but one that had to
take account of a variety of conceptual horizons in establishing its
own language. These are present in the text in the way in which
received language is incorporated, engaged, and reaccented.

BESPOKEN AND SPEAKING: DISCOURSE AND SUBJECTIVITY

Discourse does not only form communities; it forms persons as well.
We first emerge as subjects in the context of language and receive
our identities from various symbolic practices. Naming, for instance,
typically inscribes gender differentiation and an identity within some
kinship structure or other system of classification.[18] But there is much
more to this process than names. Tracking down the discourse of
the self in a given culture is a matter, as Clifford Geertz puts it, of
"searching out and analyzing the symbolic forms—words, images,
institutions, behaviors—in terms of which, in each place, people actually represented themselves to themselves and to one another."[19] The

---

[17] Bakhtin, *Dialogic Imagination*, 280–82; Voloshinov, 86. See also the similar analysis by Bourdieu, *Language and Symbolic Power*, 77.

[18] Various aspects of the social and cultural functions of names are discussed by
Kippenberg, "Name and Person in Ancient Judaism and Christianity."

[19] Geertz, *Local Knowledge*, 58.

outlines of a specific discourse of the self often emerge when an individual tries to specify who he or she is. Even when identity is not the explicit issue, the qualities and behaviors that are expected of a person, the motives and possible roles, in short, what it means to be a person, are all articulated in the way particular societies talk about any number of things. At least some of these features will be differentiated by gender, clan, social class, or other category but it is precisely in discovering one's specific and proper identity that one becomes a subject in a social discourse.

"Discovering" is perhaps the wrong word. In a well-known analogy Louis Althusser suggests the active role taken by discourse, or "ideology" in his terminology, in forming subjects. He imagines ideology as an authoritative voice, like that of a policeman who hails an individual, "Hey, you there!" The individual addressed turns around, and by this gesture becomes a subject within the ideology that hails him. The term "subject" is meant to convey a dual sense, that the individual is an aware participant (the active sense of subject) but also is one who is subjected to the system of meaning that has addressed him. The crucial element of the process, however, is the moment of recognition, when the individual addressed recognizes "that the hail was 'really' addressed to him."[20] The imagined scene is a mythos, of course, since there is never a time when one is not a subject of ideology. It does, however, express the way in which ideology continually addresses persons as subjects and secures their recognition.[21] One is always "bespoken"—spoken for in the act of being spoken to.

One of the limitations of Althusser's analogy is that it suggests a more monolithic picture of ideology and subject position than is actually the case. Even in relatively homogeneous societies a person is "hailed" by numerous discourses that offer different subject positions, and thus different models of what it means to be a person. The identities of a person are never singular but multiple, never unified but in some sense fragmented, never static but always in process.[22] The historical and cultural complexity of a society means that there are likely to be various discourses of the self that have developed

<hr>

[20] Althusser, *Lenin and Philosophy*, 174, 182.
[21] Althusser, 172–73. For a survey of recent critique and reformulation of Althusser's discussion see S. Hall, "Who Needs 'Identity'?"
[22] S. Hall, 4.

over time and exist as alternatives. Richard Harvey Brown has suggested that one can usefully think in terms of a "language of possible selves," analogous to Sassure's *langue*. The specific utterances and symbolic performances through which one makes an expression of selfhood are meaningful by reference to this language of possible selves that is part of the habitus of the culture.[23] The development of new forms of subjectivity, or the self-conscious cultivation of distinctive discourses of the self, may also be a form of resistance to a dominant discourse.

Subjectivity is also formed in crucial ways through the act of speaking. Very little is more closely identified with one's own self than speech. As a physical process, it engages the body but is also an activity of the mind.[24] In speaking one actively takes up a subject position within a discourse. Ownership of the discourse, and the identity that comes from it, is strongly enhanced through the act of speaking in its terms and its accents. People do this in many casual ways, without attending to it. For instance, the various forms of etiquette and speech tact that persons almost automatically use reinforce identification with a given social order. By the same token, deviation from such forms of etiquette can enact resistance to the proffered identities of the discourse. For a Southern black to say simply "No" instead of "No Sir" or "No Ma'am" to a white person was a fundamental rejection of the proffered identity of the Jim Crow world. For a white to say "Mr. Jones" or "Mrs. Jones" to a black person was an acknowledgment of a profoundly changed set of identities.

This discursive approach to the formation of subjectivity is obviously rich in implications for the study of Second Temple Judaism, where it is possible to discern the discourses of a number of "possible selves" and to locate the cultivation of a distinctive form of subjectivity at Qumran as a part of its work of contesting other discourses. What makes it particularly attractive for understanding the formation of subjectivity at Qumran is the extent to which self-referential speech was cultivated there, both in the community's requirement that each person give an annual account of his insight

---

[23] R. Brown, *Society as Text*, 55–63.
[24] And, of course, it is also a form of social activity. See the analysis of inner and outer speech in relation to the authoring of selves in Holland et al., *Identity and Agency*, 169–91.

and deeds and in the extensively cultivated genre of first person singular prayer found in the Hodayot. The cultivation of a theoretical language of the structure of the self is also present in the Two Spirits section of the Serek ha-Yahad. These issues are taken up more extensively in the chapters that follow.

What There Is to Talk About: Discourse and World

Clifford Geertz once offered a definition of human beings. "We are, in sum, incomplete or unfinished animals who complete or finish ourselves through culture—and not through culture in general but through highly particular forms of it: Dobuan and Javanese, Hopi and Italian, upper-class and lower-class, academic and commercial."[25] As his remark suggests, it is not just ourselves that we finish but our worlds as well. Discourse may create subjects, but it creates objects as well. This is most evident, of course, in the realm of cultural values. Love, hypocrisy, honor, humility, sincerity and authenticity are all very real objects in particular cultural worlds. But language can be said to create objects even in the physical realm in the sense that they are constituted as objects of significance. It may be that the alleged fifty different Inuit words for snow have proven to be something of an academic legend, but it is apparently the case that until recently Japanese had no word for the color blue. In any event one recognizes the process involved. Wittgenstein's dictum that the limits of language are the limits of the world is largely true.

It would be a mistake, however, to collapse the categories of world and language. There is a physical world of things to bump against; a social world of cooperation and conflict; an economic world of production, distribution, and consumption; a historical world of events and, quite often, of force. None of these are unrelated to language, but not by any stretch of the imagination are they simply equivalent to language. They may indeed "signify," but they do other things as well.

Since I am concerned with a community whose activity was intensely verbal, I am interested in the relation between discourse and world, but not so much as a general theoretical issue as with

---

[25] Geertz, *Interpretation of Cultures*, 49.

their particular discourse and their particular world. To get a better sense of that relation, however, it is necessary to do a bit of theoretical reflection. My starting point is the well-known observation of Kenneth Burke that utterances are "strategies for the encompassing of situations."[26] For Burke texts and utterances are not repositories of ideas but symbolic acts. As acts, texts do not merely reflect the world but do something in it and to it. The way in which texts act in and on the world is distinct from an act of direct force because a text exists in the realm of the symbolic.

Fredric Jameson has clarified and developed Burke's notion, exploring the nature of the relationship between text and world. Jameson insists on a tensive relationship. The world is not simply a linguistic construct; but the world is not available to us in itself but only as we are able to textualize it, to bring it into the realm of the symbolic. Insofar as a text takes the world into itself, as its subtext, then the world can be acted upon in the symbolic work of the text. Working primarily with literary texts, what Jameson's analysis attempts to uncover is what he calls the "political unconscious" of a text, the way in which it serves to rewrite or restructure a prior historical or ideological subtext. Specifically, for Jameson the symbolic act of a text is "the function of inventing imaginary or formal 'solutions' to unresolvable social contradictions."[27] Jameson also, however, has underscored the limitation of the type of "symbolic action" to which Burke directs attention. The phrase is irreducibly ambiguous. Where does the emphasis go? Is the work of a text truly a symbolic *act* or merely a *symbolic* act? Such ambiguity points, as Jameson says, "to the fundamental equivocality of the symbolic itself, at one and the same time the accomplishment of an act and the latter's substitute, a way of acting on the world and of compensating for the impossibility of such action all at once."[28]

Although most of the sectarian texts from Qumran are not, properly speaking, literary, their religious language and aesthetic structures are fully amenable to the type of analysis that Burke and Jameson propose. Both in the study of particular texts and in the comparison of numerous texts in different genres, one recognizes the

---

[26] Burke, *Philosophy of Literary Form*, 1; see also 296–300.
[27] Jameson, *Political Unconscious*, 79.
[28] Jameson, "Symbolic Inference," 151.

symbolic patterns in which the community has the greatest investment. Even a superficial reading of the sectarian literature from Qumran is sufficient to show that the most frequently recurring symbolic motif in Qumran literature is that of the binary relationship, most often figured as dualism.[29] Dualism of various sorts is explicitly present in many texts as a structuring feature of linguistic, aesthetic, psychological, social, political, and metaphysical phenomena. It also appears as a feature in rituals and as a stylistic device in certain texts. Other closely related symbolic images, such as references to separating and uniting or the contrast of clean and unclean, may not be specifically dualistic, but they do reflect the pervasiveness of binary symbolization at Qumran.

Is it possible, however, to see in this obsession with the formal patterns of dualism "a symbolic enactment of the social within the formal and the aesthetic" or to determine what form of social contradiction finds its imaginary resolution in these symbolic acts? At least in one case I think that it is. In Chapter 3 I will attempt to show with respect to the Two Spirits section of the Serek ha-Yahad why, in this particular time and place, a discourse of the self might take the form of a conflict of two spirits and how it can be read as a symbolic response to (and possibly a compensation for) a social contradiction that was not accessible to more direct resolution.

THE CULTURAL POLITICS OF LANGUAGE: DISCOURSE AND COUNTER-DISCOURSE

In any society one can speak of a dominant discourse. Although elusive, it can be described either from the bottom or from the top, so to speak. In a paradoxical way the dominant discourse can be identified as precisely what goes without saying.[30] It is what everybody knows, what does not have to be specified, what is thoroughly internalized, so that it is produced and reproduced without much fanfare. Alternatively the dominant discourse can be identified as the practices of the establishment. It is what those in power expect and require and receive, both in material terms and in symbolic and attitudinal terms. In a similar fashion E.P. Sanders attempted to define

---

[29] The best analysis of the dualisms in Qumran literature remains that of Huppenbauer, *Der Mensch zwischen zwei Welten.*
[30] Terdiman, 61.

"common Judaism" in terms of "what the priests and the people agreed on," that is, the dominant discourse of Judaism.[31] Counter-discourse on the other hand secures a place for itself by rendering problematic something that the dominant discourse takes for granted. Although counter-discourse may be polemical, often its relationship is not directly oppositional. It is, however, always interruptive or disruptive. It disturbs the smooth flow of what everyone takes for granted and in so doing calls attention to itself and gains a measure of cultural power by doing so. Whatever its particular strategy, counter-discourse presupposes and depends upon the existence of the dominant discourse in order to articulate itself.

Earlier in this chapter I discussed the model of culture as conversation and pointed out that the analogy has certain drawbacks, most notably its tendency to obscure the conflictual nature of social discourse. One may, of course, exaggerate the role of conflict. The Marxist perspective that sees the discourse between classes as *essentially* agonistic seems to me to do so.[32] Bakhtin's celebration of parody and carnival laughter as forms of the disruption of dominant speech helpfully intertwines the notion of conflict with that of playfulness.[33] More profoundly, Kenneth Burke's ironic account of mystery and courtship in the rhetoric between classes thoroughly complicates any simple conflictual model.[34] Playfulness is also a hallmark of Burke's general account of the human passion for classification, division, and the rhetorical appeal he calls "pure persuasion." But Burke qualifies his account in a significant way and reintroduces a note of social conflict: "Resources of classification, of abstraction, of comparison and contrast, of merger and division, of derivation, and the like, may characterize the thinking of man *generically*, over and above the nature of his social or personal problems. But his social and personal problems provide the incentive for the particular emphases of his expressions. You are not finished when you have analyzed the formal or dialectical devices implicit, say, in a doctrine of 'white supremacy.'"[35]

[31] Sanders, *Judaism*, 47.
[32] Jameson, *Political Unconscious*, 84.
[33] An idea developed in particular in Bakhtin, *Rabelais and His World*.
[34] Burke, *Rhetoric of Motives*, 208–33, 267–94.
[35] Burke, *Rhetoric of Motives*, 285.

For all the playfulness, exuberance, and apparent talk for the sake of talk that characterizes much social discourse, issues of interest and advantage are never wholly absent. The urge to say something is tinged with the struggle to be heard, the struggle to set the terms of the discourse, the struggle to dominate the conversation. The reason is not hard to find. What is at stake is power. Michel Foucault puts it strongly: "Discourse is not simply that which expresses struggles or systems of domination, but that for which, and by which, one struggles; it is the power that one is striving to seize."[36] Discourse is power because it is what gives meaning to the world. An established discourse connects values, actions, and attitudes in ways that make them appear self-evident and inevitable. Where discourse is secure, conflict is minimal and force is unnecessary, since individuals will act according to the roles and expectations inscribed for them in the order of discourse. But no discourse is ever wholly secure. In part it may be prey to the generic itch for division and (re)classification that Burke alludes to. What gives direction to the subversion is the fact that every particular discourse privileges the interests of some groups over others. The relatively disadvantaged know that by modifying the discourse or disrupting it and making it problematic they can secure attention, influence, and other benefits. The struggle for meaning is paramount, because where meaning goes, power follows.

The Discourse of Qumran in Its Second Temple Setting

In the essays that follow I wish to use these categories of discourse analysis to investigate certain aspects of the way in which the Qumran community actively constructed itself as a community and engaged its larger social context. Although I analyze a variety of socially symbolic discourses, the most important of these is the discourse of the self. Whether framed as a theoretical exploration of anthropology, as the creation of the individual subject in the context of a disciplinary institution, or the explicit cultivation of new forms of subjectivity in the practices of prayer, the self emerges as a particularly productive symbolic space in the sectarian world.

---

[36] Foucault, *L'ordre du discours*, 12, quoted and translated by Terdiman, 55. See also the analysis of Bourdieu, *Language and Symbolic Power*.

The book is organized as follows. Chapter two offers a schematic account of various counter-discursive jostlings over the central cultural symbol of torah and the development of competing ideologies of knowledge in the cultural politics of Second Temple Judaism. Chapter three is also concerned with the ideology of knowledge, but from a different perspective. Using the theoretical discourse about anthropology in the Two Spirits section of the Serek ha-Yahad, it explores the symbolic structure of knowledge in this Qumran text and attempts to comprehend that structure as an instrument for symbolic action.

Chapter four is explicitly concerned with the making of sectarian community and sectarian identity in the Serek ha-Yahad. As a document for the socialization of members to a new form of community, the Rule itself is a novel genre, composed of samples of various sorts of speech practices from the community's life, worked together to form a book of instruction in the ethos of the community. As a rhetorical work, it serves the function of separating the sectarian from his previous community and uniting him to the Qumran community by remaking his language and providing him with a newly "figured" world. It also reveals the extent to which the community can be understood as a form of disciplinary institution within which various "technologies of the self" were the prime means by which the community equipped itself to carry out its purposes.

Chapters five and six focus on the Hodayot. As a collection of first person singular poetic prayers, the Hodayot draw attention to the speaking subject. In keeping with the well-recognized distinction between Hodayot of the leader and Hodayot of the community, I divide my discussion between two chapters. Chapter five investigates the way in which the Hodayot of the community generate a structure of subjectivity that is distinctively different from other forms of subjectivity represented in biblical and extra-biblical Israelite and Jewish texts. The creation of a new form of the self obviously serves the formation of sectarian community by providing members with an identity experientially grasped as different from their previous sense of self. As part of this process, these Hodayot normalize certain characteristic values of the sect, and in so doing, serve as counter-discourse to the values and subjectivity of other ways of being in Second Temple Judaism.

In Chapter six, which is concerned with the Hodayot of the leader, I pick up certain issues raised already in Chapter five concerning the normalization of the disciplines of the community. Here, however, I am particularly interested to see how the self-presentation of the leader serves as a vehicle for exercising symbolic power. The Hodayot of the leader provide an important way in which the boundaries of the community are identified and maintained by associating images of affinity and estrangement personally with the leader. Moreover, these Hodayot also negotiate a perennial problem in the formation of sectarian communities, that of disaffection.

These studies are in no sense exhaustive. They do not attempt to address all the interpretive issues posed by the texts and, in the case of the Hodayot, deal only with a limited portion of the text. Many other sectarian compositions (e.g., the *pesharim*, the War Scroll, and various liturgical compositions) are not treated at all. What I hope to accomplish through the studies presented here, however, is to model a way of reading the sectarian texts that draws attention to how the discourse of the community creates an alternative figured world and self-identity, thereby critically engaging other forms of contemporary Judaism.

CHAPTER TWO

TORAH, KNOWLEDGE, AND SYMBOLIC POWER: STRATEGIES OF DISCOURSE IN SECOND TEMPLE JUDAISM

One of the most important and most intensely contested terms in Second Temple Judaism was that of torah. The intersecting currents of talk about torah provided a means by which various individuals and social groups could achieve symbolic power, that is, the social power that comes from the ability to define the meaning of common cultural symbols.[1]

It is—significantly—difficult to give a definition for the term torah, which has more than one meaning already in preexilic discourse. To say that it always is used in relation to instruction in norms of conduct or to the norms themselves is to provide a minimalist definition that only underscores the extent to which the social significance of the term depends on the particular discourse in which it is embedded. Obviously, the concrete content of behavior implied by the term differs greatly depending on whether one encounters it in the context of Ezra-Nehemiah or that of Proverbs. The sapiential and legal accentuations of the term are not rigidly segregated, however, as both the books of Deuteronomy and Sirach indicate. Indeed, these two accentuations continue to jostle each other throughout the Second Temple period, often in ways that exploit the polyvalency of the term.

A different sort of slippage occurs with the (partial) textualization of torah. Already in preexilic times torah can be associated with written texts and the scribes who handle them (e.g., Jer 8:8), a representation of torah that becomes increasingly prominent in the

---

[1] Bourdieu (*Language as Symbolic Power*, 170) describes symbolic power as "a power of constituting the given through utterances, of making people see and believe, of confirming or transforming the vision of the world and, thereby, action on the world and thus the world itself, an almost magical power which enables one to obtain the equivalent of what is obtained through force (whether physical or economic), by virtue of the specific effect of mobilization."

Second Temple period (e.g., Neh 8:1; Sir 24:23).[2] The textualization of torah is related to the phenomenon of the emergence of
scripture.[3] One should remember, however, that torah, though closely
related to scripture, is not identical with it. Not all that was regarded
as scripture was torah or formed the basis for specific norms of conduct, and not everything that was believed to be required by God
had a textual basis in scripture. Significantly, there were certain ways
of talking about torah, as Jon Levenson has shown in relation to
Psalm 119,[4] that said very little about scripture as a source of divine
instruction.

Despite these caveats, the emergence of the Pentateuch and its
increasingly recognized role as a privileged repository/source of torah
marked a decisive change in the discourse of torah. One of the
differences effected by this change, especially at the level of popular
discourse, was that torah could be represented by a physical symbol:
the book. Already in Ezra-Nehemiah one can see the social role of
this physical symbol as an object of orientation for the people who are
assembled to hear Ezra read from the "book of the Law of Moses
which YHWH had given to Israel" (Neh 8:1). Equally, the physical
symbol of torah could be an object of insult, as in the mutilation
and burning of the "books of the law" recorded in 1 Macc 1:56.[5]

The textualization of torah had even greater implications for specialist discourse. Although, as noted above, torah was never simply
equivalent to the Pentateuch, the privileged role of that document
generated new types of speech activity and literature. Self-conscious
interpretation of the text, various forms of intertextuality, and the

---

[2] See Watts, *Reading Law*, 15–20, for a discussion of the references to various
books of torah in the Bible.

[3] By scripture I mean religious texts that have a recognizable authority for a
given community. The authority of such texts may be observed as they are variously read on public and solemn occasions, are cited as sources of legitimation for
practices or beliefs, become the subject of secondary literature (e.g., commentary,
intertextual reference, pseudepigraphical writings), and—as physical objects—receive
ceremonious treatment. By the late Second Temple period scripture in this sense
included the Pentateuch, the Former and Latter prophets, Psalms, and perhaps certain other books. The category of scripture is a looser one than that of canon.

[4] Levenson, "Sources of Torah."

[5] The veneration of the physical torah scroll increased in the late and post Second
Temple periods, as Goodman argues ("Texts, Scribes, and Power," 100). This veneration may also have contributed to the status of the scribes who produced such
texts (107).

imitation of Pentateuchal texts in pseudonymous compositions all attest to the way discourse about torah was affected by the emergence of a primary text of torah.[6]

It is not possible to talk about the role of torah and especially the role of the textualized torah in Second Temple Judaism without attending to the social and political factors that made it a cultural symbol of such central significance. Already during First Temple times torah was recognized as one of the fundamental constituting elements of Judean culture, and its mishandling was the subject of public criticism (see, e.g., Jer 2:8; 8:8). The book of Deuteronomy, even in its preexilic recension, represented torah as that which constituted the people of Israel. Ezekiel could use complex casuistic analysis in talking about torah (e.g., Ezekiel 18), apparently assuming an exilic audience familiar with such forms of talk. The postexilic discourse of torah is in part a continuation of the way in which talk about the norms of divine instruction had previously been carried out.

In the postexilic period, however, a number of factors gave torah an even more central place in the cultural life of Judaism. In part these were negative factors. The absence of kingship and of an autonomous status among the nations deprived Israel of a traditional means of articulating itself in terms of international political activity. At the corresponding level of literary discourse the writing of contemporary political history (either as annals or as narrative history) virtually ceased to be practiced with the end of the monarchy and was only revived by the Hasmoneans.[7] The reconstitution of Judean society instead took its impetus from the reconstructed temple. The centrality of this institution gave an increased social significance to the priesthood and to the torah for which it was responsible.[8]

---

[6] For the re-presentation of the revelation at Sinai in pseudonymous documents from the Second Temple period, see the recent study of Najman, *Seconding Sinai.*

[7] I hold to the "two-edition" theory of the composition of the Deuteronomistic History, understanding it to have received its primary composition during the monarchy and a second edition in the early exilic period. Ezra-Nehemiah is the exception that proves the rule concerning the writing of political history. Arguably historiographical in intent, its gaps, seams, and chronological problems bespeak an intellectual and literary context quite different from that of the Deuteronomic history. Although the Chronicler is a historian, he shows either no interest in or ability to write about contemporary events. Genealogy replaces history in his account of the period after the fall of the Judean kingdom.

[8] On the civic structure of postexilic Judaism see Blenkinsopp's modification of Weinberg's hypothesis in "Temple and Society in Achaemenid Judah."

Although the notion that the Pentateuch received its formation in response to Persian insistence on a constitution based on traditional law can no longer be accepted in the form in which it was once proposed,[9] most scholars agree that the Pentateuch probably received its fundamental redaction and uniquely authoritative status as part of the reconstitution of the Judean community in the Persian period. As Jean Louis Ska put it, "the Pentateuch contains the 'official and national archives/library' of the Second Temple community," acquiring through its status as a text "the quality of a normative and irrevocable document about Israel's origins and juridical organization." As a "theological document about Israel's identity," it provided the necessary ideological basis for national survival in the Persian empire.[10] Public reading and teaching of torah that was acknowledged to be authoritative was thus an important part of the formation of a national consciousness for the people of Yehud.[11] Imperial recognition of torah also defined an important part of the community's identity in relation to the empire of which it was a part. The relative autonomy for conducting internal affairs according to ancestral laws that is presumed by the Ezra narratives (Ezra 7:14, 25–26) was affirmed explicitly in the Hellenistic period in the decree of Antiochus III (Josephus, *Ant.* 12.142) and remained the standard during the Hellenistic period, with the only attempt to abrogate this arrangement resulting in a fiasco during the time of Antiochus IV Epiphanes.

The official sanction of ancestral law and the cultic practices with which it was closely connected, coupled with the absence of any comparable institutional focus of national identity, gave torah a cen-

---

[9] The classic form of the theory is presented by Frei and Koch, *Reichsidee und Reichsorganisation im Perserreich*. For a balanced and thorough reexamination of the thesis see the essays in Watts, ed., *Persia and Torah*, which also contains bibliography of previous critical discussion.

[10] Ska, "'Persian Imperial Authorization'," 169–70.

[11] Runesson (*Origins of the Synagogue*, 277) overstates the role of the Persian authorities, but otherwise articulates well the function of emerging scripture and its public role. "The emphasis on knowing torah and, consequently, the necessity of reading it publicly and teaching it to the people should be understood as a massive attempt to transform the symbolic universes of the heterogeneous population and establish the ruling authorities in Jerusalem as legitimate. The re-building of the temple, the centralisation of the cult in Jerusalem and the public reading and teaching of torah are thus different parts of an overall strategy orchestrated by Persian appointed officials and the religious leadership in Jerusalem, initiated and supported by the Persian government." Watts (*Reading Law*, 24–25) argues that the practice of reading law originated in the preexilic period.

tral place in the formation of the community, but it also played a role in the formation of individual character. The emergence of what is sometimes called "torah piety" of the sort that finds expression in Psalms 1 and 119 is a new kind of language of the self at prayer, one that articulates the self in relation to meditation on and delight in torah. It gives evidence for the development of a new type of "possible self," to use Richard Harvey Brown's terms,[12] one quite distinct in its contours from other languages of the self. It would be misleading to represent torah piety in too homogeneous a fashion, however. Meditations on the desire to fulfill what God commands became an arena for articulating differences as well as common values. Despite recognizable parallels, the torah piety of Qumran, as expressed in the Hodayot, has very different accents from that of Psalm 119, as I will discuss in more detail in a later chapter.

The dynamics that encouraged the emergence of torah in the Persian period as a central cultural symbol, both in its textual and nontextual modes, were not identical with the dynamics of its further development in the Hellenistic period. In his study of the emergence of the synagogue, Anders Runesson distinguishes between the largely centralized and state controlled practices of reading and interpreting torah in the Persian period and its decentralization as local groups and voluntary associations increasingly conducted such activities during the Hellenistic period. Although I think Runesson overstates the direct role of the Persian imperial powers, he is certainly correct in his assessment of the proliferation of cultural activity regarding torah in the succeeding era.[13]

Not only decentralization but also the encounter with different cultural assumptions in the Hellenistic period may have changed the nature of the discourse concerning torah. Elias Bickerman has suggested

---

[12] R. Brown, 55.

[13] "As we shall see, while state control over the torah, its reading and interpretation was maintained during the first part of this [Hellenistic] period, in the latter part of the period of political stability and economic growth, i.e., shortly before 200 BCE, the torah is no longer exclusively under government supervision but becomes more and more the possession also of local groups and associations" (Runesson, 304). "The Early Hellenistic period presents us with a transition from officially controlled public teaching (in public assemblies in the cites of Judah) to a decentralised authority over the torah. This decentralisation of authority and reduction in authority range grew with the development of the scribal class and resulted in semi-public assemblies, or schools, transmitting certain understandings of the canonised traditions" (Runesson, 319).

that an additional reason why torah emerged as such an important cultural object arose from the dialogue between Judaism and Hellenism, a development that is reflected in Ben Sira's way of talking about torah. "The Greek idea of *paideia* was based on a book, that of Homer, whose poems were memorized. . . . What could a Jew oppose to the bible of the Hellenes? Ben Sira had an answer: Moses."[14] For Ben Sira torah was no longer something to be studied only by the priests and legists who were responsible for it in their official capacities. Reinterpreting the traditions of the Israelite *hakam* in light of Greek custom, Ben Sira's attitude is that torah "must be the central subject of Jewish culture and education."[15] Bickerman even suggests that the methods of torah study that emerged during the late Hellenistic and Roman periods were influenced by Greek models of inquiry and discussion rather than rote memorization. Although there is little specific evidence by which this thesis might be proven or disproven, it represents a plausible reframing of the cultural significance of torah in the encounter with Hellenism. Without reference to Bickerman's suggestion, Robert Doran recently argued that it is similarly plausible to imagine the curriculum of Jason's gymnasium as consisting of works analogous to those of Demetrius the Chronographer, Aristobulus, and Ezekiel the Tragedian, that is, works that interpreted the traditional Jewish texts via Greek methods of exegesis, philosophical analysis, and dramaturgy.[16]

Taken together, the various impulses from Persian period political reorganization, the Judean priestly community, emerging pietistic practices, and the encounter with Hellenistic culture created the conditions for a lively cultural conversation about torah. As torah and the written scripture to which it was closely connected became cultural objects of increasing importance, so the incentive increased for different segments of the community to find in talk about torah a means to define themselves and to compete for influence.

---

[14] Bickerman, *Jews in the Greek Age*, 171.
[15] Bickerman, *Jews in the Greek Age*, 171.
[16] Doran, "High Cost of a Good Education," 105. Doran (86–87) notes that there is evidence for the adaptation of the gymnasium to local culture and literature in several Hellenistic cities.

Torah: Common Possession, Special Possession

Who were the major participants in the cultural conversation about torah during the Second Temple period? Traditionally, it was the priest who was the interpreter and arbiter of torah (Lev 10:11; Deut 17:8–11; 33:8–10; Jer 18:18; Mic 3:11; Zeph 3:4; Ezek 22:26; Mal 2:6–9), and to the end of the Second Temple period the priests' role was acknowledged as central (Sir 45:17; Josephus, *Ant.* 4.304).[17] Given the significance of torah in Second Temple Judaism, however, explicit references to the priestly responsibility for torah seem comparatively sparse. Seldom does one encounter anything like a rhetorical exploitation of the priestly prerogative with respect to torah. Far from suggesting a diminution of priestly authority, however, this comparative silence may simply reflect the fact that the priests' role vis-à-vis torah was one of those things that "goes without saying."[18] Such invisibility is a characteristic aspect of dominant discourse. It is those who wish to contest, to engage in counter-discourse, who are more likely to raise the issue.

That the priests possessed expertise in torah and that their privileged relation to torah was crucial to their honor seems clear. But it is not entirely clear what in practice constituted their obligation to "teach torah to Israel." The responsibility of the priests for teaching Israel torah may have consisted primarily of rendering decisions when sought out by lay persons (see e.g., Deut 17:8–13; 21:5; Ezek 44:23–24; Mal 2:6; Hag 2:11–13; Zech 7:2–3). There is little indication that the priests carried out general, systematic instruction of the populace. Even Deut 31:9–13 provides for the priests to read the law to the people only once every seven years, and the initiative for public reading and teaching of the law in Second Temple

---

[17] See the discussions of Fraade, "Early Rabbinic Sage" and the rather polemical account in Sanders, *Judaism*, 170–82. Priests who did not have proper knowledge of the law doubtless existed, as the provision for the inexpert priest in the Damascus Document makes clear, but even there it is a Levite with expertise who is to supply the lack (CD 13:3–4).

[18] Concerning the episode in which Josephus' conduct of his military responsibilities in Galilee was investigated by a committee of four, "of different classes of society but of equal standing in education" (*Life*, 196–98), Sanders (*Judaism*, 172) concludes that "what is interesting about this is that Josephus assumes that the reader will know that the priests knew the law; he has to explain that the two non-priestly Pharisees, even though they were from the ordinary people, nevertheless knew the law."

sources is represented as coming from a variety of different loci.[19] For the Persian period at least, the extant sources suggest that initiative came from central political authority, whether local or imperial, but that the prominent representation of priests in such initiatives was essential for credibility.[20]

A continuing debate exists as to whether the struggle over interpretation of torah should be seen more as a shift of discursive authority from priestly to lay circles (the traditional view)[21] or whether it should be seen largely as a competition for influence within a socially divided priesthood.[22] To set the issue in these terms is slightly misleading. In the Second Temple period factions of the priesthood could and did dispute with one another concerning proper interpretation of torah. But these intra-priestly arguments were set within the context of a broad popular knowledge of and concern for understanding and doing what torah commanded. For all its leading role with respect to torah, the priesthood did not monopolize the discourse of torah in Second Temple Judaism, in contrast to the role of the priesthood in relation to sacred texts and knowledge in many other Near Eastern cultures.[23]

As suggested above, the impulse to what one might call popular instruction does not originally seem to have come from the priesthood but rather from other segments of the society and to have

---

[19] In 2 Kgs 23:2 the reading is carried out by King Josiah himself, although priests, scribes, and prophets are key figures in the narrative. In 2 Chr 17:7–9 initiative for public teaching comes from King Jehoshaphat, carried out by officials, Levites, and priests. In Neh 8:1 the people request the reading, which is performed by Ezra, identified as both priest and scribe. In Neh 13:1 the passive voice obscures the source of the initiative for public reading, but context makes it unlikely that such instruction was the brainchild of the priestly authorities, since it results in conflict between Nehemiah and the priest Eliashib concerning the use of temple space. These accounts have varying claims to historical probability, but my interest is less in historicity and more in how the authors of the texts represented the promulgation of torah. It appears that although priests are frequently *involved* in reading and teaching torah, the priesthood as an institution does not seem to have been the source of the social impetus toward broadening public knowledge of torah.

[20] This is at least the image projected by the Ezra narratives (note how frequently Ezra's priestly as well as scribal credentials are mentioned) and by the Chronicler's anachronistic account of Jehoshaphat's program for teaching torah. Although, there, priests represent only two of the fifteen or sixteen members of the panel, they may well have been the supervising members (see Japhet, *I & II Chronicles*, 750).

[21] For instance, Bickerman, *From Ezra to the Last of the Maccabees*, 17–18.

[22] So Fraade, 421–22.

[23] Bickerman, *Jews in the Greek Age*, 173; A. Baumgarten, "Torah as a Public Document," 17.

served different social interests, though it drew on the priests' expertise and social authority. Already in the preexilic Deuteronomic movement, building a community of consensus through instruction in torah appears to have proceeded under royal sponsorship and to have drawn on the resources of administrative scribes.[24] To be sure, there is no anti-priestly animus in Deuteronomy. Indeed, the priests, along with elders, are the special guardians of the law, responsible for its sabbatical public reading (Deut 31:11). What is distinctive about Deuteronomy is not the role of the priests vis-à-vis torah, or even the role of torah itself, but rather the way Deuteronomy talks about torah. The rhetorical distance between Leviticus and Deuteronomy is significant. Although Leviticus is punctuated with periodic notices that Yahweh said to Moses, "Speak to the people of Israel and say . . .," the literary setting is a revelation to Moses, and the focus is on the content of the laws themselves. In Deuteronomy the moment of transmission, the process of learning, and the meaning of knowing the laws and the community's history shape this intensely rhetorical text. Listening to, remembering, and teaching the torah of God and the story of the giving of the torah to Israel serve to shape the identity and moral character of the people (Deut 4–11; 27–31, passim; 17:18–20; 26:16–19; 32:45–47). In Deuteronomy it is not just torah but talk about torah that constitutes and reconstitutes Israel.[25]

Knowledge itself is represented in a distinctive way in Deuteronomy. Although Deuteronomy is obviously the product of a professional scribal group, knowledge is not presented as the special province of a sapiential elite. Knowledge of torah is transparent and unproblematic. All that is needed is careful attention (e.g., 4:1; 5:1) and a commitment not to forget but to transmit the teachings to the next generation (4:9–10). In terms that are so explicit that one wonders

---

[24] My wording intentionally fudges the complex issues of the composition and redaction of Deuteronomy and its promulgation. See the discussion of Weinfeld in *Deuteronomy and the Deuteronomic School*, 158–78, concerning royal scribal activity in relation to Deuteronomy. A brief but incisive argument against Levitical composition of Deuteronomy is given by Blenkinsopp, *Wisdom and Law*, 98–101.

[25] On Deuteronomy as the constitution of Israel see McBride, "Polity of the Covenant People." Watts (*Reading Law*, 62) rightly argues for the rhetorical shaping of the Pentateuch in its various parts and as a whole for purposes of both instruction and persuasion. He, too, notes the distinctive rhetoric of Deuteronomy, which "works to merge the voices of YHWH and Moses into a unifying rhetoric of authority" (120).

if they are designed to counter alternative perceptions, Deuteronomy insists that the word that is commanded is wholly accessible, not in heaven, not beyond the sea, but "very near to you; it is in your mouth and in your heart for you to observe" (31:14). For all the stress on learning and doing, however, no warrant is given for participation in interpretative innovation. Judicial cases too difficult for local resolution are to be decided by a central authority whose rulings are not to be disregarded upon pain of death (17:8–13). On the other hand royal power, too, is hedged about by the discipline of reading the words of torah (17:18–20). The discourse of knowledge in Deuteronomy attempts to constitute Israel as a consensual community by popularizing the pedagogical language and values of a professional scribal class and by attaching them to the symbol of torah.[26] The borrowing is not all in one direction. The sapiential discourse that characterizes Deuteronomic rhetoric has its roots in familial instruction. In Deuteronomy, however, it is reaccented with the overtones of professional scribalism (e.g., in the references to study and writing and formal instruction) and then offered back as a language for the formation of the entire people. Although in many respects a utopian document, the strength of the Deuteronomic idiom in postexilic literature suggests the extent to which it succeeded in establishing the terms of discourse about torah in Israel.

An instructive comparison with the role and representation of knowledge of torah in Deuteronomy is provided by the postexilic works of Ezra-Nehemiah and 1–2 Chronicles. A long and unresolved history of debate exists concerning the nature of Ezra's mission and the relative significance of Ezra's representation in the dual roles as priest and scribe in connection with his promulgation of the law. My concern here is less with the historical realities that lie behind the text than with the socio-religious assumptions embedded in the way the text represents events. While the text represents the source of Ezra's *authorization* as an edict of the Persian king, the primary symbol of *authority* is "the law of your God which is in your keeping" (Ezra 7:14).[27] Both Ezra's status as priest (7:1–5; cf. 7:11, 12) and his status as "a scribe expert in the torah of Moses" (7:6; cf.

---

[26] Watts (*Reading Torah*, 116–22) discusses the characterization of Moses in Deuteronomy in terms of the ethos of the ancient scribe.

[27] Knoppers, "Achaemenid Imperial Authorization?", 121.

7:11, 12) function to credential him in relation to this symbol of authority.[28] Notably, not only is Ezra's expertise stressed but also the effort required to achieve such expertise. To become a "scribe expert in the torah of Moses" (7:6) he had "focused his mind on studying the torah of YHWH" (הכין לבבו לדרוש את־תורת יהוה; 7:10). Knowledge of torah requires discipline and hard work. As in Deuteronomy, it is not merely the status of torah that matters but the formation of a community through the process of teaching and observing torah. Ezra's personal motivation for his disciplined study was, according to Ezra 7:10, "to study the torah of YHWH in order to observe it and to teach Israel statutes and rules" (לדרוש את־תורת יהוה ולעשׂת וללמד בישראל חק ומשפט). Similarly, a significant part of Ezra's official task, according to the words of the firman, was "to appoint magistrates and judges to judge all the people . . . *who know the laws of your God, and to teach those who do not know them*" (7:25).

The influence of Deuteronomy on Ezra-Nehemiah is evident even more strikingly in the classic scene of the reading of the torah in Nehemiah 8. The presence of the entire people is stressed: "Men and women, all who could hear with understanding" (cf. Deut 31:9–13). As in Deuteronomy, the goal of instruction is to establish the consensual unity among those who possess a common understanding. Shared knowledge of torah constitutes the community.[29] There are other continuities with Deuteronomy. Just as Deuteronomy had concluded with the writing down of the torah by Moses (31:9, 24), so a written document is the form of Ezra's torah. Ezra himself is the embodiment of Deuteronomy's model of proper orientation to the torah (Ezra 7:10). The most striking difference between the representation of knowledge in Deuteronomy and in Ezra-Nehemiah, however, is in the role of Levitical intermediaries. Whatever the exact nature of the Levitical activity (whether careful reading by phrases and units, translation, and/or explicit interpretation),[30] knowledge of

---

[28] Whether or not Ezra was a professional scribe in the Persian imperial administration, which he may well have been, the author interprets this role in relation to his expertise in the torah of Moses/YHWH. See Schams, *Jewish Scribes in the Second Temple Period*, 54–56.

[29] The book of Malachi suggests the extent to which public discourse about torah had become a space of social contention in the early fifth century. It presents the negative mirror image of the community represented in Nehemiah 8 as one united by a common understanding of torah.

[30] For a discussion of the meaning of the terms used in Neh 8:8 see Fishbane, *Biblical Interpretation*, 108–9. See also Blenkinsopp, *Wisdom and Law*, 139.

torah is not the immediate experience that it is represented to be in Deuteronomy. No longer is torah unproblematically "in your mouth and in your heart" (Deut 31:14). The ordinary Israelite requires assistance to understand. The self-effacing scribes of Deuteronomy, whose presence was experienced only in the pedagogical and sapiential language of that book, have now received embodiment in a class of interpreters who mediate between the priest/scribe who reads and the people who are to hear with understanding.

The ideology of knowledge of torah that characterizes Ezra-Nehemiah is physically manifested in the scene: a priest/scribe, authorized by the Persian king, stands on a raised platform, flanked by prominent lay members of the community. He reads from a written book of torah as a group of expert interpreters mediates the knowledge to the assembled community, who hear, understand, and respond. Knowledge of torah forms and unites the community but it also articulates it in a hierarchical manner. And yet the desire to know originates with the people themselves, for it is they who are said to have requested the reading and instruction (Neh 8:1). A similar idealized representation of the social location of torah and torah instruction is present in the Chronicler's anachronistic description of Jehoshaphat's reforms.[31] The Chronicler envisions Jehoshaphat sending out a team composed of five prominent lay persons, nine Levites, and two priests to teach the book of the torah of Yahweh throughout his kingdom (2 Chr 17:7–9). Royal initiative, a concern for community formation through instruction, orientation to a written document, and authority shared among priestly, quasi-priestly, and non-priestly but noble segments of the social order are all prominent in this depiction.

Something of a cultural contradiction exists in the way knowledge of torah is represented. On the one hand, the destinateurs of torah are the whole people of Israel, whose ability to understand is a necessary assumption of the existence of a society founded upon torah. But on the other hand knowledge of torah is problematized to a greater or lesser extent and represented as the special provenance of priests, Levitical interpreters, or others who possess expertise. Torah is both a common possession and a special possession. For

---

[31] See Japhet, 748–50; Knoppers, "Jehoshaphat's Judiciary," 63–65; Runesson, 305–8.

official society the terms of the contradiction would be mediated through a hierarchy of knowledge and through institutionalized interpretation, much as it is ideally represented in Ezra-Nehemiah and Chronicles. But one of the consequences of this contradiction is that it would be extremely difficult to establish a monopoly on the interpretation of torah, even by groups with official status. Indeed, we do not know if any attempt was ever made. In any case the way was open for those who lacked political authorization or institutional status or who were otherwise marginalized nevertheless to acquire cultural power by engaging in the discourse of torah, and especially by problematizing its modes and/or contents.[32] Although one can imagine other possibilities, the form that contestation took was overwhelmingly the development of rival claims to expertise rather than a denigration of expertise itself.

Before turning to look at some of those rival claims and the terms in which they engaged one another, a few words need to be said about the ultimate success of the program to establish a community of consensus founded on torah. E.P. Sanders has attempted to describe what he calls "common Judaism," defined in schematic terms as "what the priests and the people agreed on."[33] In terms of my inquiry, what Sanders is delineating is the dominant discourse of later Second Temple Judaism, the set of assumed values, beliefs, and ways of doing things that was "based on internal assent . . . backed up by common opinion."[34] One could certainly contest various particular claims that Sanders makes; and he sometimes moves with disconcerting

---

[32] Runesson, 319, 329–30. As Watts (*Reading Torah*, 146) notes concerning the representation of Moses in Deuteronomy within the redacted Pentateuch, ". . . as recorder and teacher, Moses provides a model for the authoritative reinterpretation of written law not just by Temple priests but by any scribe competent to handle the materials. In other words, if the legal traditions of the Judean lay leaders and their allied prophets have been placed in a reduced, secondary role, the publication of authorized Judean Temple law made the role of scribal interpreter available publicly, and the contradictory nature of that law made this role absolutely necessary. Thus the gain in lay scribal influence (including that of Deuteronomistic scribes) offset the loss of authority by Deuteronomistic prophets. The history of Second Temple Judaism shows clearly the religious marginalization of prophets and the increasing religious importance of lay teachers (rabbis) and scribes alongside the continuing power of the Jerusalem priesthood. The Pentateuch foreshadowed and encouraged this development by restricting Moses' prophetic characterization and emphasizing his instructional and scribal activities."

[33] Sanders, *Judaism*, 47.

[34] Sanders, *Judaism*, 47.

ease from what a text says (whether the biblical text, Josephus, Philo, or the Mishnah) to an assumption that it indeed happened like that. Despite particular reservations one might have, Sanders generally succeeds in making a persuasive case that there was a broadly consensual religious culture within Judaism, especially in the Palestinian area that is his focus. In general terms Jews believed that the sacred books were holy scripture, treated the temple as an object of devotion, respected and supported its priesthood, brought the sacrifices required of them when they came for pilgrimage feasts, set aside tithes for the priests (though less frequently for the Levites) and the other agricultural offerings. They had their sons circumcised, recited the Shema, and made daily prayers in the morning and evening. On the Sabbath they refrained from work, and many attended the synagogue to hear scripture read and expounded and to engage in other acts of worship and instruction. Not only did people do what was necessary to avoid contaminating the temple with impurity but came to regard purity as "a positive good, the proper state to be in, *whether or not* one was about to enter the temple,"[35] as evidenced not only by the widespread occurrence of immersion pools but also by references to nonbiblical customs of purification in the literature of Palestinian and Diaspora Judaism. Jews had a common moral ethos that placed a high value on charity and love and shared a general set of theological beliefs that Sanders has characterized, somewhat controversially, as "covenantal nomism."[36] It would be misleading, however, to take Sanders' delineation of the dominant discourse of "common Judaism" simply in terms of its unifying function. As Clifford Geertz has remarked, "commonality of ideological perception may link [people] together, but it may also provide them . . . with a vocabulary by means of which to explore more exquisitely the differences among them."[37] The exquisite exploration of differences is what the continuing talk about torah and scripture was concerned with. But who were those who sought to engage the popular concern with torah and sought to benefit by contesting or making problematic those things that everyone agreed mattered?

[35] Sanders, *Judaism*, 218 (italics in original).

[36] See the recent reassessment of Sanders's thesis in Carson, O'Brien, and Seifrid, *Justification and Variegated Nomism*. Although many of the essays establish the need for significant modification of Sanders's thesis, the concluding essay is in my opinion unduly negative about the value of his work.

[37] Geertz, *Interpretation of Cultures*, 206.

Setting and Contesting Agendas: The Roles of Scribes

With written documents playing an increasingly important role in the discussion of torah, the scribe's literacy and expertise with texts made him a central figure in the widening circles of those who engaged in the discourse of torah. Unfortunately, given the nature of our sources, a social history of the scribe in Second Temple Judaism cannot be written.[38] Part of the problem in discussing the role of the scribe is with the vagueness of the term, which may refer to anything from the modestly literate and lowly village scribe to the highest government official. Scribes were employed in various institutions and social contexts (in the temple and in the governmental bureaucracy, by private landowners and merchants, perhaps as teachers) and with a variety of functions (as administrators, as jurists, as copyists, etc.). Although there is no evidence that scribes as such formed a distinct social class, there are some indications that a professional ethos did emerge, though one in which differences as well as similarities can be detected.[39]

Already in the late First Temple period Jeremiah refers to "handlers of the torah" (Jer 2:8) and to the false pen of the scribes that turns torah into a lie (Jer 8:8–9). In Jeremiah's critique these legal

---

[38] The most recent survey of ancient sources is that of Schams, *Jewish Scribes in the Second Temple Period*. Although her analyses are extremely valuable, the usefulness of the work is limited by her privileging what one reviewer (Wright, 553) called the "etymological meaning" of the term *sopher*. See also Orton, *The Understanding Scribe*. Schams (23) criticizes his work, with some justification, for its "conflationist" treatment of the sources. The more sociologically oriented study of Saldarini, *Pharisees, Scribes and Sadducees*, remains especially valuable. See also the well-reasoned analysis of Davies, "Judean Scribes, Schools, Archives, and Libraries," in his *Scribes and Schools*.

[39] The type of scribe I am concerned with here is the one characterized by learnedness and for whom learnedness is connected with the study, production, and interpretation of books. This activity and the ethos associated with it I refer to as "scribalism." I would also distinguish from such self-conscious "scribalism" those persons and communities who are also "book oriented" but for whom scribal activities are not a prominent part of identity and self-presentation—as for instance the Qumran community. The status and meaning of books, of the production of books, and of those who produced them in the mixed oral/literate communities of the Persian, Hellenistic, and Roman periods is extremely complex. Books functioned there in different ways than they do in a print culture. Especially before the development of the codex, the written book in the form of a scroll was perhaps more important as a form of permanent record than as a source to be frequently consulted, though the contrast should not be exaggerated. See the important study of Niditch, *Oral World and Written Word*, and the review of the issues by Jaffee, *Torah in the Mouth*, 1–27.

experts are closely connected with the priesthood, but whether they represent a specialist development from within the ranks of the priest-hood[40] or non-priestly technical assistants is not clear. The double designation of Ezra as priest and scribe has been variously interpreted both with respect to its historical accuracy and the way it was under-stood by the author/editors of Ezra/Nehemiah,[41] but could point in the direction of scribal expertise as a specialized priestly function, especially within the Babylonian diaspora.[42] It does appear that in the early Second Temple period the Levites were particularly asso-ciated with interpretive and teaching functions.[43] It has also been argued that the scribes referred to in the New Testament are Levites, though that remains a deeply disputed question,[44] and it is often assumed that the specialization of the Levites with respect to exper-tise in torah was related to their exclusion from sacrificial service.

In addition to the Levites, non-Levitical lay jurists appear to have been part of the official administration of the province of Jehud. The Chronicler's description of Jehoshaphat's reforms (2 Chron 17:7–9 and 19:8–11), alluded to above, is generally assumed to reflect Persian period conditions.[45] He describes Jehoshaphat as sending out teams of lay officials (שרים), Levites, and priests to teach the people by means of the "book of the torah of YHWH" (ספר תורת יהוה) and establishing a judiciary in Jerusalem composed of Levites, priests, and heads of families. What this may suggest, as Bickerman argues,[46] is that by the Chronicler's time the scribe-as-jurist was a professional category that cut across other social identities. Presumably the sort of activity in which these jurists engaged is represented in the exam-ples of inner biblical halakic exegesis reflected in the books of Ezra-Nehemiah and 1–2 Chronicles.[47]

---

[40] So Blenkinsopp, "Sage, Scribe, and Scribalism," 314.

[41] See Hoglund, *Achaemenid Imperial Administration*, 226–28; Williamson, *Ezra-Nehemiah*, 91–92, 100.

[42] Blenkinsopp, "Sage, Scribe, and Scribalism," 312–13.

[43] Fishbane, *Biblical Interpretation*, 108–111; Blenkinsopp, "Sage, Scribe, and Scribal-ism," 310–11. Levites, of course, had other functions as well. See Knoppers, "Hiero-dules, Priests, or Janitors?"

[44] See the discussion of Schwartz, "Scribes and Pharisees."

[45] Japhet, 749. Knoppers, "Jehoshaphat's Judiciary," 62, 80, rightly cautions that the Chronicler does not simply mirror conditions of the postexilic period but rep-resents an idealized picture in which "the competing interests represented by the priests, Levites, military, clan chiefs, and royalty become coordinated and complementary."

[46] Bickerman, *Jews in the Greek Age*, 162–63.

[47] See Fishbane, *Biblical Interpretation*, 107–62.

THE SCRIBE AS *HAKAM*: BEN SIRA

The scribe-as-jurist would have been professionally concerned with torah and the interpretation of torah. But not all scribes were jurists, nor were all scribes employed by the temple or governor's palace. Nevertheless, one can ask about the extent to which knowledge of torah and knowledge of the emerging body of scripture constituted the primary education for all scribes and the common basis of expertise to which other specialized skills and competencies were added. Although he undoubtedly overstates the case somewhat, E. P. Sanders has argued that at least in late Second Temple times "knowledge was not divided into sub-categories"; expertise in torah was fundamental and indeed was the basis for imputing other sorts of expertise to someone—even knowledge of how to run a rebellion (referring to the panel of experts assembled to assess Josephus' conduct of his command in Galilee).[48] Although some scribes were simply reading and writing functionaries, the literary references to scribes in the Second Temple period indicate that an important segment were assumed to be knowledgeable in the law and traditions of Israel.[49] Perhaps a legitimate inference is that literacy was gained by learning to read and write the scriptural texts that formed the national religious literature of Israel. Thus such knowledge would not only be the foundation for competence in a variety of professions but might also be cultivated as a cultural value, one that gave its possessor status within the community.

Ben Sira's account of the scribe in relation to other occupations stands in an ancient tradition of scribal self praise,[50] but it serves to indicate how he understood knowledge to confer status. Although Ben Sira is in no sense polemicizing against the rhetoric of torah that one finds in Deuteronomy, his words are a reply (in Bakhtin's sense) to that earlier discourse of torah. Ben Sira makes knowledge

---

[48] Sanders, *Judaism*, 171–72.

[49] This view is most common in the New Testament and in early Rabbinic literature but also occurs in Ben Sira's description of the scribe (Sir 38:24–39:11) and in Ben Sira's grandson's description of his grandfather in the prologue to the book. M. Goodman (107) suggests that the association of scribes with expertise in torah may derive from their role in copying scripture. See also Schams, 302–4.

[50] See the ancient Egyptian texts, "The Satire of the Trades" (Lichtheim, *Ancient Egyptian Literature* I, 184–92), Papyrus Lansing and "The Immortality of Writers" (Lichtheim, *Ancient Egyptian Literature* II, 168–78).

of torah problematic in that he links it to the issue of leisure. However admirable and skillful the accomplishments of other occupations, since they do not allow for leisure, they cut one off from the opportunity to "devote oneself to the study of the law of the Most High." Like the representation of knowledge of torah in Ezra/Nehemiah and Chronicles, it is an elitist model. The contradiction between torah as common possession ("an inheritance for the congregations of Jacob," Sir 24:23; "an overflowing river," 24:25–27) and as special possession characterizes Ben Sira as well. His resolution of the contradiction, like theirs, is the mediation of the expert (24:30–34; 51:23). Whether or not Ben Sira was a priest,[51] he never connects his expertise with such a status but draws on the ancient model of the wise father/teacher (e.g., 2:1; 3:1; 4:1). This mediating role is clearly expressed in the grandson's prologue, where he describes Ben Sira as "acquiring considerable proficiency" in the books of scripture and then writing his own work so that "those who love learning should make even greater progress in living according to the law." The institutional form that this learning and its transmission takes is the "house of instruction" (בית מדרש; 51:23), which is generally understood to refer here to a private school.[52]

But what does "study of the law of the Most High" mean for Ben Sira? Is Bickerman correct, for example, when he claims that for Ben Sira "in order to be wise, one had to ponder not only the intricacies of ritual impurity, but also the statute concerning parapets on roofs?"[53] Or does Bickerman implicitly anachronize, making the later rabbinic ideal the measure for the "torah scholar" that Ben Sira cel-

---

[51] Stadelman, (Ben Sira als Schriftgelehrter, 4–26) and Olyan ("Ben Sira's Relationship to the Priesthood") have argued that Ben Sira was a priest, noting his concern for the livelihood of the priests (7:29–31) and his admiring descriptions of Aaron (45:6–22), Phineas (45:23–25), and Simon the Just (50:1–21). But as Grossman has shown in her study of first century CE texts, much talk about priests—what she calls "thinking with priests"—may have to do with the phenomenon of "interpretive competition," attempts to articulate "competing claims—to authority, authenticity, and identity—grounded in the interpretation of a shared literary and cultural tradition" (117). Ben Sira may indeed have been a priest, but his concern for and praise of priests is no certain proof of that status. Horsley and Tiller ("Ben Sira and the Sociology of the Second Temple") have suggested that Ben Sira be understood as a "scribe-sage" from the "retainer class" who acted as an intermediary between the priestly class and the common people.

[52] Crenshaw, Education in Ancient Israel, 228–30, 271; Byrskog, Jesus the Only Teacher, 68–69.

[53] Bickerman, Jews in the Greek Age, 171.

ebrates? There is no doubt that when Ben Sira refers to "the book of the covenant of the Most High God" (24:23) he refers to the Pentateuch. Nor is there any doubt that Ben Sira makes explicit references to halakah, a feature that strongly distinguishes him from the sages responsible for the book of Proverbs. It may be that Ben Sira was capable of carrying on a highly technical halakic discourse. Especially if Ben Sira were a priest, one could assume that he did indeed have the sort of technical expertise in torah that Bickerman attributes to him. But even if he did, that is not the way in which he talks about torah in the book that bears his name. It is not through halakic discourse that he carries on the education of his readers. Nor is it through such a voice that he models what it means to be wise. In fact, in terms of halakah, Ben Sira does not say much more than could be considered common knowledge. My point is not about what Ben Sira the person did or did not know but rather how he represented torah in the speech that was most characteristic of his self-identity as scribe/sage. The issue is precisely that of the way he inflects the term in question—in this case the culturally central term torah—with the particular accents of his own social dialect. Ben Sira sapientializes the term torah, in keeping with the nuance of "instruction" that it traditionally had in wisdom discourse. To be sure Ben Sira, like many others in his culture, knows what the torah requires in terms of purity and impurity, but he subordinates those details as he appropriates torah to serve his moral instruction. Wisdom is the master discourse into which the discourse of halakah is inserted. In his teaching in 34:28–31, for example, halakah concerning corpse impurity becomes one example among others for illustrating a general moral principle.[54] Similarly, when Ben Sira displays his knowledge of the narrative and prophetic texts of scripture, his account of them is in terms of moral exemplars and cultural heroes. It is possible to understand Ben Sira as both claiming a share of the cultural value of torah to validate the role of the sage in a new cultural world, and implicitly contesting the limits of the legist's discourse of torah from his own location within the sapiential tradition.

---

[54] Compare also the integration of cultic obligations into a more traditional sapiential discourse concerning social responsibilities in Sirach 35.

APOCALYPTIC SCRIBALISM: DANIEL

So far in this section I have talked about two types of scribes: the
scribe as jurist, whose work is represented in the interpretive and
exegetical work of the books of Ezra-Nehemiah, and the scribe as
hakam, represented in the figure of Ben Sira. There is also another
type represented by the fictionalized scribe Daniel.[55] Although Daniel
is a fictional character, the depiction of him in the narratives of
Daniel 1–6 is often regarded as representing an idealized model of
the administrative scribe/sage in the eastern Diaspora.[56] More transparently, the character of Daniel in the apocalyptic chapters of Daniel
7–12 is considered to be a mouthpiece for the modes of understanding
and values of the author(s) of these chapters. Even less than Ben
Sira is Daniel preoccupied with specifically halakic discourse, though
the interpretation of prophetic scripture is central to the book. What
makes Daniel important to this discussion is that he helps to clarify
how knowledge itself was constructed and contested among scribes.

A comparison of Ben Sira's description of the ideal scribe with
the figure of Daniel illumines the extent to which there was a common
scribal ethos. It also shows how differently such scribes construct
knowledge: what its proper objects are, how it is produced, what
functions it serves, with whom it is to be shared, and so forth.
Although most readers have an intuitive sense of the difference
between the two characters, it is striking how well Ben Sira's description of the ideal scribe in Sir 38:33–39:11 fits the character of
Daniel.[57]

Ben Sira's description includes the following salient features. The
scribe is above all a specialist (38:24; 39:1a). His expertise is defined
primarily in relation to knowledge of torah, wisdom, and prophecies
(39:1), a statement that apparently refers to the emerging body of
scripture in Israel. The following two verses, however, remark on
the mode of knowledge as much as its source. There is something
akin to a hermeneutic of suspicion in Ben Sira's references to the
subtleties, hidden meanings, and obscurities of parables and proverbs.

---

[55] Although the term "scribe" is not used of Daniel, Orton, 99–102, demonstrates that Daniel's aptitudes, training, and desires are those of the scribe.

[56] Wilson, "From Prophecy to Apocalyptic," 88; Redditt, *Daniel*, 16; Davies,
"Scribal School of Daniel," 257–8.

[57] Similarly, Orton, 101; Collins, *Daniel*, 49.

Real meaning is not surface meaning, and it is the scribe who has access to real meaning. Verse 4a, along with 38:33, describes the social role of the scribe. They are givers of advice about public matters, persons whose opinions are sought out even by the highest rulers. Moreover, they know how to give sound judgment in judicial matters. Although v. 4b could refer to moral judgments about "the good and evil among persons," the reference to travel in foreign lands suggests rather that the phrase has to do with judicious appreciation of alien wisdom, what is "good" and what is "worthless." The following verse emphasizes the piety of the scribe in prayer, petition, and seeking pardon. Such piety is not peculiar to scribes, of course, but it is significant that Ben Sira mentions it so specifically. Piety is apparently so much a part of the scribal ethos that his description of the scribe naturally includes it. (See also Eleazer in 2 Maccabees 7 for an example of the pious scribe as character type.) It is not accidental that Ben Sira mentions piety in the verse immediately preceding the description of divinely given understanding, though he does not specifically draw a link between petition and reception of wisdom. Finally, the understanding the scribe receives from God is presented in terms of an almost prophetic understanding (Sir 39:6–8).

Virtually all of these features are embodied by the character of Daniel, both in the narratives and in the apocalypses. Although the training regimen described in the book pertains to Chaldean wisdom, Daniel is initially selected for qualities that include previous accomplishment in the intellectual arts (Dan 1:4). As the apocalyptic chapters indicate, his ability was assumed to include knowledge of scripture, specifically prophetic texts (9:2) but also matters that are "written in the law of Moses" (9:11). Throughout the book knowledge is represented as the ability to discern hidden meanings, though Daniel exercises this skill on dreams and cryptic divine inscriptions rather than the proverbs and parables of which Ben Sira speaks. Daniel's social role is in keeping with Ben Sira's image of the scribe as counselor, and, if one includes the story of Susanna, Daniel's insight is also used in judicial contexts. As an exile, Daniel's "travels in foreign lands" were involuntary, but the knowledge of other cultures that Ben Sira alludes to is also part of the intellectual repertoire of Daniel. In a way that Ben Sira probably would not have approved of, the *author* of Daniel has himself examined foreign modes of thought and found at least one of them worthy, since the four-kingdoms schema that is used in chapters 2 and 7 is a piece of foreign wisdom, and various other elements of Babylonian tradition are employed throughout the book. Daniel's ability to discriminate between the good and the worthless in the moral sphere is exemplified in his differing interactions with the three kings, Nebuchadnezzar, Belshazzar, and Darius. The quality of piety is certainly fundamental to the depiction of Daniel. Most importantly, the relation between piety and insight is the same as that implied by Sir 39:4: petition, giving of insight, thanksgiving (Dan 2:17–23; see also Daniel 9). Although the media of revelation are more vividly developed, at least in the apocalyptic chapters, the "spirit of understanding" and meditation on divine "mysteries" of which Ben Sira speaks (Sir 39:6–7) are also characteristic of Daniel in the narratives (Dan 2:22–23; 4:15). The recognition that Ben Sira assumes is the reward of the successful scribe is echoed in the promotion to authority that Daniel receives and also in his popularity as a narrative figure.

What this comparison is intended to suggest is the existence of a common scribal ethos even among scribal figures whose ideologies of knowledge are quite different. The similarities between the two characters only set into sharper relief how differently they develop their scribal personae. The primary object of knowledge is different. For Ben Sira, as for the traditional sage, it is wise conduct in a domestic or interpersonal setting. For Daniel it is the divinely ordained historical process as it manifests itself in the fates of kingdoms and rulers. Ben Sira explicitly excludes speculation on cosmological secrets, knowledge of "what is too difficult for you . . . what is beyond your power . . . what is hidden . . . matters too great for human under-standing" (Sir 3:20–22), whereas this is precisely what the book of Daniel offers (Dan 2:22, 30; 7:15–16; 8:15–17; 9:22; 10:7). Although the opposition is not as explicit, the predestinarian assumptions of Daniel, which are necessary presuppositions for the kind of knowl-edge he cultivates, would not be admitted by Ben Sira (Sir 15:11–20). The problematic quality of knowledge is emphasized in a striking way in Daniel, especially in the apocalyptic chapters. The figure of Daniel as expert, developed in the narratives, is used explicitly as a foil in the apocalypses, where the expert appears repeatedly baffled. *Esotericism replaces expertise as the model of knowledge.* Its otherworldly quality is emphasized—far beyond Ben Sira's mild language of inspi-ration—through the media of dream visions and angelic interpreters, as well as through the physically devastating effects of revelation.

Finally, there is in Daniel a complex interplay between withholding and disclosing knowledge that is quite alien to the model of the sapiential teacher in Sirach. This is as true in the narratives as in the apocalypses. In Daniel 2, Daniel tells Nebuchadnezzar the truth, but not the whole truth. The reader, however, is implicitly invited to discern certain meanings that Daniel has declined to share with Nebuchadnezzar. The apocalypses present themselves in the guise of knowledge that has been concealed for centuries ("secret and sealed until the end of time," 12:9; cf. 12:4) and yet is disclosed in the act of reading the putatively now unsealed book.[58] According to Daniel the "wise" are to disclose their knowledge to "the many." Knowledge in Daniel thus also serves to form community, but not in the way that it is depicted in Deuteronomy, Ezra-Nehemiah and Chronicles, and not in the way it is described in Ben Sira. Here, knowledge not only includes but excludes: "None of the wicked shall understand, but those who are wise shall understand" (12:10). Although there is no likelihood of an overt polemical relation between Ben Sira and the author of the narratives and apocalypses of Daniel, they do implicitly contest each other's construction of the image of the scribe, of the content and modes of knowledge, and of the social functions of such knowledge.

Although the particular events of the Hellenistic crisis of 175–163 BCE unquestionably have an impact on the way in which the apocalypses of Daniel are developed, the fundamental model of knowledge that they embody can be identified in apocalyptic writings that antedate the crisis, for instance, in the earlier written parts of the books of Enoch (1 Enoch 1–36 and 72–82).[59] Daniel and Enoch on the one hand and Ben Sira on the other represent systemically different types of scribal knowledge, which were undoubtedly developed in different social contexts.[60] Unfortunately, we are terribly ignorant about the social determinants that shaped these two ways

---

[58] See Davies, "Reading Daniel Sociologically," 356–57, concerning the role of the "secret" in Daniel.

[59] For Enoch as scribe see Orton, 77–99; Schams, 90–98. The presentation of Enoch in Jubilees is different in significant respects from that of 1 Enoch, not least in that in Jubilees Enoch is credited with the revelation of halakah.

[60] See Wright's attempt to delineate some of the intellectual and social topography of Ben Sira, the earlier parts of 1 Enoch, and the Aramaic Levi documents in "Putting the Puzzle Together: Some Suggestions Concerning the Social Location of the Wisdom of Ben Sira."

of knowing within the scribal tradition. The one social factor that seems beyond question is that the apocalyptic scribalism of Daniel and of Enoch is developed in conversation with Mesopotamian wisdom.[61] Ben Sira arguably looks west toward Greece,[62] but in any event is not significantly influenced by Mesopotamian traditions. What we do not know is how or why that orientation is connected with other social factors. Were there economic or social class differences between those scribes who identified with the figure of the traditional *hakam* and those who cultivated mantic wisdom and favored the designation *maskil*? If mantic wisdom was more associated with the eastern Diaspora, by what conduits did it become transmitted to Palestine? What sorts of people who were literate but not scribes were likely to be attracted to each type of literature; that is, who would identify with Ben Sira's invitation to "those who love learning" and who with the Danielic category of "the many"? Unfortunately, the questions are easy to ask but virtually impossible to answer.

One other question that has to be posed is whether the near absence of talk about torah in Daniel is fortuitous or not.[63] Did moral instruction in general and halakic interpretation in particular form an object of knowledge for apocalyptic scribalism? The character of Daniel in chapter 1 is concerned about "defilement" through food (1:8), but there is not enough detail to know whether and how Daniel's concern is related to biblical or nonbiblical food laws. The apocalyptic chapters speak about the egregious desecration of the sanctuary (9:27; 11:31) and the changing of "the times and the law" (7:25), but these things were widely perceived as a violation by many who would have little technical knowledge of the practices that kept the temple and its sacrifices pure. Daniel 11:32 does refer to "those

---

[61] For Enoch see the study of VanderKam, *Enoch and the Growth of an Apocalyptic Tradition*, 33–51. Concerning Daniel, see Collins, *Daniel*, 48–55. For both, see Kvanvig, *Roots of Apocalyptic*.

[62] Although arguments for specific Stoic or Epicurean influence on Ben Sira are inconclusive, it is indisputable that Ben Sira is familiar with a number of topoi of Hellenistic popular philosophy. Compare, for example, his treatment of the danger of excessive emotion in 38:16–23 with the Greco-Roman consolatory tradition.

[63] Hoffman (*Das Gesetz in der frühjüdischen Apokalyptik*, 78–121) discusses the general discourse of law in Daniel, noting its associations with issues of cult and calendar in Dan 7–12, as well as the deuteronomistic influence in the prayer in Dan 9. Yet although Daniel *refers* to matters of torah, the book does not make *interpretation of torah* central to its work, as it does the interpretation of Jeremiah's prophecy.

who violate the covenant," though the concrete actions that constitute violation appear to be the whole attempt to abrogate rule according to ancestral laws. Significantly, it is only when the scribe Daniel
speaks the cultural language of Deuteronomistic prayer in chapter 9
that the word torah occurs (9:10, 11). That apocalyptic scribalism
shared the common cultural values represented by torah is evident,
but it is simply not possible to say whether the authors and primary
audience for Daniel made specialized study and interpretation of
torah a central object, that is to say, whether they were legists.
Comparison with other apocalyptic literature that features scribal
figures as its spokespersons (the apocalypses of 1 Enoch, 2 Baruch,
4 Ezra) suggests that the orientation to historical and cosmological
knowledge is characteristic of the apocalyptic scribal tradition in a
way that specifically halakic discourse is not. Though there is an
interest in cultivating right behavior according to divine norms (e.g.,
1 Enoch 2–5), moral instruction is contextualized by historical and
cosmological knowledge (the Enochic corpus is an excellent example) in a way that is quite alien to traditional sapiential "torah of
your father/mother." Similarly, though one might note the cosmological and historical interests of the Priestly writer or the Deuteronomist
as part of their construal of knowledge, the specificity with which
they discuss the legal norms of individual and community behavior
is simply lacking in the apocalyptic traditions represented by Daniel,
1 Enoch, 2 Baruch, and 4 Ezra. Although it is difficult to discern
legistic specialization in a figure like Daniel (and in those for whom
he is a representative figure), interpretation of scripture for the purpose of the interpretation of historical events is a well developed skill
of apocalyptic scribalism, as 1 Enoch 85–90 indicates even more
clearly than Daniel 9.[64] The background for this particular orientation
to knowledge is probably to be sought in the confluence of prophetic
divination and mantic wisdom, as well as the phenomenon of the
textualization of prophetic activity in early Second Temple times.[65]

---

[64] Reese, *Die Geschichte Israels*, 21–45; Tiller, *Animal Apocalypse*, 21–60.
[65] VanderKam, "Prophetic-Sapiential Origins of Apocalyptic Thought," 169–70;
Grabbe, "Social Setting of Early Jewish Apocalypticism," 27–47.

EXCURSUS: APOCALYPTIC DISCOURSE AND THE RHETORICAL POWER OF MARGINS

One finds in apocalyptic scribalism an alternative construction of knowledge to that represented by Ben Sira or the legists, one that cultivates the claims of mantic wisdom to disclose the hidden unities in history and to provide a basis in cosmological knowledge for making moral judgments.[66] Equally significant is the fact that apocalyptic is an "outsider" discourse: not a language of the oppressed but a language of those who elect a stance of marginality and seek to use that marginal status to find a place in the cultural conversation. My claim is about the rhetoric of apocalyptic, not necessarily about the social condition of its authors. I do think that those who opt for a rhetoric of the margins are unlikely to have been those who controlled institutions, but they may well have been persons who had various forms of social capital (education, most obviously), as well as material resources.[67] Marginality should also not be equated with weakness. Though it does not call upon the authority of institutional structures (as does Ezra) or evoke the authority of traditionally hallowed forms of speech (as Ben Sira so effectively does), discourse from the margins can be a position of power in the same way that a fulcrum can privilege a physically eccentric position.

Apocalyptic scribalism actively uses a variety of rhetorical devices

---

[66] Sapiential texts that mediate between these two types include 4QInstruction (4Q415–418) and 4QMysteries (4Q299–300).

[67] The term "social capital" is taken from Pierre Bourdieu, whose discussion of discursive give and take are highly suggestive for the situation of Second Temple Judaism. See especially *The Logic of Practice* and *Language and Symbolic Power*. The discussion of Grabbe in "The Social Setting of Jewish Apocalypticism" offers some helpful correctives to the traditional discussion about how apocalyptic fit into Jewish society. He rightly objects to the misleading term "relative deprivation" as a way of categorizing those who are attracted to apocalyptic. As he notes concerning apocalyptic eschatology among today's conservative evangelical Christians, "many such individuals are from the middle class, and there is not an inconsiderable number of fervent evangelicals among the wealthy oilmen and millionaires of the American Bible belt" (31). But Grabbe gives an incomplete picture. Because he does not also take discourse analysis into account, what Grabbe fails to see is that contemporary apocalyptic is a discourse of the margins in that it is contesting the dominant discourse of modernity. See Ammerman, *Bible Believers*, 7–8. One cannot simply equate modern and ancient apocalyptic, of course, and the cultural function of ancient Jewish apocalyptic's rhetoric of the margins has to be considered on its own terms. I doubt that we will ever have the information to identify the social demographics of the practitioners of ancient Jewish apocalyptic with any specificity.

to mark its marginal stance. For one, it may represent its knowledge as being ancient, coming from the other side of that great boundary, the deluge (e.g., Adam, Seth, Enoch, Noah). Often it represents its knowledge as hidden, not widely known or shared, either sealed or privately transmitted. Marginal with respect to common knowledge, it appropriates the cachet of what is rare or esoteric. Similarly, its means of acquiring knowledge include modes that were regarded ambivalently in Israelite culture (e.g., dreams, visions, trances) and which are characteristic of psychologically liminal states. The heroes of apocalyptic may be characters from the dominant discourse (notably, Moses and Ezra), but in such cases the apocalyptic communication is often marked with some feature that stresses its difference from the public communications of those figures (e.g., the life/death liminality of Moses in the Testament of Moses or the herbally induced visions of Ezra in 4 Ezra). In the earlier apocalyptic traditions of Enoch and Daniel the content of the apocalypses is marked with the imprint of Mesopotamian culture and wisdom. As it was for Greek society, so for Palestinian Judaism, Mesopotamian wisdom was a "boundary" discourse that gained a hearing precisely by being from the margins of what was traditional. Even though the eastern influences in the Enochic traditions are never noted explicitly, as they are in Daniel, Enoch's marginality or liminality is manifest in other symbolic ways. He has an ambiguous status vis-à-vis heaven and earth, life and death. As a pre-Israelite sage, but one anchored in and vouched for by the canonical literature, his nontraditional wisdom need not be construed as competing with the dominant discourse based on Mosaic traditions but as encompassing it, a relationship already modeled by the way the Pentateuch itself situates Israel's origins in a wider cultural context.[68]

Daniel is in many respects a less powerful figure with which to work than is Enoch, since the character of Daniel is not grounded in the Pentateuch or in prophets.[69] In all probability the apocalyptic appropriation of Daniel rests on the strong popularity of the earlier Daniel story cycle. But Daniel, too, has various traits of marginality

---

[68] For the same reasons, Enoch appealed to various nonapocalyptic intellectuals, such as Eupolemus and pseudo-Eupolemus, who were concerned with the dialogue between Judaism and the Greco-Roman Hellenistic world.

[69] I do not take the reference to Dan'el in Ezekiel 14 and 20 to be a reference to the exilic character Daniel but to the Canaanite king Dan'el.

that would make him a fit spokesperson for outsider intellectuals. Daniel is represented as one who participates in the liminal state of exile. His story extends from the year that Nebuchadnezzar besieged Jerusalem (Dan 1:1) to the first year of Cyrus the king (1:21); yet his own fate is left unspecified (12:13). His role is both one of servant and judge of foreign kingdoms, and the modes of revelation that underwrite his knowledge (dream, dream-vision) were traditionally regarded with ambivalence. The apocalyptic perspective of Daniel attaches itself to dominant discourse through its explicit act of interpreting prophetic scripture. Implicitly, the claim of the book of Daniel is that it is precisely from this position of marginality that it is able to open up the true meaning of a central text. Such an act of interpretation represents an odd combination of conscious deference to and unconscious power over received tradition. The Jeremianic text is acknowledged as authoritative and as possessing the power to conceal its full meaning from the character Daniel, despite his expertise. It is a reservoir of mystery. (Contrast Ben Sira who does not invoke the image of the impenetrability of texts as he describes the powers of the scribe.) The scriptural text and the interpretation offered by the book of Daniel mutually reinforce each other's authority by together making sense of a contemporary historical situation. Ultimately, of course, it is the interpreter who (through divine revelation) unlocks the concealed meaning of the text and in an odd sense replaces its surface or public meaning. The interpretation itself, however, is articulated in an allusive or even coded form (9:24–27), suggesting that truth has yet further reserves of mystery. The one located in liminal space (in exile, between cultures, at the point of transition between empires, and at the intersection of heaven and earth) is the one who has access to the truth that conceals itself in scripture.

Priestly and Apocalyptic Scribalism: Jubilees

Apocalyptic scribalism shared a common scribal ethos and similar interpretive and exegetical methods with legists and with traditional sapiential scribes such as Ben Sira. In that sense they all occupied the same common field of symbolic production, the "knowledge industry" of Second Temple Judaism, and shared in the status open to scribes as "intellectuals." As specialists, each produced a different type of knowledge and competed with one another for attention in the cultural conversation and the ability to inflect the conversation with the accents of their own discourse. The legist had the advantage of producing knowledge about matters that were central to the praxis of Second Temple Judaism. Although it is evident that various groups differed in their understanding of certain norms for social organization and behavior, the historical sources clearly show the attempt of Persian-approved priestly scribalism to foster, organize, and dominate legistic discourse. One can see in Ben Sira's appropriation of the language of torah and incorporation of halakah as moral example the success of legists in inflecting sapiential discourse with the accents of their discourse. But one also sees Ben Sira attempting to contextualize the discourse of torah in a broader intellectual framework, including, if Bickerman is right, the cross-cultural dialogue with Hellenism. On another flank Ben Sira contests the claims about knowledge production made by apocalyptic scribes in an attempt to keep the cultural conversation about wisdom focused on the traditional competencies of the *hakam*. Yet his very reply to them is an indication of their success in entering the conversation. Part of apocalyptic scribalism's appeal is to be found in its exploitation of the rhetorical possibilities of marginality and in the highly visual and numerically patterned quality of its symbolic imagination. Through its frequent claims to have been transmitted from the distant past, apocalyptic appealed to the widespread cultural interest in remote antiquity and the lore of origins. Perhaps most important, however, was the comprehensiveness of its interpretive structures and their ability to organize the phenomena of history as a totality and to anchor them in transcendent and immutable realia. Although the early apocalyptic literature represented by Enoch and Daniel did not, so far as one can tell, engage in legistic activity, its own intellectual orientation to the cosmological, the transcendent, and the primordial made it an appealing discourse for a certain type of priestly scribalism to appropriate. The priestly writer of the Pentateuch already reflects the intellectual common ground that made such a cultural conversation possible, but it is in the priestly scribalism of the book of Jubilees that one finds legistic discourse fully accented with the intellectual outlook of apocalyptic. Although it is the astronomical and calendrical knowledge of the Enochic tradition that forms the bridge between priestly legistic interests and apocalyptic, Jubilees shows a much deeper interanimation of these two discourses than simply a borrowing of calendrical lore.

First, it is important to indicate how the scribal and priestly identity of Jubilees is manifest. The self-conscious scribal ethos of the book of Jubilees is evident above all in the author's concern to establish something like a history or genealogy of the scribal arts.[70] Thus Enoch is identified as "the first who learned writing and knowledge and wisdom" (Jub 4:17; trans. Wintermute). Several persons are said to have taught their sons to write (Arpachshad teaches Cainan, 8:2; Serug teaches Nahor, 11:8; Terah teaches Abraham, 11:6; Amram teaches Moses, 47:9). Books are written by Enoch (4:23), by Noah (10:10–11), and by Jacob (32:20–26). Similarly, the act of the writing of Jubilees itself is repeatedly mentioned at the beginning of the book (1:5, 7, 26, 27; 2:1). Heavenly books and scribal activity are often noted. The transmission of written documents is referred to several times. Cainan copies the antedeluvian inscription of the watchers (8:2–4), Noah entrusts his book to Shem (10:10–14), Abraham (who has been taught Hebrew by God) copies and studies Terah's books (12:25–27; 21:10), and Jacob entrusts "all his books and his father's books to Levi, his son, so that he might preserve them and renew them for his sons until this day" (45:15; trans. Wintermute). Given the narrative setting of the book, "this day" would refer to Moses' time, but the statement undoubtedly is intended also to identify the priesthood as the repository of such ancient lore even in the author's own day.

Levi's place as the final recipient of this inherited body of texts and lore in the book of Jubilees, and the parallel between Levi's role and what the author of Jubilees is in fact doing, strongly suggests that the author of Jubilees is himself a priestly scribe, perhaps a Levite.[71] The strongly halakic interests of the book, too, comport with the traditional priestly area of expertise. This is not to say that

---

[70] See now the important study by Najman, "Interpretation as Primordial Writing," especially pp. 381–88.

[71] Brooke ("Torah in the Qumran Scrolls," 116) refers to the "particular Levitical ideology" that characterizes both Jubilees and the Temple Scroll. VanderKam ("Origins and Purposes of the Book of Jubilees," 19), however, notes that although Jubilees 31 "has been taken by some to point to levitical connections . . . the more broadly priestly orientation of the book is evident in the reward given to Levi after he helped avenge the rape of Dinah in which both priests and levites are mentioned (30:17)."

the author of Jubilees speaks for all priests. Far from it. The author of Jubilees represents only one voice in the inner-priestly dialogue to which Fraade refers.[72] The positions advocated by Jubilees were certainly not those of the Hasmonean priests, and it is unlikely that in general they represented prior "establishment" practices displaced by the Hasmonean regime.[73] It is more likely that Jubilees represents a reformist, utopian voice, which would also comport well with its appropriation of certain aspects of apocalyptic discourse.

As is well known, Jubilees' substantive agenda includes the demonstration of the divine origins of the 364 day calendar, the immutability of various laws (written on heavenly tablets or "without limit of days"), the patriarchal antiquity of a number of festivals explicitly commanded in Mosaic law, details of sacrificial practices, and a particular concern for endogamous marriage and pollution by blood. With respect to calendar, festivals, and sacrifices, it is close to the agenda of the legists responsible for the Temple Scroll.[74] In contrast to the Temple Scroll, however, Jubilees presents that agenda in the context of narrative, specifically rewritten biblical narrative.[75] Najman has interpreted Jubilees' interest in the narratives as a rejection of the notion that "these narratives could have been of historical, non-legal import." Rather, "these narratives had to be shown to be crypto-legal texts."[76]

---

[72] Fraade, 421–22.

[73] The solar calendar may be an exception. Jaubert ("Le calendrier des Jubilées et de la secte de Qumrân") attempted to make the case for the use of the solar calendar as the official temple calendar in the early Second Temple period. Although acknowledging the indirect nature of the evidence, VanderKam ("Origin, Character, and Early History of the 364 Day Solar Calendar" and "2 Maccabees 6,7A and Calendrical Change in Jerusalem") has argued that Antiochus IV's attempt to change "the times and the law" (Dan 6:25) is an allusion to the substitution of the luni-solar calendar for the traditional solar calendar, an innovation that the Hasmoneans then perpetuated. See, however, the reservations of Davies, "Calendrical Change and Qumran Origins: An Assessment of VanderKam's Theory."

[74] See now VanderKam, "Temple Scroll," who refutes the arguments of Schiffman which claim incompatibility between the Temple Scroll and Jubilees.

[75] Brooke ("Torah in the Qumran Scrolls," 117) suggests that Jubilees, the Temple Scroll, and 1Q22 The Words of Moses, may be related documents that together form a reworked Pentateuch that was characterized among other things by "the primacy of the Levites as interpreters of the Law," a feature he sees as particularly characteristic of 1Q22. See also Brin, "The *Temple Scroll* and the Book of *Jubilees*," 108–9. If this is the case, then the reworked Pentateuch represented by these texts simply amplifies the tendency in the original Pentateuch to cluster narrative material in Genesis and the first part of Exodus and to emphasize legal material in the latter part of the document.

[76] Najman, "Interpretation as Primordial Writing," 395.

While this is certainly part of the dynamics, Najman may underestimate the entertainment value of these parts of Jubilees. The engagement with narrative may suggest that the author is directing his appeal not to other legists only but also to a broader audience who were consumers of various types of biblical retellings. The incorporation of legendary supplements to the biblical account and the moral editing of the biblical story perhaps suggest an overlap with the audience for such texts as the Genesis Apocryphon and the diverse testamentary literature.

But what about the author's ideology of knowledge? Some assumptions about how to produce knowledge are common ground, for instance the assumption that scripture contains puzzling hints that can be decoded to produce new knowledge.[77] Where Ben Sira discerns moralizing instruction and Daniel finds oracular prophecy, the author of Jubilees finds the exegetical clues that prove that the patriarchs celebrated various festivals on the calendrically appropriate days and otherwise obeyed laws that were inscribed on the heavenly tablets but not explicitly revealed until Sinai.[78] One of the most characteristic features of the ideology of knowledge in Jubilees is its privileging of a special tradition of ancient, revelatory books and its attempts to locate itself in that tradition. These books, however, each represent a different sort of knowledge, so that taken together, they suggest the scope of the objects of knowledge that Jubilees values, its intellectual horizons. The Enochic books hold pride of place in Jubilees, above all for their astronomical lore, essential for proper understanding of the calendar. The author of Jubilees also takes note of Enoch's knowledge of the details of heavenly realia, his proleptic account and moral analysis of human history until the day of judgment, as well as his account of his witness against the Watchers. Noah's book contains herbal remedies for illnesses caused by evil spirits. Jacob's book concerns the future history of Israel. The objects of knowledge that the author of Jubilees privileges are those characteristic of apocalypses. Though the author undoubtedly knows many

---

[77] Kugel (*Traditions of the Bible*, 15) lists as the first of four common assumptions shared by the diverse ancient interpreters the assumption that "the Bible is a fundamentally cryptic document."

[78] VanderKam, "Temple Scroll," 218–21; Najman, "Interpretation as Primordial Writing," 395–97.

other books, these are the only ones represented as part of the "library" of books transmitted from antiquity.

By situating his own book in this series, he makes a claim not only about the authority of his legistic teachings but also about the intellectual and social context within which such legistic discourse properly takes place. The characteristics of torah (its immutability, its numerological symmetries, its foundations in cosmic realia and primordial events, its uniting of heaven and earth) can only be adequately comprehended by those who understand the mysteries of cosmic structures and of history. Thus the speech of those who talk about torah without such comprehensive intellectual contexts is likely to be defective. Such claims about intellectual contexts also have social correlates. Since the books containing such matters are said to have been entrusted specifically to Levi for preservation by his sons, the author makes a case for the privileged role of the priestly scribe among those who engage in apocalyptic speculation. Simultaneously, the claim implies that those priestly scribes who reject the intellectual connection between halakah and apocalyptic speculation have betrayed their heritage and responsibility as guardians of ancestral knowledge. One can see in this kind of self-presentation the claims and counterclaims that are part of the contest of voices on the field of symbolic competition. Although the ideology of knowledge and the way it influences the discourse of torah in Essene writings is taken up below, it should be noted here that the priestly scribalism of Jubilees with its apocalyptic overtones is very close to that of the Qumran community.

NONSCRIBAL EXPERTISE

Not all forms of expertise in torah and scripture emerged from professional scribes, of course. Literacy was sufficiently widespread for many who were not professional scribes to be conversant with sacred texts. Moreover, oral media remained an important means of education.[79] The emergence of the synagogue provided an institutional basis for a basic popular familiarity with scripture and its interpretation.[80] The family, too, was a crucial institution in the

---

[79] See Jaffee, 15–27 and more generally, Niditch, *Oral World and Written Word.*

[80] Runesson (193–235) makes a strong case that torah reading was "the characteristic

reproduction of a culture of torah.[81] Thus it was possible for various pietist groups which were not part of the scribal "knowledge
industry" to participate in the cultural conversation with their own
claims of expertise. Although it is perilous to make any firm claims
about the Pharisees in light of the complex and incomplete historical record, I would identify the Pharisaic movement as cultivating
this sort of nonscribal expertise. By way of contrast, in looking at
the evidence for scribes, I have discussed individual authors or representative characters who either display a distinct "book consciousness" or claim for themselves an identity as a dedicated or professional
knowledge expert specifically concerned with writing and interpreting texts. There is no evidence that these scribes in any way constituted a movement or even a group in the sociological sense, though
I do argue that there was a certain common ethos, differentiated in
ways that one can discern in the different ideologies of knowledge
represented in the various texts. These differences do have sociological bases, even if one can no longer trace them in detail. But
there is far less evidence for these scribal authors as leaders of social
movements than is often thought.

With the Pharisees one has a different phenomenon. The simple
fact that a name is attached to them by others and that persons,
such as Josephus, could identify themselves with that name is evidence of a type of group identity. The social origins of the Pharisees
have been hotly debated, but occupationally and in terms of other
social markers they seem to have been reasonably diverse.[82] Though

---

activity of early synagogues" (193) in the first century CE and that the practice has
its roots in the public reading of torah originating in the Persian period. Similarly,
Levine (*Ancient Synagogue*, 139) puts the probable date for the institutionalization of
torah reading "as the central component in the non-sacrificial liturgy" sometime
between the fifth and third centuries BCE.

[81] As Bickerman (*Jews in the Greek Age*, 170) says, "children, instructed by their
families, learned by doing (for instance, by observing the Sabbath). The pious
Susanna was no biblical scholar, but she was taught by her parents how to live
according to the Law of Moses."

[82] In his survey of the evidence Sanders (*Judaism*, 406) adopts in modified form
the arguments of Finkelstein and Ginzberg that the Pharisees may have been modest merchants and traders or small independent landowners. With a somewhat
different emphasis Saldarini suggests that they were "subordinate officials, bureau-
crats, judges and educators . . . retainers who were literate servants of the governing class" (284), a definition that would certainly include scribes. Baumgarten
(*Flourishing of Jewish Sects*, 47) is less inclined to be specific but finds evidence that
"members of these groups [i.e., Qumran and the Pharisees] were men likelier to

scribes were undoubtedly among the ranks of the Pharisees, just as priests were, there is no indication that their participation is what gave the movement its identity or ethos. The New Testament references to "Pharisees and scribes," though difficult to interpret, also indicates a perception of difference.[83] What one would like to know is if the Pharisees created alternative forms for the production of knowledge as they engaged priests and scribal legists on the symbolic field of torah interpretation. The early rabbinic culture of argumentation, for instance, owes much to forms of oral debate that are strikingly different from the scribal book consciousness of a work like Jubilees, though it is not possible to say whether those Rabbinic modes for the production of knowledge owe their origin to Pharisaic discourse.[84]

It is now increasingly argued that the Pharisees, a largely lay group, did not control institutions, either the synagogues or the Sanhedrin. Though Josephus is generally conceded to have exaggerated the influence of the Pharisees in the life of late Second Temple Judaism, his analysis points in the right direction. It was through their reputation as learned and exact interpreters of torah that they gained influence. This is not to say that people actually did what Pharisees said they should do with respect to various categories of halakah. There are many reasons for thinking that Pharisaic interpretations were often restricted to the Pharisees themselves.[85] It is, however, quite possible to fail to change behavior and nevertheless achieve considerable standing in the society for having staked out the high ground in a matter of broad cultural concern.[86] Indeed

---

come from the economic, social and educational elite—the 'middling sort' (to the extent that there was such a class in antiquity) and better. . . ." He, too, finds that the research of Ginzberg and Finkelstein concerning the Pharisees "still retains some validity; it proves that at least some Pharisees reflected the social perceptions of the middle classes in their halachic positions" (47, n. 31).

[83] Occasional references to "the scribes of the Pharisees" also occur (e.g., Mk 2:16 in some manuscripts; Acts 23:9). See Schams's thorough discussion of the relevant New Testament texts (143–201) and especially her treatment of the association of scribes and Pharisees in Mark (161). Daniel Schwartz ("Scribes and Pharisees," 93–98) has argued that the New Testament scribes may be identified with Levites.

[84] Jaffee (39–61) argues forcefully that the *ideology* of oral torah is a much later phenomenon and that the evidence for tracing its origins to Pharisaic thought and practice is insufficient. While I think he is too skeptical concerning some of the evidence (in particular his treatment of CD 1:18 [42–44] and *m. Yad.* 4:6–7 [55–57]) one can certainly not simply project later Rabbinic understandings upon the Pharisees.

[85] See the discussion in Sanders, *Judaism*, 448–51.

[86] During the controversy in Britain over John Hicks' book, *The Myth of God*

it may be an error to think of the Pharisees as having an agreed upon program. Sanders has made the point that much of the deposit of Pharisaic material that can be recovered from the Mishnah and Tosephta does not consist of rules but of debates.[87] The Pharisees may thus have achieved their reputation in part by *not* having a single interpretation. Through their ability to represent torah as infinitely problematic and themselves as masters of a highly subtle discourse, they achieved status and influence within the society, whether or not many people did as one or another Pharisaic teacher said they should.

The question has been posed about the areas of expertise cultivated by the Pharisees. Although the evidence is difficult to come by and tedious to develop, Neusner's researches have suggested that the Pharisees did not engage extensively in debate about temple practice but rather cultivated the areas of purity, tithing, and agriculture.[88] One should be somewhat cautious about this picture. When Josephus talks about the changing fortunes of the Pharisees in regard to their influence with different Hasmonean rulers, he refers to the rulers adopting or abrogating practices or customs that the Pharisees or the Sadducees favored. Since neither the Hasmoneans nor anyone else could by fiat control the individual behavior of all Judeans, Saldarini is undoubtedly correct when he says that these matters "pertained to public and significant behavior."[89] The temple as the major institution subject to Hasmonean control would presumably be the focus of some of these policies and practices. Such reservations do not necessarily argue against Neusner's basic picture of the areas of Pharisaic concern. Given the central place of the temple in Judaism, it would be difficult to imagine that a pietistic group engaged in a struggle for influence with ideologically distinct opponents would not have any opinions about the temple that served to differentiate it from its opponents. If Neusner is largely correct, however, it would appear that the Pharisees' development of halakah focused primarily on those areas of behavior within the control of the individual.

Incarnate, a London cabbie said to the Rev. Peter Gomes, as he was on his way to a ceremonial occasion at Lambeth palace, "I'm not a religious man m'self, but I think that them what are ought to believe more than that!" His respect was reserved for those whom he perceived to be the rigorists in a matter that was part of his general cultural world but not his personal world.

[87] Sanders, *Judaism*, 414.
[88] Neusner, *Judaism*, 69–71.
[89] Saldarini, 89.

That is to say, they engaged dominant discourse, those matters the importance of which everyone grants, at the level where it was least subject to priestly or other institutional control. Even if few people actually followed Pharisaic practices, the Pharisees' strategy would be to talk about (and render problematic) precisely those things that people did have to decide to do one way or another. Thus they entered the cultural conversation at a popular level. Although the point is debated, some scholars understand the Pharisees as also developing a kind of populist interpretation, for example, by interpreting halakah in ways economically favorable to those of modest means. Despite many uncertainties, the general picture of the Pharisees as a largely lay group that gained influence through a reputation for expert knowledge of torah and pious practices seems quite secure.[90] The issue of the Pharisees' models of knowledge is taken up below.

ALTERNATIVES TO EXPERTISE

The strategy of promoting expertise in torah or even esoteric claims to knowledge about torah, scripture, and the will of God is such a common phenomenon in Second Temple Judaism that it is sometimes difficult to remember that it was not the only strategy for achieving cultural influence. Not everybody was interested in making knowledge the key to the will of God. Writing in support of the Hasmoneans, the author of 1 Maccabees attempted to establish "zeal for the torah" as the key term.[91] The will of God was to be discerned in the success of this family, and such categories as "righteous" and "lawless"—moral categories from the language of torah—could in effect be redefined in terms of cooperation with or opposition to the family's leadership. Although in one encomium Simon is said to have "searched out the law" (1 Macc 14:14), the theme of knowledge is virtually absent from 1 Maccabees. This is not to say that the Hasmoneans

---

[90] See Baumgarten, "Pharisees," 658, on Pharisaic *paradosis and akribeia*.

[91] The classic study of "zeal" in late Second Temple Judaism is Hengel, *The Zealots*. For 1 Maccabees see pp. 149–154. As Hengel (154) notes, "what is remarkable in this context is that, in contrast to the Old Testament, this zeal is no longer directly related to God. It is rather related to the law." Similarly, Smiles ("The Concept of 'Zeal,'" 285) argues that zeal does not so much have to do with Jewish distinctiveness or separatism but that "in all cases zeal functions to protect *the Law* as the guarantor of the covenant and of Israel's election" (italics in original).

or the author of 1 Maccabees were not well acquainted with torah
and scripture. On the contrary there is every evidence from genre,
style, and in the way in which Judah is depicted as heeding the dic-
tates of torah that the author knows scripture thoroughly and expects
a high level of knowledge from his readers. But in the representation of the heroes of the story, knowledge per se is not a value by
which the author of 1 Maccabees attempted to establish the legitimacy of the Hasmonean family's leadership. For the Hasmonean
apologist of 1 Maccabees the torah is represented as an object that
can be attacked or defended, abandoned or embraced, invoked or
repudiated, but not primarily as a ground of interpretive conflict.
Although Judah is presented as scrupulous in his adherence to the
laws of holy war, when the matter of fighting on the Sabbath is at
issue, the author of 1 Maccabees eschews exegetical justification in
favor of purely pragmatic grounds (1 Macc 2:29–41). By highlight-
ing zeal rather than knowledge as the key term, 1 Maccabees strategically simplifies the cultural phenomenon of torah and valorizes
militant leadership at the expense of those whose cultural authority
was grounded in knowledge. Indeed the pietists and the scribal
"experts" are presented as naive and in need of protection against
more clever Gentiles and renegade Jews (see especially 1 Macc
7:12–18). It is not that scholars of torah are the subject of overt
polemic in 1 Maccabees; rather, they and their discursive practices
are marginalized, visible only at the edges of the symbolic world of
1 Maccabees. Nevertheless, it is precisely in these attempts to mar-
ginalize such segments of society that one can perceive, at least dimly,
the danger they posed for the establishment of Hasmonean supremacy
by offering alternative interpretations of the issues at stake in the
crisis between Judea and its Seleucid overlords. Although the
Hasmonean dynasty did establish itself with considerable security, its
troubled history of cooperation, co-optation, and conflict with the
Pharisees suggests that such movements did possess a kind of social
power with which it was necessary to engage.

Cross-Talk

An example of this social power and its limits can be seen in the
anecdote that Josephus tells about the encounter between John
Hyrcanus and the Pharisees (*Ant.* 13.288–98). While this account is

not to be taken as a verbatim transcript of the episode, it does illustrate well the complex and overlapping discourses by which the parties involved related to one another. As Saldarini notes, the social context in which the Pharisees dine with Hyrcanus is that of the patron/client relationship[92] but another social relationship grounded in a very different discourse is also in play. The Pharisees represent themselves and are acknowledged as instructors of Israel. At the banquet Hyrcanus engages them in a way of talking that accepts them in that role and casts himself in the role of one instructed by them. That Hyrcanus would engage them in that way indicates the power of a traditional model of the political leader's subordination to the representatives of torah (already delineated in Deuteronomy's law of the king). Moreover, it indicates the Pharisees' socially successful claim to occupy such a role of moral leadership. How are the two models to be coordinated? As everyone is presumed to know, the patron/client relationship is supposed to prevail. Having been graciously offered the symbolic gift of Hyrcanus' request for moral correction, the Pharisees are supposed to reply that they find him to be in need of no correction (as indeed they say). This does not mean that the Pharisees have no influence. They do, or they would not be there or be the object of such a symbolic gesture. Through this exchange, however, they are also being asked to give a symbolic recognition of the limits of their power. The complex exchange falls apart when one of the Pharisees, Eleazar, reverses the hierarchy of the two sets of relationships, takes Hyrcanus at his word, and criticizes him for holding the high priesthood when there is a cloud on his parentage. Although Josephus refers to him as a man "who had an evil nature and took pleasure in dissension" (*Ant.* 12.291; trans. Thackeray), Eleazar's model is recognizably that of the prophet who confronts a king.

The sequel is equally interesting for revealing the way in which the cross-talk of multiple discourses could be manipulated and exploited. Jonathan, a Sadducean rival of the Pharisees, knows of the reputation of the Pharisees for leniency in judgment and engineers a situation in which the Pharisees' words will be misread by Hyrcanus. Arguing to Hyrcanus that Eleazar spoke with the connivance of the

---

[92] Saldarini, 87.

others, he suggests that the Pharisees be asked to recommend what punishment Eleazar should receive. Jonathan correctly judges that Hyrcanus, sensitive of his dignity as high priest and secular ruler, will misread the Pharisees' typical leniency as evidence of their approval of Eleazar's rebuke. The entente of Hyrcanus and the Pharisees is disrupted by the ability of the rigorist Eleazar and the representative of a rival interest group, Jonathan, to exploit the ambiguities in the cross-talk of different social discourses. By doing so, they diminished the Pharisees' influence with the official sphere for many years.

The way in which Essenes engaged the authority of the political rulers, and especially the ways in which they used their cultural standing to do so, are harder to trace. That the Hasmoneans saw the Qumran Essenes as a threat is indicated by the direct and violent confrontation of the Righteous Teacher by the Wicked Priest (in all probability Jonathan the Hasmonean). What is more difficult to determine is the nature of the perceived threat. If, as some believe, the Righteous Teacher had been serving as high priest from 159–52 BCE,[93] then Jonathan's motives are simply to remove or intimidate a rival for the official position on which his authority largely rests. There is, to be sure, an awareness of different cultic calendars and a willingness to exploit the discrepancy, much as the Seleucids and later enemies of the Jews used the Sabbath to military advantage. If the incident is understood in terms of the high priesthood, then it does not necessarily say much about the role of the Qumran community's ideology in Judean cultural politics. If, however, the Righteous Teacher was not a displaced high priest, as most believe, one has to rethink the nature of what motivated Jonathan's action. The Qumran texts, as has often been noted, do not polemicize against Jonathan's non-Zadokite genealogy but rather accuse the Hasmonean "priests of Jerusalem" of having profaned the temple through impurity (1QpHab 8:9–13; 12:9). It is possible that in the volatile years after the Hellenistic crisis and in the wake of the restoration of temple service, that accusations of defiling the temple, especially when leveled by dissident priests, were themselves sufficiently threatening to provoke direct confrontation. The document known as Miqsat Maase ha-Torah has been interpreted by its editors as a letter from

---

[93] So Stegemann, *Die Entstehung* 212–14; Murphy-O'Connor, "The Damascus Document Revisited," 239.

the Qumran community to its priestly opponents in Jerusalem, laying out the halakic differences that separate the two and their followers.[94] The rhetoric of the document is quite mild, but if the editors are correct, it could well be seen as part of the initial stages of an attempt to bid for Hasmonean concurrence in Essene halakah, an attempt that later came to grief and resulted in the confrontation mentioned by the Habakkuk Pesher.

Although the Nahum Pesher indicates that the Qumran community continued to be quite well aware of Judean and Seleucid politics, neither Qumran literature nor other historical sources indicate whether in later years the Qumran Essenes attempted to use their status and influence in matters of cult and torah to contest publicly the authority of the Hasmonean dynasty. Josephus does provide one interesting piece of information concerning how the Essenes took advantage of their reputation for a different kind of knowledge during the rise of Herod. Although he may or may not have been connected with the Qumran group, one of the Essenes foretold Herod's eventual rise to power.[95] We do not know, of course, precisely how the statement was used by Herod, but the fact that Josephus knows about it and refers to it in his history is clear evidence that the Essene prediction was valuable to Herod in more than a purely personal way and became part of what was publicly known about him. This "transaction" with the Essene allowed Herod to borrow from the Essenes' reputation in order to present his ascendancy as fated. In return, both Herod's eventual accession to power and his concession to the Essenes in excusing them from taking an oath reinforced their own honor and reputation within the Jewish community. This is not to say that the Essene prediction was a particularly important moment in the history of Herod; in all probability it was not. It does indicate, however, one of the ways in which knowledge and claims to knowledge were objects of value in the symbolic economy and could be exchanged to mutual benefit.

Many social groups excluded from institutional authority shared

---

[94] Strugnell and Qimron, 1.

[95] Knohl (*The Messiah before Jesus*, 60–62) not only connects this figure with the Qumran community but also with the Menahem mentioned in Rabbinic sources (*y. Hag.* 2:2 [77b]; *Midr. Song Zuta* 8:14), though, as he himself admits, it is merely a speculative hypothesis. In my opinion the identification and the conclusions Knohl draws are unlikely.

a common interest in problematizing knowledge in order to participate in the cultural power it gave access to. Although such knowledge might be used directly in confrontation or mutual co-optation
with official authority, the terms of such a discourse ensured that,
despite their common interest, these groups would dispute as much
with one another as with representatives of official authority. In
Qumran literature the Hodayot and the Damascus Document are
replete with references to rival interpreters. In part this appears to
be an Essene/Pharisee rivalry. The phrase "the seekers of smooth
things" (CD 1:18, דרשו בחלקות; 1QH[a] 10:32, דורשי חלקות) is often
taken as a critical pun for "seekers of halakah" (דורשי הלכות), depict-
ing the Pharisees as insufficiently rigorous in their interpretation.[96]
Whether there is evidence of a schism within the Essene movement
over interpretive differences is debated,[97] but the (mis)use of torah
knowledge in internal conflicts is clearly alluded to (e.g., in 1QH[a]
13:23–25). Rabbinic tradition describes a less volatile kind of conflict
in the disputes of the Houses of Hillel and Shammai. Even though
the representation of these disputes is highly schematized, the model
of conflicting authorities is so thoroughly ingrained in Rabbinic discourse that it surely developed out of a tradition of disputation.
Rather than being a question of factional splitting, however, disputation in this context may have been developed as a kind of culture
of argumentation, a way of producing knowledge.

    There is an important sense in which such conflicts, whether of
the collegial or of the factional type, are also unconscious acts of
collusion. A dispute over correct interpretation manages to place certain issues at the level of unquestioned assumption: the central importance of interpretation itself, its deeply problematic character, and
the significance of expertise. If the broader community can be persuaded of those claims, then interpreters as a class will possess real
social power. A "dispute" need not be a formal, public debate. A

---

[96] See, however, the reservations of Meier, "Is there *Halaka* (the Noun) at Qumran?"
155.
[97] See, variously, Murphy-O'Connor, "Essenes and Their History," 235; Jeremias,
Der Lehrer der Gerechtigkeit, 86–87; García Martínez and van der Woude, "A Groningen
Hypothesis," 537–38; García Martínez, "Origins of the Essene Movement," *The People
of the Dead Sea Scrolls*, 95–96; but see the rebuttal by Collins, "Origin of the Qumran
Community," 172–77, who interprets the dispute with the Man of the Lie in terms
of conflict with a rival group, most likely the Pharisees. Cf. Stegemann, *Die Entstehung*,
227–28.

symbolic act, such as the refusal of a member of one Jewish group
to eat with or to marry or to have certain kinds of commercial transactions with the members of another group may be enough to sig-
nal the existence of a dispute to the whole community. Josephus'
representation of himself as a sort of "comparison shopper" among
the various teachers and groups offering knowledge indicates one
way in which the perception of difference enhanced the value of
each (*Life* 9–12).

CONTRASTING WAYS OF KNOWING AND THEIR SOCIAL IMPLICATIONS

Although conflict between rival groups claiming correct interpretation of torah may have been mutually beneficial in helping to ingrain
the belief in the wider public of the significance of proper interpretation, one should not minimize the competition for influence between
rival groups, a competition very much tied to the way in which the
rivals constructed and produced alternative discourses of knowledge.
As noted above, it is usually assumed that the major rivals of the
Qumran community were the Pharisees. One would like to be able
to compare the discourses of knowledge of Pharisees and of Qumran
Essenes, but unfortunately the sources of information on Pharisaic
thought are both limited and extremely difficult to interpret. Daniel
Schwartz, however, has attempted to examine what we do know of
Qumranic and Rabbinic halakah, looking for systematic differences
in the way they are formulated.[98] What he discovered is of considerable
significance for identifying their different constructions of knowledge.
Although he carefully notes that he is making a phenomenological
comparison, since his sources are not contemporaneous, it seems
likely that the contrast he draws would hold for Qumran/Pharisaic
differences as well. Not only does it seem likely that there was a
general continuity between Pharisaic and Rabbinic movements,[99] but
in one of the concrete examples of halakah examined by Schwartz,
the position of the Qumran opponents agrees with Rabbinic halakah.

The basic difference, as Schwartz summarizes it, between the
priestly halakah of Qumran and Sadducees and that of the Rabbis
is that, to borrow terminology from medieval philosophy, "priestly

---

[98] Schwartz, "Law and Truth," 229–40.
[99] See the careful analysis by Cohen, "The Significance of Yavneh, 36–41."

jurists seem to have been mainly realists while rabbis were mainly
nominalists."[100] The realist assumptions of Qumran halakah can be
seen in the following examples. The Qumran writings are more likely
to justify their halakic positions by reference to the structure of reality, as in the Damascus Document, where a man's remarriage while
his first wife is alive is excluded because "the principle of creation
is, 'Male and female he created them'" (CD 4:21).[101] Again, concerning the edibility of locusts, "And as for locusts, according to their
various kinds they shall plunge them alive into fire or water, for that
is what their nature requires" (CD 12:14–15). Marriage of a man
with his niece is excluded because "although the laws against incest
are written for men, they also apply to women" (CD 5:8–10), a position not endorsed either by Qumran's apparently Pharisaic opponents or the later Rabbis. As Schwartz notes, the logic of the argument
of the Damascus Document depends on the assumption that God
forbad incest because it was wrong (that is, wrong by nature), not
that it is wrong because God forbad it.[102] Qumranic halakah is based
on realist epistemology; Rabbinic halakah assumes a nominalist epistemology. The contrast can be seen in the different conclusions about
the impurity of animal bones. Scripture declares only that human
bones are impure (Num 19:16). The Temple Scroll (51:1–6) and the
Sadducees (*m. Yad.* 4:7) conclude that animal bones also are sources
of impurity. After all, bones are bones. The Rabbis, however, do
not consider animal bones as sources of impurity, since scripture
speaks only of human bones.[103] Although Schwartz provides additional examples, these should suffice to show the contrast.

Different halakic positions thus correlate with different structures
of knowing. Different structures of knowing do not arise arbitrarily,
however. They are developed in different social locations, though
the spokespersons for such perspectives may not be aware of it.
Schwartz—correctly in my view—correlates the realist outlook, which
characterizes not only Qumran halakah but also Sadducaic halakah,
with a priestly orientation. One has only to think of the Priestly
source in the Hebrew Bible to recognize the energy with which it

---

[100] Schwartz, "Law and Truth," 230.
[101] Translations from the Damascus Document follow Rabin, *Zadokite Document*,
unless otherwise noted.
[102] Schwartz, "Law and Truth," 231.
[103] Schwartz, "Law and Truth," 232.

correlates the proper order of the natural world with the proper order of the human community.

That priests formed an important segment of the Qumran community is beyond doubt but they were not the sole source of the community's membership, as the Community Rule makes explicit. Like Pharisaism, Essenism both in the Qumran community per se and in the towns and villages throughout Judea drew on persons from a variety of occupational and social backgrounds. The question, however, is not about the social origin of individual members but is about the intellectual leadership and formation of the ethos and world view of the community. That ethos was, unquestionably set with a priestly stamp, in contrast to the Pharisaic movement.

Schwartz makes an important observation about the interrelationship between the social status of priesthood and its realist epistemology when he remarks on the risks of realist approaches to law. He notes that a judgment based on realist assumptions is always subject to disconfirmation. One may discover that reality is different from what one had thought. Schwartz argues that priests could afford this insecurity, since their authority was itself based on nature, their "Aaronite genes."[104] For the Rabbis (and, I would add, for the Pharisees), authority was based on the law and their interpretation of it. Consequently, there was a greater investment in an intellectual position that holds that "the law is what the judge says it is," to borrow an idiom from American jurisprudence. Thus the content of halakah may have been the explicit grounds on which the Qumran community fought with its Pharisaic opponents. That content, however, grew out of different symbolic systems of knowledge embedded in different social locations. This analysis concretizes the dictum of Pierre Bourdieu, that "the field of ideological stances thus reproduces in transfigured form the field of social positions."[105]

Other contrasts between the Qumran Essenes and Pharisees suggest systemic differences in the modes of discourse as well as the structures of knowledge. One can at least make a plausible case that Pharisees showed a preference for oral rather than written forms, had a particular interest in identifying the "genealogy" of particular arguments, and were more oriented toward the concrete identities

[104] Schwartz, "Law and Truth," 237.
[105] Bourdieu, *Language and Symbolic Power*, 167.

(or at least the personal names) of revered teachers, and engaged in a different culture of argumentation (preserving and organizing debates according to antithetical positions) than did the Qumran Essenes. It is not accidental that the two movements chose different terms to designate those who possess knowledge, the Qumran community favoring *maskil* (with its affinities with Daniel and Enoch, as well as the Levitical tradition) and the Pharisaic-Rabbinic movement favoring *hakam* (with its rootage in the traditional pragmatic wisdom of ancient Israel).

One of the continuing debates about the Pharisees concerns the repertoire of their objects of knowledge, specifically whether the dominance of halakic knowledge and the absence of nonhalakic forms of knowledge (e.g., either traditional forms of aphoristic wisdom or apocalyptic speculation) or literary genres (e.g., a corpus of prayers or hymns) is characteristic of the range of what they talked about or is simply the result of what a later Rabbinic tradition cared to preserve. It is a mistake to think of this as a question of what interests a particular individual might have.[106] The question is how Pharisaism as a movement constructed its objects of knowledge. What "hung together" as necessary or as mutually reinforcing in the pursuit of their central object, detailed, and precise interpretation of torah? Schwartz's analysis of the contrasting structures of knowledge suggests one reason why the dual cultivation of speculative cosmological knowledge and halakic knowledge may have been more characteristic of the Qumran Essenes than of Pharisees. But other factors are involved, most significantly the structure and self-understanding of the Qumran community.

QUMRAN: HOW KNOWLEDGE OF TORAH REQUIRES KNOWING OTHER THINGS

Despite all the emphasis the Qumran community placed on its expertise in the interpretation of torah, the collection of an extraordinary number and variety of biblical scrolls and nonbiblical manuscripts, and the creation of novel literary genres (e.g., *serakim, pesharim, hodayot*), it would be an error to see the Qumran community as another of the "scribal" movements discussed above. Although many scribal

---

[106] *Pace* Sanders, *Judaism*, 414.

activities occurred at Qumran—reading and interpreting scripture; keeping written records of property transfers, community rank, and formal rebukes; composition, revision and copying of community documents; copying of biblical manuscripts—the sectarian compositions never draw attention to writing and the written word in a manner similar to Jubilees, nor do they invoke the image and ideology of the learned scribe as a form of self-identification, as one finds in Ben Sira and Daniel. Indeed, as Schams's careful survey reveals, there is an "almost complete lack of reference to scribes in the sectarian texts from Qumran."[107] This situation should not be surprising. Like the Pharisees, the Qumran community was a voluntary society, not a professional guild. The ways in which they authorize their claim to superior knowledge of torah are made in relation to the nature of the community itself.

The community represented itself as a reconstituted Israel (1QS 2:22), formed of those who "freely offer themselves to observe the statutes of God in a covenant of loyalty" (1:7–8) and who "separate themselves from the congregation of the men of deceit in order to form a community with respect to torah and possessions" (5:1–2). The conceptual center of community's identity is thus the concept of covenant and the obligations of obedience that follow from it. Simply to say that, however, provides little clue as to what made the Qumran community's discourse concerning torah distinctive, how knowledge of torah was related to other objects of knowledge cultivated by the community, or how such knowledge was linked to a unique form of social organization.

The opening lines of the Serek ha-Yahad identify the purpose of the community as "to seek God . ⸜. in order to do what is good and upright before him according as he commanded by the hand of Moses and by the hand of all the prophets" (1QS 1:1–3). The central role of torah study in shaping the focus of the community is further reflected in the requirement that in an assembly of ten persons it is required that there be "a man who searches the torah day and night" and that for a third of every night the community keep watch in order "to read in the book and to study the law and to bless together" (1QS 6:6–8). The separation of the community from greater Israel is interpreted in terms of the prophecy of Isaiah 40:3

---

[107] Schams, 251. See further 257–60.

as the building of a highway for YHWH in the wilderness, an act
that is glossed with the comment that "this is the study of the torah
which he commanded by the hand of Moses" (1QS 8:15).[108]

In common with others who sought cultural influence through the
discourse of torah, the Yahad understood correct knowledge of torah
to be deeply problematic, though in a way that distinguished them
from others. Where the Pharisees authorized their knowledge of torah
in part as accurately preserved teachings from antiquity ("the traditions of the elders"), the Qumran community represented their knowledge in relation to categories of revelation. In common with the
tradents of Jubilees they understood torah to have a temporal dimension.[109] Thus the obligation of torah was not simply "to walk before
him perfectly" but "to walk before him perfectly [according to] all
that has been revealed at the times appointed for their revelation"
(1QS 1:8–9; trans. adapted from Knibb). Moreover, the coupling of
references to Moses with parallel references to "the prophets" suggests both that the community considered the disclosure of torah to
Moses to have been a form of prophetic revelation and that the revelation of torah was continued by later prophets. The passage in
1QS 8:15–16 that interprets Isa 40:3 in terms of study of torah con-
tinues by saying, "This is study of the torah w[hic]h he commanded
by the hand of Moses, in order to act according to all that is revealed
from time to time and according to what the prophets revealed
through his holy spirit."

Both the temporality of the revelation of torah and the role of
God's spirit are integral conceptual components of what was perhaps the most distinctive feature of Qumran's discourse of torah, the
distinction between the laws that were revealed and those that were
hidden but which could be discerned through exegesis. According
to 1QS 5:11–12 the men of iniquity cannot be considered as part
of the covenant "because they have not sought and have not examined his statutes in order to know the hidden things in which they
went astray, incurring guilt; and with respect to the revealed things
they have acted presumptuously." The claim that the sect makes,
however, is not simply one of expertise. It is not the case that anyone might discern the hidden things by an effort of diligent study.

---

[108] The citation of Isa 40:3 is not present in the text of 4QS^d (4Q258) but does
appear in 4QS^e (4Q259).

No longer is torah both a common possession and a special possession. True torah can be known *only* in the sect.

Here is where the sect makes use of the close relation between
the concept of covenant and torah, already established in the Sinai
traditions of the Pentateuch,[110] to claim such exclusivity. In contrast
to the biblical traditions and even to the way in which Jubilees treats
the covenant as applying to all Israel, the sectarians of Qumran
understood covenant more restrictively, as the relationship between
God and those Jews who undertake a particular commitment of obedience.[111] Indeed, in the Serek ha-Yahad the expression "to enter
the covenant" is effectively the equivalent of "to enter the community."[112] "All those who come into the order of the community will
enter into a covenant before God to do all that he has commanded"
(1:16–17). The relationship between this restrictive notion of covenant
and the "hidden things" that is assumed in the Serek ha-Yahad is
made explicit in the Damascus Document. "But with those who held
fast to the commandments of God, who were left over from them,
God established his covenant with Israel for ever, revealing to them
the hidden things in which all Israel had gone astray: his holy sabbaths and his glorious feasts, his righteous testimonies and his true
ways, and the desires of his will which a man must do that he may
live through them" (CD 3:12–16; trans. Knibb).[113]

Knowledge of the "hidden things" is thus a gracious divine response
to the initial and continuing commitment of its members to live a
life of perfect obedience. But this is no "cheap grace." Both obedience to commandments already known and the further understanding of the commandments of God embedded in scripture require an
extraordinary discipline, one that can only be undertaken within the
community (1QS 5:1–13). For this reason the community's efforts to

---

[109] Anderson, "Status of the Torah Before Sinai," 15–19.
[110] As Christensen (46–47) notes, "because the Old Testament has the giving of
the law as a central idea to the covenant establishment at Sinai, an identification
of law and covenant is almost inevitable."
[111] Christensen, 158.
[112] Metso, "Qumran Community Structure and Terminology," 435, observes that
in the Serek ha-Yahad the terms יחד and ברית are often used synonymously.
[113] The relationship between the communities described in CD and S remains
one of the most vexed questions in Qumran scholarship. I think it is a reasonable
assumption, however, that this interpretation of the sect's (pre)history would have
been accepted as valid by the authors/tradents of the Serek ha-Yahad.

know the torah of God also required the cultivation of other sorts of knowledge. Discipline, as Foucault has shown, is not simply a matter of rules, inducements, and punishments. It is also complexly related to the generation of new knowledge, even new kinds of knowledge.[114] This connection is readily seen in the Serek ha-Yahad. Concerning every person who seeks to join the community the rule requires that "they examine [ודרשו] his spirit in community, distinguishing between one man and another according to his insight and his deeds in torah" (1QS 5:21; cf. 6:13–23). In a slightly different formulation provision is made for a yearly review of members' "spirit" and "deeds" (1QS 5:24). These procedures lead not only to the development of a practical knowledge concerning individuals but to the development of a highly sophisticated theory of the person in the Two Spirits Treatise, a theory that combines anthropology, pneumatology, and angelology. In order to create a community capable of the disciplined searching of the scriptures that leads to the revelation of hidden torot, one must also have such a knowledge of human nature.

The understanding of torah as possessing a historical dimension similarly requires the cultivation of knowledge concerning the nature of history, its epochs, and the mysteries of the plan of God that are embedded in its structure and events. Thus the type of historiographical and eschatological speculation one finds in apocalypses and related works becomes an object of knowledge for the sect. The Maskil is required "to learn all the wisdom that has been discovered throughout the times and the rule of time" (1QS 9:13–14). This interest in the mysteries of history is reflected not only in the nonsectarian works that were collected and read within the community (e.g., 1 Enoch, Jubilees, the Genesis Apocryphon, 11QMelchizedek, 4QVisions of Amram, 4QInstruction), but also in the distinctive works of the sect itself (e.g., 4QAges of Creation, the various pesharim, the hortatory section of the Damascus Document). Indeed, there are often discernible traces of influence between these nonsectarian texts and the compositions of the sect.[115]

---

[114] This topic is explored in more detail in Chapter 4.

[115] For example, see the discussion of Tigchelaar (*To Increase Learning*, 194–207) concerning the common vocabulary in 4QInstruction and 1QS 3–4 and 1QH[a] 5. He is, however, cautious—perhaps overly cautious—about tracing the lines of influence among the texts.

These various objects of knowledge are not compartmentalized but are part of an integrated way of knowing that gives the construction of knowledge at Qumran a distinctive aspect. Knowledge is often represented as having two axes. The Maskil is told to "walk with every living being according to the rule appropriate to each time and according to the weight of each man" (1QS 9:12; trans. Knibb; cf. 1:14–15; 8:4). An even more complex relationship of axes of knowledge introduces the Two Spirits Treatise, which requires that the Maskil "instruct and teach all the children of light concerning the history [or genealogy; תולדות] of all the sons of man according to the types of their spirits in accordance with the signs revealed in their deeds in their generations and according to the visitation of their chastisements together with the periods of their reward."

Several things thus contributed to the distinctive Qumran way of knowing and to the development of its particular repertoire of objects of knowledge, among them priestly "realism," the nature of the community as a disciplinary society, and the entailments of certain assumptions about covenant and torah. What a group knows and claims it is important to know is not merely a matter of content, however, but is often related to the social uses of knowledge.

TRANSACTIONS IN KNOWLEDGE

What the Pharisees and the Qumran community chose to do socially with their knowledge—what one might call their transactions in knowledge—is also linked to the way they constructed knowledge out of their distinctive social contexts. Again we are troubled by a lack of evidence, but it does seem clear enough that the Pharisees, although they engaged in some practices that involved limiting social interactions with others, were characterized by an orientation to the common, public domain in their transactions in knowledge.[116] Various traditions represent the Pharisees as engaged in public disputation. Although the New Testament's accounts of disputes between Jesus and certain Pharisees may be historically unreliable, the depiction of

---

[116] Baumgarten (*Flourishing of Jewish Sects*, 13) aptly characterizes the Pharisees as a "reformist" sect, which played an active role in public life, institutions, and debate. Saldarini (281) says that "the Pharisees' association probably functioned as a social movement organization seeking to change society."

this type of confrontation between rival teachers is generally accepted as plausible.[117] The Pharisee Simon b. Shetah is associated in certain Rabbinic traditions with the establishment of broadly based primary education (*y. Ketub.* 8.32c).[118] This tradition, too, may be historically questionable,[119] but it is suggestive that a prominent Pharisee would be remembered in connection with the development of a system of schooling. Josephus depicts the Pharisees as concerned to translate their halakic expertise into political influence, although they clearly did not succeed to the extent that they wished. The public, engaged nature of Pharasaic activity may also have involved proselytizing activity among Gentiles.[120] For the Pharisees, public transactions of knowledge were an important part of the way in which they gained status and influence.

The Qumran community, by contrast, carefully regulated transactions in knowledge. Knowledge played a central role for the community as an instrument of social definition. Relationship to knowledge is what forms the boundary between the sect and the outside world. Wherever the language of community formation is used, there one finds the language of knowledge (e.g., 1QS 1:8–10; 5:8–11). Consequently, transactions in knowledge are the subject of strong regulation. A "spirit of secrecy" governs the Maskil's relations with the "men of the pit" (9:22). Even debate with them is restricted in order not to compromise the control of knowledge exercised by the sect (9:17). By contrast the exchange of knowledge within the community serves as a bond that unites members. There is even a positive command to exchange knowledge among "perfected" members: "And nothing that was hidden from Israel but found by the man who studies shall he hide from these [members] through fear of an apostate spirit" (8:11–12). To exchange knowledge is to practice trust and to build up the community.

The last phrase of the quotation, "fear of an apostate spirit," also underscores the boundary-marking quality of knowledge. The alienation of the community's knowledge is an act of aggression and an

---

[117] Saldarini, 283.

[118] Safrai, "Education and the Study of the Torah," 947. Baumgarten, *Flourishing of Jewish Sects*, 120.

[119] Another tradition associates such activity with the high priest Joshua b. Gamla (see Safrai, 948).

[120] McKnight, *Light among the Gentiles*, 106–7; Runesson, 225–26.

attack on the integrity of the community. In one of the Hodayot often associated with the Righteous Teacher, the speaker complains of defecting members that "all who are associated with me in fellowship speak ill of me with evil lips. . . . and with the secret you have hidden in me they go about as slanderers to the children of destruction" (1QHᵃ 13:23–25). The speaker, however, hastens to give reassurance that God has protected the community's knowledge: "In order to magnify my w[a]y, and on account of their guilt, you have hidden the spring of understanding and the foundation of truth" (13:25–26). Alienation of knowledge is probably also what the Serek ha-Yahad refers to when it decrees expulsion for "one who goes about slandering the community" (1QS 7:16–17). Given the role of knowledge in defining the limits of community, it is not surprising that the Qumran community does not give evidence of what scholars have called the missionary impulse.[121] That the members of the Qumran community were prohibited from engaging in public disputes or from disclosing the "hidden things" revealed to them, however, does not mean that they failed to make an appeal based on knowledge. Their very reserve served as a powerful instrument of appeal, enhancing their reputation for possessing valuable secrets. In a similar fashion the difficulty of entering the community—and the total commitment required of one who did—served to give the Qumran sectarians a certain cachet among the groups competing for influence. If one takes up Baumgarten's image of Jewish sects as marketers of intellectual merchandise and of interested Jews as comparison shoppers,[122] then the Qumran sectarians not only staked out the high end of the market but also enhanced the desirability of their goods by making them so difficult to inspect or obtain. Through these various means they cultivated symbolic power by engaging in the competitive social discourse of Second Temple Judaism concerning torah, the identity of Israel, and the will of God.

---

[121] McKnight, 54–55.
[122] Baumgarten, *Flourishing of Jewish Sects*, 51–58.

CHAPTER THREE

KNOWING AS DOING: THE SOCIAL SYMBOLICS OF KNOWLEDGE IN THE TWO SPIRITS TREATISE OF THE SEREK HA-YAHAD

LANGUAGE AS SYMBOLIC ACTION

In the previous chapter I attempted to locate distinctive features of the Qumran community's construction of knowledge—its contents, modes, and uses—in relation to the cultural conversation of Second Temple Judaism concerning torah. But the forms of knowledge cultivated at Qumran had other social functions as well. In this chapter I wish to explore certain ways in which *knowledge as a symbolic form* is related to the specific conditions of history within which the sectarian community existed. The text that I will examine is the teaching about human nature in the Two Spirits section of the Serek ha-Yahad (1QS 3:13–4:26). Commentators have long been aware of similarities between this text and apocalypses that have a more explicitly political concern.[1] No sustained inquiry into the nature of this relationship has been conducted, however. Examining the symbolic forms of knowledge in which knowledge is articulated by means of the lens of ideological criticism allows a clearer understanding of how something as abstract as a mode of knowing is nevertheless deeply engaged with concrete historical conditions.

The starting point for my inquiry is Kenneth Burke's notion of language as symbolic action. Burke frequently spoke of utterances and texts not as repositories of ideas but as symbolic acts. As acts, texts do not merely reflect the world but do something in it and to it. They are, as he puts it, strategies for encompassing situations.[2] It is fairly easy to see how a traditional speech of political persuasion does this, but Burke was referring to all sorts of utterances, including both everyday commonplaces as well as abstract, symbolic, and

---

[1] E.g., Collins, *Apocalyptic Imagination*, 153–57.
[2] Burke, *Philosophy of Literary Form*, 1.

aesthetic texts, where the relationship to the situations they are
designed to encompass is far from obvious.

The problem of the relation between text and world, never fully
explicit in Burke, has been critiqued and "rewritten as a model for
contemporary ideological analysis" by Fredric Jameson.[3] The way in
which texts act in and on the world is distinct from an act of direct
force because a text exists in the realm of the symbolic. As Jameson
notes, the world is not simply a linguistic construct. But the world
is not available to us in itself but only as we are able to textualize
it, to bring it into the realm of the symbolic. Insofar as a text takes
the world into itself, as its subtext, then the world can be acted upon
in the symbolic work of the text. More specifically, for Jameson the
symbolic act of a text is "the function of inventing imaginary or formal 'solutions' to unresolvable social contradictions."[4]

Jameson has shown how the socially symbolic work of texts does
not all take place in the clear light of conscious intention. Much of
it operates at another level, as a work of the unconscious, employing the resources of the primary processes. In psychoanalytic terms
one would talk about condensation, displacement, and overdetermi-
nation; in literary terms, about metaphor, metonomy, and polyvalency.[5] The task of ideological analysis, as Jameson describes it, is
to "rewrite" the symbolic construction so that "it may itself be grasped
as the rewriting or restructuration of a prior ideological or historical subtext" to which it is in some sense a response.[6] Even at the
level of a particular writing the relationship between text and world
is subtle and complex. What interests me here, however, is not just
this specific text but the *structured way of knowing* that is present in it
but not limited to it. A "way of knowing" is also a symbolic form
and, as such, is dynamically related to historical conditions. There
is no suggestion here that in any simple or superficial sense such a
structured way of knowing has been "caused" by a particular set of
historical conditions. The roots of any way of knowing are deep and
diffuse, without a single moment of origin. Both priestly and apocalyptic scribal traditions of considerable antiquity are present in the

---

[3] Jameson, "Symbolic Inference," 139.
[4] Jameson, *Political Unconscious*, 79.
[5] See the discussions of these categories in Silverman, *Subject of Semiotics*, 87–125.
[6] Jameson, "Symbolic Inference," 141.

assumptions about knowledge in 1QS 3–4. What I am suggesting is
that the inherited structures of knowing represented in this tradition
were shaped and transformed by the necessity of grappling with the
historical contradictions of Second Temple Judaism—especially the
persistence of political domination by international empires—and that
a significant moment of this process can be uncovered in 1QS 3–4.

THE TWO SPIRITS TREATISE (1QS 3:15–4:26)

The Two Spirits Treatise is not ostensibly about concrete historical
or political realities. Rather, 1QS 3–4 presents itself as a teaching
for the Community's Instructor (the Maskil) about universal human
nature (3:13–15). It begins at the beginning—or even before—with
an account of the plan of God, which predetermines the ways and
fates of all beings (3:15–17). In its account of the nature and destiny of humankind, the discussion begins in the cosmic plane, with
an account of the angelic spirits of truth and perversity and their
effect on human behavior (3:17–4:2). The discussion then moves to
an account of the manifestation of these spirits in the personal characteristics of individuals (4:2–14) and even in the divided psyche
(4:15–18). The text closes with an account of the eschatological resolution of the struggle and the removal of the "spirit of perversity
from within the flesh" of persons (4:18–26).

   Is it possible to discover how the construction of knowledge about
human character and existence in this text is at the same time an
attempt to provide a formal solution to an intractable contradiction
in the realm of ideology and history? This is not a reductionist procedure. What the text says it is about is indeed what it is about—
the genealogy and teleology of human existence. But ideological
criticism asks additional questions. Why does the self become a symbolic space? Why is that topic of so much interest? What provides
the energy? Why does the explanation take the particular form that
it does? What makes it such a satisfying explanation? Does it satisfy
needs not explicitly acknowledged? What this text "knows" must be
sought not only in what it tells but in what it models as it goes
about the act of telling.

   Cultural assumptions about what passes for knowledge, what the
objects of knowledge are, what knowledge is good for, and the process
by which one comes to know something may or may not be explicitly

stated, but these assumptions are inevitably embedded in acts of speech. By this I mean to draw attention not only to the self-conscious things one says about knowing but also to the quite unconscious ways of speaking about anything. Metaphors, figures of speech, even syntax are part of the implicit model of knowledge with which speakers operate. In order to inquire about these things at Qumran, it would probably be possible to take almost any extended passage of Qumran literature and deduce a great deal about the construction of knowledge. But one can get to the issues more quickly by taking a passage like the introduction to the Two Spirits Treatise because it not only presents itself as a teaching but also makes a number of self-conscious statements about knowledge.

If one asks what the object of knowledge is in this text, it would appear to be stated in the phrase תולדות כל בני איש. But one is immediately entangled in all the qualifying phrases that follow in dense syntactical interlinkage: לכול מיני רוחותם באותותם למעשיהם בדורותם ולפקודת נגיעיהם עם קצי שלומם (1QS 3:13–15). The object of knowledge is not simply the "genealogy of humankind," but "the genealogy of humankind with respect to all the types of their spirits (recognizable) in the characteristics of their deeds in their generations and with respect to the occasion of their punishments and the periods of their reward." That is quite a mouthful. But anyone familiar with Qumran literature recognizes the habits of syntax and style that it represents: the passion for specification, qualification, and closer definition (especially in the Rules, e.g., 1QS 1:1–15; 1QSa 2:11–22; 1QSb 1:1–3; 1QM 2). I would be prepared to argue for the significance of this feature for the construction of knowledge at Qumran, even if it did not occur in a sentence that is explicitly concerned with delineating an object of knowledge; but in this context its significance is particularly clear. Even at the level of syntax the passage claims that one cannot really know one thing without knowing many other things and their relationships. Things are joined together in webs of significance. If one wants to know about human character or why the righteous sin, one has to know about the plan of God for all of creation from beginning to end. If one wants to know about the eternal destiny of humankind, one will inevitably find oneself attending to concrete details of human behavior, to acts of patience or greed.

There is another element of style in 1QS 3–4 that is also an element of the structure of knowledge—the use of balanced pairs, espe-

cially antonyms (light and darkness, truth and perversity) and phrases
such as "in equal measure." In part this is a simplifying device.
Where syntactical linking and the piling up of qualifying phrases create complex categories, balanced pairs provide a powerful analytical
tool for rendering the complexity intelligible. The two devices together
serve a common purpose. Exhaustive in their reach, they serve to
totalize knowledge. Nothing escapes the operations of linking and
sorting. Nothing is left unaccounted for, unknowable. This concern
to totalize is evident also in the often noted repetition of the word
"all" (כול), a word that sometimes seems to occur as often in Qumran
literature as "ya' know" does in a sports interview.[7] This use of כול
was probably a virtual reflex of speech, but it is not the less important for being so. It represents the integration into the surface style
of speech of a profound orientation to the totality of things. One
could go on adding confirming evidence of this characteristic orientation. The use of temporal expressions for immeasurable lengths of
time (עד, נצח, עולם), for example, reinforces the sense of comprehensiveness.

KNOWLEDGE AND TIME

The way in which time figures in relation to knowledge in the Serek
ha-Yahad, both as a condition for knowing something and as the
object of knowledge, requires a somewhat closer look. Time conditions knowledge, of course, in the sense that God provides for the
disclosure of knowledge at different times in history. This is most
apparent in the rule for the Maskil in references to statutes specific
to particular times: "according to the rule appropriate to each time
(לתכון עת ועת, 1QS 9:12), "according to all that is revealed from
time to time" (ככול הנגלה לעת בעת, 1QS 9:13), "according to the
rule of the time" (כתכון העת, 1QS 9:18), and so forth. It is not simply a matter of knowledge having a "history," however, either in
terms of a history of revelation or of a sequence of statutes pertinent to successive ages. Rather, one might say that temporality is
one "axis" of knowledge, which must be coordinated with other axes
for correct knowledge. Consider the introductory line of the Two

---

[7] E.g., 1QS 1:3–19 (20 occurrences in 17 lines).

Spirits section again: בתולדות כול בני איש לכול מיני רוחותם באותותם
למעשיהם בדורותם ולפקודת נגיעיהם עם קצי שלומם. Knowledge of human
existence involves both a temporal axis (here, specifically "genealogical," תולדות) and an analytical one, having to do with the atemporal "kinds" of things (מיני). This double axis of knowledge is indeed
carried through in the development of 1QS 3–4. On the one hand
there is a strong genealogical orientation to the explanation, as the
conditions of human existence are traced back to the creation of the
two spirits and ultimately to their origin in God's plan (1QS 3:15–4:1;
e.g., "From the God of knowledge comes everything that is and will
be," 3:15). Similarly, the teleology of this process is described in
the concluding paragraphs (4:15–26). In between the text provides
the atemporal analysis of types of spirits and corresponding fates
(4:2–14).

This pairing of temporal and atemporal is not simply fortuitous.
In the rules governing the conduct of the Maskil, he is instructed to
conduct himself "with every living being according to the rule appropriate to each time and according to the weight of each man" (עם
כול חי כתכון עת ועת ולמשקל איש ואיש, 9:12 trans. Knibb). Time and
"weight" (or as we might say, "substance") are the two variables that
the Maskil must consider in order to find the right relationship
between himself, the rule, and the other. Even the pairing of "rule"
and "time" by itself, a pairing that is repeated several times in this
section, contains the two axes of knowledge. A rule orders relations
synchronously, whereas the notion that each "time" has its appropriate rule introduces a historicizing dimension into the notion of
order. One can even see this double axis model at work in figures
of speech. In the introductory section of the Community Rule, where
the aims of the community are given, perfect conduct is summed
up as follows: "They shall not depart from any one of all the commandments of God in their epochs, neither anticipating their times,
nor falling behind any of their appointed times, not turning aside
from his true statutes to go to the right or to the left" (1:13–15).
Perfect conduct is represented as the intersection of the coordinates
of time and space.

The most encompassing pairing of the temporal and atemporal
structures is that between history in its totality (כול הויה ונהייה, "all
that is and will be") and the plan of God (מחשבת כבודו, "His glorious plan," 3:15–16). In this ultimate relationship, of course, the two
elements do not have the same status. The temporal order is com-

pletely dependent on the plan of God. It is merely the manifestation in time of that plan, without any changes (3:15–16). This relationship has implications for the status and purpose of knowledge.
After all, what is presented in 3:13–4:26 is not merely a teaching
about the conditions of human existence but a teaching that discloses the plan of God, insofar as it is capable of being grasped by
human beings.

Although the human knower is located in the temporal realm, the
ultimate object of knowledge, the plan of God, is not. From the perspective of that plan past, present, and future are simultaneously
available. The construction of knowledge in the Two Spirits Treatise
is sensitive to the temporal and atemporal axes of reality but ultimately offers a transcendence of the temporal through knowledge of
the plan of God. This knowledge is clearly of greatest importance
in explaining the nature of the "realized eschatology" that has been
recognized as so characteristic of the Qumran ethos. The ideological significance of this feature will be taken up again below.

A Semiotic Model of Knowledge

The perception that knowledge at Qumran is constructed with a
concern for totality, for the interrelationship of aspects of reality, and
especially for the relationship of temporal and atemporal dimensions
leads to the observation that the model of knowledge is implicitly
semiotic.[8] To understand the meaning of various phenomena, such
as particular actions, traits of character, or events, one does not
attempt to account for them as expressions of individual wills or
intentions but rather seeks their meaningfulness primarily as *elements
in a system of relationships*. As the text explicitly says, deeds are *signs*
(אותות) of spirits (3:14). Similarly, the various behaviors and characteristics outlined in 4:2–14 are signs or symptoms to be interpreted
in light of a system of contrasts and resemblances. The task of knowledge is not to ask about the meaning of an act of generosity or

---

[8] I use the term "semiotic" as a counterpart to "hermeneutic," to indicate a contrast between two complementary types of understanding. Semiotic understanding
is formal and structural, as Zerubavel (*Time Maps*, 7) puts it, a "claim that meaning lies in the manner in which semiotic objects are systemically positioned in relation to one another."

impatience per se, but to establish the conditions that endow that act with meaning and significance.

Of course, one cannot assume that the theory of knowledge articulated in 1QS 3–4 is identical with postmodern semiotics.[9] There are important differences in the metaphysical assumptions each begins with. The deterministic constraints on individuals are explained as cultural codes by postmodern semiotics, but as divinely ordained at Qumran. The concern for origins and ends so prominent in Qumran thought is rejected by postmodern semiotics. Whereas postmodern semiotics proclaims the "death of the author" as a source of meaning, Qumran thought, in common with its culture, posits God as ultimate author of meaning and object of reference. So long as one does not lose sight of the differences between the assumptions of ancient Judaism and modern semiotics, the comparison can be useful in bringing into focus certain aspects of the way in which knowledge is constructed at Qumran. But the differences in some instances may be a matter of semantics. I would argue that even the notion of God as author of meaning is nuanced at Qumran by semiotic assumptions about knowledge. The source of all is expressed in 1QS 3–4 not simply as "God" but as אל דעות, "God of knowledge." What endows the phenomena of the world with meaning is not the impulse of an acting/reacting deity but that set of structured relationships called מחשבת כבודו, "His glorious plan."

There are other points in common between postmodern semiotics and the theory of knowledge implicit in 1QS 3–4. Both operate as acts of demystification. Postmodern semiotic analysis often describes culturally determined codes governing social behavior but operating at an unconscious level, so that those who participate in these behaviors are accustomed to giving a different and more personal explanation of their motivation. So, too, with the explanation of behavior and character offered by 1QS 3–4. Where the wisdom tradition and indeed much paranetic literature appealed to individuals to embrace

---

[9] Although semiotics was most intellectually fashionable in the 1970s and 1980s, its more fundamental insights remain an important part of humanistic and social scientific inquiry. See, for example, the recent study of social memory by sociologist Eviator Zerubavel, *Time Maps: Collective Memory and the Social Shape of the Past*. But it is the "classic" semiotics of early postmodernism that bears such an intriguing resemblance to the Two Spirits Treatise. For an account of literary semiotics and cultural criticism see Jonathan Culler, *The Pursuit of Signs* and Kaja Silverman, *The Subject of Semiotics*.

or avoid virtues and vices like those in 1QS 4:2–14, the Serek ha-Yahad demystifies the paranetic appeal. To one who has understood 1QS 3–4 it is not the authority and personal appeal of the father in Proverbs 1–9 or of the ancestors of Israel in the Testaments of the Twelve Patriarchs that affect the response of the one who heeds them. The capacity to respond to such appeals is disclosed in 1QS 3–4 to be a matter of the degree of "inheritance" each person has in the two spirits.

When this semiotic model of knowledge is employed in an analysis of human nature, traditional understandings of the self are transformed. In postmodern semiotics this transformation is often referred to as the "decentering of the self." Rather than posit the individual as an autonomous subject capable of endowing objects with meaning, semiotics sees the individual as the product of the intersection of various impersonal systems of meaning.[10] Though the systems understood to be at work in the Serek ha-Yahad are not cultural but metaphysical, an analogous decentering of the self is evident. The self can be spoken of not as an independent will but as the locus of a system of conflicting forces. In 1QS 3–4 these forces are organized in an explicitly dualistic fashion.[11]

Before turning to draw out the socially symbolic activity of the construction of knowledge in general and of the self in particular, there is one other aspect of the semiotic model of knowledge in 1QS 3–4 to be discussed: the construction of knowledge through intertextuality. In the formulation of Jonathan Culler, "literary works are to be considered not as autonomous entities, 'organic wholes,' but as intertextual constructs: sequences which have meaning in relation to other texts which they take up, cite, parody, refute, or generally transform. A text can be read only in relation to other texts, and it is made possible by the codes which animate the discursive space of

---

[10] Culler, 33. One needs to be careful in drawing a comparison between the modern semiotic or poststructuralist critique of the modern subject and the Qumranic transformation of the traditional ideology of the self in Israelite thought. There is a striking analogy, but the traditional construction of the subject in ancient Judaism is in significant respects different from the autonomous individual of modern subjectivity. See Fisch, "Psalms: The Limits of Subjectivity," pp. 104–35 in *Poetry with a Purpose.*

[11] In the Hodayot, too, it is possible to identify the decentering of the self, though in a nondualistic fashion. See Chapter 5 below.

a culture."[12] Explicating the intertextual space that surrounds a given text is a task that is both theoretically and practically infinite. The Two Spirits Treatise is in dialogue with a large and complex body of discourse that includes not only Israelite but also Mesopotamian, Persian, and perhaps Greek traditions. But there is one identifiable text with which 1QS 3–4 has a particularly marked relationship: Genesis 1. The reader is made aware of this relationship through the number of words common to both texts: ברא, צבאות, אותות, מיני, תולדות, אור, חושך, מלא, ממשלת. That a relationship between these two texts exists is clear enough, but the nature of the relationship is less clear. The text of 1QS 3–4 cannot be said to be an exegesis of Genesis 1 in any straightforward sense. The individual words are not necessarily used in comparable contexts. But the thick cross-referencing of vocabulary suggests that one cannot fully understand 1QS 3–4 without understanding its relationship to Genesis 1. It presupposes Genesis 1 as "already read," to borrow Roland Barthes' phrase.

If Genesis 1 is assumed as a literary pre-text to 1QS 3–4, the logical relationship between the two texts is just the reverse. Read by itself, Genesis 1 evokes a sense of flat and rather absolute beginning. Though it obliquely acknowledges some antecedent situation in its reference to תהו ובהו, its opening words ("When God began to create . . .") firmly orient the discourse to the moment of beginning and to its consequent moments. But what 1QS 3–4 manages to do is to open up a space behind Genesis 1 and to insert itself into that space. It establishes itself as the pre-text for Genesis 1. Where Genesis 1 is concerned with creation, 1QS 3–4 is concerned with the מחשבת that grounds creation. It is not just that 1QS 3–4 is to be read in the light of Genesis 1, but that henceforth Genesis 1 must be read in the light of 1QS 3–4. The effect, when one does this, is quite striking. Consider Gen 1:4b–5: "God divided the light from the darkness. And God called the light day and the darkness he called night. And there was evening and there was morning—day one." Where formerly this statement disclosed only God's organization of the created world, now it alludes as well to an antecedent spiritual reality that informs the structures of creation: "From a spring of light come

---

[12] Culler, 38.

the generations of truth, and from a well of darkness the generations of perversity. . . . He created the spirits of light and of darkness, and upon them he founded every deed" (1QS 3:19, 25; trans.
Knibb, adapted). Even the aesthetic feature of balanced pairs in
Genesis 1 now takes on a moral resonance.

The intertextuality does not merely transform Genesis 1 as a text.
It also makes available a reading of the physical world as a sign. /
Now the very alternation of day and night becomes a sign on the
physical level of the struggle between the spirits of light and darkness which are established "in equal measure until the last time"
(1QS 4:16). The lights in the firmament which separate the day from
the night are signs (אתת, Gen. 1:14), as deeds are signs (אותות) of
spirits in 1QS 3:14. The commands to fill the seas and the earth
(ומלאו, Gen. 1:22, 28) now serve as confirmation that all things do
indeed "fulfill" the plan of God (ימלאו, 1QS 3:16). The dominion
(ממשלת) of sun and moon over day and night (Gen 1:16) is analogous to the dominion (ממשלת) of humankind in the world (1QS
3:17–18).

The allusions, echoes, and parallels between 1QS 3–4 and Genesis
1, as these last examples suggest, often link different levels or aspects
of reality (e.g., luminaries/humankind) by associating each with the
same key word. They tease the reader with hints of mysterious correspondences never made explicit. In so doing they nurture the same
construction of knowledge that was identified above in the syntactical practices of complex interlinkage. Equally, the intertextual relations of a signifying cosmos, a scriptural text, and a sectarian teaching
also implicitly confirm the principle of the homology of reality that
is made explicit in the teachings about the presence of the two spirits in both the cosmological and anthropological realms. The serious play with the priestly creation text and its teaching about origins
points toward the secret of the relationship between the temporal
and the atemporal in the mystery of knowledge, as it also hints at
the absorption of all knowledge in the totality of the divine plan.

KNOWLEDGE AND THE CONTRADICTIONS OF HISTORY

It is now time to see whether and in what way specific features of
Qumran's construction of knowledge can be understood as an engagement of the particular historical conditions that defined Second

Temple Judaism. It may seem odd to posit 1QS 3–4 as a text that responds to the politics of empire. There are other Qumran texts that speak quite directly about international political figures (as in the specific references of the pesher on Nahum and in the account of the defeat of the Kittim in the War Scroll), but 1QS 3–4 ignores these realities and concerns itself with universal human experience. In its attempt to construct the self that is the subject of its discourse, the text appears to bypass the sphere of collective action where one ordinarily locates the political.

One can, however, fairly easy recognize a political subtext rewritten in the abstract and formal structure of 1QS 3–4 because other sorts of texts exist in which the response to historical contradiction is more direct. One has only to place 1QS 3–4 with its abstract struggle of light and darkness and its comprehensive, periodized temporality alongside more self-consciously political apocalypses, such as Daniel 2 and 7 or 1 Enoch 85–90. Indeed, many of the constituent elements of the symbolic speech of 1QS 3–4 can already be discerned in Second Isaiah's attempt to resolve the ideological contradiction between Babylonian and Persian power and the sovereignty of Israel's god: the long temporal vistas; periodization; predetermination; confrontation of opposing divine powers and human agents; eschatological resolution; and so forth.[13] In apocalypses such as Daniel and 1 Enoch a narrative transformation of ideological contradiction into a plot of conflict and resolution works its symbolic magic. In 1QS the formal structures of conflict and resolution remain identifiable; there is even a vestigial narrative quality. But the political derivation of these symbolic constructions is repressed, and all that appears on the surface is an account of metaphysical realities and the structure of the human self.

It is precisely the "evaporated" quality of the political subtext in 1QS 3–4 that is so intriguing. The symbolic work of the text is rather like that of a machine that transforms one kind of energy into another (as heat into rotary motion). Our ability to identify the derivation of the formal and symbolic structures of 1QS 3–4 points to the historical and political contradiction that supplies the energy to power this symbolic engine. The particular form that knowledge

---

[13] See Osten-Saken, *Die Apokalyptik*, for the close relationship between Second Isaiah and Daniel 2. Also Fröhlich, "Daniel 2 and Deutero-Isaiah."

of human nature takes in this text is closely determined by the fact that the intractable ideological and historical contradiction of the time is the continued domination of Israel by Gentile powers. Concern about political domination can be displaced onto anthropology, reshaping the structure of the human self according to the dynamics of the repressed struggle. It is the specific construction of knowledge in 1QS—especially its sense of the complex interlinkage of things—that provides the transformative gears, facilitating the displacement of the ideological and historical contradiction into the realm of character and anthropology. Perhaps, though, it would be more appropriate to say that the historical contradiction and the necessity of finding an imaginary resolution for it transformed the various antecedent elements of a priestly/scribal mode of knowing into a sophisticated and powerful intellectual system for the knowledge of human nature.

Given the extent to which Qumran theorizes the homology of levels of reality, it is likely that they were aware of the correspondence of patterns between the construction of human nature and that of history. But that is not to discount the extent to which the "magic" of displacement works at the unconscious level. This displacement accounts for the energy that can be invested specifically in knowledge of the nature of the self. On that level the contradiction can be grasped and overcome not only through symbolic speech but even in the practices of daily life. Although 1QS 3–4 looks forward to an eschatological resolution of the contradictions of the divided subject, one should remember the immediate literary context of 1QS 3–4 in the Serek ha-Yahad with its elaboration of the disciplines that make it possible for a person to enhance "his insight and the perfection of his way" (1QS 5:24). Thus the almost obsessive cultivation of a properly ordered character at Qumran is at least in part an attempt to resolve symbolically the ideological and historical contradictions created by the political domination of international empires. One only uncovers this, however, by analyzing the symbolic structures and tracing the displacement and repression of the political motive.

There is finally one other way in which the historical contradictions are symbolically resolved in this text, a way that takes one back to another aspect of the construction of knowledge, specifically to the relation between knowledge and temporality. The temporal is, of course, the realm in which the conflict between truth and perversity must be endured, and the realm in which even the righteous are subject to the influence of evil. And although the text makes no

explicit reference to it, the temporal is also the sphere of the political. But all of this conflict, including its origin and its resolution,
can also be said to exist in the atemporal plan of God (1QS 3:15–16).

Since 1QS is a teaching of the plan of God, at least insofar as
human beings are capable of grasping it, it is knowledge that allows
one to transcend the temporal and with it to transcend subjection
to conflict and contradiction. Knowledge becomes an experience of
power over the temporal, even while one is still subject to it. Such
knowledge, however, is available only to one who has "persevered
in the conversion of his life," as the Community Rule puts it (חזק
למשוב חיו, 3:1). Thus, the disciplining of the self through obedience
to the will of God is validated despite its apparent inability to make
a difference in the world, because it is through obedience that one
receives knowledge and through knowledge that one experiences now
the overcoming of subjection to contradiction.

In the relation between knowledge and temporality and in its symbolic forms of knowledge that facilitate the displacement of political
conflict into the realm of the self, 1QS 3–4 does indeed offer "imaginary solutions for unresolvable social contradictions." And thus it
serves as an act of ideological resistance against the international
political context in which Second Temple Judaism found itself. As
with all symbolic acts, it is an ambiguous one. A symbolic act is, as
Jameson notes, "a way of acting on the world and of compensating
for the impossibility of such action all at once."[14] By enacting their
victory in the symbolic structures of knowledge, language, and the
self, the Qumran community found it possible to postpone action in
the realm of history for generations. Whether in the end they attempted
to act or were simply overtaken by history is difficult to say. The
charred rubble and Roman arrowheads found at Khirbet Qumran
remain silent on that point.

---

[14] Jameson, "Symbolic Inference," 151.

CHAPTER FOUR

HOW TO MAKE A SECTARIAN: FORMATION OF LANGUAGE, SELF, AND COMMUNITY IN THE SEREK HA-YAHAD

If by some time-machine magic one could ask a member of the Qumran community what his purpose was in joining the sectarian community, he might well reply with something like the opening words of the Serek ha-Yahad: "to seek God with a whole heart and soul in order to do what is good and just before him, as he commanded by Moses and by all his servants the prophets" (1QS 1:1–3). What is remarkable about this statement is how unremarkable it is. There is nothing distinctly sectarian about it. It would be difficult to find any Jew of the Second Temple period who would disagree with the centrality of these matters or with the way in which they were expressed. Only as one persuaded this member of the Qumran community to elaborate would it become apparent that for him the meaning of the concept of divine commandments and of a life lived in accordance with them was inflected with a distinctive pattern of accentuation. Some of these inflections one would recognize as having priestly overtones or apocalyptic ones. Others would be ordinary words used in a slightly distinctive way, the nuances of which one would gradually learn by listening to the sectarian talk. Although very little in his speech would be unique, the combination of the various features would produce a way of talking that was not quite like that of any other community within Second Temple Judaism. As the sectarian continued to speak, it would become apparent that a distinctive form of self-understanding and distinctive patterns of community were embedded in his language, not only in the direct assertions of his statements but also in his choice of figures of speech, metaphors, and even verbal style. As James Boyd White remarked, "There is an intimate and necessary connection between the organization of language and the organization of community—between 'text' and 'constitution'—and between both of these and the organization of the individual mind."[1] Making a sectarian is, above all,

---

[1] White, 199.

a matter of remaking the language he speaks. Within the Qumran literature, the text that is most self-consciously concerned with the formation of language, self, and community is the Serek ha-Yahad.

CONSTRUCTED SELVES AND FIGURED WORLDS

The framework I use for studying sectarian rhetoric in relation to the formation of self and community has been discussed at some length in chapter one. I wish to supplement that discussion here with a brief account of the approach to the social and symbolic construction of selves and communities recently developed by anthropologist Dorothy Holland and her associates.[2] Naturally, there are many things that anthropologists can investigate, working with living communities and persons, that are not accessible to someone working with the textual deposits of an ancient community. But much of what engages Holland and her colleagues are the discourses and practices of the self as they occur in particular communities. Such things may include first-person speech, speech that construes others and their actions in particular ways, as well as more theoretical discussions about the nature of selfhood. Since these topics are of explicit concern in the Serek ha-Yahad and in the Hodayot, Holland's approach lends itself—with appropriate limitations—to a study of these documents. Care must be taken, of course, not to import alien or anachronistic notions of the self into the discourse of another culture. But the culturally specific notion of the self can be elicited by attending carefully to the particular words, symbolic forms, and practices by which people represent themselves.

Holland and her associates share much in common with Geertz's approach, particularly the crucial role of symbolic forms. But they place rather more emphasis on the dynamics of the self as a practice. Persons develop a sense of who they are in many ways. Social norms for bodily practices are one significant means, because of the close identification of a person with his or her body. How one positions and moves the body helps to form a sense of the self in terms of gender, social position, religious identification, and so forth. How one clothes the body and what foods one eats or does not eat—and

---

[2] Dorothy Holland, et al., *Identity and Agency in Cultural Worlds*.

with whom—join any number of other symbolic practices to construct identity. Although physical and nonverbal symbolic practices
are of great significance in the construction of identities, language
takes pride of place among the symbolic tools for the fashioning of
selves and worlds. The terms used to refer to self and others, the
vocabulary of insult and praise, the words that locate a person in
relation to a larger community, those that articulate aspirations or
fears, the little narratives that connect events in meaningful sequences
and construct possible futures all work together to create a richly
textured world in which the person locates him or herself. Such discourses that shape self and world are not developed in isolation but
are fundamentally social practices.

Identities, of course, are not singular but plural. Even in relatively
simple societies (if there are such), persons are regularly engaged in
many different, and often competing, discourses of the self. One has
many identities of varying scope and significance—professor, wife,
hiker, Episcopalian, southerner, political liberal, dog fancier. These
plural identities are often compartmentalized, although at times they
can be used over against one another to resist or critique proffered
identities and roles. Identities, of course, are only intelligible in relation to larger social and cultural constructs, what Holland and her
associates call figured worlds.[3]

Figured worlds are the "as if" structures that persons take as
meaningful reality. They are "as if" in the sense that they are culturally constructed, furnished with model narratives, typical character

---

[3] Although Holland et al. (60) do not give a formal definition, the following
description is helpful. "As we situate [the concept of figured worlds] among the
related concepts of fields, practices, activities, and communities of practice, the place
of figured worlds takes a clearer shape. It is a landscape of objectified (materially
and perceptibly expressed) meanings, joint activities, and structures of privilege and
influence—all partly contingent upon and partly independent of other figured worlds,
the interconnections among figured worlds, and larger societal and trans-societal
forces. Figured worlds in their conceptual dimensions supply the contexts of meaning for actions, cultural productions, performances, disputes, for the understandings
that people come to make of themselves, and for the capabilities that people develop
to direct their own behavior in these worlds. Materially, figured worlds are manifest in people's activities and practices; the idioms of the world realize selves and
others in the familiar narratives and everyday performances that constantiate relative positions of influence and prestige. Figured worlds provide the contexts of meaning and action in which social positions and social relationships are named and
conducted. They also provide the loci in which people fashion senses of self—that
is, develop identities."

roles, objects and activities that are part of the social performances conducted within these worlds, sets of appropriate and inappropriate emotions and responses to recurrent situations, posited beliefs about the nature of reality, and so forth. In this regard figured worlds bear considerable resemblance to game-playing and fantasy, except that the "brackets" put around those activities to emphasize their fictionality are generally not in play in the figured worlds of everyday reality.[4] The figured worlds of social life include the various institutions of a given community (e.g., the business world, the academic world, the military world, the medical world, the world of a religious community), but they also include smaller social niches and less formalized realms. Holland and her associates explore, for instance, Alcoholics Anonymous and the world of college romance as examples of figured worlds.

Figured worlds, along with the character roles they offer and the structures of meaning they provide, are not just given realities but must be entered. Whether the process is formal or informal, persons enter into figured worlds as novices and become both more proficient and more shaped by the worlds as they continue to engage in their discourses and practices. By the same token, however, the historical and contingent nature of figured worlds means that they exist only by being enacted. Thus no matter how real such a world may appear, it is always under construction and modification by those who participate in it. Selves and worlds are co-produced. Since figured worlds must recruit persons, they are always in various fashions engaged in rhetorical persuasion. They often tout their goods in terms of narratives of aspiration and achievement or of reward versus punishment, but in some instances the strategy involves the creation of the image of a counterworld. In such counterworlds, "motives are askew and actions are opposed to the course of events appropriate to the world's topos." In just such a manner, Holland suggests, the figured world of conservative talk-show hosts constructs the counterworld of "secular humanists and multiculturalists."[5]

The usefulness of this type of analysis for studying the literature of the Qumran community is obvious. Although figured worlds are

---

[4] It is possible, however, for a fantasy world to move into the public, political realm. Holland et al. (239–47) describe just such a process in the "publicization of courtly love."

[5] Holland et al., 250.

part and parcel of every aspect of human culture, sectarian movements must be particularly explicit and intentional in constructing the language and practices that will give tangible shape to their world. Since entry into such a world is so much more clearly marked than, for example, recruitment into the system of gender and family relations typical of the general social world, the cultivation of a model identity is likely to be the subject of rather intense concern. The typically agonistic relationship of sectarian movements to the larger social body fosters the creation of counterworlds that help to define sectarian identity, both individually and collectively. Since our sources for the Qumran community are not only literary but in some sense "official" texts, what one cannot examine is the way in which specific individuals internalized the figural identities offered them, negotiated among various identities, became agents within the figured worlds, and perhaps also resisted or modified the identities offered. But what is available are the models of the language and symbolic forms by which the figured world and its characters were articulated, as well as references to some of the practices by which they were realized.

The Figured World of a Disciplinary Institution

One might attempt to get a sense of the particular nature of the figured world of Qumran by comparing it with other sectarian movements, both in Second Temple Judaism and in other cultural contexts. Although he was not particularly focused on rhetoric and the formation of self in relation to sectarian community, Albert Baumgarten provides much of this kind of analysis in *The Flourishing of Jewish Sects in the Maccabean Period*. Important aspects of the Qumran community, however, might be overlooked if they were to be compared only with other contemporary sectarian movements. Thus I wish to situate the Qumran sectarian community in relation to another quite different frame of reference, namely, Michel Foucault's account of disciplinary institutions and the disciplinary power they construct. In addition, Foucault's investigation of various interpretive "technologies of the self" also lends itself helpfully to understanding the relation between language, community, and self at Qumran.[6] Foucault,

---

[6] See especially Foucault, *Discipline and Punish* and "Technologies of the Self."

of course, was not generating a general theory of power, knowledge, and the subject but rather investigating the specific historical context within which certain forms of power developed. Although one must respect the limits set by Foucault's historicism, it is possible to draw on his work for insight into other periods. Foucault himself acknowledged that, even though disciplinary power only became a socially pervasive form of power in the eighteenth and nineteenth centuries, it existed in more restricted social forms (e.g., monastic houses) in earlier periods. Similarly, Foucault's work on confession as a practice that relates power, knowledge, and the self came to focus increasingly on the ascetic practices of Greco-Roman paganism and early Christianity. As helpful as Foucault can be in providing a framework for understanding the social nature of disciplinary practices, there are "symbolic dimensions" to the practices and discourse of the Serek ha-Yahad that his type of inquiry cannot illumine; hence the importance of attending also to the more socio-linguistic and symbolic approach of Holland. Since Foucault is not a staple of Qumran scholarship, it is important to give a somewhat extended introduction to those aspects of his work that are most relevant to this inquiry.

Disciplinary power is a technology of control that takes the body as a primary object of power. Whatever the discipline's concrete purpose, it has the general aim of producing human beings who are both productive and docile. The parade examples of the products of such disciplinary technology are the soldier, the factory worker, the student, and in somewhat different ways, the prisoner and the hospital patient. Control of the body is an essential element. Indeed, in some disciplines the body may even be subdivided into constituent parts, as when separate drills are used to train the legs and arms of a soldier for their particular functions. Although some types of control of the body are clearly instrumentally related to the aims of the discipline (e.g., the motions necessary for efficient shooting of a rifle), in other cases the relationship is less direct (e.g., the training of a student in how to sit "properly" at a table for instruction or how to stand for reciting). Foucault himself notes the way in which Philo describes the Therapeutae as learning the discipline of listening in part by "always assum[ing] the same posture when listening."[7] The

---

[7] Foucault, "Technologies of the Self," 32.

concern for seating order and decorum at Qumran assemblies is a similar form of such discipline. The organization and training of bodies is never incidental in the exercise of disciplinary power, for it subjects the individual to a form of control which eventually becomes a form of self-control. "The motto of the disciplines might be: Get hold of their bodies—their hearts and minds will follow."[8]

Along with operations on bodies themselves, disciplinary power exercises itself through the organization of space and, in particular, the organization of bodies in space. Two features are characteristic: separation (e.g., the separate enclosure for the factory, schoolroom, army camp, prison) and internal organization, the grid within which bodies are arranged. The internal organization of space may be a feature of architecture (e.g., the physical configuration of the hospital or the prison building), but it may also be accomplished by arranging bodies themselves (e.g., the formation of soldiers in lines and units for military review, the seating arrangements in a classroom). As Foucault notes, "discipline organizes an analytical space" that accounts for each individual.[9] Such organization of space and bodies serves many purposes, one of the most important of which is surveillance, which Foucault understands as essential to the functioning of disciplinary power. "The exercise of discipline presupposes a mechanism that coerces by means of observation; an apparatus in which the techniques that make it possible to see induce effects of power, and in which, conversely, the means of coercion make those on whom they are applied clearly visible."[10] Surveillance is most effective if it is dispersed and continuous. This "disciplinary gaze" is not merely a feature of architectural or physical arrangements but also of social and organizational ones. Foucault gives as an example the forms of surveillance instituted in elementary teaching in the eighteenth century, in particular the system of observers, monitors, and tutors, senior students who were responsible for supervising aspects of the behavior and learning of their classmates, and who were themselves supervised by teachers.[11]

Surveillance makes possible, among other things, the exercise of "normalizing judgments," what Foucault calls the "small penal mechanism" at the heart of all disciplinary systems. This system imitates

---

[8] Ransom, *Foucault's Discipline*, 47.
[9] Foucault, *Discipline and Punish*, 143.
[10] Foucault, *Discipline and Punish*, 170.
[11] Foucault, *Discipline and Punish*, 176–77.

the legal/judicial penal system in certain ways, although the behaviors it seeks to regulate are not those that are the concern of the law, nor matters of serious moral concern, but rather minute, subtle, and often quite personal matters. Attention to detail and the control of the minute is characteristic of the exercise of disciplinary power.[12] "The workshop, the school, the army were subject to a whole micro-penalty of time (lateness, absences, interruptions of tasks), of activity (inattention, negligence, lack of zeal), of behavior (impoliteness, disobedience), of speech (idle chatter, insolence), of the body ('incorrect' attitudes, irregular gestures, lack of cleanliness), or sexuality (impurity, indecency)."[13] One might almost think Foucault compiled his list from the schedule of punishments in col. 7 of the Serek ha-Yahad.

Not all normalizing judgments in a disciplinary system have this quasi legal/judicial character, however. Discipline is not simply concerned with proscribed behaviors and attitudes but also with what does not measure up or meet the standard. Systems of rewards and punishments are used as inducements to motivate achievement of the standard level of performance. These judgments evaluate behavior not simply in terms of a binary good/bad classification, as in a legal/judicial system, but in terms of better/worse, thus creating a hierarchy of skill or achievement, so that persons are distributed according to rank or grade. Thus rank itself becomes a form of reward and punishment, especially if it is made visible by some token or enacted in daily activities. Foucault concludes,

> The art of punishing, in the regime of disciplinary power, is aimed neither at expiation, nor even precisely at repression. It brings five quite distinct operations into play: it refers individual actions to a whole that is at once a field of comparison, a space of differentiation and the principle of a rule to be followed. It differentiates individuals from one another. . . . It measures in quantitative terms and hierarchizes in terms of value the abilities, the level, the "nature" of the individuals. It introduces, through this "value-giving" measure, the constraint of a conformity that must be achieved. Lastly, it traces the limit that will define difference in relation to all other differences, the external frontier of the abnormal. . . . The perpetual penalty that traverses all points and

---

[12] Foucault, *Discipline and Punish*, 140.
[13] Foucault, *Discipline and Punish*, 178.

supervises every instant in the disciplinary institutions compares, differentiates, hierarchizes, homogenizes, excludes. In short, it *normalizes*.[14]

Although surveillance and normalizing judgment are exercised in a variety of ways, the technique that brings them together is the examination. Often highly ritualized, the examination combines a ceremony of power with the form of an experiment, in that the exercise of power leads to the establishment of some truth about the one examined. As will be explored below, the system of annual examinations described in the Serek ha-Yahad serves just such a purpose.

Foucault argues that disciplines "produce" individuals. They do this first by creating in persons certain qualities, behaviors, and skills that were not there before but which become integral to the person and part of his or her identity. Surveillance and the examination also make the individual an analyzable object whose peculiar achievements and limits become the focus of attention both for the person and for the examining authority. Finally, hierarchical ranking distributes, and thus individualizes, by placing each person in relation to others.

One of Foucault's most important observations has to do with the relationship between disciplinary power and knowledge, which he understands as being mutually produced. In various ways the exercise of disciplinary power requires and therefore produces knowledge. There is, for instance, the creation of entire fields of empirical knowledge about bodies, populations, and so forth, which are generated by various disciplines' "need to know." More pertinent here, however, is the way in which certain techniques of power, such as the examination, produce knowledge about persons. Such information is often documented in writing, so that the individual becomes a "case," an object of knowledge. But knowledge can also underwrite and generate the exercise of power. Foucault pursued this topic most explicitly in relation to his study of sexuality. In the nineteenth century certain theoretical discourses posited sexuality as the essence of the individual and the key to personal identity. Foucault attempted "to analyze the practices by which individuals were led to focus their attention on themselves, to decipher, recognize, and acknowledge themselves as subjects of desire, bringing into play between themselves

---

[14] Foucault, *Discipline and Punish*, 182–83.

and themselves a certain relationship that allows them to discover, in desire, the truth of their being, be it natural or fallen."[15] These discourses of (truth) both necessitated and justified the development of various techniques of power by which an individual could learn the truth about himself. The individual confessed his private thoughts and practices to a figure of power, the doctor or psychiatrist, who required and directed the nature of the disclosures, but who was in turn able to interpret the meaning and significance of the self-disclosure. In this relationship was an interplay of truth and power that held out the promise of healing and liberation. Thus the examination became a type of confession and the individual not simply an object of knowledge but a subject of knowledge as well. At Qumran, of course, the discourse of truth did not concern (sexuality) but the "spirit" of a person as it can be discerned by an examination of his knowledge and deeds of torah.

Despite certain obvious differences from those studied by Foucault, the community described by the Serek ha-Yahad is recognizable as a disciplinary institution. One of the differences between the Yahad and institutions studied by Foucault is the role of "meaning" in relation to the institution. Whereas many of the nineteenth century disciplinary institutions were utilitarian in character (a factory does not primarily "mean" something), the Yahad and the activities that took place within it were saturated with meaning. Nevertheless, one should not overlook the fact that the Yahad also understood itself as a place of production. What it produced was acts of obedience to God according to torah, and more precisely according to the proper interpretation of God's torah. Such acts of obedience further served to make expiation for the sins of the community (1QS 5:6) and for the land (8:10), and to effect the judgment of the wicked (5:7; 8:10). The instruments required to accomplish this purpose are the individuals who join the community. In their unimproved state, however, they cannot adequately serve that function. To do so they must enter into a necessary system of discipline, as the Serek ha-Yahad explicitly states (1:11–13). Thus they become simultaneously the objects of disciplinary power and its instruments. Since we lack an adequate range of sources that would allow for a reliable reconstruction of the life of the community either at a particular moment or over

---

[15] Foucault, *The Use of Pleasure*, 5.

time, it is important to keep in mind the focus of this study. It is an analysis of a text, not a society. But the nature of the Serek ha-Yahad is such that it presents itself as an intentional instrument for the formation of a figured world that takes the form of a disciplinary community.

THE NATURE, PURPOSE, AND STRUCTURE OF THE SEREK HA-YAHAD

A glance at the terms by which scholars have attempted to characterize the Serek ha-Yahad suggests some of the difficulty of finding a modern genre designation that is apt. Among other things, the work has been designated a "manual of discipline," a "handbook," a "rulebook," a "code," and a "constitution." One can intuit from these terms something of what scholars are trying to indicate about the work: that it is in some sense a normative account of the practices of the community that pertains both to individual and group behavior. Some of the terms suggest the formative or foundational nature of the text. Others draw attention to the specificity of the norms included. But all seem problematic in various ways. The difficulty is not simply one of anachronism, as modern Western analogies are sought to clarify the nature of the document. Moshe Weinfeld's comparison of the Serek ha-Yahad with various official organizational documents from Hellenistic-Roman guilds and religious associations underscores the fact that, despite various parallels, the Serek ha-Yahad is *sui generis*.[16]

Perhaps the best place to begin is with the text's own designation of itself as a *sefer serek*. Philip Alexander's study of the semantics of *serek* demonstrates that the word has a range of meaning approximating that of Greek *taxis*. Both words have to do with organization, administration, procedure, regulation, or, as Alexander puts it,

---

[16] Weinfeld, *Organizational Pattern*, 46–47. The closest generic parallel from antiquity would be the early church orders, which were composed more than two centuries later than the Serek ha-Yahad. See the study of Audet, "Literary and Doctrinal Relationships of the 'Manuel of Discipline'." Klinghardt ("The Manual of Discipline in the Light of Statutes of Hellenistic Associations") argues that the similarities between the Serek ha-Yahad and the rules of the Hellenistic associations warrant understanding the Yahad as a religious association of the Hellenistic type. In my opinion he overstates the case. See also the critical comments of Collins, "Forms of Community," 100–104.

"the order or rules according to which a group of people is to be organized and to conduct its affairs."[17] The term *serek* occurs in four texts—the War Scroll, the Damascus Document, the Community Rule, and the Rule of the Congregation. When the word is used to refer to the text itself, it seems primarily to designate the content of what is to follow (e.g., "this is the order for . . ."). Nevertheless, there appears to be an incipient sense of genre in those works that attempt to give an account of the order by which the community is to organize itself or conduct certain activities, though they differ from one another in many ways.

Concerning the purpose of the Serek ha-Yahad, the most plausible suggestion is that it was composed as a guide for the community's teacher, the Maskil, who was charged with a crucial role in the admission, instruction, and advancement of the members of the society.[18] Because the beginning of the text is broken, there is some question whether the Serek ha-Yahad is addressed to the Maskil alone or to the Maskil and the community at large, although the most plausible reconstructions favor an address to the Maskil alone.[19] It is a separate question, however, whether the Maskil was the primary reader of the text or, as some have suggested, that the Serek ha-Yahad was used directly in the instruction of new members, as a sort of written extension of the Maskil's teaching function.[20] In

---

[17] Alexander, "Rules," 799; Yadin, *War of the Sons of Light*, 148–50.

[18] Vermes, *Complete Dead Sea Scrolls*, 97; Roop, "Form Critical Study of the Society Rule," 335; Alexander, "Redaction-History of Serekh ha-Yahad," 439. The Two Spirits section is specifically introduced by a reference to the Maskil's responsibility for teaching, and a special set of rules for the Maskil begins in 1QS 9:22. A reference to the task of bringing new members into the sect (1:7) also suggests to some that the document is addressed to the leaders of the community (see Knibb, 79). For the role of the Maskil in the formation of the community, see Newsom, "The Sage in the Literature of Qumran: The Functions of the *Maskil*."

[19] Carmignac ("Conjecture," 85–87) suggested that the opening line of the text be restored as follows, "For [the Maskil . . . for the me]n his brothers" (. . . למשכיל לאנשים לחיו). That suggestion has been refuted by Metso (*Textual Development*, 111) and by Alexander and Vermes (*Serekh ha-Yahad*, 32). More probable is Metso's (112) own suggestion, למשכיל ללמד את אנ]שים לחיו ספר סרך היחד, "For the wise leader, to instruct the men for (during?) his life, the book of the order of the community."

[20] So Charlesworth (*Rule of the Community*, 1), who suggests that "portions of the *Rule of the Community* were probably to be memorized during the two years probationary period (1QS 6.13–23). Probably 3.13–4.26 (or at least sections of it) were known by heart by all members of the community." Whether or not Charlesworth is technically correct, his remarks contain an important insight. For identities to be conferred and the figured world of Qumran sectarianism to be maintained, the discourses and practices of the sect had to become by some means the internalized

either case the document's function has more to do with "formation" than information. The Serek ha-Yahad lacks the level of detail that would be needed if it were to be a sort of "owner's manual" for the operation of the sect. Yet neither is it, despite its composite nature, a mere loose-leaf notebook of odds and ends. As Alexander and Vermes note, its unity, both thematic and functional, is best understood in relation to its purpose as a "guide" for the Maskil in his preparation for his responsibilities as teacher and spiritual head of the community.[21] This is especially clear in the recension of 1QS. Not only does the document begin with a directive to the Maskil, but two other sub-sections are similarly introduced (3:13; 9:12), the latter of which contains instructions specific to the Makil's own responsibilities and behavior and concludes with a first-person hymn attributed to the Maskil. Thus, although the document contains material that the Maskil used in teaching and forming new members, 1QS also has the rhetorical shape of a work of formation for the Maskil himself.

RECENSIONS

Publication of the Cave 4 copies of the Serek ha-Yahad has shown that the document existed in several different recensions, the relationship among which is still debated. Both for practical reasons and because I find it the most rhetorically interesting recension, my investigation will focus on 1QS. But a brief account needs to be given of how the various copies of the document compare with one another. The manuscript copies of the Serek ha-Yahad differ from one another in two primary ways. First, some of them contain large blocks of material that are absent in others. Second, some contain numerous explanatory phrases and scriptural proof-texts that others do not. The two main accounts of the recensions of the Serek ha-Yahad have been published by Metso and by Alexander and Vermes. In their edition of the Cave 4 fragments, Alexander and Vermes suggest that four recensions of the Serek ha-Yahad existed.[22] Recension

words by which each member of the community thought and spoke. We cannot know, however, the means by which the Maskil carried out his teaching.

[21] Alexander and Vermes, 10.

[22] Alexander and Vermes, 12. In his earlier study, "Redaction-History of Serekh

A is represented by 1QS (Hasmonean semiformal script, ca. 100–75 BCE); Recension B by 4QS^b and 4QS^d (both early Herodian formal script, ca. 30–1 BCE);[23] Recension C by 4QS^e (late Hasmonean/early Herodian semicursive with semiformal features, ca. 50–25 BCE); Recension D by 4QS^g (late Hasmonean/Herodian semicursive, ca. 50–1 BCE). It is also possible that 4QpapS^a (early Hasmonean cursive, ca. 125–100 BCE) was an early draft of the document, containing some material not found in other versions.[24] Metso reconstructs an (unattested) original version of the Serek ha-Yahad which contained the equivalent of 1QS 5–9. In the extant manuscripts, two lines of textual tradition can be discerned, one represented by 4QS^e, the other by 4QS^b and 4QS^d. A compiler who knew both lines of tradition produced the recension represented by 1QS.[25]

Although Alexander and Metso generally agree in their recensional groupings, they disagree as to their relationship and consequently on the place of 1QS in the history of the development of the Serek ha-Yahad. In an article published in 1996, Alexander argued that in the absence of compelling evidence to the contrary,

---

ha-Yahad," Alexander proposed three recensions, the first represented by 1QS and 4QS^c, the second represented by 4QS^e, and the third represented by 4QS$^{b, d}$.

As the best preserved text, 1QS forms the basis of comparison, though it does not otherwise have a privileged status. For recensional analysis Alexander and Vermes consider the presence or absence of the following blocks of material to be significant: (1) 1QS 1–4, the introduction, the account of the covenant renewal ceremony, and the Two Spirits Treatise; (2) 1QS 8:15–9:11, the so-called Manifesto; (3) 1QS 10:5–11:22, the Hymn of the Maskil; (4) 1QSa, the Rule of the Congregation, and 1QSb, the Rule of Blessings. To take these units in order, manuscript 4QS^d does not contain the material represented in 1QS 1–4 but begins with the equivalent of 1QS 5, though with a different heading. Of the other manuscripts 4QpapS^a, 4QS^b, 4QpapS^c and 4QS^h all contain some material from this section. The so-called Manifesto (1QS 8:15–9:11) is not contained in 4QS^e, but is found in 4QS^d. The Maskil's Hymn is also not found in 4QS^e, though it appears in 4QS^b, 4QS^d, 4QS^f, 4QS^j. In place of the Maskil's hymn 4QS^e contains the calendric text known as Otot. Only 1QS attests 1QSa and 1QSb. This listing of major differences only begins to reflect the complex recensional picture, however, since the patterns of variant readings do not necessarily correspond with the inclusion or omission of the larger units of text.

[23] Since 4QS^b and 4QS^d differ concerning the inclusion of 1QS 1–4, Alexander and Vermes (12) suggest that this recension be subdivided, B^1 = 4QS^b and B^2 = 4QS^d.

[24] The assignment of other manuscripts to these recensional groups is uncertain because of their fragmentary state, although 4QS^f may belong with 1QS and 4QS^c, and 4QS^g (probably ca. 50–1 BCE) may belong with 4QS$^{b, d}$. See Alexander and Vermes, 10–12, and Metso, *Textual Development*, 90–95.

[25] Metso, *Textual Development*, 146–47.

the paleographical dates of the manuscripts should be taken as evidence of the dates of development of the various recensions. Although his recensional analysis in that article differs somewhat from the analysis in the *editio princeps*, he assumes that 1QS represents the oldest available recension. The composite nature of 1QS, however, points to a history of development that extends back behind the available textual evidence. What is most difficult to explain in Alexander's model is the nature of the differences between 1QS 5:1–10 and the shorter text in 4QS[b, d] and the differences between 1QS 8:15–9:11 and the parallels in 4QS[d], though Alexander offers possible explanations for such development. Metso argues differently. Provisionally setting aside the issue of the paleographical date of the manuscripts and concentrating on the likely patterns of redactional development as they can be inductively determined, she comes to the opposite conclusion and argues that the recension found in 1QS is later and more developed than that in 4QS[b, d] on the one hand and 4QS[e] on the other. The issues are complex and the evidence ambiguous. Considerable work remains to be done before the issue can be settled with certainty. Although it would be desirable to know more about the history of the composition and revision of the Serek ha-Yahad and the place of 1QS within the history of that development, the limits on what can be established requires that one work more modestly, taking 1QS simply as one version among others.[26] Because of the differences, each recension would have had a somewhat different rhetorical force. Since the Cave 4 texts exist only in fragments, it is seldom possible to compare and contrast their rhetorical strategies, though I will note differences between the texts from time to time.

THE RHETORICAL STRUCTURE OF 1QSEREK HA-YAHAD

Since the Serek ha-Yahad is a composite text, formed by joining preexisting materials of diverse sorts, its unity does not derive from a sustained argument or from the presence of a single rhetorical

---

[26] In contrast to the optimism of some earlier interpreters, such as Murphy-O'Connor ("La genèse littéraire"), I do not think that one can correlate the stages of redaction with particular events or stages within the history of the sectarian community.

voice or even a consistent set of words and images but rather from the arrangement of the sections and their relation to one another. That the author/redactor did operate with a sense of the whole is indicated in the way in which the opening lines (1QS 1:1–15) foreshadow several of the parts to follow. In her analysis of the introductory passages that are found throughout the Serek ha-Yahad (1:1–15; 5:1–7; 8:1–13a+15a), Metso noted that although there are certain themes that recur in all (e.g., commitment to torah, ethical obligations of the members), 1QS 1:1–15 contains two that are distinctive: the polarities of light/darkness and love/hatred (1:3–4, 9–10), and the admission of members into the covenant (1:7). These clauses anticipate the language and themes of the Two Spirits Treatise (3:13–4:26) and the account of the liturgy for entry into the covenant (1:16–3:12). Other themes, such as property (1:13; cf. 6:18–21) and the calendar (1:9, 13–14; cf. 10:1–8) anticipate issues that are dealt with in later sections of the document.[27] Thus the introduction in 1:1–15 seems to have been developed as an introduction to the document as a whole and not for cols. 1–4 only.[28]

Whether 1QS has an overall rhetorical structure has been a debated question. Pierre Guilbert has made the most forceful attempt to argue for a logical and intentional plan for 1QS, a plan conceived and executed by an author who controlled his materials closely.[29] Despite many astute observations Guilbert's theory has rightly been judged to overstate the case for the unity and logical coordination of the Serek ha-Yahad. Although Devorah Dimant assumes the composite nature of the text, she has argued for a chiastic structure that orders the sections of 1QS and gives unity to the whole.[30] Undoubtedly significant echoes and parallels between sections of 1QS exist, but in my opinion a chiastic analysis similarly overstates the unity of the document. Nevertheless, I am not inclined to say that 1QS is simply a random assemblage. It is important, however, to think both about the diachronic development of the text as well as its synchronic shape.

---

[27] Metso, *Textual Development*, 122.

[28] This finding argues against Stegemann's contention (*Library of Qumran*, 107–12) that 1QS 1:1–3:12 is a separate rule from 1QS 5–11.

[29] Guilbert, "Le plan de la Règle de la Communauté."

[30] Dimant, "Qumran Sectarian Literature," 497–502.

I am generally persuaded by Metso's theory of the growth of the Serek ha-Yahad. In her scenario the oldest discernible version contained the short recension of the material found in 1QS 5–9, without 8:15b–9:11 (whether 4Q Otot was included in this recension is uncertain). In one line of textual tradition (A) many small additions were made to 1QS 5–9, supplying scriptural legitimation and emphasizing the theme of the community as the keeper of the covenant with God. Otot was transmitted in this line of tradition. In another line of tradition (B) the short text of 1QS 5–9 was supplemented with a version of 1QS 8:15b–9:11, and the Maskil's hymn (9:26a–11:22) was added in place of Otot. At some point the material found in 1QS 1–4 was added. Finally, a redactor or compiler drew on both redactional streams to produce what we know as 1QS.[31]

Given such a complex history, overall structures are likely to be formed more from an intuitive sense of the appropriate sequence of general topics than by a careful plan or chiastic design. But such a sense of sequence can be discerned. Both in the older form of the Serek ha-Yahad (= 1QS 5–9) and in the form represented by 4QSᵇ and 1QS 1–11 the text opens with a motivational paragraph couched in infinitives, followed by a treatment of a ritual of entry (the oath in 1QS 5, the covenant ceremony in 1QS 1–2), and finally material concerning the order of life in the society. The instructions for the Maskil, who has a specialized leadership role within the society, are appropriately placed at the end of the document. Thus the Serek ha-Yahad is roughly shaped to recapitulate the stages of life as a sectarian: from motivation, to admission, instruction, life together, and leadership. Although the inclusion of 1QS 1–4 creates a slight reduplication of the pattern, the fundamental rhetorical movement remains clear. The strong verbal echoes between the description of the covenant ritual in 1QS 1–2 and the material pertaining to the Maskil in 1QS 9:12–11:22[32] not only serve as a literary inclusio but also encourage one to see in the character of the Maskil the telos of the disciplines and teaching that the Serek ha-Yahad has described.

[31] Metso, *Textual Development*, 146–147.
[32] Weise, *Kultzeiten*, 64–68, 71, n. 79; Falk, *Daily, Sabbath, and Festival Prayers*, 110–11.

The Figured World of the Serek ha-Yahad and the Construction of the Subject

1QS 1:1–15. Introduction

Since the heading is broken, one cannot be certain how the text began. Virtually all reconstructions, however, assume that the text is addressed to the Maskil, and that, as in the directive to him in 3.13, he is charged with instructing the members.[33] Following this initial charge, the text gives the title of the document that will prepare him for his duties: ספר סרך היחד. The heading thus sets a tone of formality and gravity. But in what follows, who speaks—and to whom? The voice of the text is never personalized but seems rather the collective voice of the community. Quite plausibly, these are actually the words of previous Maskilim, written down for future use.[34] Thus, even though the text is formally addressed to the Maskil, it is better understood as providing him with a model for his own speech as he addresses members of the community. Indeed the first section of the Serek ha-Yahad seems rhetorically designed specifically to address new members. The text begins, not with exclusively "insider" language, but rather with a sophisticated rhetorical movement that takes the language of the broader linguistic community of Judaism and gradually transforms it into the distinctive accents of the sectarian community.

Such a beginning is particularly apt, since to enter the community is to learn a new language, one distinct in its choices of diction, syntax, structure, and genre, as well as its content. Such a language cannot be too novel or foreign, however, but must begin on common ground. Bakhtin notes that this orientation is actually a part of all speech. The speaker orients himself toward the conceptual horizon of the addressee as the ground upon which he will attempt to construct his own utterance. By incorporating what is familiar and even "owned" by the addressee, the speaker facilitates

---

[33] Metso, *Textual Development*, 111–12.

[34] Although Tigchelaar ("In Search of the Scribe of 1QS," 452) does not use the term Maskil, his analysis of the scribal practices of 1QS suggests that "the scribe may have been one of the leaders of the Community, entitled to insert his scriptural interpretation into the Community's Rulebook. This might explain why someone who was 'careless' and 'less competent' as a scribe was nonetheless entrusted to copy the 1QS scroll, and why this scroll was preserved so well."

the process by which his alien speech can be appropriated by the addressee not just as an external, authoritative word but as "innerly persuasive" speech.[35] So here, even though the long, developed sequence of infinitive clauses with which the text begins is often taken as a peculiarly Qumranic style, it echoes the style with which the book of Proverbs begins.[36] This echo suggests that, like Proverbs, the Serek ha-Yahad presents itself as a book of instruction and formation. The infinitives identify the desire of the reader ("to learn wisdom and discipline" in Proverbs, "to seek God" in the Serek ha-Yahad) and represent the book as the means toward fulfilling that desire.

Comparison with Proverbs takes one only so far. The further significance of this construction for the Serek ha-Yahad has to be sought within the logic of that text itself. Although it is often observed that infinitives may be used in Qumran Hebrew as the equivalent of finite verbs,[37] the construction of such a long chain of infinitives suggests an intentional stylistic strategy, one used not only here but also at the beginning of other introductory sections of the Serek ha-Yahad (1QS 5:1–7; 9:12–23; cf. 8:1–13). The choice of the infinitive exploits an important nuance of grammar. Where finite verbs include information on subject, aspect, and mood, the infinitive expresses only purpose: "in order to seek God . . . to do what is good . . . to love . . . to hate . . . to keep away . . . to cling . . . to conduct oneself." The vocabulary of motives first given to the reader of the text is a vocabulary of pure intention. This is an apt language, since a voluntary society is not constituted by the givens of blood, marriage, or geographical location, but only by the motives provided by a common purpose.

Equally prominent in the opening lines are polar terms (e.g., good/bad; love/hate; choose/reject; light/darkness) and paired terms (e.g., heart/soul, good/upright, Moses/the prophets). Most of these pairs have a history in the common language, though they are not

---

[35] Bakhtin, *Dialogic Imagination*, 282.

[36] In commenting on the statement of purpose in Prov 1:2–6, Fox (*Proverbs 1–9*, 58) comments that "the syntax of this passage—a noun defined by a long series of infinitives of purpose—is without parallel in the Bible. It is later employed in the Rule of the Community from Qumran (1QS I 2–11), probably in dependence on Proverbs."

[37] Wernberg-Møller, *Manual of Discipline*, 44. See Qimron, *Hebrew of the Dead Sea Scrolls*, 70–72, for a linguistic analysis of the predicative use of the infinitive in Qumran Hebrew.

elsewhere used in such a dense clustering. Common language is thus subtly inflected by stylistic emphasis, creating a rhetoric of distinction and division. Words are given meaning not through stipulated definitions or through concrete examples but formally, through the linguistic resources of synonymy and antinomy. The linguistic world, like the social world of the sectarian, is constituted by the paired actions of separating and uniting. The very language he is taught to speak is an icon of the life he will live.

Another notable feature of the language here and elsewhere in the Serek ha-Yahad is the passion for qualification and specification. One does not simply desire "to seek God" but "to seek God—with a whole heart and soul—in order to do what is good and right before Him—as he commanded—by the hand of Moses and by the hand of all his servants the prophets." An even more involved syntax introduces the Two Spirits Treatise, as was discussed in the preceding chapter. To a certain extent this tendency may simply be part of the ethos of scribes who delight in glossing texts. The various glosses, scriptural citations, and other small expansions that one can recognize through a comparison between 1QS 5–9 and the comparable sections of 4QS^b and 4QS^d reflect this scribal tendency.[38] But one should not think of the Serek ha-Yahad as composed in an original lean syntax, subsequently glossed. The elaborate and qualified style seems to be a characteristic of the mode of composition itself. Although this stylistic tendency is less transparently related to the ideology of the sect than is the fondness for polar terms, it does reflect a recognizable feature of the ethos of the community. The Serek ha-Yahad repeatedly displays a concern for the production of exact and precise knowledge. This concern is reflected not only in the disciplines of the society that produce knowledge about persons and about the will of God, but also in the way in which knowledge is described. So here, the very habits of speech are shaped by a concern to qualify and specify.

At the formal level, elements of the distinctive language of the Yahad are present from the first line of the text, but in terms of diction and content the language with which the Serek ha-Yahad begins sounds much like the ordinary, unmarked language that a

---

[38] Metso, *Textual Development*, 68–106. See Fishbane, *Biblical Interpretation*, 44–77, for an analysis of forms of scribal glossing in the Hebrew Bible.

nonsectarian might use to express his desires and intentions: to seek God; to do what is good and right; not walking any more in stubbornness of heart. On first impression the language strikes one as vaguely deuteronomistic,[39] but that is only to say as one of the most widely used idioms of moral and religious discourse in the Second Temple period. The Serek ha-Yahad thus opens with a passage that uses the common coinage of moral language. As one who instructs probationary members, the Maskil has to be able to use a language that operates within the shared conceptual world, even as he inflects that discourse with an intense rhetoric of purpose, synonymy, and antinomy.

A more attentive listener will discern something else in those opening lines. More than simply an evocation of vaguely deuteronomistic language, the initial statement of purpose is a dense network of scriptural allusions and echoes (2 Chron 15:12; Deut 6:18; 12:28; Josh 14:2; 21:2; 2 Kgs 17:23; Isa 7:15–16; Am 5:15; Jer 7:24; 9:13, 23; 22:5; Ezek 6:9; Isa 52:2; etc.).[40] By invoking this intensely intertextual language immediately following the heading, "book of the order of the community," the Serek ha-Yahad acknowledges the language of scripture as the dominant discourse within which it situates its own speech. Biblical allusion is a characteristic of virtually all of Second Temple literature, so this aspect of the Serek ha-Yahad's speech is also a part of the conceptual horizon of the addressee. But the sheer density of allusion is unusual. As Colleen Conway observes, with the "tight interweaving of the other's word (the Rule) with the reader's own word (Scripture) the lines between the two are made practically imperceptible,"[41] thus facilitating the appropriation of the new discourse as the addresee's own. It also models what the sectarian will learn: how to speak a language saturated with the power and holiness of scripture, and also how to see in scripture references and allusions to the life and values of the sect itself.

To understand the rhetoric of the introduction, one must also attend to the structure of the passage as a whole. The long sequence of infinitives serves to throw emphasis upon the point in the text in which the writer switches to a finite verb in line 11 (יביאו), but more

---

[39] Cp. Deut 6:18; 12:28; 29:18; Jer 7:24; 9:13; 11:8.
[40] See Wernberg-Møller, "Biblical Material in the Manual of Discipline," 41 n. 1.
[41] Conway, "Toward a Well-Formed Subject," 118.

subtle patterning and shifts in grammar and diction also divide the
first section of the introduction into two parts, lines 1–7a and lines
7b–11a. As most translations recognize, not all of the infinitives in
these initial lines have the same function. Some structure the main
line of thought, whereas others add explicating or qualifying comment. Although readers might interpret such an involved structure
in slightly different ways, the basic architecture of the passage is
clear. The structuring signals are the preference for paired infinitives
and the mostly consistent use of *waw* both to introduce the second
member of a pair and also to introduce a new pair of main infinitives.
Inclusio and mirror image repetition further contribute to the structure. These devices are better seen in a schematic chart of the infinitives. The main infinitives are placed on the right with the subordinated
infinitives to the left.

Lines 1–7a

		לדרוש
		ולאהוב
		ולשנוא
	לרחוק ולדבוק	
		ולעשות
לעשות		ולוא ללכת

(לעשות)

Lines 7b–11a

		ולהבי
	לעשות	להיחד
	ולהתהלכ	
		ולאהוב
		ולשנוא

To seek God with [a whole heart and soul] **in order to do** what
  is good and right before Him as he commanded by the hand of
  Moses and by the hand of all his servants the prophets;
And to love all that he has chosen,
And to hate all that he has rejected, **in order to keep far** from all
  evil **and to cling** to all good works;
And to do truth and righteousness and justice in the land,
And not to walk any longer in the stubbornness of a guilty heart
  and promiscuous eyes, **to do** all manner of evil.

And to bring in all those who volunteer freely **to do** the statutes of
  God in the covenant of grace,
To be united in the council of God, **in order to walk** before Him

> in perfection [according to] all that he has revealed with respect to the times appointed for them;
>
> **And to love** all the children of light, each man according to his lot in the council of God,
>
> **And to hate** all the children of darkness, each man according to his guilt in the vengeance of God.

Although the entire introduction receives its orientation from the primary desire "to seek God," lines 1–7a are marked out by the inclusio of the qualifying infinitive לעשות. Within that section, the paired infinitives "to love … to hate" and "to do … not to walk" serve as the main structuring verbs. The end of the first section may also be signaled by the distinctive use of a negative infinitive. That lines 7b–11a form a distinct but mirroring section is suggested by the fact that the four main infinitives of lines 1–7a are repeated, although "to do" and "to walk" appear as qualifying rather than main infinitives in 7b–11a. Also, the initial infinitive in this section is, uniquely, a causative. But the most important marker is not grammatical but semantic. In the first section the speaker uses primarily unmarked moral language. Specifically sectarian terms and concepts appear only in the second section, where they cluster thickly (e.g., "council of the community," "things revealed at their appointed times," "sons of light/darkness," "lot"). The pivot term that stands between the two sections is the causative verb, "to bring in." "They shall bring all who willingly offer to do the statues of God into the covenant of grace, and they shall be joined to the council of God" (1:7–8).

What the introduction models in its structure is that as persons are brought into the community, so is their language. Immediately following the reference to entry into the community, two of the previously stated moral imperatives are reinterpreted with distinctly sectarian meanings. Where before it was said "to do what is good and upright before him according as he commanded by Moses and by all his servants the prophets," now one understands that intention as "walking before him in perfection [according to] all that is revealed with respect to the times appointed for them" (1:8), that is, the specifically sectarian understanding of laws appropriate to various epochs. Moreover, the previous statement about loving all that he has chosen and hating all that he has rejected is interpreted as "loving all the children of light … and hating all the children of darkness. …" (1:9–10). The common language of moral discourse is not defective or false but it is revealed to have hidden significance. Until it is brought within the language community of the Yahad, its full meaning cannot be discerned.

What one can see taking place with respect to bringing language within the disciplines of the sect the text makes explicit in the third section in terms of the sectarian's knowledge, ability, and (mental) capacity. Just as the sect was to "bring in those who freely offer themselves" (line 7), so those who offer themselves are to "bring in" their דעת, their כוח, and their הון (line 11).[42] Knowledge must be brought into the community to be "purified" (לברר, line 12), and ability and (mental) capacity must be brought into the community to be "disciplined" (לתכן, line 12) by means of the communal practices of perfected conduct and right counsel. In this section the language of the Serek ha-Yahad models an example of the reorderings of which it speaks.

Along with offering to reorder the knowledge of the sectarian and the language with which he articulates that knowledge, the introduction to the Serek ha-Yahad also offers the sectarian a new term of identity. In line 7 and again in line 11 those who enter are called הנדבים, "those who willingly offer." At one level the term simply alludes to the fact that entry into the community is a voluntary act, a feature also present in the rhetoric of infinitives of purpose. The term הנדבים, however, is also redolent of motives that qualify the nature of the act and thus the persons who do it. As Aloysius Fitzgerald has shown in his study of the root נדב, although the term has both military and cultic connotations, exilic and postexilic writings strongly associate the root with generosity to the temple and the sacrificial cult.[43] In particular, Fitzgerald argues, it is the narrative of 1 Chr 29:1–22, in which David collects contributions for the building of the temple, that provides the background for the Qumran usage. Whereas the community leaders gave gold, silver, bronze, iron, and precious stones for the building of the temple, the addresses

---

[42] The context favors taking הון not in its biblical Hebrew sense of "property" but in the sense it has in Mishnaic Hebrew and in Jewish Aramaic of "(mental) capacity." See Wernberg-Møller, "Biblical Material in the Manual of Discipline," 54, n. 1, citing Dupont-Sommer, Sukenik, and Marcus.

[43] Fitzgerald, "*MTNDBYM* in 1QS." Fitzgerald (495, n. 1) takes הנדבים in 1QS 1.7 as a niphal participle, "semantically equivalent" to the hithpael.

of this teaching bring their knowledge, ability, and (mental) capacity. The evocative metaphor analogizes the Qumran community to the temple, an identification made explicitly elsewhere, but it also does something else. By correlating the sectarian's knowledge and personal capacities with the material offerings of the leaders of Israel, it makes those qualities the dedicated possession of the community. To embrace this metaphor is to naturalize the disciplines of the sect in a profound way.

The last lines of this section (1:13–15) complement the preceding instruction about reordering one's life within the community with a series of four injunctions phrased in the negative (ולוא לצעוד ... ולוא להתאחר ... ולוא לסור ... לקדם). Although the temporal language in these lines led some scholars to assume that the injunctions have to do with the proper times for celebrating yearly festivals,[44] the context does not favor such an interpretation. The orientation of the preceding lines to comprehensive terms (e.g., "the truth of the statutes of God," "His perfect ways," "His right counsel") leads one to expect general instruction here, too. Manfred Weise is undoubtedly correct when he argues that the issue here is the same as in col. 9, the claim of the sect that distinct laws and behaviors are appropriate to each historically determined epoch.[45] Wernberg-Møller reasons similarly, "that an action, in order to be morally perfect, should not only formally comply with a commandment, but should also take place at the right time," citing as a parallel the comment about Abraham in Jub. 17:18, "Neither was his soul impatient, nor was he slow to act."[46] The passage in Jubilees, however, seems more akin to the traditional sapiential belief that wisdom inheres in doing the right act at the right time, whereas the background here has to do with revelations of the mysteries of God.

More striking and more significant is the way in which spatial and temporal figures are interwoven in these lines. The text makes use of the familiar deuteronomistic cliche of not turning to go to the right or the left (cf. Deut 5:32; 17:11, 20; 28:14; Josh 1:7; 23:6). The image of walking a path undeviatingly is an obvious sort of moral analogy (cf. Prov 4:27). But the Serek ha-Yahad does something

---

[44] E.g., VanderKam, *Calendars*, 45.
[45] Weise, 66–67. See also Leaney, *Rule of Qumran*, 120, 123.
[46] Wernberg-Møller, *Manual of Discipline*, 49.

distinctive by combining the received trope of spatial orientation with its own language of temporal orientation. The two categories are first combined in one statement: the sectarian is one who does not "step aside" or "depart" (ולוא לצעוד) from the words of God "in their times" (בקציהם). Next the categories are developed in separate phrases: "not advancing their times nor delaying any of their appointed times, and not turning aside from his true statutes by walking to the right or to the left." At one level this is merely a figure of speech; but as cognitive linguists have shown, figures of speech are also figures of the mind and so warrant investigation. The fact that similar figures of speech show up three more times in the Serek ha-Yahad (see 8:4; 9:12, 18) makes it all the more likely that these express something characteristic about the nature of the sect's perception. In each case a temporal expression is paired with another kind of measure. In 8:4 the members of the community are instructed "to walk with all according to the measure of truth and according to the rule of the time." In 9:12 the rule for the Maskil is that he should "walk with all the living according to the norm of every time and according to the weight of every person." And in 9:18 he is to teach the members of the community "each according to his spirit [and] according to the norm of the time." In this figure of a double analytic, correct action is achieved only at the intersection of two coordinates, one of which is knowledge of the times and the other of which is knowledge of another sort.[47] The trope is an image of the way in which knowledge is precisely configured at Qumran. True knowledge requires not only being able to make graded distinctions along various continua (e.g., the spirit of a person, the relation of one time to another) but also to bring the different dimensions of knowledge to a point of intersection.

Although the specific details of community life and teachings are taken up only in later sections of the Serek ha-Yahad, the opening lines of the document do a remarkable job of creating a sense of the figured world of the Qumran community and of the new identity it offers to the one who would enter it. Beginning with the desires and motives of the person who is inclined to membership, these lines introduce such a person to a way of speaking—and thus a way of

---

[47] See the analysis of this representation of knowledge in the Two Spirits Treatise in chapter 3 above.

thinking—that embodies key elements of the sect's figured world. They point to the sect as the locus of the true meaning of inherited language (1:1–11), available only to the one who makes a total commitment to the sect and its disciplines (1:12–13) and who embraces the conviction that to obey the commandments of God requires understanding their relation to the epochs of time (1:13–15). The most fundamental work of this passage, however, lies in the tropes that permeate the language itself: the complex qualifying phrases with their patterns of synonyms and antonyms, and the double analytic of time and space. These tropes, and others closely related to them that will occur later in the Serek ha-Yahad, figure not only the habits of speech but also forms of knowledge, the structure of the self, and the social organization of the community, both in its internal and external relations.

1QS 1:16–3:12. The Covenant Ritual

The moment of entering the covenant community is decisive for constituting the identity of the persons to whom the Serek ha-Yahad is addressed. The term covenant has a different meaning in the Serek ha-Yahad than it possesses in the Hebrew Bible and in many other contemporary Jewish writings. As Ellen Juhl Christiansen has demonstrated, the covenant is not represented in terms of "a relationship between God and ethnic Israel" but as *"a particularistic covenant relationship."*[48] Drawing on the imagery of priestly covenant commitment, the Serek ha-Yahad places the emphasis on "covenantal obedience and a status of perfection" rather than membership by birth.[49] Thus the passage describing the covenant ritual in 1QS 1:16–2:25 contains primary images that define both the self-understanding of the community and the character its members must possess.

The beginning of the passage, which refers to "all who enter into the order of the community" (וכול הבאים בסרך היחד), has suggested to some that what follows is an initiation ceremony for novices.[50] As a later part of the passage shows, however, this is also an annual

---

[48] Christiansen, 157 (italics in original).
[49] Christiansen, 158.
[50] So Dupont-Sommer, "Observations sur le Manuel de Discipline," 16, 19, 22–23. *Nouveaux aperçus*, 127.

event in which all members participate (1QS 2:19–25).[51] The confusion is actually instructive. The language in which the action is represented ("coming into" [הבאים ב-], "crossing over into," [ועברו ב-]) are metaphorical terms that employ the imagery of spatial movement across a marked boundary or threshold to describe a change in status.[52] A new identity is conferred in the act of crossing over. Yet even though entering the covenant is a definitive act, it is one that is never completed once and for all. Through the yearly ritual the sectarian repeatedly reenacts the movement of "crossing over" and "entering in" that constitutes his identity. Ritual repetition that serves to reinforce identities occurs in many ways and in communities of every sort. The socially and historically contingent nature of figured worlds requires that identities be constantly reaffirmed. But not all communities do this by reenacting the moment of entry. Given the particular understanding of covenant in the Yahad, however, this ritual serves to reinforce the "separation from" and "uniting with" that is at the heart of the sect's moral imagination.

One should remember that although the account of the entry into the covenant community refers to a ritual event, in the Serek ha-Yahad it is a textual event. Its place in the text, however, does imitate its place in the life of the sectarian. Coming very near the beginning of the text, it follows the development of initial motivation and serves as the entryway to the knowledge and formation that lie beyond. Like the annual ceremony, it is reexperienced with every reading. Although presented in a descriptive and prescriptive framework, the account of the covenant ceremony is a careful combination of summary and quotation. From the perspective of rhetoric, it is significant that it is specifically the performative words that are quoted: the words of confession, of blessing, of cursing, and the community response of affirmation. While one does not actually enter the community or renew the covenant by reading the Serek ha-Yahad, its dramatic form recreates the gateway experience for the reader of the text, the moment of self-examination and decision.

One cannot know how the account given in the Serek ha-Yahad compared with any particular ritual enactment. The existence of sev-

---

[51] Knibb, 88.
[52] Christiansen, 171. She, however, remains agnostic as to whether the ceremony describes an initiation rite or a covenant renewal.

eral texts that appear either to reflect or describe the covenant ritual suggest that there was some variation in the performances.[53] Thus
it is important to remember that the account of the covenant ritual
given here has been adapted for the purposes of the Serek ha-Yahad,
that is, to serve as a text of instruction and formation. This adaptation is particularly apparent in the way in which the account of
the ritual itself melds into a discussion of the types of character that
can and cannot be present in the community (2:25–3:12). This concern for character may also be reflected in the choice of material
excerpted for "quotation" rather than summary. Certainly the structure of the account, whether it reflects the sequence of the actual
ceremony or is a reorganization of it, places a concern for character at an emphatic point.

   The structure of the ceremony as represented in the text is symmetrical and chiastic:

> Priests and Levites together bless God
>   Response of those entering the covenant: Amen, Amen
> Priests recite mercies of God to Israel
> Levites recite iniquities of Israel
>   Confession of those entering the covenant
> Priests bless the members of the lot of God
> Levites curse the members of the lot of Belial
>   Response of those entering the covenant: Amen, Amen
> Priests and Levites together curse the one who enters the covenant
> hypocritically
>   Response of those entering the covenant: Amen, Amen.

As is often noted, the covenant ceremony contains echoes of earlier,
paradigmatic ceremonies. Through textual allusions it refers back to
and appropriates the ceremony prescribed by Moses in Deuteronomy
27 for the time when the people enter the land and also the ceremony for the renewal of the covenant in Moab described in Deuteronomy 29. There are also echoes of the solemn convocation of
Nehemiah 8 and of the Day of Atonement in Leviticus 16. The confession is framed in highly traditional language, particularly close to
Ps 106:6. Similarly, the priests' blessing is an interpretive expansion

---

[53] Falk, *Daily, Sabbath, and Festival Prayers*, 219–36, surveys the various texts from
Qumran that describe the covenant ceremony or were perhaps liturgical texts used
in connection with it, including not only 1QS but also the Damascus Document,
5QRule, and 4QBerakhot.

of the Aaronic blessing, a text that also serves as a point of reference for the development of the levitical curse.[54] Such evocations are part of the way the sect claims for itself the identity of Israel and contests the claims of others to that identity. As with the rest of the community's speech practices, one can see here appropriation and reaccentuation of the common language of worship. Weise, for instance, has indicated the extent to which various elements of the liturgy in 1QS are part of a common postexilic tradition. The sequence of praise, confession, Aaronic blessing, and curse can also be identified in the postexilic prayers of confession, such as Nehemiah 9, Ezra 9, Daniel 9, and Bar 1:15–3:8.[55] Similarly, the expansions of the Aaronic blessing have significant parallels in later rabbinic interpretation and in the synagogue liturgy.[56]

Alongside the general pattern of similarities, the distinctive Qumranic reaccentuation is evident in a number of ways. It is present first of all in the morally weighted aesthetic of symmetry and antithetical balance in the structure of the ceremony. More explicitly, words that seem most evidently part of a "common possession," such as the words of confession, are weighted with sectarian implications because the sins confessed are characterized as having been committed "during the dominion of Belial" (1QS 1:23). The figured world of sectarian identity is most evident in the blessing and cursing. In contrast to the biblical usage in which both blessings and curses are addressed to those who enter the covenant, here the blessings and curses establish the boundary between insiders ("all the men of the lot of God") and outsiders ("all the men of the lot of Belial")[57] and establish in a symbolic fashion the space of separation necessary for the constituting of a disciplinary institution.

Most intriguing is the emphatic position given to the cursing of the one who would enter the covenant hypocritically. It is the final act of the ritual and forms the counterpart to the blessing of God. Why is such a person so threatening to the community? The motive for the curse draws first on the imagery of idolatry. "Cursed for the idols of his heart," which he serves,[58] is the one who enters this

---

[54] Falk, *Daily, Sabbath, and Festival Prayers*, 219–230, analyzes the intertextual echoes.
[55] Weise, 81–2.
[56] Weise, 82–93.
[57] Nitzan, *Qumran Prayer and Religious Poetry*, 125–26.
[58] Reading לעבוד instead of לעבור.

covenant while the stumbling block of his iniquity he sets before himself, in order to backslide by means of it" (2:11–12). The language clearly evokes Ezek 14:4, which refers to persons who "take their idols into their hearts, and place their iniquity as a stumbling block before them, and yet come to the prophet." In Ezekiel the crucial element is not simply the idolatry but the intentional holding on to the iniquity of idolatry while coming to seek God from the prophet. The horror is in the willful duplicity. In the Serek ha-Yahad what is analogous to "coming to" the prophet is "coming into" the covenant. That duplicity—and not simply idolatry—is also the focal issue for the Serek ha-Yahad[59] is confirmed through the citation of Deut 29:18, Moses' warning against the "poisonous and bitter root" of the one who enters the covenant with duplicitous intent. With only a single substantive change ("covenant" for "oath") the Serek ha-Yahad appropriates the Mosaic language as follows: "And when he hears the words of this covenant he blesses himself privately and says, 'Peace be with me, even though I walk in the stubbornness of my heart'" (1QS 2:13–14).

Such a person poses a mortal danger to the community because he recognizes but is at peace with his own moral duplicity. He is immune to the rhetoric of distinction, division, separation, and purification that stands at the center of the linguistic and symbolic world of Qumran. Thus he is resistant to the disciplinary regimens of the community. His subjectivity is constituted by an autonomy that repudiates the relation between self and community practiced at Qumran. The hypocrite is one who cultivates a private place, an interiority utterly alien to the construction of the self in the Qumran community. It is not by accident that the hypocrite is represented as engaging in a private and self-referential act of blessing when the rest of the community is engaged in a public and communal act of confession, blessing, and cursing. As later sections of the Serek ha-Yahad make evident, the community takes priority over the individual. Only by a rigorous practice of submission to the hierarchical order of the community and an internalizing of its forms of speech does one receive the transformed selfhood in which one is a confidant of the counsel of God and an associate of angels. The hypocrite cannot be taught or disciplined because he holds back what should be

---

[59] Contra Laubscher, "Literary Structure of 1QS 2:11–18," 54.

brought into the community to be set in order (cf. 1:11). The disciplinary power of instruction and the system of rules of penance that govern members who enter in sincerity are consequently ineffective against him. Only the performative language of the curse (2:14–17, adapting Deut 29:18–20) can close the gates of the community against such a threat.[60]

In contrast to the hypocrite who represents a confusion of motives, attempting to enter without submitting, a description of the well-ordered community concludes the account of the covenant ceremony (2:19–25). Once again the language of distinction and division prevails. Here, however, it is not the binary distinction between outside and inside, God and Belial, curse and blessing. Rather, it is the traditional Second Temple division of Israel into priests, Levites, and laity (see, e.g., Ezra 9:1), subdivided according to the groupings of the wilderness march (thousands, hundreds, fifties, tens; cf. Exod 18:21; Deut 1:15), now combined with the sect's own ordering of each category according to a hierarchy of spirit (לפי רוחותם זה אחר זה, 1QS 2:20). A binary division that distinguishes the sect from outsiders is thus complemented both by an order of inherited status and by the infinite gradation of more and less spirit (cf. 1QH^a 6:8–22). The moral imagination that expresses itself in this vision of the well-ordered community is one that has strong continuities with the priestly tradition and its passion for classifying and ordering. But the materials on which the formal symbolic patterns are mapped are not only the traditional priestly ones, but also the phenomenology of spirit manifested in the individuals who comprise the sect. That is to say that the self becomes a critical symbolic space for the moral imagination of the community. The ritual described is not only a recommitment ceremony, as its echoes of Deuteronomy 27–30 and Nehemiah 8–10 suggest, but also a *tableau vivant* of the spirit of holiness and truth in the world. Like the description of Ezekiel's temple with its zones of holiness, it is a map of spirit.[61] Although temple imagery, which is elsewhere used of the community is not explicitly invoked here, the use of purity language in the following section about the

---

[60] Just how important is the problem of the person who cannot be disciplined is further indicated by the fact that the topic is taken up again at the conclusion of the discussion of the covenant ritual (2:25–3:12), immediately before the discussion of human nature in the Two Spirits Treatise.

[61] Smith, *To Take Place*, 56–71.

recalcitrant member suggests that the analogy is implicit here as well.

The importance of the order described in this section of the Serek ha-Yahad is underscored by the insistence that no one should move down or move up from the place allotted to him. The phraseology used (ולוא ישפול איש מבית מעמדו ולוא ירום ממקום גורלו, 1QS 2:23) evokes Ps 75:8, with its grounding of status in divine decision ("For it is God who judges; one he makes low; another he makes high"; כי אלהים שפט זה ישפיל וזה ירים). When one asks, however, what value the text places on each one "knowing his place in the community of God according to the eternal plan" (2:22–23), the answer is given in terms of moral community: "for they shall all be in a community of truth, virtuous humility, kindly love, and right intention toward one another in a holy council, and they shall all be members of an eternal fellowship," 2:24–25; trans. Knibb). Proper relations and even proper sentiments can flourish only when the spirit is properly ordered in the precedence of the community.

The nature of the relationship between individual and community implied in this symbolization is vastly different from that which governs the relationship between individual and community in what, with Sanders, one may call "common Judaism." Certain consequences follow from this different symbolic order. One is the necessary development of a new language of the self or a transformation of old languages of the self to make them adequate for the discrimination of spirit required for the formation of the community described here. Both the Hodayot and the Two Spirits Treatise contribute to this reformation of language of the self. Another consequence is the intensely focused attention on the cultivation of the individual in the disciplines of the community. Since it appears that the measure of spirit is not fixed in a person but is a perfectible quality, the community had to develop what Foucault would call various "technologies of the self." These technologies, discussed below in more detail, include the practices of social etiquette, the community disciplines, the experience of yearly examinations, and certain practices of piety, such as the first-person prayers of the Hodayot.[62]

---

[62] Although Foucault does not discuss the Qumran community, he does comment on Philo's account of the Therapeutae ("Technologies of the Self," 21, 32), noting the attention given to the physical discipline of the proper posture to assume in listening to the discourse on scripture. It is tempting to connect the increased focus on the cultivation of the individual at Qumran with the broader Hellenistic

Communities of discourse create subjects in part by providing what Richard Harvey Brown calls "vocabularies of motive" and "a language of possible selves."[63] The hypocrite who is the focus of attention in the concluding covenant curses is, one might say, a kind of "impossible self" for the ethos of the community, one that must be excluded by a curse. A related type of "impossible self" is explored in 1QS 2:25–3:12, as the text considers one who "refuses to enter [the covenant of Go]d" (2:25–26; cf. 5QRule). As Knibb points out, the question is not one of a "formal refusal" but rather a matter of the "attitude" with which a person enters the covenant.[64] Like the hypocrite, the recalcitrant is a type of autonomous self, characterized by "stubbornness of heart." The recalcitrant seems either unable to perceive crucial distinctions or willfully to invert them ("he gazes on darkness as the ways of light," 3:3). His failure is located in his abhorrence of discipline ("his soul has rejected the disciplines of knowledge," 2:26–3:1; cf. the expulsion ceremony in 4QD[a] 11, which uses similar language). Criticism of a stubborn nature that refuses to submit to discipline and correction is a staple of Israelite moral discourse. Although most explicitly present in the wisdom literature (e.g., Prov 12:1; 13:1; 15:1), it occurs also in other biblical texts, most notably in deuteronomistic rhetoric (e.g., Deut 9:6; 10:16; 31:27; Jer 7:24–26; 11:7–8; Neh 9:16–17; Ps 81:12–13). What is novel in the way the Serek ha-Yahad talks about the recalcitrant is how the consequences of the autonomous self are articulated, that is, in the cultic language of atonement and purification (1QS 3:3–12, passim).

Although Jonathan Klawans has rightly argued that the language of atonement and purification in this passage is to be taken at face value, I think he is wrong to say that the language is therefore not metaphorical.[65] The work of this passage *is* the work of metaphor,

concern for the self. There are, however, significant differences in the languages of the self in Second Temple Palestinian Judaism and in Greco-Roman culture. The question should not be posed in terms of "influence" but rather a search for reasons why the self became an increasingly important symbolic space in so many different cultures of the Hellenistic era. See the analysis of Burkes (*Death in Qohelet and Egyptian Biographies*, 235–59) concerning the formation of conceptions of individual identity and death in Judea and Egypt in the Hellenistic period.

[63] R. Brown, 55–56.

[64] Knibb, 91. Similarly, Lichtenberger (*Studien zum Menschenbild*, 118) describes the situation as one in which the possibility exists that someone will become a member of the community but not truly enter into the covenant of God.

[65] Klawans, *Impurity and Sin*, 85.

if metaphor is understood in the way that cognitive science has framed it, that is, "understanding and experiencing one kind of thing in terms of another."[66] This passage superimposes various elements of the language of purity/impurity, drawn from a number of texts and contexts,[67] onto a novel situation, the implications of a recalcitrant and stubborn disposition for a sectarian community in which the self is an important symbolic locus. The work of metaphor is to organize perception of the lesser known by means of the categories of the better known. Facilitating this conceptual transformation is the submerged metaphor of the community as the sanctuary, an equation that is elsewhere more explicit. Just as it is unthinkable to introduce pollutants into the sanctuary, so that which pollutes cannot be brought into the Qumran community. And, as Klawans has shown, sin at Qumran is understood as defilement.[68] The radical problem posed by the recalcitrant is not just that he is seen as like something that pollutes but that he is like something that cannot be cleansed of its pollution. Being incapable of repentance (3:1), he cannot be purified (3:4–5).[69]

What is the community to do? Inverting the language used earlier in the introduction concerning the entry into the community of those "who willingly offer themselves" (הנדבים, 1:11), here the text says of the one who is recalcitrant that "his knowledge and his ability and his (mental) capacity *shall not be brought* into the council of the community" (3:2). As Wernberg-Møller has noted, the text of 3:5–6, "Unclean! Unclean shall he be all the days that he rejects the precepts of God" (טמא טמא יהיה כול יומי מואסו במשפטי אל) combines elements of both Lev 26:43 (concerning rejection and abhorrence of the statutes of God) and Lev 13:45–46 (exclusion of the unclean leper from the camp).[70] The text shrewdly manages to transform the

---

[66] Lakoff and Johnson, *Metaphors We Live By*, 5.

[67] Including at least Leviticus 13, 16, 26; Numbers 19; and perhaps others.

[68] Klawans, 67–91.

[69] Drawing on the work of anthropologist Mary Douglas, Conway (113) argues that purity language is particularly prominent in this discussion of initiation since initiation ambiguates the boundaries of the community. Outsiders are impure; insiders are pure. But is the initiate outside or inside the community? Pure or impure? Although a successful transfer and transformation of the initiate is the aim of the ritual, the process is fraught with the danger that impurity may be unintentionally brought into the community.

[70] Wernberg-Møller, *Manual of Discipline*, 60–61.

one who would reject the disciplines of the community into the one rejected and excluded.

While it may be the case that the presence of impurity within the community would prevent it from carrying out its functions of atonement for itself and for Israel, that is not the rhetorical force of the passage. The consequences of the recalcitrant attitude are described not in terms of the community but of the individual. Rhetorically, the burden of this passage and the following concluding section is to discourage the reader from identification with the attitudes of the recalcitrant and to move him toward identification with the proper disposition of the sectarian.

In the concluding section of the introductory part of the Serek ha-Yahad the type of self that the Serek ha-Yahad seeks to construct is characterized by receptivity to truth ("through a spirit of true counsel," 3:6) and by submissiveness ("and through a spirit of uprightness and humility," "the submission of his soul to the statutes of God," 3:8). The motivating consequences are cast in the same language of atonement, purification, and sanctification in which the fate of the recalcitrant was given.[71] Echoes of the first lines of the Serek ha-Yahad describing the purposes of the community and the disposition of those who enter it crown the conclusion of the account of the proper self (בכול, 1:8; ולהתהלך לפניו תמים, 3:9// להלכת תמים; 1:2–3 כאשר צוה, 3:10// כאשר צוה; 1:13 כתם דרכיו, 3:10// דרכי אל; 3:10// ולוא לסור ימין ושמאול, 1:9 למועדי תעודותם, 3:10// למועדי תעודתיו; ואין לצעוד על אחד מכול דבריו . . . ולוא לסור, 1:15 ללכת ימין ושמאול; 3:10–11// ולוא לצעוד בכול אחד מכול דברי אל, 1:13–14). The inclusio not only signals the conclusion of the entire introductory part of the Serek ha-Yahad but also links the themes of proper character and entry into the community. Rhetorically, 2:25–3:12 offers the reader two contrasting models of the self. One, the recalcitrant, he must reject, for to embrace it means to be excluded from the community, as the unclean leper is excluded from the camp. Identification with the other, the submissive self, is connected with the benefits of the community, as the text concludes: "Then he will be accepted through soothing atonement before God, and it will be for him a covenant of the eternal community" (3:11–12; trans. Knibb).

---

[71] Conway (115) has observed that 2:26b–3:6a is shaped by a chiastic structure that encourages an imaginary journey down the path of dissension and back again.

Taken as a whole 1:1–3:12 forms a rhetorical equivalent to the probationary period and entry into the community of the novice member. It lays before the reader the purposes of the community, teaching a new language through which to understand what God has commanded. The fateful quality of entry into the covenant and exclusion from it is dramatically enacted. Finally, the reader is given a vocabulary of motives for the formation of the character necessary and proper to the covenant community.

1QS 3:13–4:26. The Two Spirits Treatise

Although the Two Spirits Treatise is generally acknowledged to be an independent composition incorporated into the Serek ha-Yahad, its function in the text is crucial. A quotation from Michel Foucault helps to illustrate why:

> Max Weber posed the question: If one wants to behave rationally and regulate one's actions according to true principles, what part of one's self should one renounce? What is the ascetic price of reason? To what kinds of asceticism should one submit? I posed the opposite question: How have certain kinds of interdictions required the price of certain kinds of knowledge about oneself? What must one know about oneself in order to be willing to renounce anything?[72]

Foucault's reversal of Weber's question is provocative. His point is not to claim a simple causal relationship between disciplinary power and the creation of knowledge about the self so much as to insist that power and knowledge are mutually produced. As the preceding section of the Serek ha-Yahad made clear, the community is preeminently the place of discipline (יסר, 3:1, 6). The correlative relationship between the disciplines of the community and the knowledge of the self explains the inclusion of the Two Spirits Treatise in the Serek ha-Yahad. This is what one needs to know about oneself in order to be willing to submit to the disciplinary power of the community. These are the qualities that the disciplinary power of the Yahad seeks to enhance and to minimize, respectively.

The Two Spirits Treatise introduces itself explicitly as a teaching about anthropology as it pertains to character, "the genealogy of all human beings according to the types of their spirits" (תולדות כול בני איש לכול מיני רוחותם, 3:13–14). In its account it covers much

---

[72] Foucault, "Technologies of the Self," 17.

more. All of the text's speculation, however, concerning predetermined divine plans, angelology, and eschatological rewards and punishments are not presented for their own sake but are in the service of its theorizing about the self. More specifically, as Hermann Lichtenberger has argued, the problematic that structures the discourse is that of why the righteous sin,[73] the very issue that the disciplines of the community attempt to remedy, insofar as that is possible in the pre-eschatological time.

An outline of the passage will serve to orient the following discussion.[74] After the introductory statement, the text establishes the metaphysical context of human nature in the eternal and predetermined plan of God (3:15–17). The description of the nature and destiny of human beings begins with an account of the angelic spirits of truth and perversity and their effect on human behavior (3:17–4:1). The discussion then traces the manifestation of these spirits in a detailed phenomenology of character, along with the "visitation," i.e., the rewards and punishments appropriate to each type of spirit/character (4:2–14). The following passage explains the condition of individuals prior to the eschatological visitation, caught in the struggle between the two spirits (4:15–18), and describes the eschatological resolution of the ancient struggle with the removal of "the spirit of perversity from within the flesh" of persons (4:18–23). The conclusion summarizes themes from the discourse, correlating the presence of the spirits that characterize behaviors and explaining the purpose of the spirits and their struggle: so that persons "may know good [and evil]" and so that God may determine the fates of all in an eschatological judgment (4:23–26).

Research on the character profiles of the two spirits has often turned to the virtue and vice lists found in didactic literature.[75] That is a logical place to look, since a concern for delineating character types and nurturing proper behavior is a feature of much sapiential and paraenetic literature. In a general sense, that tradition undoubt-

---

[73] Lichtenberger, 129, 136–41.

[74] Whether the Two Spirits Treatise was composed as a literary unity (so Puech, *La croyance*, 430–32) or reached its present form through a complex redactional process (so Osten-Saken, *Gott und Belial*, 17–18; Duhaime, "L'instruction sur les deux esprits," 566–94) is debated. In either case I am concerned with the form in which it appears in 1QS.

[75] See Wibbing, *Die Tugend- und Lasterkatalogue*, 43–61.

edly stands behind this text. At the level of specifics, however, the
parallels are not impressive, especially for the characteristics of the
spirit of truth. As von der Osten-Saken has shown, these qualities
do not correspond to traditional catalogues of "virtues" but can be
coordinated with the effects of the spirit of holiness that, according
to the Hodayot, members receive upon entering the community.[76]
The individual qualities, however, are not necessarily untraditional,
and many of the phrases echo scripture and the moral discourses of
other Second Temple literature. Rather, the selection, combination,
and accentuation of them delineates the distinctive sectarian character, not to mention the claim that these are not qualities of persons per se but rather qualities of spirit that form the character of
a person.

The diagnostic qualities, for which the sect looks in its examination of new members and which it seeks to enhance through its disciplinary power, are as follows: "a spirit of humility and patience,
and abundant compassion, and eternal goodness, and insight and
understanding and powerful wisdom, which trusts in all the deeds
of God and relies on the abundance of his kindness, and a spirit of
knowledge in every plan of action, and zealousness for the precepts
of righteousness and a holy purpose with a firm intent, and abundant kindness toward all the children of truth, and glorious purity,
detesting all impure idols, circumspect behavior with discernment of
all things, and concealing the truth of the mysteries of knowledge"
(4:3–6). The first four qualities (humility, patience, compassion, goodness) were widely shared character values in Second Temple Judaism.
They are nuanced, however, by their contextualization in the Serek
ha-Yahad. What "humility" means has to be understood by reference to the immediately preceding section of the document in which
the recalcitrant member is contrasted with the one who has "an
upright and humble spirit" with respect to the disciplines of the community (2:25–3:12). Similarly, "humility" and "compassion" are qualities with which reproof is to be administered, according to 5:25.
These are not abstractions but dispositions that are part of the daily
praxis of the sect.

Not surprisingly, terms for knowledge have a prominent place in
the catalogue of spiritual qualities: "insight and understanding and

---

[76] Osten-Saken, *Gott und Belial*, 137.

powerful wisdom . . . and a spirit of knowledge," with the latter two terms bearing qualifying phrases about the mode and content of knowledge. Knowledge, too, was a value widely shared in Second Temple Judaism, but the nuancing that distinguishes the sectarian from others formed through identification with knowledge is evident in the way the terms for knowledge are qualified. "Powerful wisdom" is specified as wisdom "that trusts in the deeds of God," an allusion to the predestinarian theology of the sect, and as wisdom "that relies on the abundance of his kindness" (ונשענת ברוב חסדו), which both echoes the reference to the "covenant of kindness" (ברית חסד; 1:8) that forms the basis of the community, and more generally to the sense of self as wholly dependent on God, a disposition explicitly cultivated in the prayers of the Hodayot. Such expressions both place the sectarian within the traditional correlation of knowledge and piety that one meets, for instance, in Ben Sira and in the figure of Daniel, but also differentiates him from them.

The next set of terms allude to what one might call "scalar" qualities of the sectarian self, terms such as "zealousness" (קנאה), "holy purpose" (מחשבת קודש), and "firm intent" (יצר סמוך). They designate the focused, intense quality of the true believer. Such intensity of attitude and affect was directed both outward and inward, as the contrasting dispositions toward the "children of truth" and the "impure idols" indicate.[77] Combined with intensity of character is the quality of control. Whatever its original meaning in Mic 6:8, the association of "circumspect behavior" (הצנע לכת) with "careful discernment" (בערמת כול) in 1QS 4:5–6 indicates that its primary nuance is that of carefully measured behavior rather than modesty. The phrase also situates itself within traditional language of the ethics of instruction, as is evident when one compares Ben Sira's use of the word "circumspect" (הצנע) in a statement about measuring out knowledge in teaching: "I will pour out my spirit by measure, and carefully will I impart my knowledge" (אביעה במשקל רוחי ובהצנע אחוה דעי, Sir 16:23). Here again, the background of the sectarian character values in the repertoire of the larger culture can be detected. All who teach must measure out knowledge appropriately. As the concluding line

---

[77] Zeal, variously understood, was an important value in Second Temple Judaism. See, for example, Smiles, "The Concept of 'Zeal' in Second-Temple Judaism and Paul's Critique of It in Romans 10:2."

of the passage in the Serek ha-Yahad makes clear, however, the received value has been inflected with the distinctive accents of the community. Careful measure and circumspection are linked with "concealing the truth of the mysteries of knowledge." By nature, or at least by second nature, the sectarian's disposition is to be guarded, especially in his dealings with those outside the sect. Thus the character type that emerges from this description displays a receptiveness to the social demands of the sectarian milieu and to its worldview combined with a quality of guarded discretion toward those outside the sect.

The quality of the moral imagination that undergirds this phenomenology of the self is a delight in discipline and order, grounded in insight into metaphysical realities. One could say the same thing, of course, about the wisdom tradition in general. The indebtedness of the Two Spirits Treatise to the traditional moral language of wisdom is even more clearly visible in the characteristics of the person formed by the "spirit of perversity" (4:9–11). Although there are a number of echoes of various biblical texts, this repertoire of behaviors and attitudes is drawn in large measure from wisdom traditions (note in particular the use of the catalogue of body parts, which metonymically indicate defects of character; cf. Prov 6:12–15, 16–19). These include not only evil (wickedness and falsehood, abominable deeds in a lustful spirit, impure ways in the service of uncleanness, a blaspheming tongue), but also aspects of unregulated excess (greed, slackness in the service of righteousness, zeal for insolence, shortness of temper, abundant folly), resistance to discipline (pride and a haughty heart, blind eyes, a deaf ear, a stiff neck, and a hard heart), and the capacity for deception that evades discipline (lying and deceit).[78]

There is very little here that seems to bear the reaccentuation of Qumran's specific figured world. One might perhaps point to the use of terminology of impurity (דרכי נוה בעבודת טמאה). A slight nuancing of sectarian perspective may also be evident in the catalogue of body parts. Proverbs tends to include "hands" and "feet" as symbols of active mischief, whereas the Qumran list has a preponderance of symbols

---

[78] As will be discussed later, a strong overlap exists between these characteristics and the behaviors listed in the schedule of punishments in col. 7, as there is an overlap with the characteristics of the hypocrite and the recalcitrant (2:11–18; 2:25–3:6) who pose such a problem for the composition of the community.

for receptivity or rather lack of it (eyes, ear, neck, heart). Yet there is no mistaking Qumran's discourse of character for that of traditional wisdom. In part the distinctiveness is a product of the form of speech, shaped in a highly schematized, formally parallel structure. Although wisdom's discourse of character makes use of antitheses, this rhetorical and conceptual feature has been "perfected," as Kenneth Burke would put it, in the Two Spirits Treatise.

But more occurs here than a simple perfecting of wisdom's discourse. In common with certain other Second Temple literature (e.g., Wisdom of Solomon, 4QInstruction),[79] wisdom discourse is here combined with an eschatological orientation. One reflex of this merging is evident in the rewards and punishments that correspond to each type of character, where traditional rewards such as peace, long life, fruitfulness, and joy are complemented by eschatological honor ("a crown of glory" and "a garment of splendor") in eternal light for those who walk in the spirit of truth. Similarly, for those who walk in the spirit of perversity there is not only terror and shame, but angelically administered punishments, and eternal destruction in "abysses of darkness" (4:6–8, 11–14). The eschatological context is underscored by the characterization of the rewards and punishments as a "visitation" (פקודה).

Although traditional wisdom and the Two Spirits Treatise share a conviction that character is related to metaphysical realities, the content of those metaphysical beliefs in the Two Spirits Treatise drastically transforms the meaning and function of the character language it borrows from wisdom. For the wisdom tradition, insight into the wisdom that is integral to creation is fundamental to the formation of character and the ability to make appropriate choices (e.g., Prov 3:19–26; 8:22–36). Although wisdom never minimizes the difficulty of disciplining unruly impulses, it is fundamentally a volitional ethic. The Serek ha-Yahad's commitment to a penultimately dualistic metaphysics that is explicitly predestinarian would seem to make its use of a sapiential character ethic difficult, to say the least. How can one combine the language of a volitional ethic with a predestinarian metaphysics? The Two Spirits Treatise not only manages to avoid simple incoherence but forges a powerful vision of the

---

[79] Burkes, "Wisdom and Apocalypticism in the Wisdom of Solomon," 27–30; Harrington, *Wisdom Texts from Qumran*, 41.

self out of the tension between these two discourses. It manages to theorize something that had been left without explanation in wisdom: why there is so much resistance to the counsels of wisdom even among those who are instructed, why some people seem to be born fools, and yet how it is possible for others to do what is right. What mediates the "tension" between the "volitional" and "predestinarian" languages in the Two Spirits Treatise is the figure of "struggle" (קנאת ריב, 4:17–18; ריבו, 4:23) and the notion of an imbalanced division between the two spirits within each individual, even though the spirits are established "in equal measure" in the world (4:15–18). As a feature of anthropology, the spirits of truth and perversity are themselves the volitional aspects of a person: the disposition and desire to do what is right or what is wrong. Thus the languages of wisdom's character ethic and of a dualistic predestinarian metaphysics are rationally coordinated with one another. The predestinarian metaphysics is the encompassing discourse, however, as the conclusion of the passage shows. The text does not exhort the sectarian to overcome his bad characteristics, as would be possible if the volitional dimension were the predominant one.[80] Instead, the text presents—as information rather than explicit motivation—the rewards and punishments that attend each spirit (4:6–8, 11–14, 26) and discloses how the person with a predominance of the spirit of truth will be purified by the eschatological action of God (4:18–22).

The construction of the self in this discourse is radically different from most of the received moral languages in First and Second Temple Judaism, which assume the self as a more or less unified moral agent. Here, however, the self is the product of the balance of spirits, an unstable construct subject to change in either direction. This teaching provides a powerful instrument of persuasion to the sectarian life. Those within the Qumran community have a preponderance of the spirit of truth and are ultimately assured that they will be purified of perversity in the eschatological cleansing. Such an

---

[80] Hortatory material occurs elsewhere in Qumran speech, even in the Serek ha-Yahad itself. In part this is because the sect never spoke a fully self-consistent language. Nevertheless by locating the capacity for the good in identifying with the spirit of truth in oneself, the Two Spirits Treatise makes a theoretical place for such language. For an analogous case see Paden ("Theaters of Humility and Suspicion," 66–67), who discusses the relationship between the trope of struggle and the affirmation that everything comes from the grace of God in the moral vocabulary of Cassian.

inheritance of the spirit of truth, however, only intensifies the distress the individual experiences in knowing that for the present he cannot escape the seductions of perversity. Although the Two Spirits Treatise does not explain the way in which the struggle between truth and perversity takes place in the individual, the larger context of the Serek ha-Yahad indicates that it is the disciplines of the community that enable the sectarian "to walk perfectly before [God] in accordance with all the things that have been revealed" (1:8–9). In part this link is made associatively. Just as the eschatological resolution of the divided self is presented in terms of purification (יברר זקק...ולטהרו...וי...כמי נדה, 4:20–22), so is the language of purity used in connection with the constitution of the properly ordered community (2:25–3:9). A further connection between the eschatological rewards and punishments described in the Two Spirits Treatise and the rewards and punishments already embedded in the hierarchy of spirit enacted in the community is indicated through the use of the same root, פקד, both for the eschatological visitation (4:6, 11) and for the yearly examination (5:24). As Foucault rightly understood, submission to the disciplines of the community requires the price of a certain kind of knowledge of the self. Once one embraces that knowledge, however, then the disciplines become the means for achieving significant rewards. In the sections of the Serek ha-Yahad that follow these disciplines are discussed in detail.

5:1–9:11. Community Practices and Procedures

Following the Two Spirits Treatise are nearly four and a half columns that contain what could be called community procedure. 1QS 5:1–6:23 is itself a rule of the community, composed of introduction (5:1–7a), an account of the binding oath taken upon admission and the consequences that follow from it (5:7a–20a), and various regulations for the conduct of community life (5:20b–6:8a). Rules for the session of the many (6:8b–13a) and for the admission of new members (6:13b–23) follow. Columns 6:24–7:25 contain a penal code. Although there is disagreement as to how it is to be characterized, 8:1–9:11 concerns the establishment of a new community. Most scholars consider the various sections of 5:1–9:11 to have been excerpted from other documents of the sect or to be portions of previous editions of the Serek, now incorporated into a new recension. But what purpose do they serve here? They are certainly not complete and definitive accounts of the community's procedures. Repetition (cf. 5:20 and 6:13–23), differences in presentation (cf. 6:24–7:25 and 8:16–9:2), substantive corrections (7:8), and what appear to be contradictions (cf. 8:16–19 and 8:20–24) are often interpreted as evidence that the documentary sources come from different periods of the sect's history. Also, it appears that various sections of the Serek ha-Yahad actually refer to different forms of Yahad communities. Some parts seem to pertain to Yahad communities in towns and villages (e.g., 6:1–8) and others to the Qumran establishment proper (e.g., 8:1–9:11).[81] Given such a state of affairs, what might be the rationale for including such excerpts in 1QS? If it is correct to understand the Serek ha-Yahad as a resource for the formation of the Maskil and his formation of the members through his teaching, then the presence of such disparate materials makes sense. They do not serve as reference materials to be consulted for information—even in the case of contradiction readers would know what was current practice and what was not— but rather as rhetorical expressions of important aspects of the community's ethos. These excerpts function in a way that Nelson Goodman once described as "serving as a sample of," that is, as something that *exemplifies* that to which it refers, much as a swatch of cloth serves as a sample of color, texture, and weave, but not of the shape of the suit into which it will be made.[82] Not only does the content of such excerpts influence the one who immerses himself in them, but also the formal and aesthetic features that are part of the sample.[83] These various sections are textual samples of the community's life, values, and ethos. When Moshe Weinfeld studied the procedural aspects of the Qumran community, he noted that many of its practices were similar to those of voluntary organizations known from the Hellenistic world. Various groups were also known to have drawn up lists of their rules. But Weinfeld found no parallel for the type of literature represented by the Serek ha-Yahad, with its combination of procedural rule and hortatory prose.[84] The peculiar nature of the Serek ha-Yahad points to the way in which "procedure" was

---

[81] Knibb, 115; Metso, "In Search of the *Sitz im Leben* of the *Community Rule*," 311; Collins, "Forms of Community," 104–7.

[82] Goodman, *Ways of Worldmaking*, 31–32.

[83] Goodman (105) insists that not only representational works but even abstract works of art can effect important emotional and cognitive changes.

[84] Weinfeld, *Organizational Pattern*, 47.

regarded in the community. It was not mere operational detail that one would consult as needed but rather something at the heart of the sect's moral imagination. For the sect truth is inseparable from right ordering. Consequently, the way in which things are done has a moral resonance that would be lacking in a society constituted along different lines.

5:1–20a. Motivational Introduction and the Binding Oath

The first of the sections in this part of the Serek ha-Yahad resembles the beginning of the 1QS, and in 4QS[d] it actually serves as the beginning of the document. It contains a heading ("this is the order for the men of the community," הסרך לאנשי היחד),[85] a term of identity for the members ("those who willingly offer themselves," מתנדבים; cf. 1:7), and a statement of purpose couched in infinitives. Paralleling the description of the annual covenant ceremony in 1:16–2:25, this portion of the text also refers to a gateway ritual, the taking of the binding oath (5:7–11). The whole passage, however, is structured by an organizing image different from that of the statement of purpose and ritual found in cols. 1–2. Here the organizing trope is one of reorientation, articulated both as turning from one thing and holding fast to another, and as separating from and uniting with ("turning from all evil and holding fast to all that he has commanded as his will, separating from the congregation of the men of perversity in order to unite together in torah and in possessions," לשוב מכול רע ולהחזיק בכול אשר צוה לרצונו להבדל מעדת אנשי העול להיות ליחד בתורה ובהון, 5:1–2; "he shall undertake by a binding oath to return to the torah of Moses . . . and he shall undertake by the covenant to separate from all the men of perversity," ויקם על נפשו בשבועת אסר לשוב אל תורת מושה . . . ואשר יקים בברית על נפשו להבדל מכול אנשי העול, 5:8, 10). Placing this presentation of the community and its purpose immediately after the Two Spirits teaching gives its symbolic shape added prominence. The community and its institutional structures form the present counterpart to the eschatological separation of truth and perversity that the Two Spirits teaching describes. The community will be the place in which that separation can proleptically be experienced.

---

[85] 4QS[d] reads מדרש למשכיל על אנשי התורה, "Interpretation for the Instructor concerning the men of the torah."

The term "separation" (הבדל), which occurs three times in this section (5:1, 10, 20) has considerable symbolic significance. Most immediately, it echoes the reformation of the Second Temple community as represented in Ezra-Nehemiah (see esp. Neh 9:2; 10:29). In a less obvious way the passage also seems to exploit the image of the separation of clean and unclean (cf. Lev 10:10; 11:47; 20:25), as Israel was set apart from the Gentiles (cf. Lev 20:24, 26), and priests and Levites set apart from the rest of Israel as holy (Num 8:14; 16:9). This overtone may influence the end of the passage, where the terms "separate," "man of holiness," "impure," and "unclean" cluster together. There is finally an echo of the separation of innocent persons from a congregation about to face divine judgment in the narrative of the rebellion of Korah, Dathan, and Abiram in Num 16:21 (cf. 5:10–13). One need not prove which of these allusions was present to the mind of the author of this passage. All are available to the reader. Indeed, by employing a style that is rich with evocations of scriptural language, the Qumran texts teach their readers an active skill of perceiving intertextual connections.

The internal structure of the passage also suggests how central the figure of separation is. Following the general introduction (lines 1–7), two references to the act of "entering the covenant" of the community occur (lines 7–10 and 20). The binding oath referred to in line 8 has both a positive and a negative component. Positively, the commitment is to "return to the torah of Moses" (line 8); negatively, the commitment is "to separate from all the men of deceit" (line 10). From line 10 until the resumptive repetition of the reference to entering the covenant in line 20 the text piles up four separate warrants for the act of separating from the men of deceit. That these various statements belong to different redactional layers[86] only underscores the fact that the topic exercised a fascination on those who sought to add to the ways in which separation might be figured and motivated.[87]

---

[86] Knibb, 110–11; Metso, *Textual Development*, 114, n. 23. The corresponding sections in 4QS[b, d] are considerably shorter. See Alexander and Vermes, 94–95.

[87] In the first warrant (lines 11b–13a) the text constructs the men of deceit as the negative mirror image of the Yahad. Because they do not do those things that the community is formed to do (seek knowledge of hidden things and obey the revealed things) they are subject to destruction. The second warrant (lines 13b–15a) has to do with danger to things interior to the community (waters, pure things, work and possessions) and invokes purity and pollution language. Alluding to Lev

The counterpart of such separation, of course, is the act of uniting with the community in the covenant of God. In the moral imagination of the sect the knowledge and discipline that enables one to
fulfill the commandments of God cannot be a purely private achievement but is resolutely social. Implicitly, the Serek ha-Yahad excludes
the possibility of a good person in a bad society. The choice that a
person makes is decisive. Even so, there remains a distrust of the
individual. Body imagery of heart, eyes, neck, and the erring will
that they depict serve to represent the individual as naturally a creature of stubbornness and waywardness (5:4–5). Only through the disciplines of the community, represented as circumcizing the stubborn
will, can the individual practice well-ordered behaviors and affects
(5:3–4). It is to the authority of the community that the sectarian is
"answerable" (משיבים; 5:2), a word that puns on the frequent references to "turning" (לשוב) from evil (5:1, 13) and turning back to the
torah of Moses (5:8). The goal is not the improvement of the individual for his own sake, however. The text motivates the submission
that it demands by means of its representation of the community as
a temple. Together such rightly ordered persons become "a sanctuary in Aaron" and "a house of truth in Israel," capable of effecting
atonement and judgment (5:5–7).

1QS 5:20–23; 6:13–23. Examination for Admission and Advancement
As Foucault observed, disciplinary institutions characteristically organize space in two ways: by separation and by the construction of an
internal, analytical space within which persons will be located. The
hortatory introduction in 5:1–20a has symbolically established and
rhetorically justified the separated space necessary for the commu-

---

22:16, which deals with the profaning consequences of allowing improper persons
to eat the priests' portions, sectarian separation is framed as the protection of the
holy from impure. The third warrant (lines 15b-16a) uses judicial imagery. Basing
itself on a scriptural admonition that Israel's judges should "keep distant from any
false thing" (Ex 23:7), this warrant insists on separation in discussing legal matters
of torah and judgment (לוא ישוב . . . על פיהם לכול תורה ומשפט). The fourth warrant (lines 16b–20) also uses a scriptural citation, this time from Isaiah 2:22 ("Have
no more to do with a man in whose nostrils is breath, for what is he worth," line
17; trans. Knibb). Although the passage puns on the word השב ("be worth"/"be
accounted [a member of the covenant]") it develops the idea of the insubstantial-
ity of breath by associating it with the futility (הבל) of the existence of those outside the covenant and with their impending destruction, thus echoing the word of
judgment of the first warrant.

nity. In what follows, this internal space and its corresponding technologies of the self are presented, most particularly in the system of
surveillance and examination that underwrites the hierarchical ordering of the community.

A person first becomes the object of disciplinary power upon seeking to join the community, a process described briefly in 5:20–23
and in more detail in 6:13–23. At the heart of the process is a verbal examination, focused on the person's spirit "with respect to his
insight and his deeds in regard to the law" (5:21; cf. 6:17–18). The
longer account describes a multi-year process of annual examinations, first by the "officer in charge at the head of the Many" (6:13–14)
to determine the candidate's suitability for the discipline (מוסר) of
the community (6:13–15), then by the Many (6:15–16) for provi-
sional admission. Annually, at the end of each probationary year the
candidate is again examined by the Many and gradually incorporated into the purity and the sharing of wealth and counsel within
the community (6:16–23). Unfortunately, we know very little about
the actual proceedings. That it was a formal and ceremonious occasion seems evident, but there is no indication of how questions were
put or how the candidate was required to give an account of himself to the authorities who judged his suitability and progress. The
language used suggests that the examination concerned halakah and
also an investigation of the type of behaviors and dispositions that
the Two Spirits Treatise identifies as characteristic of the spirits of
truth and perversity.

As Foucault argues, all such examinations work to *produce* an individual. Just this person and just these particular qualities become the
focus of attention. Knowledge about the person, previously unknown,
is generated through the examination and becomes available, not
only to the authorities who have required it, but also to the person
who speaks of himself. The object of the inquiry at Qumran is a
deeply intimate one, indicative of the individual's essential self, his
"spirit." Yet the individual, although he is required to disclose information, cannot himself interpret and evaluate the significance of what
he discloses. That power belongs to the examining community.

The individuating effect of the examination is also evident in the
requirement that the examination be used to distinguish "between
one man and another" (5:21), the results being documented in a
register ("They shall write them down in order, one before another,"
5:23; cf. 6:22). What results is rank. Such ranking, however, is not

a static order, or something that affects only new members. Each
year all members of the community are reviewed with respect to
their spirits and their deeds and receive advancement or demotion
according to the results of the examination (5:23–24). If the hierarchy were merely in the form of a register, it would not have such
effects of power. But the normalizing judgment embodied in the
hierarchy is continuously and ubiquitously enacted. Rank order governs daily practices of submission in matters of work and money
(6:2; cf. 5:23). In the council assembly, seating (6:4) and the order
of speaking (6:8–13) proceed by rank. And in the ceremony of the
annual covenant renewal, both procession and seating are hierarchical, with the solemn proviso that "no one shall move down from
his position or move up from his allotted space" (2:23).

The peculiarity of the hierarchical seating arrangement becomes
evident if one asks what it represents or symbolizes. Foucault contrasted symbolic ways of arranging bodies in space (e.g., royal displays arranged to represent the king's sovereignty) with disciplinary
arrangements which represent nothing except the normalizing judgment of the discipline.[88] In the case of the annual covenant ceremony the precedence of the priests and Levites might be taken as an
instance of a symbolic arrangement, representing the fixed status of
the priestly orders. But the rank order of the community represents
simply the results of the yearly examination.

Such arrangements are what Foucault calls "the first of the great
operations of discipline . . . *tableaux vivants*', which transform the confused, useless or dangerous multitudes into ordered multiplicities."[89]
They are not merely the results of discipline, that is, rewards and
punishments for performance; they are also active instruments for
discipline. One knows simply by looking, what is better, what is
worse. Since rank governs the order of speaking, the performances
of the higher ranking members serve as models and norms for the
performances of the lower ranking persons, who are nevertheless eli-
gible (perhaps even required) to speak (6:4, 9–10).

1QS 5:24–6:1. The Practice of Reproof
Surveillance and discipline in the community were not only exercised in relation to hierarchy and in the annual examination but

---

[88] Foucault, *Discipline and Punish*, 187–88.
[89] Foucault, *Discipline and Punish*, 148.

were also dispersed into a continuous and ubiquitous presence through the system of mutual reproof. Reproof was a widely shared value in the moral culture of ancient Judaism. Although corrective in its intent, it was not necessarily punitive. In the Second Temple period, reflection on the topic often took the form of interpretation of the divine commandment in Lev 19:17 ("You shall not hate your brother in your heart; you shall indeed reprove your neighbor, and so you will not bear guilt yourself").[90] In the Serek ha-Yahad that verse is also the starting point, but the moral problem of self and community addressed by each text is rather different. In Leviticus the issue is the corrosive effect of a grievance nurtured in private. Leviticus recommends open and direct confrontation so that the aggrieved person does not himself become guilty of harboring a grudge (see Lev 19:18). The moral focus is on the aggrieved party. Unlike Leviticus, the Serek ha-Yahad does not preface the discussion by an initial reference to hatred in the heart; rather it simply says, "each man shall reprove his neighbor" (5:24–25). This is not advice for an individual dealing with an occasional situation but a directive for community praxis. In this respect the sect's practice of mutual reproof has more in common with the wisdom literature, where the focus is on the educative value of reproof (e.g., Prov 3:12; 9:8; 15:12; 28:33). Following as it does the discussion of the yearly assessment of each member's status in the community according to his insight and deeds (5:23–24), the directive for reproof seems to function as a means for refining those qualities. There is a characteristic difference, however, between the context of reproof as envisioned in the wisdom literature and its practice at Qumran. As the concluding line of section 5:24–6:1 makes clear, reproof is not merely a matter of moral improvement but part of the judicial discipline of the sect: "and furthermore, no one may bring a case against his fellow before the Many except after reproof before witnesses" (6:1).[91] Thus, in the Yahad, reproof was integrated into the system of punishment. A record of such reproofs, which are directed both at disapproved behaviors (anger, boastfulness) and at

---

[90] See Kugel, "On Hidden Hatred and Open Reproach: Early Exegesis of Leviticus 19:17."

[91] See Schiffman, *Sectarian Law*, 92–98, for a thorough discussion of the judicial context of reproof in the Serek ha-Yahad and in the Damascus Document.

violations of halakah (forbidden sexual relations) is to be found in 4Q477 Rebukes Reported by the Overseer.[92]

One should not overlook, however, the deep concern the text has for the reprover, yet in a different manner than one finds in Leviticus. Whereas Leviticus concerns itself with the moral consequences of not speaking what is in the heart, the Serek ha-Yahad concerns itself extensively with the spirit in which reproof is made. Reproof is to be conducted "in tr[uth] and humility and kindly love toward a man. Let him not speak to him in anger or in complaint or in stub[born-ness or in] mean-spirited [jealousy], and let him not hate [. . .] in his heart" (1QS 5:25–26). Of all the reflections on Lev 19:17 dis-cussed by Kugel in his survey of the reception of this passage, only in the Serek ha-Yahad is such attention paid to the disposition of the reprover in speaking. There are reasons, both in the ideology and in the organization of the community, that would have made the practice of reproof both desirable and fraught with danger. The practice of reproof was an important mechanism for the achieve-ment of the community's purposes. At the same time the commu-nity's ethical rigor would have made it easy for reproof to be carried out with a level of intensity detrimental to the unity of the sect. Even more complex would have been the effect of the hierarchical organization of the sect. Reproof and the judicial practices connected with it would have been essential for establishing "insight and deeds of torah," but the practices of reproof could easily have been co-opted by envy, resentment, and desire for advancement. Such is per-haps the background to the requirement that reproof should be carried out "on the same day, so that he not incur guilt because of him" (5:26–6:1). The reason is somewhat clearer in the parallel dis-cussion of reproof in the Damascus Document, which treats the mat-ter of hoarding information for a strategic denouncement as involving the culpability of "bearing a grudge and taking vengeance" (CD 9:26, alluding to Lev 19:18). The contradictory impulses invited by the practice of reproof leave their traces in the concern that the Serek ha-Yahad shows for the proper spirit in which reproof is to be administered.

---

[92] For discussion of this text see Eshel, "4Q477: The Rebukes by the Overseer"; Hempel, "Who Rebukes in 4Q477?"; Reed, "Genre, Setting and Title of 4Q477." Reed (148) plausibly speculates that such written records of reproof may have been used as part of the annual examination and evaluation of members.

1QS 6:1–8a, 8b–23. Communal Organization and Work

As is often noted, 6:1–8a appears to represent a communal context somewhat different from the surrounding material. The reference to discrete, small groups ("in every place where there are ten men of the council of the Community") who are said to live in "their places of sojourning" (מגוריהם, 6:2) does not seem to reflect the reality of the Yahad at Qumran. Perhaps the section derives from an earlier stage of the development of the Yahad,[93] or, as seems more likely, to the organization of the Yahad in cities and towns throughout Judea.[94] The inclusion of such material here only serves to underscore the impression that the Serek ha-Yahad is not so much a book of reference as a book of resources for the formation of the ethos of the community by the instruction of its members. The principles of composition appear to be topical and associational. As Metso has pointed out, the term הרבים occurs toward the end of 5:20b–6:1b, near the end of 6:1c–8a, and at the beginning of 6:8b–13a.[95]

More than word association is involved, however. In the previous section attention was focused on the disciplinary practices that form the individual as a sectarian: examination, rank order, and the practices of mutual reproof. Although an intense discipline of the self is essential to the community, self-culture is absolutely not the goal of its activity. The purpose of such discipline is that of constituting a community that can be "a sanctuary in Aaron and a house of truth in Israel" (5:6). Thus in this section the attention shifts from the formation of the individual to the work of the community as a whole. Although rank order and the obedience it structures are constitutive of the social organization of the community (6:2, 4), the emphasis here is on the fundamental collectivity of the society's form of being and acting. Echoing the term chosen to designate the community, the Yahad, the text enjoins that "*together* they shall eat, *together* they shall pray, and *together* they shall take counsel (ויחד יואכלו ויחד יברכו ויחד יועצו, 6:2–3). The completeness of the community is further figured in two ways, first by the stipulation of a minimum of ten

---

[93] Leaney, 33, 180.

[94] Knibb, 115.

[95] Metso, *Textual Development*, 115. See also pp. 133–135 for her more detailed analysis of the different *Sitzen im Leben* of the two passages and the similarities of vocabulary that apparently encouraged a redactor to combine them by means of a bridge passage in 1QS 6:7b–8a.

men (6:3b, 6b), a religious unit known elsewhere in ancient Judaism, and second by the presence of a priest (6:4a). Thus constituted, the community can fulfill its functions (6:4–6). But there is one more necessity for the completeness of the community, namely, the presence of a "man who studies the torah day and night." Although the syntax initially makes it sound as though this is an individual figure, like the priest (ואל ימש . . . איש דורש, 6:3–4; אל ימש מאתם איש כוהן, בתורה יומם ולילה, 6:6), it soon appears that this task is distributively borne, "each man replaced by his fellow" (על יפות איש לרעהו, 6:7).[96] The section concludes with a further reference to the communal work of the Yahad, twice more emphasizing the adverb "together." "And the Many shall keep watch together for a third of all the nights of the year, reading scripture, and searching out judgment and praying together" (6:7–8).

What does it mean within the ethos of the community to engage in an act "together"? Although this ideal will have been realized differently depending on the activity in question, the unit in 6:8–23 describes in some detail the activity of taking counsel together in "the rule for the session of the Many." Here one may see how collective speech is produced from the speech of individuals in the assembly.

It is unfortunate that we know so little about cultural models of taking counsel in First and Second Temple Judaism. Biblical narrative does provide brief descriptions of royal counsel, as when Absolom seeks the advice first of Ahitophel and then of Hushai (2 Sam 16:15–17:14), or when Jehoshaphat and Ahab seek counsel from the court prophets and Micaiah (1 Kgs 22:5–28). This latter example incorporates a further description of counsel in heaven among the spirits of God (1 Kgs 22:19–22). In all these examples the king initiates and terminates the session. The reputation of the counselor for past advice is important but not decisive in reaching consensus. These narrative examples include instances of polite disagreement (2 Sam 17:5–7), acrimonious disagreement (1 Kgs 22:24–25), and simple diverse opinion ("one said one thing, and another said another," 1 Kgs 22:20b). The general impression is of a fairly informal protocol subject to the king's direction. The process of counsel produces

---

[96] Assuming with Qimron (in Charlesworth et al., 26, n. 170) that על יפות = חליפות.

two or more distinct options and ideally results in a consensual decision in favor of one of the positions (2 Sam 17:14), though in the
absence of such consensus the king decides for himself (1 Kgs
22:26–27). The one example of judicial counsel, the narrative of
Jeremiah's arraignment before the officials of Judah in Jer 26:7–19,
suggests a similar model. There the sharp conflict between the priests
and the prophets on the one hand and Jeremiah and his support-
ers on the other hand is presented through conflicting speeches interpreting what Jeremiah has said (Jer 26:11, 12–15). Although Jeremiah's
speech in defense of himself is presented by the narrative as largely
persuasive, the common ground that validates a consensual judgment
is provided by the elders who invoke a prior example. Neither of
these models, however, the royal or the judicial, provides much of
a parallel for the counsel described in the Serek ha-Yahad.

Closer models for the Qumran Community's session of the Many
appear to be found in the protocols for meetings of voluntary associations, where rules of speech tact are part of the discipline of communal meetings,[97] and in the session of the Sanhedrin according to
the Mishnah, where fixed seating is prescribed, and where the order
of speaking is regulated according to seniority (m. Sanh. 4.2, 4).[98] Of
course, part of the reason for the apparent similarity might be one
of genre. Biblical narratives do not stress protocol; rules and accounts
of procedure schematize actual practice. Nevertheless, there are good
reasons for thinking that the moral imagination that informed the
Qumran community's sense of how to organize communal speech
was more similar to that of the Iobacchi or the Mishnah's construct
of the Sanhedrin than to the ad hoc royal and judicial councils
described above. Despite their other dissimilarities, these organizations are all voluntary associations of some sort. Although many
things give associations their identity, few are so important as the
assembly. It is there that the group is physically constituted as an
entity, its identity made visible. The discourse of the assembly has
to do either with matters that give the group coherency (admissions,
expulsions, disciplinary matters, collective use of resources, etc.) or
identity (ceremonially acting out its self-identity in ritual, producing
knowledge, performing the judicial functions that the larger community

---

[97] Weinfeld (Organizational Pattern, 26) cites in particular the code of the Iobacchi.
[98] Weinfeld, Organizational Pattern, 27.

has entrusted to it, etc.). Formalizing etiquette and speech tact underscores the role that communal speech plays in constituting the group
as such.

The regulation of communal speech in such organizations, however, would have had a different moral resonance in each depending on the way speech itself was related to the ideology of the group.
The ideology of truth that one finds so prominently in the literature
of the Qumran community gives a distinctive significance to the production of communal speech. Only rightly ordered proceedings could
produce rightly ordered speech. As one would expect, the principle
of hierarchy is fundamental. The very first words of the account are
"each man in his rank" (1QS 6:8). The categories of priests, elders,
and people are specified, followed by a repetition of the injunction,
"each man in his rank." Not only seating but the order of inquiry
follows rank. As important as the principle of hierarchy, however, is
the inclusivity of the process. Counsel is not a specialized function,
but like possessions, something that is put at the disposal of the community (see 6:22–23). The discipline of speech practiced in council
includes both the positive requirement to share knowledge and the
prohibition of sharing it improperly.

√ Provision for including all members in the discourse of the community should not be confused with a truly dialogical speech community. It is difficult to imagine a process that would produce a
more thoroughly monological discourse. Those who spoke first were
already recognized as persons possessing the greatest share of insight
within the community. It would be difficult for a junior member of
the society to contradict the judgment of a senior member. The
space of discourse that would be left for lower ranking members
would be that of speaking within bounds. There are other indications of the care that was taken to maintain a consensual discourse
from beginning to end. One sees these in the careful concern for
speech tact, such as the prohibition on interruption. More difficult to
interpret is the statement that "in a session of the Many no man
shall say anything which is not approved by the Many and, indeed, by
the overseer of the Many (ובמושב הרבים אל ידבר איש כול דבר אשר לוא
להפץ הרבים וכיא האיש המבקר על הרבים, 6:11–12; trans. Knibb).[99]
While the role of the overseer in relation to the assembly is not

---

[99] Emending להפץ to להפץ.

entirely clear, I am more concerned with the question of whether the issue is one of protocol or content. Although the rest of the passage is concerned with the order of speech, here the words כול דבר ("any matter") point rather to the content of what is said. Exactly how disapproval is expressed is not specified, but apparently members may be silenced for broaching topics or opinions perceived to deviate from the accepted bounds of the community's discourse. This is not to claim that nothing new could ever be said within the community, but any novum would had to have been couched in language that anchored it securely within the modes of thought and speech held to be normative within the Yahad.

The assumption that underlies the distinctive practice of taking counsel together described in 1QS 6:8–23 is that the discourse of the community is a collective product. It does not belong to any individual but is produced through the rightly ordered practice of communal speech. Although the Serek ha-Yahad does not speak of it theoretically, it is fairly easy to see what other assumptions underlie the practice. According to 1QS 3:13–4:26, although individuals have greater and lesser shares in light and darkness, truth and perversity, none is wholly free of perversity. In the community, although those who have greater measures of the proper spirit should speak first, their pronouncements cannot be assumed to be free of error. Correspondingly, even those with the least understanding also have a share in the spirit of truth. But in the community as a whole, the spirit of truth predominates over that of perversity, since it is constituted by those whom God has chosen as children of light. Consequently, although any one opinion might be subject to error, the systematic process of the assembly can be relied upon to produce a discourse of truth. In this way the whole is indeed more than the simple sum of its parts. Submission to the authority of this community is not submission to an alien authority but to the truest part of oneself.

This concern for ensuring the proper production of the discourse of the community is evident in the passage that follows, 6:13–23. Because this section includes information about entry into the community, commentators often read "through" the text to the social reality to which it refers, the three-stage probationary membership. Although that is a valid inquiry, it tends to obscure the function of the passage in the structure of the Serek ha-Yahad. As the repetition of key words indicates, the topic is taken up in just this place because the concern is to show how the community of discourse is maintained and protected from contamination. Line 13, which begins to speak of the admission of new members, refers to one who desires "to be added to the council/counsel of the community," and the final sentence of the section concludes "and so his counsel will be (available) to the community, and his judgment" (6:22–23). What the passage describes is the care that is taken in selecting and preparing those who will participate in taking counsel. During this time, too, the potential member has been required to give an oral account of himself four times before the *paqid* (6:14) and the session as a whole (6:15–16, 18, 21), so that his own speech is heard and tested. The correlation between access to the pure food and pure drink of the community at the end of the final year of probationary membership and participation in the counsel and judgment of the session of the Many underscores the concern for the proper regulation of speech as essential to the work of the community.

1QS 6:24–7:25. The Penal Code

Even though 6:24 is clearly marked as a new section in the document by a partially blank line, indentation, and heading, its link with the preceding material about the session of the Many is equally marked by allusion. The preceding section describing the cautious process of adding new members to the community ended with a syntactically awkward sentence ("and so his counsel will be [available] to the community, and his judgment"). The emphasis on the word "judgment" is immediately picked up in the heading of the new section ("these are the judgments by which they shall judge in the inquiry of the community" ואלה המשפטים אשר ישפטו בם במדרש יחד). This detail is important for assessing the rhetorical function of the passage. The following rules and penalties are not included here, *pace* Schiffman, for the purposes of instruction in behavior.[100] Rhetorically, the reader is not instructed about what he may or may not do but rather how he, as a member of the session, shall judge. He is addressed as one who is to exercise disciplinary power rather than as one who is subjected to it, although that fact is assumed.

---

[100] Schiffman, *Sectarian Law*, 157. It is certainly possible that they may have been used for such a purpose in another context, but that is not how they are presented here, where the heading clearly concerns itself with the decision making process in the session.

But in the composition of the Serek ha-Yahad, this section, together
with the preceding one, forms what James Boyd White would term
a rhetorical constitution: how the community organizes the etiquette
of its formal speech in a session of the Many, how it constitutes the
range of participants in such speech, a sample of the sort of things
it will talk about, and the categories that will direct its speech.[101]

The specific topics selected for inclusion here concern gateway
issues (admission, expulsion, readmission), plus a number of behaviors that threaten the order of the community. Perhaps not surprisingly, a large percentage of these involve improper speech or
interference with the speech of the community: lying, speaking obsti-
nately or impatiently, ignoring a command, improper use of the
divine name, insulting a colleague, speaking foolishly, interrupting a
colleague, sleeping, leaving, or spitting during a session of the Many,
foolish laughing, rude gesturing, slandering a colleague or the community, and complaining about a colleague or the community.

In the preceding remarks I have drawn attention to the immediate context of 6:24–7:25. But there are other contexts to be considered. As Moshe Weinfeld has demonstrated, the rules in col. 7
have many parallels in the list of regulations of voluntary societies
in the Hellenistic-Roman world.[102] The Qumran community thus
can be seen to have participated in the general cultural assumptions
of what is necessary and proper for the social form of a voluntary
association and for the forms of speech in which these norms are
given expression. It gives its own distinctive accentuation to this form
of speech however, as Weinfeld also notes, in the way it contextu-
alizes its ordinances in a "religious-moralistic rhetoric." It is the context of that rhetoric that provides a sense of the significance for the
Qumran community of rules that bear a superficial resemblance to
the rules of other organizations. Weinfeld rightly analogizes the contrast in contextualization to the similar distinction between the rhetorical "sermonizing and appeal to the emotions" in Israelite law and
the lack of such motivation in ancient Near Eastern codes.[103] There
is surely a distant echo of Deuteronomy in the rhetorical shape of
the Serek ha-Yahad as a whole, with its motivating introduction,

---

[101] White, 89.
[102] Weinfeld, *Organizational Pattern*, 23–43.
[103] Weinfeld, *Organizational Pattern*, 47.

middle section of community procedure and rules, and its conclusion with poetry. In the Serek ha-Yahad the discourse of procedural rules drawn from the world of Hellenistic associations is brought together with the discourse of Israelite law to produce a unique form of speech.

I would make one objection to Weinfeld's way of framing the issue. He contrasts the listing of the laws with "religious-moralistic rhetoric," as though legal language were not itself a form of rhetoric. All forms of speech, however, are rhetorical, and the rhetoric of rules is an interesting topic on its own terms, as is the particular rhetoric of these rules. By their nature, rules simultaneously expose and reinforce lines of fragility in a human community. Although rules are seldom made against wholly nonexistent behaviors, one should not simply assume that rules offer a transparent window onto social reality. What shows up in rules is not necessarily the undesirable conduct most rampant in the community or even the conduct that an outsider would judge most dangerous. Rather, it is the conduct that preoccupies the attention of society as most in need of control. There is thus a symbolic dimension to the content of rules. Naming such conduct in the formulation of rules gives it a visibility in the community's discourse that may serve to magnify it beyond its actual incidence, but it also places such conduct within a rhetoric of control. One can see that clearly in the casuistic form of statement used in 1QS 6:24–7:25, in which the disturbing behavior is immediately answered by the stipulated punishment.

If one looks at the categories of behaviors that these rules seek to control, one finds, not surprisingly, a strong degree of overlap with the concerns raised in the hortatory passages about proper and improper character in 2:25–3:12, in the listing of the qualities of the spirit of perversity in 4:9–11, and in the hortatory material in 5:1–7. The most harshly punished behaviors are those involving disrespect for holy authority (misuse of the divine name and expressions of anger at the priesthood), deception of the community or undermining the authority of the community's hierarchy (lying about wealth, rejecting the authority of superiors, slandering the community or complaining about its authority, departing from the community), and undermining its solidarity (groundlessly insulting a fellow, bearing a grudge or seeking revenge).[104] Lack of self control characterizes the

---

[104] A textual correction "upgrades" the behaviors of bearing a grudge and taking revenge by increasing the punishments from six months to one year.

lesser offenses (in order of seriousness: deceitful words or conduct
with a fellow member, going naked, negligence, speaking foolishly,
disrupting a session by sleeping, leaving during a vote or spitting,
laughing inappropriately, carelessly exposing oneself, gesturing inappropriately, leaving a session too often, interrupting a fellow). Stubborn
willfulness is at the heart of the most serious offenses; an inability
to discipline the self at the heart of the lesser ones. Here, as before,
what preoccupies the discourse of the community is the problem of
the unruly and self-regarding impulse, though here the sources of
that problem are not examined in a theoretical fashion, as they are
in the Two Spirits Treatise.

Unlike the hortatory material of 2:25–3:12 and 5:1–23, which
appeals with promises and threats, and unlike the didactic material
in 4:2–9, which appeals to the intellect by setting such behaviors in
a comprehensive theoretical framework, the rhetoric of rules makes
its appeal not just by means of its explicit punishments but by symbolically aligning the entire community against the imputed transgressor. The active "characters" in the discourse of the rules are "the
man who"/"whoever," on the one hand, and "they"/the "midrash
Yahad" on the other. This isolation of the transgressor is also emphasized in the symbolic nature of the punishments. The most severe
punishment is expulsion, through which the insider is once again
made into an outsider (7:1–2, 16–17, 22–25). Serious but less severe
punishments involve a return to the liminal status of the probationary member, who cannot touch the pure food or drink of the community or participate in the council, and who must be reexamined
before his rank is returned (7:18–21). Other serious punishments also
speak of exclusion from "the purity of the Many" for a year (6:24–27;
7:2–3, 15–16). The term for exclusion is הבדיל, "to separate," the
figure that is so important in establishing the identity of the community. Schiffman has argued that the phrase "the purity of the
Many" refers in these cases only to the liquids (and so implies the
status of second-year probationer),[105] but the term is characteristically used of solid foods (restricted even from first-year probation-
ers). In either case a return to the liminal status between outsider
and insider is clear. The least serious offenses do not involve explicit
separation from the community but involve "fines" of one-quarter

---

[105] Schiffman, *Sectarian Law*, 167.

of the transgressor's food for a set period of time, such fines also
being levied against those separated from the purity for more serious offenses. The symbolism of food, especially in a community that
ritualized certain meals, is resonant. Hunger and weakness are the
conditions of life for one who would set his undisciplined will in
opposition to the requirements of the community.

1QS 8:1–9:11. The Constitution of an Elite Community
Since the issues I am pursuing have to do with the rhetoric of the
Serek ha-Yahad as it appears in 1QS, I have generally avoided discussions of the redaction of various sections. Nevertheless, in the case
of 8:1–9:11, some discussion of the redactional issues is unavoidable.
As the text stands, a clearly recognizable structure appears in 1QS
8:1–9:11, marked out by a brief introduction followed by three paragraphs, each introduced by the phrase "when these exist in Israel"
(בהיות אלה בישראל, 8:4, 12; 9:3). The tone of the text is often described
as "idealistic" or "programmatic," terms that are quite justified, as
I will discuss below. Certain sections of the extant text, however,
which are either introduced by distinctive formulae or are graphically set apart from the surrounding text (8:10–12; 8:16–19; 8:20–9:2),
suggest to some that material was subsequently added to a base text.
One copy of the Serek ha-Yahad from Cave 4 (4QS^e) does not contain the text of 1QS 8:15b–9:11. Opinions differ as to the significance
of this data. Some consider all of 8:15b–9:11 to be an interpola-
tion.[106] Others recognize 8:16b–19 and 8:20–9:2 as interpolations,[107]
while considering the omission in 4QS^e to be the result of scribal
or redactional shortening.[108] The extensive interlinear corrections of
1QS 8 also lend an impression of considerable scribal activity, although
the actual history of the development may never be resolved. The
result, however, is a mosaic-like effect of thematically related but
verbally distinguishable units. However the text might have reached
the form in which it appears in 1QS, it is both intelligible and rhetorically coherent, as I will argue below.

---

[106] Metso, *Textual Development*, 72–73.
[107] Murphy-O'Connor, "La genèse littéraire," 532–33; Knibb, 136; Hunzinger,
Entwicklung der Disziplinarordnung, 242–43.
[108] Hunzinger, 242–43; Murphy-O'Connor, "La genèse littéraire," 532; Pouilly,
La Règle de la Communauté, 18; Dohmen, "Zur Gründung der Gemeinde," 95.

Since the influential study by Sutcliffe in 1959,[109] the distinctive character of this section has been generally acknowledged. Sutcliffe's interpretation, that it was the program or charter for the establishment of the Qumran community itself, as it emerged out of a broader movement, has won considerable though not universal support.[110] In a recent study of forms of community in the Dead Sea Scrolls, Collins similarly characterizes the community described in this unit as an elite formation (presumably the Qumran community itself) specially trained for a life of particular knowledge and discipline. "They complement the larger movement and bring it to perfection."[111] Those who argue for redactional stages in the form of the document as it appears in 1QS also see these additions as updating of the document needed to address the practical problems of sectarian life: the problem of disobedience (8:16–19; 8:20–9:2)[112] and perhaps the issue of the incorporation of new members (8:10–12).[113] While that certainly could be the case, the model of the fall from idealism into the hard realities of everyday life seems a bit facile. At least in the case of 8:20–9:2, as I will discuss below, the level of idealism in addressing disciplinary matters is no less high than in the base document.

If the interpretation of this unit as the program for the establishment of an elite community is correct, it is easy to see why it is included in the Serek ha-Yahad and placed where it is. As a description of the most dedicated and highest form of community life, it serves not merely as yet one more account of community procedure but rather as an expression of its highest potential and its telos. Similarly, following and complementing this description of the perfected

---

[109] Sutcliffe, "The First Fifteen Members of the Qumran Community."

[110] Metso, *Textual Development*, 118, argues that 8:1–15a "formed an introductory passage for the following sections addressed to the wise leader," thus not a manifesto but an introduction comparable to those in cols. 1 and 5.

[111] Collins, "Forms of Community," 106. Collins plausibly interprets lines 10–12 as referring to a two-year period of special training. The spiritual status of this community is marked by their complete access to knowledge. In contrast to the cautious control of knowledge that marks the Maskil's teaching of persons "each man according to his spirit" (9:13), here it is explicitly stated that "nothing that was hidden from Israel but found by the man who studies shall he conceal from these from fear of an apostate spirit" (8:11–12).

[112] There is disagreement as to whether 8:16–19 and 8:20–9:2 represent two stages of response to disobedience or whether 8:16–19 refers to disobedience to sectarian rules and 8:20–9:2 to disobedience to Mosaic torah. The issue is discussed below.

[113] Knibb, 133.

community is the rule for the Maskil, the individual who has achieved
the highest spiritual perfection. The placement of these two sections
at the end of the Serek ha-Yahad help to give it the rhetorical shape
of a document that directs the reader from entry, through knowledge and discipline, to an understanding of the spiritual perfection
toward which the disciplines of community life lead.

The conceptual center of 8:1–9:11, and what organizes its various tropes and rhetorical gestures, is the identification of the function of the community: to make expiation for the land (8:6, 10; 9:4).
In order to effect this result three things are necessary: separation
from the men of iniquity, accurate knowledge of the torah of God,
and perfection of way within the community. Of these three things
the most emphasis is given to the achievement and maintenance of
the community's perfection of way. The primary metaphor that facilitates the discourse is that of the community as temple.

The necessary conceptual context within which this passage must
be understood is the distinctive Qumran understanding of the relationship of moral and ritual impurity, as these have been clarified
by Jonathan Klawans. As Klawans demonstrates, in documents from
the Hebrew Bible ritual and moral impurity have different logics,
different consequences, and different remedies. Ritual impurity "is
natural, more or less unavoidable, generally not sinful, and typically
impermanent. . . . It is not sinful to be ritually impure, and ritual
impurity does not result from sin."[114] Moral impurity, however, is
the result of heinous and sinful acts. The result is that the sinner,
the land of Israel, and the sanctuary are morally, but not ritually,
defiled. The ultimate consequence of such defilement would be the
expulsion of the people from the land of Israel (Lev 18:24–30). Moral
purity is considerably more difficult to restore than ritual purity. The
most effective course of action is not to commit the defiling acts in
the first place. The stain of defilement, however, can be removed
from the sanctuary and the people by the sacrifices performed on
the Day of Atonement (Lev 16:11–19, 20–22). But, Klawans argues,
"these sacrifices do not appear to purify grave sinners, or the land
upon which the grave sins were committed. Such sinners either live
out their lives in a degraded state (like the guilty adulteress) or suffer
capital punishment (like apprehended murderers). The land, it appears,

---

[114] Klawans, 41.

likewise suffers a permanent degradation" (cf. Num 35:33–34).[115] The people are thus at risk of expulsion from the land.

At Qumran the two concepts of "ritual" and "moral impurity" are merged into a single system.[116] One of the consequences of this melding of the concepts of ritual and moral impurity is that it brings what had been outside the sphere of remedial action—making atonement for the land—theoretically within the reach of such action, and specifically, within the reach of the sectarian community's action. The notion of the purification of the land from the defilement of sin is typically an eschatological hope. Here, however, the practices of the community allow it to begin to be realized.[117] This sense of purpose is what gives the teaching in 1QS 8:1–9:11 its heady idealism. It also ties together the various images of identity, statements of purpose and obligation, and concomitant practices that constitute the figured world of the council of the community as it is articulated here.

Two potent images of identity are provided for the community. The first occurs in the introductory paragraph (1QS 8:1–4) in its ostensibly matter-of-fact specification of the numbers and religious status of the members: "in the council of the community (there shall be) twelve men and three priests, perfect in all that has been revealed from the whole torah" (8:1). In some sense the council of the community is to be a reconstituted Israel and a reconstituted priesthood. The symbol of a reconstituted Israel is a resonant one in late Second Temple Judaism,[118] made powerful not only by the biblical narratives of the fragmenting of a preexilic Israel that was anything but "perfect in torah" but also by the postexilic experience of a deferred and incomplete restoration. The imagery of the three priests, however,

---

[115] Klawans, 30.

[116] Klawans (75) summarizes the evidence under five heads. "First, very frequently, sins—and not just those enumerated in Leviticus 18, but all sins—are described as impurities. Second, outsiders, who by definition sin, are assumed to be ritually [im]pure. Third, insiders are not to sin, and those who do are likewise considered defiling. Fourth, initiation involves not only moral repentance, but ritual purification. Finally, instances of ritual defilement among insiders seem to be assumed to result from sin: The ritual purification of insiders involves repentance too."

[117] Klawans (88, n. 114) takes the phrase בדהוה העה (1QS 8:4) to refer to an eschatological future. But the unit as a whole appears to refer to the establishment of present communities (in particular, 8:12–13). See the analysis of Klinzing, *Die Umdeutung des Kultus*, 72–73.

[118] See the texts listed by Sanders, *Jesus and Judaism*, 95–98.

gives a distinctive accentuation to this vision of restoration. In contrast to the more common symbolism of the twelve tribes, it also suggests the restoration of the three priestly families.[119]

The suggestion of redemptive purpose, hinted at by the symbolically reconstituted Israel perfect in torah, is developed more fully in the first of the three main sections of the text (8:4–12), which provides the reader with the central set of metaphors that interpret the significance of the council of the community. As virtually every commentator has recognized, the dominant metaphor that creates identity for the community in 8:4–12 is that of the community as temple, which, as Bertil Gärtner has observed, is a quite unprecedented transference of meaning.[120] But the metaphor is more complex than is sometimes noted.

Several of the metaphorical images invoked by the passage are architectural ones: "foundation" (סוד, יסודות), "wall" (חומה), "corner" (פנה), and, more generally, "house" (בית) and "dwelling" (מעון). Even the term for "planting" (מעטת) is, as Wernberg-Møller notes, closely associated with terms for house and house-building in Ben Sira.[121] These terms have more than one level of meaning, of course. In ordinary discourse such words have "associated commonplaces" that include the values of stability and security. Such meanings are especially important for a community in the initial stages of existence, when secure establishment cannot be taken for granted. The architectural metaphors, however, are not exhausted by such connotations, since they appear in the Serek ha-Yahad already marked with traces of previous metaphorical usage, especially from prophetic rhetoric. Intertextual allusion in lines 7–8 ("it is a tested wall, a precious cornerstone that will not shake, and whose foundations will not be shaken from their place," היאה חומת הבחן פנת ירק בל יזדעזעו יסודותיהו ובל יחישו ממקומם) invokes Isa 28:16 ("See! I am laying in Zion a stone, a tested stone, a precious cornerstone, firmly founded. The one who trusts will not be alarmed," הנני יסד בציון אבן אבן בחן פנת יקרת מוסד מוסד המאמין לא יחיש). The allusion to Isaiah serves as an implicit assertion that the foundation of the community is a decisive act of God. Moreover, in the larger context of Isa 28:16–18 the

---

[119] Milik, *Ten Years*, 64–65.
[120] Gärtner, *Temple and Community*, 47.
[121] Wernberg-Møller, *Manual of Discipline*, 124.

theme of judgment is introduced through the distinction between the new foundation and what is rejected. Finally, the reference to Zion in Isaiah 28:16 facilitates the transfer of temple associations to the new foundation, both in Isaiah and in the echo of that passage in 1QS 8.

The metaphor of the community as temple is introduced in subtle ways. Of all the expressions used, actually only one ("and to offer a soothing odor," ולקריב ריח ניחוח, 8:9) is exclusively a cultic term. The others have noncultic connotations as well as cultic ones. It is not the presence of any particular term, however, so much as it is the density of possible allusions that establish the governing metaphor (e.g., "house," בית, and "dwelling" מעון, which are often used of the temple or of God's heavenly dwelling; the use of the terms קודש and קודש קודשים with Israel and Aaron, echoing the two main divisions of the temple building; and the use of nouns and verbs that often refer to cultic functions, לכפר, לרצון).

What does the community learn about itself and claim for itself through the invocation of such metaphorical language? Metaphorical assertion, as is well known, has an irreducibly paradoxical quality, what Ricoeur frequently calls the "is and is not" quality of metaphor. The council of the community manifestly *is not* the temple. Metaphor does not permit the collapsing of the two things compared. Paradoxically, however, the only adequate language for the truth of what the community is, *is* the language of temple. Metaphorical assertion is also selective in the way it transfers categories and relations from one semantic field to a new and unstructured domain. As the particular terms make clear, it is the mediatorial functions of the temple that are appropriated. Atonement, acceptability, and the offer of soothing odors are all part of the traditional vocabulary for restoring ruptured relations between the divine and the human (see, e.g., Gen 9:20–21; Exod 28:38; Lev 1:3–9; 16:30–33) Even the terms "house" and "dwelling" allude to the presence of the divine among the people that is only possible when conditions of holiness are maintained (see Ezekiel 8–11, 40–48). The reference to the temple in terms of holiness also gives a particular framing to the community's impulse to separation from the larger society. The metaphor of sanctuary holiness construes that separation not in terms of rejection but in terms of being set apart as holy in order to perform the mediatorial function (cf. 1QS 8:11). One of the things characteristic of metaphorical assertion is the fluidity with which different aspects of the donor field may be appropriated. Just as the terms "house," "dwelling," and "holy place/most holy place" appropriate the language of the temple building, and as the verbs of action ("to make atonement," "to offer") appropriate the activities of the priesthood, so the expression "and they will become an acceptable thing" identifies the community in terms of the sacrifice offered to God.

Perhaps the more interesting question is the social implication of such a metaphor as counter-discourse. In the Serek ha-Yahad the community appropriates to itself a unique function that the temple was supposed to provide for the people as a whole—atonement. Indeed, it goes beyond what was traditionally understood as within the scope of such atoning action to claim that it can make expiation for the land itself. The counter-discursive force of the temple metaphor is not simply the implicit claim that the Hasmonean temple has failed. At the same time that the temple metaphor structures an identity for the sectarian community, it also restructures thought about the temple. The cognitive force of metaphor flows in both directions. Because the community appropriates the metaphor of the temple for its identity, what it further says about its own identity reorganizes discourse about the function of the temple. An inclusio of infinitives of purpose defines the function of the community in lines 6–7: "to atone for the land and to return to the wicked their due"; the interlinear addition above line 10 reads "and they will become an acceptable (sacrifice) in order to atone for the land and to determine the judgment of wickedness."

The text juxtaposes the discourse of atonement with that of judgment against the wicked. Although the relation between the two is not spelled out, they are in some sense related functions. That is not, of course, the way in which atonement is represented in the priestly writings.[122] It is not just that Leviticus and Numbers do not address the issue of atonement for the land. When they do speak of atonement, theirs is a rhetoric of restored wholeness for the community. Because the Qumran community has merged the categories of moral and ritual impurity and is particularly concerned about the

---

[122] Klinzing (69, 71) would correlate the function of atonement with "Aaron" and recompense of the wicked with "Israel," but this does not seem necessary. Moreover, his argument is based on a complex and unpersuasive reconstruction of the redaction of 1QS 8:5–10.

effects of moral impurity on the land, it combines the language of atonement with one of the few traditional remedies for moral impurity—the punishment of the sinner. Juxtaposing atonement and judgment recontextualizes both categories in a grammar and ideology of dualism. The wholeness of atonement is here achieved in the context of the destruction or expulsion of wickedness. In this context wickedness is defined according to the halakic disputes between the Qumran community and its opponents, as is evident from the further expression of purpose in line 10, that the community should "establish the covenant of the eternal statutes," referred to in line 9 as a "covenant of judgment" (ברית משפט). It is noteworthy that the expression "to return to the wicked their due" has its closest parallels in biblical texts concerning the Gentile enemies of Israel (Ps 94:2; Lam 3:64; Obad 15). The language of the outsider is appropriated to characterize those Israelites who do not keep the "eternal statutes." The radical nature of the purpose of the community is summarized in the final phrase, "and there shall be no more iniquity" (ואין עולה), a phrase that is elsewhere used in the Two Spirits Treatise to characterize the eschatological purification (1QS 4:23). Used here, the phrase is no mere hyperbole but the serious self-understanding of the community, which already begins to effect eschatological realities.

This self-understanding of the community as temple and the transformed understanding of the atoning work of the community/temple explains the intense focus on the notion of perfection in this teaching. If the community is understood as the temple, and if the notions of moral and ritual impurity have been merged, then the community/temple would be polluted and unable to carry out its functions if sin is present. But perfection of way plays a positive role, too. Several aspects of the community's life are seen as instrumental in effecting expiation. 1QS 8:5 refers to "the practice of justice and (enduring) affliction." In 1QS 9:4–5 the place of burnt offerings and the fat of sacrifice in making expiation for the land is taken by "the proper offering of the lips" and "perfection of way," which are respectively analogized to the cultic "soothing odor" and "freewill offering." The author is not attempting to construct a technical correlation, of course, but an associative one. Perfection of way is essential both to protect the necessary holiness of the community/temple and to serve as the equivalent of cultic offerings.

Although the discussions of community discipline in 8:16b–19 and 8:20–9:2 are often seen as later redactional additions, they are

nevertheless logically related to the larger topic of the section that
began in 8:1 concerning the nature and function of the community.
While the Yahad appropriates to itself the atoning work of the temple,
the community's mediatorial action is performed not through a
sacrificial ritual system but through its piety and acts of torah. To
invoke Foucault's terms, it carries out its work as a disciplinary institution dedicated to the production of acts of torah obedience. As
the highest degree of holiness is essential to the temple and its
sacrifices, so is the perfection in torah essential to the community.
Not surprisingly, the rhetoric of perfection is almost obsessive in
8:1–9:11. Several different phrases involving the term תמים occur
(e.g., "those who walk perfectly," "perfect of way," "men of perfect
holiness"). Just how much of a leitmotif perfection is in this section
is reflected in the fact that of seventeen occurrences of such phrases
in 1QS, eleven are in this section. The only other document with
a similar fondness for the term תמים is CD, where related phrases
occur some six times. In other Qumran sectarian literature the term
is found with this sense three times in 1QS[a] and 1QS[b], twice in the
War Scroll and the Songs of the Maskil, and once each in 1QH[a]
and in the Sabbath Songs.

This is the context within which the nature and gravity of torah
disobedience are considered in 8:16–19 and 8:20–9:2. These sections
have drawn the attention of many commentators because of the
apparent contradiction between the treatment of offenses in 8:16b–19
and 8:20–9:2. Why is the deliberate sinner in 8:16b–19 treated like
the one who sins inadvertently in 8:24b–9:2, whereas the deliberate
sinner in 8:20–24a is punished much more severely? I will suggest
a possible solution to this anomaly presently, though my primary
concern is with the way in which the practices of the community
with regard to infractions of torah are related to the figured world
of the community as temple. Rather than treating the passages in
order, I wish to begin with the problem of the sinners in 8:20–9:2.

The section in 8:20–9:2 introduces itself with a heading, "These
are the rules by which the men of perfect holiness shall conduct
themselves, each with his fellow" (8:20). What follows, however, is
a reference to transgression of the torah of Moses, which one might
think is more properly a matter of conduct with God rather than
conduct with one's fellow (cf. 8:2, which similarly transforms Mic
6:8 into a statement about intra-community ethics). As the heading
suggests, the problematic that the passage explores is evidently not

the same as that taken up, for instance, in Leviticus 4–5 or Numbers 15. In those passages the issue is how expiation is to be accomplished and the forgiveness of God achieved for the individual and the community in the aftermath of a transgression. In 1QS 8:20–9:2 neither expiation nor God's forgiveness is mentioned; indeed, there is no reference to God at all. This is not because of the difficulties of offering sacrifice at a temple deemed corrupt. The difference has to do rather with the different problem with which each text deals. Leviticus is concerned with how to repair the breaches that inevitably occur; the Serek ha-Yahad is concerned to eliminate the possibility of such a breach within a community of perfect holiness. Far from being a concession to the disappointing reality that even the men of perfection are subject to sin, as some commentators have understood it, this paragraph is an expression of the most remarkable idealism about the possibility of a life of perfection within this community of discipline.

The first category taken up in 8:20–24a is that of transgressing "with a high hand" (כול איש מהמה אשר יעבר דבר מתורת מושה ביד רמה, lines 21–22). The phrase "with a high hand" is an explicit allusion to Num 15:30, where sins committed presumptuously are considered in contrast to those committed "inadvertently" (בשגגה). Such sins, because they show contempt for God, cannot be expiated by sacrifice. The only remedy is כרת. Although the exact meaning of that punishment in its original context remains debated, it involves some form of definitive separation of the individual from the sanctuary. Analogously, the member of the Yahad who sins deliberately is "sent out" from the community with no possibility of return. Nor may community members have anything to do with him in matters of property or counsel (8:22–24a). By means of a punning assonance (ביד רמה או ברמיה; 8:22) this severe punishment is extended also to violations of torah committed "high-handedly or *underhandedly*," as one might translate. Although רמיה can refer to negligence, "with a slack hand,"[123] elsewhere in Qumran literature רמיה most often carries the connotation of "deceit."[124] The end of "all deceitful works" (כול מעשי רמיה) is one of the characteristics of the eschatological resolution (1QS 4:23).

---

[123] So, Wernberg-Møller, *Manual of Discipline*, 34; Knibb, 135; Leaney, 209.
[124] E.g., 1QS 4:23; 7:5; 9:8; 1QH^a 10:16, 34; 12:7, 10, 19, 21; 20:16.

The treatment of sins committed "unwittingly" (בשגגה) reflects more clearly the different contexts and concerns of Numbers and the Serek ha-Yahad. Both texts assume that such sins create real effects. In Numbers, and in the similar discussion in Leviticus 4, inadvertent or unwitting sin creates moral pollution that must be remedied by the offering of a proper sacrifice. But it is a straightforward matter. The priest makes expiation, the person is forgiven, and that is that. With respect to the understanding of the effects of the sin, Jonathan Klawans has shown that Qumran differs from the biblical texts in holding that such a sin creates not only moral but also ritual pollution—hence the requirement of separation of the sinner from the "purity" of the community (8:24). There is another difference that deserves notice, however, one that has to do with the understanding of what it means to act בשגגה, "inadvertently" or "unwittingly." As Milgrom has shown, "inadvertent wrongdoing may result from two causes: negligence or ignorance. Either the offender knows the law but involuntarily violates it or he acts knowingly but is unaware he did wrong. . . . [U]nconsciousness of the sin and consciousness of the act are always presumed. . . ."[125] The connection between lack of perception and inadvertent sin is reflected in several texts (where inadvertence is associated with סכל in 1 Sam 26:21, פתי in Ezek 45:20, אולת in Pr 5:23, בין in Job 6:24). The impossibility of having adequate knowledge to prevent all such inadvertent sins is presumed in the plaintive cry in Ps 19:13, "Who can be aware of errors?" (שגיאות מי־יבין).

As becomes evident from the Serek ha-Yahad's treatment of inadvertent sin, the sectarian community would not take the psalmist's question as a rhetorical one. For this community, torah must be understood perfectly. There is no room for inadvertence. Consequently, the proper response to such sin is to return the sinner to the status of probationary member. Because he poses a danger of moral and ritual pollution, he is removed from the purity of the community; but because his knowledge is defective, he is also removed from participating in its counsel, judgments, and collective explication of scripture for two years (8:24–26). Although the text does not specify whether specific remedial instruction or discipline is applied, the two-year period of probation is a period of testing (9:2), during which

---

[125] Milgrom, *Leviticus 1–16*, 228.

time the individual must demonstrate his "perfection of way" (8:25; 9:2). And, it appears, there is only one such second chance (על כיא שננה אחת; 9:1).

If perfection is such a hallmark of this figured world, what is one to make of the apparently lenient treatment of the sinner in 8:16–19, who also acts deliberately (וכול איש מאנשי היחד ברית היחד אשר יסור מכול המצוה דבר ביד רמה; 8:16–17)? Scholars who assume that this text refers to the same situation as that in line 22 posit that the two regulations come from different periods in the sect's history, though they do not agree as to which is older.[126] Some have argued, however, that the differences in terminology between the two sections point to different referents. One difference is between the substantives, "command, regulation" (מצוה) on the one hand and "torah of Moses" (תרות מושה) on the other. Schiffman, who has made the most sustained attempt to clarify the halakic terminology of the sect, has argued that in the Serek ha-Yahad and in the Damascus Document מצוה designates divine commandments derived by the sect from study of torah, elsewhere referred to as things that are "hidden" (נסתר). The phrase "torah of Moses," by contrast, would refer to the body of law explicitly formulated in scripture.[127] Although this differentiation is possible, it does not completely satisfy, since it leaves without explanation why a deliberate violation of a divine command, even one not explicitly formulated in scripture, would be treated by the community by anything less than expulsion, as the allusion to Num 15:30 (ביד רמה) would suggest it ought to be.

The difference may have to do with the status of the person.[128] Several differences in wording between the two passages suggest that the section in 8:16–19 refers to a person who is still in the initial probationary period. Compare the treatment of this individual with that of the inadvertent transgressor of 8:24. In the latter case the full member is "separated" from the purity and from other privileges that he was already exercising. In the former case in 8:17–18

---

[126] Cf. Murphy-O'Connor, "La genèse littéraire," 533; Hunzinger, 243; Metso, *Textual Development*, 127–28.

[127] Schiffman, *Halakah at Qumran*, 47–49; *Sectarian Law*, 166–67. Alternatively, Leaney, 224, argues that "anything that is commanded" in 8:18 refers to the rules of the community, not to the torah of Moses (8:22). The context in 1QS (following the reference to the study of torah in line 15) does not favor this interpretation, however.

[128] Forkman, *Limits of Religious Community*, 59–61.

there is no reference to separation; rather the individual is not allowed
to "touch the purity" or be part of the process of counsel *until* (עד
אשר) he has been purified by his association with the men of perfection. Only then will they "bring him near" (וקרבהו) the council
to enlist him in its ranks. The summary statement also identifies this
procedure as pertaining to "everyone who is to be added to the
Yahad" (לכול הנוסף ליחד). Thus I would suggest that the greater
leniency has to do with the fact that this individual is still in the
liminal stage of probationary membership.[129]

In the redaction of the Serek ha-Yahad represented by 1QS, 9:3–11
serves both as recapitulation and as conclusion for the section that
began in 8:1. Echoing once again the phrase of initiation of the
community ("when these exist in Israel"), the passage recapitulates
the primary images of identity and purpose for the community that
were articulated in 8:4–10, specifically the functional replacement of
the temple and its atoning function by the community. The particular phrases rarely overlap, although many words and roots are common to the two sections (e.g., התכונים in 9:3 and נכונה in 8:5; ליסוד

---

[129] An alternative line of analysis also suggests itself. Following Schiffman's lead
that the solution might be sought in terms of the halakic assumptions, one might
look at the difference in the verbs rather than the substantives. In the second passage the verb is עבר, "transgress." In the first passage, however, the verb is יסור,
often translated "strays from," or the like. But the passage appears to make an
intertextual allusion to Josh 11:15 ("Just as the Lord had commanded His servant
Moses, so Moses had charged Joshua, and so Joshua did; he left nothing undone
of all that the Lord had commanded Moses"; trans. NJPS). The verb there is
לא־הסיר, and one might also translate the qal verb in 1QS 8:17 as "turn away
from" in the sense of "leave undone." The significance of this may rest in what
Jacob Milgrom (*Leviticus 1–16*, 229) has referred to as a distinction between performative commandments and prohibitive commandments. In Leviticus, performative commandments "are violated by refraining from or neglecting to do them. The
omission of a religious duty is a personal failing; but the sinner alone is affected.
Because no act was performed, his sin carries no impact upon his environment.
The violation of prohibitive commandments by contrast, involves an act. It sets up
reverberations that upset the divine ecology." The exclusion of the individual from
the purity of the community suggests that the Qumran community did see such
failure with respect to performative commands as having ritually polluting effects,
since it proscribes the person from touching the purity (cf. Num 15:22 on inadvertent failure to fulfill performative commands), but the Yahad may in its own
way have continued to preserve the distinction between performative and prohibitive commandments. Thus the deliberate violation of a prohibitive commandment
would require more serious response than the deliberate omission of a performative commandment. Nevertheless, because of the prominent rhetoric of "perfection
of way" in this document, I prefer to see the distinction as based on the status of
the offender rather than on the nature of the violation.

in 9:3 and יסודותיהו in 8:8; אמת in 9:3 and 8:5; כפר in 9:4 and 8:6, 10; רוצן in 9:4 and 8:6, 10). References to sacrificial terminology, introduced by ריח ניחוח in 8:9 are elaborated in terms of זבה, עולות, תרומה, and מנחה in 9:4–5, and similar allusions to a house of holiness for Aaron and Israel occur in 9:6 and 8:5–6.

Rhetorically, the concluding provisions in 9:8–11 frame the life of the community in the familiar pattern of coordinated spatial and temporal figures. The forbidding of "mixing" property with those who have not "separated" from deceit recalls the important image of physical and symbolic separation in 8:13. Similarly, the spatial image of those "who walk in the perfection of way" and who do not "go out to walk in the stubbornness of their heart" echoes not only the earlier references to ways and walking in col. 8 but the similar imagery in 1:1–15. Temporally, the life of the community is framed between the beginning of understanding and the disciplined life it makes possible ("the first statutes by which the men of the community began to be instructed") and the eschatological culmination signaled by the coming of the prophet and the messiahs of Aaron and Israel.[130] The idealism and programmatic commitment to the perfection that will atone for the land through the assimilation of the community to the image of the temple is thus set within the contours of the eschatological plan of God.

1QS 9:12–11:22. Instructions to the Maskil and the Hymn of the Maskil
The assumption that has guided my investigation of the Serek ha-Yahad follows Alexander and Vermes in seeing it as a "manual to guide the Maskil in his duties as the spiritual head of the Community."[131] To this point the document has provided samples of various topics and teachings. But except for occasional references to the obligation of the Maskil to teach (3:13 and presumably 1:1), the Maskil's own character and responsibilities have not been explicitly addressed. With the unit that begins in 1QS 9:12, however, attention is directed explicitly to the figure of the Maskil and remains on him to the end of the document. Rhetorically, placing the sections

---

[130] This reference is missing in 4QS^c, which does not contain the equivalent of 1QS 8:16–9:11. It is not certain whether the phrase occurred in 4QS^d (Alexander and Vermes, 111).

[131] Alexander and Vermes, 10.

concerning the Maskil at the end of the document emphasizes the leadership role he exercises and, as I have suggested, helps create a rough structure for the document that begins with issues of entry, proceeds to the knowledge and discipline of the community, and finally focuses on the image of the leader who represents the spiritual ideal of the sect.

Not all manuscripts of the Serek ha-Yahad end in the same way, however. Six manuscripts preserve material from the end of the composition (1QS, 4QS[b], 4QS[d], 4QS[e], 4QS[f], and 4QS[j]). Apparently all contained the third-person instructions addressed to the Maskil.[132] In 4QS[e] this instruction is followed by a calendrical teaching concerning intercalation, the Otot document. In the other copies the concluding section is not Otot but a first-person hymn of the Maskil. Scholars differ as to whether the recension represented in 4Q[e] represents an early version of the Serek ha-Yahad[133] or a later revision of the document.[134] The rhetorical shaping of the document, however, is quite different, depending on whether it concludes with Otot or with the first-person hymn of the Maskil.[135] With Otot, the focus on the figure of the Maskil in the instructions is quickly subordinated to the content of his teaching. His presence in the document is no more vivid than that of the members described in the accounts of community procedure. The inclusion of the Maskil's first-person hymn, however, not only gives the Maskil a voice and presence but also provides the Serek ha-Yahad a much more forceful rhetorical structure and even something like a genuine conclusion. The Maskil's hymn should not be mistaken for the personalized expression of an individual, of course. It is utterly formulaic in its sentiments and expression. But this is scarcely surprising. Even in figured worlds that claim to value unique personal expression, confessional speech and testimony is often strongly shaped by role expectations and implicit speech norms.[136] Indeed, it is by learning how to speak about one-

---

[132] There is no direct evidence for 4QS[j], which includes only material corresponding to 1QS 11:14–22.

[133] So, e.g., Metso, *Textual Development*, 70–74; VanderKam, *Calendars*, 81.

[134] So Alexander, "Redaction-History," 448–53. García Martínez, "Calandarios en Qumran (I)," 341, considers both possibilities.

[135] It is possible that one manuscript, 4QS[b], might contain material following the end of the Maskil's hymn, but the status of the fragment in question is uncertain. See Alexander and Vermes, 63.

[136] See, e.g., the examination of the personal stories told in Alcoholics Anonymous in Holland et al., 66–97, or the conversion stories in evangelical Protestantism.

self in just such a formulaic way that one develops the type of character that fits within the figured world.

Although the Maskil's hymn deals with certain aspects of the responsibilities addressed in the instructions, much of its content does not have to do with those things that distinguish him from other members of the Yahad. In this regard the self-presentation of the Maskil provides a model of the ideal sectarian self. If one is properly shaped by the teachings and disciplines of the community, as they have been described in the Serek ha-Yahad, then this is the kind of voice with which one will speak. Thus the Maskil's hymn itself is an element of his teaching. Similarly, the dense network of echoes between the Maskil's hymn and the language of the covenant ceremony[137] not only provides a literary inclusio for 1QS but also suggests that the process of the shaping of sectarian character, which begins with entry into the covenant community, finds its telos in just such a self. The similarity between the Maskil's hymn and the poetic compositions of the Hodayot indicates that those compositions, too, play an important role in the formation of the proper sectarian character, a topic that will be taken up in the following chapters.

Structure and Content

Like many other sections of the Serek ha-Yahad, 1QS 9:12–11:22 is composed of several separate units, probably originally independent and recycled from other contexts, even though they have been put together with a discernible rhetorical sensibility. Two sets of instructions to the Maskil are identified by similar headings in 9:12 ("These are the regulations for the Maskil in which he is to walk with all the living according to the norm of every time and according to the measure of every person") and 9:21 ("These are the norms of conduct for the Maskil in these times with respect to his love and his hate"). In the first, following brief instructions concerning the knowledge that the Maskil must have (9:13–14a), the instruction initially takes up the Maskil's responsibilities for properly constituting the membership of the community (9:14a–16a), and then the proper control of knowledge in relations with outsiders and insiders (9:16a–21a). The second set of instructions is concerned more with the proper dispositions of the Maskil and the conduct that follows from them,

---

[137] Weise, 64–68, 71, 79 n. 2; Falk, *Daily, Sabbath, and Festival Prayers*, 110–11.

dealing first with his relations with the men of the pit, now and on
the day of vengeance (9:21b–24a), and second with the complete
conformation of the Maskil's desires to the will of God (9:24b–25).
The fact that 4QS^c apparently concludes this section with the phrase
ולמשפט אל יצפה תמיד (= 1QS 9:25)[138] suggests that a new unit begins
in line 26 concerning the obligation of the Maskil to bless God. This
transition is unfortunately obscured in 1QS because of a break in
the text at the beginning of 9:26.

   Opinions differ as to the structure of 9:26–11:22. Translators often
assume that the Maskil's hymn is introduced not only by the verbal
sentences in 9:26–10:1 but also by a lengthy enumeration of the
times for praise, with the Maskil's own speech beginning in 10:5
(after the vacat)[139] or in 10:6 (with the first-person verb).[140] In their
edition of the 4Q fragments, however, Alexander and Vermes now
argue that the hymn proper begins with the words בראשית ממשלת אור
(4QS^d 8:11 = 1QS 10:1). The short introduction in 1QS 9:26–10:1
is composed from phrases taken from the opening lines of the hymn
proper.[141] Thus 9:26–10:1, which also has the form of a directive,
grafts the Maskil's hymn onto the second instruction to the Maskil
in 9:21–25. The long catalogue of times for praise is an integral part
of the Maskil's first-person hymn.

   The Maskil's hymn consists of several sections. Although they are
not always clearly divided, a discernible structure exists that is important for the way in which the Maskil constructs himself in the act of
speaking. The poem opens with a list of times for praise (10:1–8),
apparently a preexisting formulation adapted to its present purpose

---

[138] See Alexander and Vermes, 150.
[139] So Vermes, *Complete Dead Sea Scrolls*, 112; Wise, Abegg, and Cook, *Dead Sea Scrolls*, 140.
[140] So Leaney, 234; Wernberg-Møller, *Manual of Discipline*, 36; Charlesworth et al., 43.
[141] In 4QS^d in col. 8, "the preface to the Maskil's Hymn begins with line 10 (after the words יצפה תימד [= 1QS 9:26], and the hymn itself probably begins with בראשית ממשלת אור in line 11 [= 1QS 10:1]. The hymn originally existed as an inde-pendent composition. A redactor of S constructed an introduction for it, built out of phrases lifted from the opening of the hymn: cf. 1QS IX; 26 שפתים יברכנו [ותרומת with X 6 תרומת שפתים הברכנו; IX 26 יספ[ר] חסדיו with X 4 למפתח חסדיו; and IX 26 ובכול קץ נעהיה with X 5 בכול קץ נהיה," Alexander and Vermes, 119. Their position is somewhat obscured by the statement in the introduction (p. 10) that the Maskil's hymn is contained in 1QS 10:5–11:22. This is the division reflected in the translation of Vermes, *Complete Dead Sea Scrolls*, 112.

by a single first-person verb in 10:6. Following this list comes a long section in which first-person verbs cluster thickly (10:8–11:2a). The Maskil variously commits himself to acts of praise, self-judgment, confession of God, and submission to God's judgment (10:8b–13a). He further commits himself to praise at the times that organize human activity (10:13b–17a). Finally, he engages in a variety of commitments concerning forms of self-discipline (10:17b–11:2a), first regarding relationships with other persons (10:17b–21a), second with respect to his speech (10:21b–24a), and third with respect to the control of knowledge (10:24b–11:2a). Following this extensive act of self-commitment, the poem takes a more reflective turn. In three sections, all introduced by כיא אני or ואני (11:2b–9a, 9b–11b, 11b–15a), the Maskil reflects on the contrasting nature of God and humankind and the gracious actions by which God has rescued him, despite his human sinfulness. This reflection and confession leads to the final section of the poem (11:15b–22), which consists of a blessing of God (11:15b–20a) and a concluding reflection on human nothingness (11:20b–22).

The Character of the Maskil

Certain aspects of the Maskil's character, as they are represented here, are dependent upon the particular leadership role that he exercises, whereas others reflect the common shape of a character formed in the Yahad. Although there is some overlap among the units, the instructions, which deal with his specific responsibilities, attend more to the traits derived from the exercise of his duties, whereas the hymn articulates the more general features. One striking element, which characterizes both types of material, however, is the preoccupation with the vocabulary and imagery of time. I wish to hold a discussion of the representation of time until later, however, since the issue of the construction and role of time is an important aspect of the figured world of the Serek ha-Yahad in general.

In describing the Maskil's responsibilities, the first instruction (9:12–21a) represents him as, above all, a person with the capacity to make exquisite discriminations. His is the ability to make the complex acts of discernment and measurement encapsulated in the expression "according to the norm of every time and the weight of every man" (9:12). Through his judgment the children of righteousness are not only "separated" (9:14) from the men of perdition and "brought near" (9:15), but their spirits, too, are "weighed" by him (9:14). To be able to perform these functions, he must possess two primary traits: a complete attunement to the will of God and an encompassing knowledge of everything that has been revealed by God throughout all times (9:13). The theme of the Maskil's attunement to the will of God is taken up more extensively in the second instruction and in the hymn.

The Maskil's role in making discriminations casts him as a gateway or boundary-marking figure. He lets in, and he keeps out. No one comes into the community except through his judgment. As a boundary figure he must face both to the outside and to the inside. Indeed, he is represented as having both an "outside" persona and an "inside" persona. With outsiders he is characterized by a profound reserve. Within a culture that was characterized by a good deal of public teaching and public disputation, the Maskil is explicitly forbidden either "to rebuke or dispute with the men of the pit and to conceal the counsel of the law in the midst of the men of iniquity" (9:16–17). This restriction is obviously related to his role as one who is charged with the control of the flow of knowledge. To invoke a slightly absurd analogy, the Maskil is somewhat like a mechanical regulator in a complex machine that controls and directs the flow of fluids in and out of the system. He keeps out the men of perdition and he does not allow the flow of knowledge to reach them. Within the community he has a positive duty to teach, but there, too, such teaching is strictly regulated, "each man according to his spirit and according to the order of the time" (9:18). Although directed to his particular responsibilities, the Maskil's reserve, discernment, and circumspection are a realization of the general sectarian character, as it is expressed in the Two Spirits Treatise, "walking circumspectly with a canny understanding of all things, and concealing the truth of the mysteries of knowledge" (1QS 4:5–6).

In his study of rhetoric in literature and society Kenneth Burke commented on "mystery" as one of the fundamental modes of rhetorical appeal, one that was especially potent when combined with a principle of hierarchy.[142] The Maskil's reserve, coupled with his reputation for unequaled knowledge of the mysteries of God, make him just such a figure of mystery. To insiders, he is the one who knows

---

[142] Burke, *Rhetoric of Motives*, 114–23.

more than he may disclose, since he measures out knowledge according to the readiness of individual sectarians and the appropriateness
of the time. But to outsiders he practices an intentionally concealed
self. This topic is treated in the second instruction (9:21–25), which
deals specifically with the discipline of the Maskil's affects—"his love
and his hate." The instruction makes a sharp distinction between
the type of behavior appropriate to "these times" and to the coming "day of vengeance" (cf. 10:18–19 in the hymn). For the present
the Maskil is advised to present a dissembled persona to outsiders.
Even the "eternal hatred" that he is to hold toward "the men of
the pit" is to be cloaked "in a spirit of secrecy." The particular form
this concealment takes is described in terms of wealth and power.
The Maskil plays a role during "these times," appearing in the humble guise of a "servant" or "lowly person" before "the one who rules
over him" (כעבד למושל בו וענוה לפני הרודה בו; 9:22–23), as he leaves
to them "wealth and the produce of hands." The true state of affairs
will be evident in "the day of vengeance." The figure of the powerful leader who must conceal his power and true identity until the
appropriate time is not a common one in the Israelite imagination.
The suffering servant in Isaiah 52:13–53:12 is a notable exception.
It may, however, have become more of a cultural type during the
time of the flourishing of Jewish sects in the Hellenistic and Roman
periods. The treatment of the "messianic secret" in the Gospel of
Mark casts Jesus in something of the same role. Even if there are
partial similarities between the cloaked or dissembled self cultivated
by the Maskil and other figures, the combination of traits he embodies is unique to the figured world of Qumran sectarianism.

The Maskil's character embodies to the fullest the disciplines that
are at the heart of the moral imagination of the Serek ha-Yahad.
As the present concealment in relation to the men of the pit describes
the disciplined nature of the Maskil's "hatred," so his relationship
with God expresses the discipline of his "love." In 9:24–25 four parallel sentences—two framed positively and two negatively—describe
the Maskil's complete conformation of his own desires to the will of
God. "Everything that happens to him he will willingly accept (רצה),
and except for the will of God he will take pleasure (חפץ) in nothing,[143] [and] in all His words he will delight (רצה), and he will not

---

[143] Taking לו as an error or phonetic spelling for לוא.

desire (אוה) anything that He has not commanded." The final lines of the instruction complement the image of perfect attunement of the desires of the Maskil by an image of focused attention, as the Maskil "watches continually" for the judgment of God (9:25).

The Maskil's hymn reiterates the discipline of perfect conformation to the will of God in the commitment the Maskil makes to the spiritual discipline of praising God both at the liturgically significant times (10:1–8) and also at the beginning of all his activities (10:13–16). Such praise orients the person repeatedly to God and so serves to give an experiential reality to the "delight" referred to above. Fittingly, the image of such perfect attunement is a musical one, as the Maskil refers to his singing and musical accompaniment as played according to "the order of His holiness" and "the line of his judgment" (10:9).

What the hymn contributes to the development of the Maskil's character that is not found in the instructions is the form of self-awareness cultivated as the Maskil contemplates the nature of God. This dynamic is frequent in the Hodayot and will be examined more fully in the following chapters. Characteristically, as the Maskil orients himself to God, he sees himself from the perspective of God and becomes aware of his sins. Here, the morning and evening recitation of the Shema and the Decalogue ("With the coming of day and night I will enter the covenant of God, and with the departure of evening and morning I will recite his statutes," 10:10) introduce the Maskil's awareness and acceptance of God's judgment on his iniquities (10:11, 13). In an important rhetorical gesture, one that is often repeated in the Hodayot, the speaker's confession of his sinfulness is paired with a confession of the saving power of God ("I say to God, 'My Righteousness,' and to the Most High, 'Foundation of my Goodness,'" etc.; 10:11–12). The knowledge and strength that come to the Maskil through his contemplation of God is what allows him to undertake the moral commitments he enumerates in 10:16–11:2. This tensive relationship of the Maskil's own incapacity and divine supercapacity becomes the dominating theme in the first כיא אנ passage. There, everything that constitutes the Maskil—his perfection of way, insight into mysteries, strength and sureness, status as part of God's eternal possession—is seen as coming from the hand of God (11:2–9).

Just as the Maskil's enumeration of the benefits of God's graciousness reaches its rhetorical pinnacle in his affirmation that God's elect are joined with the heavenly assembly, he plunges immediately into an abyss of awareness of his own nature (יאנו) as part of the "assembly of deceitful flesh" and "assembly of maggots" (11:9–10). The downward plunge of horrified self-recognition is again reversed in the recollection (אני; 11:11b) that God's plan and power is the source of everything. These sharp reversals of the angle of self-perception and the rapid changes of emotional tone are a part of the practice of the construction of the self, as will be seen more fully in the Hodayot. In the present context, the discipline of such self-examination enables the Maskil to see that even though, as a human, he stumbles, commits iniquity, and becomes impure, he receives perfection of way, salvation, atonement, and purification through the mercy of God (11:10–15). Indeed, the Maskil sees in this dynamic the purpose of his existence: to praise God for just such gracious rescue of him from the impurity and sinfulness that is the human condition (11:14–15). Only now after some forty lines of stating his intention to bless God, does the Maskil address God directly. The content of the praise is shaped according to the same structure as his preceding reflections—the nothingness of humankind that corresponds to the fullness of the divine. The poem ends, however, not with contemplation of divine glory but with images of human decay, corruption, and inability to understand.

What constitutes the Maskil's character is not so much conceptual knowledge about the plan of God and the nature of humankind as it is an experience of that dynamic in his own psyche. Reciting the hymn creates a vertiginous experience that might well be described as the cultivation of the masochistic sublime. The positive pleasure of seeing oneself as constituted and destined for heavenly reward by means of the overwhelming power and mercy of God is grasped and intensified precisely by perceiving and articulating one's natural human sinfulness and loathsomeness.

The character constructed for the Maskil in the instructions and hymn is one that embodies the values of the sect in a particularly pronounced fashion. His ability to make subtle distinctions, informed by a knowledge of mysteries and a sense of eschatological destiny, his reserve with outsiders, amounting even to a dissembled self, creates a sense of mysterious power that constitutes part of his appeal both to outsiders and insiders. His disciplined orientation to God's will is shaped by practices of nearly continuous temporally structured worship, and his sense of self is formed through the cultivation of a focus on the radical alterity between divine and human nature and gratitude for being saved from human sinfulness and its consequences.

Qumranic of the self
discipline quite unlike
common
Judaism

Though one might find individual points of similarity, these various features come together to create a persona quite unlike one constructed by the figured worlds of "common Judaism," by ordinary priestly service, or by participation in another of the sects and religious movements current in late Second Temple Judaism. The characteristic language, communal disciplines, roles, and practices of the figured world at Qumran produce a self uniquely configured.

The Construction of Time and the Figured World of the Serek ha-Yahad

The preoccupation with time in this portion of the Serek ha-Yahad is striking, most particularly in the first instruction and in the hymn of the Maskil (9:12–20). In the first instruction the word עת occurs some ten times in eight expressions and is repeated again in the heading to the second instruction in 9:21. The Maskil's hymn begins with an elaborate listing of the times for praise that moves from the daily cycle through the cycle of jubilee periods. Slightly later in the poem comes a catalogue of the times for praise as defined by the rhythms of daily life. Who the Maskil is, is significantly defined in terms of his relation to time.[144] These materials also provide an occasion for examining other representations of time in the rest of the Serek ha-Yahad, in order to consider how the construction of time is part of that figured world and serves to construct a self different from those in other Jewish subcultures. In previous research the role of calendrical disputes in the emergence of Qumran sectarianism has been thoroughly studied,[145] as have the various calendrical texts found at Qumran.[146] The terminology of time has also received scrutiny.[147] The questions I wish to explore, however, are somewhat different, for they have to do with cultures of time and their social implications.

Time is not a simple concept, in part because it is socially constructed and serves a variety of purposes. The title of a recent book by Robert Levine reflects this well: *A Geography of Time: The Temporal Misadventures of a Social Psychologist, or How Every Culture Keeps Time Just a Little Bit Differently*. Even this title oversimplifies, however, since

---

[144] Note the similar catalogue of times for praise introducing one of the Hodayot attributed to the Maskil in 1QH[a] 20:4–9.

[145] Most notably by Talmon, "Calendar Reckoning," 166–68.

[146] See Glessmer, "Calendars in the Qumran Scrolls," and VanderKam, *Calendars in the Dead Sea Scrolls*, and the literature cited there.

[147] Brin, *The Concept of Time in the Bible and the Dead Sea Scrolls*.

there are also multiple forms of time in play in a given society. The role of time in cultural analysis is widely recognized as fundamental. As Allen Bluedorn succinctly put it, "time is used to generate meaning."[148] But time often intersects with other dimensions of reality in the generation of meaning. Bakhtin, for instance, made the chronotope, the representation of the relationship of time and space, a fundamental criterion for understanding the sense of reality of various cultures and literature.[149] Although the space-time relationship may have a certain privilege, it is only one of many meaning-giving combinations.[150]

To provide a framework for analyzing various modes of time Bluedorn suggests the terms fungible time and epochal time. Fungible time is time that has no qualitative differentiation. One unit is the same as another. All minutes are the same and thus are, in this way of thinking, exchangeable or fungible. Although they fall one after the other in the sequence of time, they are qualitatively indistinguishable. This is the "absolute time" so characteristic of modern science. Fungible or absolute time serves as a framework within which various events can be located. Although fungible time is particularly characteristic of the modern scientific world, Jubilees's set of Anno Mundi dates is also an example of fungible or absolute time.[151] Epochal time, by contrast, is time defined by events, for instance, "harvest time" or "the year of the invasion." Such times are qualitatively different from other moments or periods. More often than not, a particular cultural formulation of time will not be purely fungible or epochal but will partake of aspects of both. Thus Bluedorn suggests that these categories be thought of as establishing a type of continuum within which a particular account of time can be situated.[152]

One means by which time organizes the structures of meaning in a culture is the way in which the temporality of one system is used to structure another aspect of life, a relationship known as entrainment. As Bluedorn defines it, "entrainment is the process in which

---

[148] Bluedorn, *Human Organization of Time*, 42.

[149] "Every entry into the sphere of meanings is accomplished only through the gates of the chronotope." Bakhtin, *Dialogic Imagination*, 258.

[150] See, in particular, E. Hall, *The Dance of Life: The Other Dimension of Time*.

[151] Though it is true, as Wintermute ("Jubilees," 38–39) observes, that Jubilees also envisions a qualitative as well as a quantitative differentiation between times in its distinction between sacred and profane days.

[152] Bluedorn, 21–35.

the rhythms displayed by two or more phenomena become synchronized, with one of the rhythms often being more powerful or
dominant and capturing the rhythm of the other."[153] This may be
as simple as the entraining effect of work times on bus schedules or
as complex as the effect of a liturgical year. Although entrainments
may occur simply as conveniences, they often also reflect and construct meaning and power relationships. Since entrainment is fundamentally relational, it is often associated with the social aspects of
rhythmic activity and with being "in sync."

Human activity is also organized along another temporal continuum, the poles of which can be described as monochronicity and
polychronicity, concepts developed by social psychologist Edward T.
Hall.[154] In monochronicity one task at a time is taken up and maintained until it is completed. Schedules organize activity and are considered fundamentally important. In polychronicity many tasks with
different time horizons are allowed to intersect with one another.
Schedules, if they are perceived to exist at all, are of less importance than the claims of personal relationships, which can reorient
the order of activities. Preferences for monochronicity or polychronicity
are strongly cultural. Although the basic preference is set by the culture of the ethnic group as a whole, particular institutions or groups
within a culture may deviate from the prevailing preference. Depending
on the dominance of monochronicity or polychronicity, social space
also will be organized differently, an example of what Bakhtin
would call a chronotope. Forms of social interaction also will differ.[155]
Although much of the work on theories of time has been done in
relation to social and institutional organization, such organizational
practices are often implicitly if not explicitly related to underlying
ideologies and world views. Since much of what social psychologists
and cultural analysts examine in living societies is no longer available with respect to the Yahad, one can only in a limited sense
recover the construction of time at Qumran. The more modest task
is to examine some of the ways in which time is represented in the
Serek ha-Yahad, beginning with the text concerning the Maskil, and
drawing, as appropriate, on other sections of the document.

---

[153] Bluedorn, 148.
[154] E. Hall, *The Dance of Time*, 41–54. For a more recent discussion see Bluedorn, 48–82.
[155] Bluedorn, 50.

Of the various accounts of time given in the sections pertaining to the Maskil, the most complex but the most interesting is the one that occurs in the first instruction in its recurrent references to עת and עתים. The Hebrew word עת is one of the most common words for referring to epochal time, that is, time as configured and given significance by events.[156] Nowhere is this more aptly illustrated than in the poem on the times cited in Qohelet 3:2–8, with its insistence that there is a time for every human activity. As this poem suggests, epochal time is closely connected with the notion of "timeliness," the effectiveness or even rightness that comes from coordinating an act with the time appropriate to it. This perception is itself a form of entrainment and is part of popular wisdom in many cultures, expressing the importance of performing the right deed at the right time. As has often been noted, the particular form of epochal time reflected in the instruction to the Maskil (as elsewhere in Qumran literature) is more historicized, even eschatologized, than what one finds, for example, in the wisdom literature. In the Serek ha-Yahad sequential periods of time have been qualitatively differentiated by God's acts of predetermination and revelation at particular times.[157] Thus the fundamental task of the Maskil is "to do the will of God according to all that has been revealed from time to time" (9:13). Knowledge is consequently historicized, and the Maskil is "to learn all the insight that has been found out in accordance with the times and the rule of the time" (9:13–14) and to teach the community "all that has been found out that is to be done at this time" (9:20). Although "the rule of the time" might refer to the very system of epochal times itself, more likely the phrase simply alludes to the conviction that knowledge which is valid at one time may not be "the rule" for another.[158]

The instruction largely takes for granted that the reader will know what the relevant times are, though it explicitly describes the present

---

[156] Speculation about a distinctive Hebrew sense of time, embodied in words like עת, was put to rest by the trenchant criticism of Barr, *Biblical Words for Time*. Although he is correct that עת may have a variety of meanings, as Kronholm ("Et," 447) observes עת "normally refers to 'the appointed time for something,' thus resembling in meaning such terms as Egypt. *tr* and *nw* and Gk. καιρoξ ."

[157] Brin, *Concept of Time*, 301.

[158] Cf. Brin, *Concept of Time*, 303: "God decides the compass of the period, its character and contents—this is evidently the meaning of the term חוק העת—so that ipso facto all events and situations are predetermined."

as "the time for preparing the way to the wilderness," a trope on
Isa 40:3 that apparently is used to signify the time of the elite sect's
separation—symbolic and literal—from the larger Jewish community
(cf. 8:13–15). Characteristic of proper behavior during this time is a
strongly differentiated relationship to outsiders and insiders, most particularly in relation to the control of knowledge (9:16–21). Insiders
are to cultivate knowledge of torah but "to conceal the counsel of
torah in the midst of the men of deceit" (9:17). The present epoch
is distinguished from the םקנ םוי (9:23; 10:19), at which time the
constraint concerning outsiders is relaxed, as they receive their due
and a rather belated recognition of reality.

One should be careful in conflating various texts from Qumran
into a single system of thought. Nevertheless, various references to
periods of time in other documents would likely be part of the horizon of understanding of sectarian readers. The references to "the
age of wrath," the "latter generations," and the time when Israel
was "like a stubborn heifer" in the opening of the Damascus Document,
as well as its account of the various generations in cols. 2–4, seem
close to the sense of the epochal times found in the instruction in
1QS 9. Similarly, the reader would think of the historical periodization of Jubilees ("what will happen in all of the divisions of
the days which are in the Law and testimony and throughout their
weeks [of years] according to the jubilees forever, until I shall descend
and dwell with them in all the ages of eternity" (Jub 1:26; trans.
Wintermute). This and the similar speculations about the ages of
the world such as one finds in 4QAges of Creation (4Q 180–181)
would presumably be the kind of comprehensive knowledge that the
Maskil is instructed to master concerning what has been "found out"
about the various times. The most immediate horizon of reference
for the reader of 1QS, however, would be the allusions in the Two
Spirits Treatise to the comprehensive plan of God, which refers to
both the "history of all humankind" (3:13) and the "appointed time
of the visitation" (4:18–19).

Such an epochal construction of time accomplishes many things.
In Burke's dramatistic terms it creates a rhetoric in which scene,
rather than act, agent, agency, or purpose, is the dominant category. Epochal time is the encompassing scene within which agents
are located, acts take place, and purposes are understood. Other
rhetorics might construe the same situation differently, as, for instance,
a highly messianic rhetoric might stress the role of the agent, sub-

ordinating the scenic element. Epochal time also creates value and interest, as different times have different qualities in relation to one another. This is so whether the larger framework is a cyclical one ("seedtime and harvest") or a more linear narrative, as is the case with eschatological time. In both cases epochal time also tends to give unity to the experience of time by locating particular times in relation to an encompassing whole (e.g., the food cycle or the plan of God for the world). The use of epochal times in an eschatological framework intensifies this feature, since it extends comprehensive meaning to the ultimate horizons of history.

Although the Serek ha-Yahad shares many of these features with other Jewish apocalyptic compositions that privilege epochal time, it also exhibits certain distinctive features. One of these, discussed in connection with 1:14–15, is the characteristic expression of proper action according to a double analytic that combines a knowledge of epochal time with some other form of measurement. Here the heading specifies that "these are the regulations for the Maskil in which to walk with all the living according to the norm of every time and according to the weight of every person" (לתכון עת ועת ולמשקל איש ואיש, 9:12). Similarly, in the instructions concerning teaching, the Maskil teaches the members of the community "each man according to his spirit [and] according to the norm of the time" (איש כרוחו כתכון העת, 9:18). Something other than simple entrainment is at work here. What is expressed in these phrases is an almost algebraic sensibility. As the course of a line may be defined precisely in terms of the intersection of x and y coordinates, so correct action is located at the intersection of two coordinates of knowledge. Although epochal time is always one of the coordinates, knowledge is configured as multi-dimensional. These phrases are an index of a distinctive way of knowing and are related to more general habits of mind in the Serek ha-Yahad and other Qumran literature, in particular to the passion for distinction and division. This tendency is expressed in binary forms (e.g., the dualistic rhetoric, the frequent references to "separating" or to "dividing") but also in forms of infinite gradation, the distinctions between more and less (e.g., the ranking produced by annual examination and its expression in the seating order of the sectarians). Epochal time is thus part of a larger system of qualitative and quantitative judgments that intersect in order to produce the knowledge necessary for a perfect alignment with the will of God. Such an orientation to knowledge, embodied not only in turns

of phrase but also in the organization of daily life, is a distinctive
and important aspect of the figured world of Qumran and of the
self-understanding of those who participated in it.

The second focus on time occurs at the beginning of the Maskil's
hymn. The introduction to the hymn is broken and is variously
restored[159] but it clearly instructs the Maskil to praise God "at the
times that he has prescribed" (עם קצים אשר חקקא; 10:1). The Maskil
then begins his hymn with a catalogue of the times at which he will
praise. These are calendrical times, which, as Alexander and Vermes
have shown, include the daily cycle of morning and evening, the
annual cycle (comprising the first days of the months, sabbaths and
other prescribed festivals, the days of equinoxes and solstices that
mark the beginning of the four seasons), and the sabbatical cycle,
including the jubilee year.[160]

Calendrical time partakes of both fungible and epochal time. It is
fungible in that it is composed of units of equivalent measure (days,
weeks, months, years, and larger units), but it often has epochal
dimensions in that calendrical time is closely connected with human
activities, whether these be matters of the agricultural cycle or events
memorialized in ritual cycles, both of which are aspects of the ritual
calendar articulated by the Maskil (e.g., "holy days appointed for
remembrance," 10:5; "on the day decreed by Him that they should
pass from one to the other—the season of early harvest to the sum-
mer time, the season of sowing to the season of grass," 10:7; trans.
Vermes). Similarly, the differentiation of sacred times and profane
times in a religious calendar give it epochal dimensions, especially
if these are coordinated with narratives of creation that relate patterns of divine activity to the differentiation of one day from another
(e.g., Gen 2:2; Exod 20:8–11). In several Jewish apocalyptic texts the
larger units of calendrical time (jubilees or weeks of years) sometimes intersect with notions of epochal times of predetermined content, as in the Apocalypse of Weeks. Here, however, in the Maskil's
hymn the intersection with eschatological epochal time is not stressed.

Because calendrical time is based on physical time, that is, the

---

[159] E.g., Falk, *Daily, Sabbath and Festival Prayers*, 105, "[At every period that will]
be he will bless his maker and at every occurrence he will de[clare. . . . (With) the
offering of] lips he will bless him at the times which he prescribed" (ובכול קץ נ[היה
[יברך עושיו ובכול אשר יהיה יספ]ר . . . ותרומת] שפתים יברכנו עם קצים אשר חקקא).
[160] Alexander and Vermes, 120.

regular movements of heavenly bodies,[161] it is fundamentally rhythmic time. Thus in the entrainment relationship calendrical time supplies the dominant rhythm to which human time is accommodated. For these reasons calendrical time can become a potent symbol of harmony, of being "in sync" with the cosmos—or not. The high degree of concern for calendrical systems at Qumran and in the intellectual and social circles from which it emerged underscores this, whether it is expressed in detailed accounts of the lunar and solar cycles and the ways in which they were to be coordinated (e.g., the calendrical documents from Cave 4, 4QPhases of the Moon [4Q 317], 4QCalendrical Document E [4Q 326–327], 4QOtot [4Q 319, part of 4QS^e]), in the coordination of priestly courses with calendrical cycles (4QMishmarot [4Q 320–325, 328–330]), or in polemics against the "irregular" lunar calendar (e.g., Jubilees).

Institutionally and sociologically speaking, in Israel calendrical time was above all priestly time. By contrast, the so-called Gezer Calendar was fundamentally an epochal system of months based on the activities of the agricultural cycle. Systems of years and dates played a role in political systems, of course, but these also tended to be measured in epochal terms (i.e., regnal years). Physical and calendrical time was the province of those who had the responsibility to see that the ritual time of sacrifices and festivals was synchronized with heavenly time. The depth of significance of such synchronization is indicated by Albani's observation on the Mishmarot texts:

> Der Grundgedanke der in 4QMischmerot repräsentierten Kalenderordnung ist die Vorstellung einer himmlisch-irdischen Entsprechung, wonach die Umläufe der Gestirne und die Zyklen der Priesterdienste einen gemeinsamen Ursprung haben. Diese Universalisierung der Tempelkultes bis zum weitesten Horizont der Weltschöpfung kann natürlich nur den theologischen Interessen priesterlicher Kreise entsprungen sein.[162]

The sophisticated instrument found at Qumran that served both for astronomical measurement and as a sundial to measure seasonal hours indicates the seriousness with which this commitment to observing precise times was taken.[163]

---

[161] E. Hall, 19–22.
[162] Albani, "Die lunaren Zyklen," 23.
[163] Albani and Glessmer, "Un Instrument de Mesures astronomiques à Qumrân."

In the Maskil's hymn, entrainment occurs between calendrical time
and the spiritual practice of prayer and praise. This is not an idio-
syncratic relationship on the part of the Maskil, of course, but belongs
to the developing prayer practices in late Second Temple Judaism.[164]
Although the distinctiveness and rationale for Qumran practice remains
debated, Daniel Falk[165] has argued persuasively that, at the least,
daily prayer in the morning and evening began to be practiced by
a variety of Jews. This was in large measure a private and individual practice and consisted of recitation of the Shema, the Decalogue,
and probably blessings. Paralleling this private activity were popular
gatherings at the Temple at the time of sacrifice which included acts
of prayer. In Falk's view two systems developed, one organized
according to the course of the luminaries and another organized
according to the times of sacrifice in the Temple. The distinction
was often blurred and eventually the two systems were "conflated to
produce the standard thrice daily prayer of the synagogue service."[166]
Both systems, however, reflect the way in which priestly practices
and concerns came to fund the piety of the broader community.
The coordination of praise with calendrical and sacrificial cycles may
also reflect another type of synchronization, that between human
worshipers and angelic ones, as reflected, in both sectarian and nonsectarian prayer and praise (e.g., 11QPs[a] Hymn to the Creator;
4QDaily Prayers [4Q503]; 4QWords of the Luminaries [4Q504],
and in the Songs of the Sabbath Sacrifice).[167]

The Maskil's frame of reference is to a cycle of prayer regulated
by the calendar, though it goes beyond the scope of the popular
practices, so far as we have evidence of them, by including the
rhythms of the entire sacred calendar from days through jubilee
cycles. Also notable is the emphasis placed on points of beginning
and transition from one part of a cycle to another. Forms of רשית
and רוש occur five times, תקופה four times, אסף three times, זה לזה
twice, and מבוא once. A few lines later the Maskil uses forms of the
root בוא to coordinate the "coming" of day and night (עם מבוא יום

---

[164] Nitzan, 41–42; Falk, *Daily, Sabbath, and Festival Prayers*, 49, 114–116; also Falk,
"Qumran Prayer Texts and the Temple," 122–123.
[165] Falk, *Daily, Sabbath, and Festival Prayers*, 47.
[166] Falk, *Daily, Sabbath, and Festival Prayers*, 47.
[167] See Chazon, "Liturgical Communion with the Angels at Qumran," which
includes analysis of texts of nonsectarian provenance.

(ולילה) with his act of "entering the covenant" (אבואה בברית, i.e., reciting the Shema and the Decalogue). More broadly, the language of
the Maskil's hymn is replete with echoes of the annual covenant ceremony in which persons entered the covenant (1QS 1:16–2:26).[168]

The figure of beginning also appears significantly in lines 13–16,
where a third kind of time is introduced, time as measured by the
activities of daily human existence.

> When I begin (ברשית) to stretch out my hand or my foot I will bless
> his name,
> When I begin (ברשית) to go out or to come in, to sit or to stand or
> when I lie down on my bed, I will sing joyously to him.
> And I will bless him with the offering of the utterance of my lips in
> the ranks of men
> And before (בטרם) I lift my hand to enjoy the delicacies of the earth's
> produce.
> When dread and fear begin (ברשית) and in the place of distress and
> desolation I will bless him for his exceedingly wondrous deeds.

The passage is based on Deut 6:7, which requires that the Shema
be recited "when you stay at home and when you are away, when
you lie down and when you get up." Both Deuteronomy and the
Maskil's hymn use the figure of merismus, the naming of paired
opposites to express totality. Both begin with images of basic activity, of movement and "coming and going," but the Maskil's hymn
expands the horizon with complementary images of physical and
emotional well-being on the one hand and distress on the other.
Thus the rhythmic nature of human experience is considered to
incorporate not simply the small gestures of life but also its larger
and more public episodes. Syntactically and stylistically, the Maskil's
hymn departs from Deuteronomy's elegant use of infinitives introduced by the preposition ב ("when," "whenever"), favoring instead
ברשית ("at the beginning of"). Thus human time, like cosmic time,
is given a subtle shaping that marks the points of beginning and
transition as qualitatively significant.

It would be difficult to say if those who learned to speak in the
idioms of the figured world of Qumran would have been conscious
of this tendency, but the frequency with which language and imagery

---

[168] Weise, 67–68, 70–71, 79, n. 2; Falk, *Daily, Sabbath, and Festival Prayers,* 111,
provides a chart of verbal correspondences.

of beginnings, entries, and points of transition occur is striking.[169] I
suspect much of it was unconscious and all the more significant for
being so. Recurrent figures that show up in a variety of contexts
reflect deeply ingrained orientations. Both the sense of identity that
is gained from the reiterated action of entering the covenant and
the sense of alignment that comes from coordinating one's worship
with the beginning of each of the calendrical periods would be part
of the shape of the self formed by the figured world of the sect.

Those who study the construction of time in various human communities often pay attention to the degree to which social synchronization occurs, the degree to which persons are "in tune" with one
another. Much of this coordination happens naturally and may even
have a biological basis.[170] But it may also be specially cultivated.
Although the Maskil's hymn is articulated in terms of a personal
commitment to synchronize his praise with the rhythms of life and
of the cosmos, it is generally believed that within the sectarian community the calendrically regulated acts of praise were not individual
but communal acts.[171] Indeed, this kind of synchronization, performing an activity together, is one of the leitmotifs of Yahad society. Nowhere is it articulated more succinctly and emphatically than
in 1QS 6:2–3: "Together (יחד) they shall eat, and together (יחד) they
shall bless, and together (יחד) they shall take counsel." (Cf. the similar instruction in 6:7 concerning the requirement to read, study, and
bless "together" during one of the watches of the night.) That the
word יחד appears to be the term of self-designation for the com-

---

[169] The introductory section in col. 1 refers to "entering" and being "brought
into" the community. Columns 1–3 describe the ritual of entry into the covenant,
a ritual that was re-experienced each year; cols. 3–4 give an intellectually sophisticated account of the cosmic beginnings of the struggle between truth and perversity; col. 5 recounts the individual's entry into the community through the oath
that separates him from the men of perversity; cols. 6–7 describe the three-stage
process of entry into full membership in the community and the way in which various disciplinary problems are dealt with by returning the individual to the condition of one just entering the community; cols. 8–9 provide a programmatic account
of the beginning of an elite community dedicated to the highest ideals of the sect.
None of these sections in the Serek ha-Yahad is voiced in quite the same way;
none of them is about precisely the same thing. But in terms of a "grammar of
motives" the symbolism of entry and beginning is given a privileged place by being
repeated as a figure within diverse materials.

[170] E. Hall, 149.

[171] Falk, *Daily, Sabbath, and Festival Prayers*, 115, indicates how rare this communal practice apparently was.

munity underscores the importance of this mode of social interaction. Synchronization does not refer simply to unison activities, however, but to the coordination of activities among the members of a group. Here, too, considerable attention is given in the Serek ha-Yahad to the intentional ordering of group activities in time. In the act of taking counsel, not only do members process and seat themselves in rank order but also speak sequentially according to rank, with none permitted to interrupt one who is already speaking (6:4, 8–11). Similarly, the task of continual study of scripture is temporally coordinated, with "one man relieving his fellow" (6:7). Although any communal activity requires a measure of such coordination, the fact that it becomes a topic for explicit instruction is an index of how much synchronization was a part of the ideology as well as of the ethos of the community.

The aspect of temporal organization that has not yet been addressed is that of monochronicity and polychronicity. Without question, ancient Judea was fundamentally a polychronous society. All ancient Mediterranean societies were, and indeed that form of social time remains characteristic of many modern Mediterranean ones. Although information about ancient Israel is limited, both narrative sources and archaeology suggest as much. Open, communal spaces such as courtyards and plazas are physical arrangements that are often the concomitant of polychronous temporality.[172] Biblical narratives suggest the use of such spaces, especially the areas around the city gates, for a variety of improvisational and unscheduled activities (e.g., Ruth 4; 2 Sam 15:1–6; Jer 26:10–11). Even the temple courts were places where persons gathered for a variety of activities with varying temporal horizons (e.g., Jer 7:1; 26:2; 28:1–11; 36:8–10; Amos 7:12–13). Polychronous time is also characteristic of societies in which networks of obligation are strongly based on family and friendship relations, rather than institutional status or contractual arrangement. This is not to say that nothing is ever scheduled in such societies but rather that schedules have a low level of importance compared with the immediate claims made by one's social connections. The striking exception to this arrangement is priestly service. Whatever else might be going on in the temple courts, the sacrificial service itself is conducted according to monochronous time. The rotation of priests

---

[172] E. Hall, 44.

on duty is strictly set, sacrifices must be offered not only on set days but at set times. Nor may they be interrupted for other activities. The time of priestly service is scheduled and focused time. It drives and is driven by the concern with calendrical time.

Although priestly time intersects with the time of the populace in general through the cycle of communal ritual obligation, at Qumran monochronic priestly time is extended much more broadly into the life of the individual and the community. As noted above, the times for blessing that structure the temporality of piety are drawn from priestly calendrical time. But more generally, the orientation to time for the organization of daily activities appears to be strikingly more monochronous at Qumran than elsewhere. The scheduling of activities for various times of the day and night suggests this, as does the presence of the astronomical measuring instrument mentioned above. Not only did it measure the solstices and equinoxes but also the seasonal hours of the day, thus indicating the length of the watches of the day.[173] So, too, the concern for strict control of the agenda and speaking order in the session of the Many indicates the concern with the structured, sequential, and uninterrupted organization characteristic of monochronous time. Thus even where the events in question are not distinctively priestly, monochronic time characterizes the temporal rhythm of the sect. This culturally unusual organization of time at Qumran was an important part of their figured world. The orientation to calendrical and monochronous time was a practice that had to be learned, but that once internalized, gave the sectarians a way of experiencing themselves and of situating themselves in the world that would have set them off from other Jews, not only in conscious ideological terms but perhaps even more importantly in terms of their fundamental habitus.

The Serek ha-Yahad and the Making of Sectarians

How does one make a sectarian? In this chapter I have suggested that the process is not formally different from the ways in which a person comes to possess any cultural identity, although it does tend

---

[173] Albani and Glessmer, 112–115. They suggest that the length of the watches of the night was measured by observing the position of the stars upon the ecliptic (114).

to be more self-conscious and direct. Becoming a sectarian requires the entry into a fictive world, though fictive only in the sense that all human cultural constructions are. It is, as Dorothy Holland aptly put it, a "figured world" in which various privileged words, tropes, embedded narratives, patterns of behavior, and constructions of time create a distinctive form of reality and selfhood. By engaging in structured social practices and learning to speak the language of the figured world, the novice both receives a new identity and contributes to the construction of the community.

The Serek ha-Yahad is both an instrument in this process and a source of information about some of the other mechanisms by means of which the Yahad created and maintained sectarian identities. Although composed of a heterogeneous set of materials, excerpted and recycled from a variety of other contexts, the Serek ha-Yahad appears to have been designed as a document to aid the Maskil as he prepared himself for the task of forming the members of the community. Whether or not it was read by or to new members one cannot know. But the rhetorical structure of the document as a whole suggests it would have been apt for that purpose, since it begins with the motives that would lead a person to seek entry into the community, vividly presents the liturgy of entry, teaches about character and identity, describes the disciplines of the community and the nature of life together, and recounts the purposes and dedication to perfection of an elite community, before concluding with an account of the duties and spiritual profile of the Maskil himself. In those recensions that end with the hymn of the Maskil, the sectarian identity that had been merely described before now becomes palpable in the voice that speaks. The Serek ha-Yahad is thus roughly shaped as a virtual experience of the discourse and praxis that members would experience as they entered the community and became increasingly proficient participants in its figured world. This is so, I would argue, whether or not the descriptions in the Serek ha-Yahad reflect the precise practices of the community at any given time. What one has here is how the community represents itself to itself, not so much in terms of precise information as in ethos, values, and sensibilities.

Another way of thinking about how the Serek ha-Yahad goes about the business of making sectarians is to ask if there is some pervasive issue that recurs throughout the varied materials assembled in the document. I believe that there is and that it gives some insight into what made the selves constructed within the figured world of the Yahad distinctive. One may begin with the ways in which the text articulates the motives of the members who join and the purposes of the community. These motives are repeatedly stated but perhaps nowhere more succinctly than in the introduction to the covenant ceremony: "to do all that [God] has commanded" (1:16). The purpose of the community is reflected in the way it is referred to as "the congregation of holiness" (5:20) and in the way the elite community is referred to as "a holy house for Israel and a most holy foundation for Aaron . . . in order to make expiation for the land and pay the wicked their reward" (8:5–7). Yet in the Serek ha-Yahad there is virtually no discussion of specific torot or rules of purity, such as one finds, for instance, in the Temple Scroll. Making a sectarian is not simply a matter of filling him with content. The Serek ha-Yahad is rather preoccupied with those preconditions that must be in place if the community and its members are to fulfill their purposes. Two things are necessary for the person who would do all that God has commanded: knowledge and discipline. As I have argued above, drawing on Foucault, these are not distinct and autonomous matters but are two sides of one coin. Thus what seems to underlie the selection and shaping of materials for the Serek ha-Yahad is a concern for instilling in the sectarian the character that is receptive to the community's discipline, the knowledge that makes the disciplines both necessary and desirable, and a sense of how the disciplines produce a community "perfect in all that has been revealed from the whole law" (8:1–2).

To this end the introduction to the Serek ha-Yahad describes the necessity for new members to bring knowledge, ability, and (mental) capacity into the community to be discplined and purified (1:11–13). But it also models the way in which entry into the community will take the very language that the person speaks and discipline it to the idioms and modes of categorization that characterize the sect. From this new way of speaking and perceiving, the sectarian gains the kind of knowledge he needs in order to be receptive to the disciplines of the community.

Similarly, while the account of the covenant ceremony in 1:16–3:12 rhetorically imitates the entry into the community, the discussion is shaped to focus on acceptable and unacceptable forms of character. Both the hypocrite (2:11–18) and the recalcitrant (2:25–3:6) have an immunity to discipline that makes them dangerous to the purposes of the community. By "contrasting" those character types and their exclusion from the community by curse and rejection with the submissive character who receives purification from his iniquities and the reward of "looking on the light of life" (3:7), the sectarian is persuaded to become the type of person amenable to the disciplines of the sect.

The Two Spirits Treatise is, I have argued, not simply a piece of anthropological and cosmological speculation but, as Foucault put it, "what one must know about oneself" in order to renounce those things required by sectarian discipline. It establishes the "connection" between the very specific behavioral and dispositional features of good and bad character and the mysteries of the plan of God. Thus the disciplines of the community can be experienced not simply as impositions of the community upon one's will and desire but as nothing less than salvific.

The various sections in the Serek ha-Yahad concerning community practices and procedures (5:1–9:11) are the most explicitly concerned with disciplinary matters, taking discipline in the broad sense in which Foucault uses it. In these sections one sees most clearly that the concern for the discipline of the individual does not emerge out of the kind of self-culture one might find in a Greco-Roman context. Rather the community and its work are primary. That the individuals are components of this primary entity is nowhere better seen than in the way the disciplined order of the assemblies is described, with the results of the individual examinations displayed in the hierarchical order of seating and speaking. In ways that bear analogy to the disciplinary institutions of armies or factories—or indeed to machines—it is the way in which the finely tooled parts work together that produces what the institution or machine was intended to do. So the Yahad—composed of individuals shaped by disciplines of the community, examined and ranked according to knowledge and deeds, and taking counsel together in a carefully regulated fashion—is able to generate the knowledge of torah and the judgment concerning persons and their deeds that result in the creation of a community of holiness capable of walking perfectly in torah. As a result of the interaction between its knowledge and its disciplines, the community can effect what the compromised temple cannot: expiation for the land.

The Maskil is a figure who can be described not only as an apotheosis of sectarian selfhood but of the sect itself, and fittingly, the

materials pertaining to the Maskil conclude the Serek ha-Yahad
(9:12–11:22). He is the master of all revealed torah, the knowledge
of the ages, and the rule for each time. Many of the roles earlier
attributed to the community as a whole concerning the admission,
ranking, and regulation of members are here attributed to the Maskil.
This is most likely not a matter of differing practices but a rhetorical condensation of the work of the community in its highest ranking figure. If he can be seen to personify the community, he also
serves as the model for a subjectivity fully formed by the knowledge
and disciplines of the community. The values, affects, and commitments articulated in his hymn form a template for the other members of the sect as they attempt to internalize the sectarian identities
offered to them in the figured world of the Yahad.

Hearing a ranking figure speak can be an important instrument
for forming identity, but a much more powerful instrument is being
called upon to speak about oneself in the presence of a community.
This, too, was one of the means by which the Yahad made sectarians, not just in the annual examinations but also in the religious
poems of the Hodayot, the subject of the following two chapters.

CHAPTER FIVE

WHAT DO HODAYOT DO?
LANGUAGE AND THE CONSTRUCTION OF THE
SELF IN SECTARIAN PRAYER

My question about what Hodayot do is not a new one. Hans Bardtke posed it and gave a tentative answer almost a half century ago, when he suggested that the Hodayot be understood as a collection of spiritual exercises. Bardtke observed that the repetition of various forms and images and even of particular emotional patterns in the Hodayot served to shape the beliefs and religious affections of those who read them.[1] Unfortunately, critical response to Bardtke's article focused narrowly on the question of personal versus cultic use of the Hodayot to the neglect of the much more important matter of discovering the specific ways in which the Hodayot formed and reformed their readers. Perhaps the intellectual climate was not right. In recent years, however, the question of the social function of texts in the formation of self-identity has been of increasing interest in the social sciences and in biblical studies.[2]

SELVES, SUBJECTS, SYMBOLS, AND WORLDS

The terminologies by which scholars speak of the formation of selves are varied and not always consistent. Some prefer to speak of "identity," others of "the person" or "the self," and still others of "subjectivity." Terms may be used interchangeably or strictly differentiated. What is at issue may vary with whether the scholar is a social psychologist

---

[1] "En d'autres termes, la récitation répétée de ces pièces représentait un exercice spirituel de grande envergure, qui, à travers une masse et formes d'images des plus variées, lui inculquait de façon permanente et réitérée une seule et même conviction de portée religieuse," Bardtke, "Considérations," 231.

[2] See, Carrithers, Collins, and Lukes, eds., *The Category of the Person: Anthropology, Philosophy, History*; Aune and McCarthy, eds., *The Whole and Divided Self: The Bible and Theological Anthropology*, and Baumgarten, Assman, and Stroumsa, eds., *Self, Soul and Body in Religious Experience*.

or an anthropologist, a culturalist or a constructivist.[3] In this study I tend to use the terms more or less interchangeably, though I find subjectivity to be a particularly helpful concept. It is a slippery term, however, and requires clear definition. In the sense in which I am using it, subjectivity refers to the culturally specific ways in which the meaning of one's self is produced, experienced, and articulated.

Several important points follow from these observations. First, subjectivity, no matter now natural it feels to an individual, is not natural but rather belongs to the sphere of the symbolic. It is a matter of representation. A person's sense of self is not just given as a part of physical existence but is constructed through the symbolic practices of a person's culture. Language is by far the most important of these symbolic practices, though other nonlinguistic symbolic practices (e.g., class, ethnic, and gender specific systems of garments and body posture) also play significant roles in constructing subjectivity.

It is not just language as such that is crucial for the formation of subjects but language as discourse, the way in which language is used to give meaning to the world, to organize it, to structure institutions and behaviors. These historically specific forms of discourse offer a person access to meaning: a sense of who one is, what experiences mean, what matters and what does not, how one is related to others, how the world works. This sense of who one is, is thus not produced in isolation from other social constructions but rather as part of them. The terms, metaphors, and images that construct a certain kind of self imply a corresponding kind of society and vice versa. In thinking about the relation of subjectivity to social discourses one begins to notice a certain double meaning in the word. On the one hand subjectivity connotes an active relation to meaning and so a kind of empowerment (to be a subject rather than an object). On the other hand it connotes a subordinate position (to be subject to a particular construction of meaning and possibility and constrained by it).[4] Because meaning is so intimately related to the distribution of power in a society, subjectivity, too, is implicated in the ways in which power is distributed, retained, or redistributed.

Consequently, it is important to remember that subjectivity is not

---

[3] For a review of some of these differences, see Holland et al., 3–18.

[4] This distinction is usually traced back to Althusser, *Lenin and Philosophy*, 169, 182, though it has become a fairly commonplace notion in recent writing about the self.

just a symbolic formation but a socially symbolic formation. This is not to imply that subjectivity is produced merely as a product or by-product of a general cultural conversation. The forms of subjectivity available in a culture are elements of its active discourse. As with other symbolic structures, the self may become the representational space in which the fundamental tensions within the culture are symbolically explored. In fact, such appears to be very much the case with one of the representations of the self at Qumran, as I have attempted to show above in chapter 3.

It is equally important to remember that there is never just one language of the self in a society, but rather multiple languages. Consequently, persons are "composites of many, often contradictory, self-understandings and identities . . . few of which are completely durable."[5] This fact is central to the social significance of forms of subjectivity. Sometimes these multiple, and often conflicting, languages of the self are compartmentalized in particular social roles, so that an individual can move from one to the other without being aware of it. But there are also situations in which tensions between rival constructions of the self can become self-conscious and acute. In these circumstances the cultivation of a distinctive subjectivity may be an act of cultural resistance. By nurturing a distinctive discourse of the self, one is progressively alienated from a socially dominant language of the self or from a previous sense of self. The content and structure of this new subjectivity serves as a condensed critique of the dominant culture.[6] With respect to the Qumran community, its status as a sectarian religious movement means that the cultivation of a language of the self would have been crucial both for the formation of its own social cohesiveness and for its role in contesting other constructions of meaning in the discursive community of Second Temple Judaism.

THE FORMATION OF SUBJECTIVITY AT QUMRAN

The Qumran community had to be intentional and explicit in the formation of the subjectivity of its members. As a voluntary society

---

[5] Holland et al., 8.
[6] See further the subsection in chapter 1, "Bespoken and Speaking: Discourse and Subjectivity."

with a sectarian character, it had to detach members from their prior identities and offer them new ones. They had to be made into subjects of a new discourse. In general, societies cohere and can reproduce themselves to the extent that members find their subject positions persuasive. The process begins so early in a person's life and is reinforced from so many directions that the discursive formation of subjectivity is rendered almost invisible. A person's subjectivity has a quality of obviousness and inevitability. The task of a sectarian community is twofold. It must simultaneously undermine the sense of obvious inevitability that characterizes the subjectivity created by the dominant discourse and provide a new subjectivity that is compellingly persuasive. The reason that the formation of the subject has to become so intentional in a sectarian community is not just that the society is often concerned with adult converts. It is also because the sect exists as a marginal phenomenon. Even for persons raised in Essene households in the villages and towns of Judea, the discourses of dominant non-Essene Judaism implicitly called into question the plausibility of Essene life. The formation of an alternative subjectivity is part of the counter-discourse of the sect, that is, the way it challenges structures of meaning taken for granted in other Jewish communities. This phenomenon is not hard to recognize in obviously polemical language, in formulations like "children of light and children of darkness." It is, however, equally if more subtly present in ostensibly nonpolemical aspects of the discourse of the self, such as the denial of an autonomous moral will, which one finds in some Qumran texts, or the cultivation of the masochistic sublime, illustrated in the Maskil's hymn. The restructuring of the self that takes place through these nonpolemical elements also serves to estrange the subject from the world outside the sect. The self who is formed in this way now has dispositions, desires, motivations, and behaviors that are incompatible with other discourses. The discourses that had previously formed a person's identity now appear inadequate. One ceases to feel at home in them or in the institutions founded on and supported by them.

The new identities offered by the Qumran community were not, of course, absolutely new. In developing its repertoire of terms and images of self-representation the Qumran community drew on highly traditional languages of the self, grounded in the familiar idioms of prayer and worship, wisdom instruction, cultic language, and much more. It is actually quite difficult to isolate elements that could be identified as unique in the discourse of the self at Qumran. Yet no one can read the Qumran sectarian literature without sensing the distinctive quality of the subjectivity it sought to produce. What happens in the language of the self at Qumran is precisely what Bakhtin called reaccentuation.[7] Ordinary words, words traditionally important for self-representation, such as "righteousness" or "spirit" may be given a slightly different nuance by being associated with a different range of terms or employed in unusual constructions. Emphases may be different. Not infrequently in the Hodayot the conventional exaggeration of pious cliches (e.g., "no one can direct his steps") may be taken not in the ordinary sense as a loose expression of pious humility but as the very basis for understanding one's situation.

The presence of traditional elements is extremely important. They allow a person entry into the discourse because of their familiarity and the value already attached to them. In the reaccentuation of terms, however, and in the new utterance that is constructed out of these traditional elements, it is possible to create the sense that one is only now understanding the true meaning of words that had long been familiar and important. The subject who is called into being is also experienced as at once familiar and new, a self that is recognizable but truly known for the first time.

One cannot give any adequate account of the formation of subjectivity at Qumran. That subjectivity was produced by the entire range of practices, utterances, and symbolic enactments that took place in the community. Everything from the etiquette among members in formal and informal settings, to the symbolism of ceremonial occasions, to the texts of prayers and hymns, to the organization of time, space, gestures, and clothing, and much, much more contributed to the formation of the way in which the sectarian represented himself to himself and to others. Concerning some of this we have limited information: from the Serek ha-Yahad (*if* it mirrors actual practices) and from Josephus (*if* he is speaking—and speaking accurately—about Qumran or a community closely related to it). Much that it would be necessary to know, however, is no longer accessible at all, because it was simply part of the texture of everyday life that is not preserved in any record. Moreover, even in a sectarian community it would be necessary to reckon with the existence

---

[7] Bakhtin, *Dialogical Imagination*, 290.

of multiple languages of the self, especially in a community that had a historical existence of over 200 years.[8]

Clearly, some kinds of questions cannot be answered because we no longer possess all the information we would need. What we do possess are some of the central writings of the Qumran community. The proper question is not one about the formation of subjectivity at Qumran in some complete sense but the formation of subjectivity in a particular text, such as the Hodayot or the Serek ha-Yahad. This narrower focus on the way in which a discourse of the self is developed in a particular text or form of speech is not a terribly disappointing restriction, since the Serek ha-Yahad and the Hodayot are both texts that are self-consciously devoted to the formation of languages of self and community. In this chapter the focus will be on the Hodayot. In order to address the question of the formation of subjectivity in the Hodayot, however, one must first pose some preliminary questions.

HODAYOT: AUTHORSHIP, REDACTION, AND *SITZ IM LEBEN*

For present purposes it really does not matter who wrote the Hodayot. The issue of authorship per se would matter only if one held to a romantic model of authorship and expressive subjectivity. Some of those assumptions can in fact be detected in the scholarly literature that asserts that in the Hodayot we have a record of the unique and personal experiences of the Righteous Teacher.[9] That position, at least in its pure form, is now seldom seriously advocated.[10] It has largely been replaced by a much more sophisticated question about the persona or personae who are represented by the "I" of the Hodayot. Whoever wrote them, does the "I" of the Hodayot, or at

---

[8] Lichtenberger's analytical work on the anthropology of Qumran, *Studien zum Menschenbild in Texten der Qumrangemeinde*, provides an inventory of many of the languages of the self employed in Qumran literature.

[9] See, e.g., Carmignac and Guilbert, *Les textes de Qumran*, I, 132–33. Similarly, Jeremias (*Der Lehrer der Gerechtigkeit*, 264), concerning those compositions he believes written by the Righteous Teacher, says that "Wir haben damit die Psalmen, in denen wir mit Sicherheit den Lehrer der Gerechtigkeit als Verfasser erkannten, besprochen. . . . [S]ie zugleich einen Einblick in das Fühlen und Wollen ihres Verfassers erlaubten."

[10] This notion has been recently revived in Michael Wise's "novelization" of the life of the Teacher of Righteousness in *The First Messiah*.

least some of them, refer to the Righteous Teacher? The case for distinguishing the Hodayot into two groups, generally identified as the Hodayot of the Teacher and the Hodayot of the community, has been made persuasively by Jeremias and refined by many others.[11] Whether and how this first group of Hodayot refers particularly to the Righteous Teacher is a question that I will take up in the next chapter. It is evident, however, that in a number of the compositions the persona of the speaker is that of a persecuted leader of the community, whether the Righteous Teacher or some other figure. These I take to comprise 1QH^a 10:3–19; 12:5–13:4; 13:5–19; 13:20–15:5; 15:6–25; 16:4–17:36.[12] The arrangement of materials in the various manuscripts from Caves 1 and 4 show a tendency to group the hymns of the leader together. In 1QH^a these cluster in cols. 10–17.[13] Whether all of the compositions in these columns pertain to the leader, however, remains uncertain.

Should the compositions pertaining to the leader be set aside as not bearing on the formation of the subjectivity of the "ordinary" sectarian? I think not. Even if they are understood as representing the perspective of a leadership class or of a single, historical leader, they would still be in many respects a model of ideal sectarian subjectivity. To be sure, a leader would have certain roles that the ordinary sectarian would not be expected to fill, but even in his distinctive situation and experiences the leader would embody exemplary characteristics

---

[11] See Jeremias, *Der Lehrer der Gerechtigkeit*; Becker, *Das Heil Gottes*; Kuhn, *Enderwartung und Gegenwärtiges Heil*. But note the reservations of Puech, *La croyance*, 336–38. The most recent examination of the issues is the dissertation of Michael Douglas, "Wisdom, Power and Praise in the Hodayot: A Literary Critical Study of 1QH 9:1–18:14." The circulation of the dissertation is currently restricted, however, so I was unable to examine Douglas's arguments.

[12] The column numbers are given according to the reconstruction of the scroll by Puech, "Quelques aspects," and by Stegemann, "Material Reconstruction," 272–74. Since no edition of 1QH^a with the line numbers reconstructed by Puech and Stegemann has yet been published, I follow the practice adopted by García Martínez and Tigchelaar, *The Dead Sea Scrolls Study Edition*, in which the column numbers reflect the reconstruction of Puech and Stegemann, but the line numbers remain the same as in the edition of Sukenik. This practice is also followed in Abegg, *The Dead Sea Scrolls Concordance*.

The transcriptions in this study are based on the photographs and initial transcription of Sukenik. I have also made considerable use of the excellent transcriptions of García Martínez and Tigchelaar, and the transcriptions and notes of Puech in "Quelques aspects," "Un hymne essénien," and *La croyance*. A new critical edition with high quality photographs is much to be desired.

[13] Schuller, "Hodayot," 74.

and dispositions that the composition would offer as an ideal model of proper sectarian character. Portraits are also mirrors. Nevertheless, I reserve those texts that directly speak of the relation of the leader to the community for examination in the following chapter. They provide an insight into different aspects of the dynamics of sectarian life than are available in the rest of the material.

The remainder of the Hodayot do not form a homogeneous collection. In most cases, however, although one can observe different thematic or stylistic groupings, there is no reason for assuming that the "I" of the text represents a figure other than an ordinary member of the community. Four of the compositions, however, are introduced by the heading למשכיל ("by" or "for" the Maskil; see 1QH^a 5:1; 7:11; 20:4; 25:10), and a fifth describes responsibilities that the Serek ha-Yahad assigns to the Maskil (1QS 6:8–22). Although his responsibilities differ from those of the ordinary sectarian, his character is described in terms similar to those used in the community hymns.[14] One quite unusual hodayah, which does not match the motif and linguistic profile of either the Hodayot of the community or of the persecuted leader, speaks in exalted terms of the speaker's place "among the heavenly beings" (1QH^a 26:24–27?; 4QH^a frag. 7). The referent of this "self-glorification" poem remains debated.[15] The publication of the Cave 4 Hodayot fragments have shown that the collections of Hodayot differed from one another, both in terms of the extent of the collections and the arrangement of the compositions within the collections. Since I am concerned with representative motifs within individual hodayah rather than with the principles of organization of the collections themselves, these differences do not affect my inquiry.

The issue of the *Sitz im Leben* of the Hodayot is both more complex and more significant for the question of the construction of subjectivity than the issue of authorship. To understand what is involved requires some thought about the nature of the pronoun "I," the linguistic basis of subjectivity, and the relationship between readers and texts. The work of French linguist Emile Benveniste and its adap-

---

[14] Puech ("Hodayot," 366–7) suggests that these headings may not be attributions of particular compositions to the Maskil but rather rubrics that serve to divide 1QH^a into five sections, perhaps in imitation of the five books of the biblical Psalms.
[15] See the discussion and references in Schuller, "Some Contributions," 282–283.

tation by literary and film critic Kaja Silverman are extremely helpful for revealing what is at stake. Benveniste's work draws attention
to the linguistic peculiarity of the pronouns "I" and "you."[16] These
pronouns do not refer to a concept in the way that a word like
"tree" does but "to something very peculiar which is exclusively linguistic: *I* refers to the act of individual discourse in which it is pronounced, and by this it designates the speaker. . . . The reality to
which it refers is the reality of the discourse. . . . And so it is literally true that the basis of subjectivity is in the exercise of language."[17]

What Benveniste is pointing to is the fact that the pronouns "I" and
"you" are empty markers that can only be filled in concrete instances
of discourse. "I" simply means the one who says "I." It is through
instances of discourse that a speaker establishes his or her identity.
Benveniste uses the term "speaking subject" to refer to the person
who produces the speech—the one who is the referent of the signifier
"I" in the act of discourse. He uses the term "subject of speech" to
refer to the "I" as signifier. The "subject of speech" is the pronoun
itself but more generally can be thought of as the representation the
speaker makes for himself or herself in the speech—all the elements
that stand in for the speaker at the level of the discourse. Clearly,
Benveniste is basing his analysis on everyday, conversational discourse. But the Hodayot, as written texts, are not everyday discourse.
In order to make use of Benveniste's insights into the relationship
of subjectivity and the pronoun "I," one has to consider the way
the peculiarities of literary texts affect the problem. Here the work
of Kaja Silverman is important.

Silverman is not interested simply in instances of first-person speech
but rather in how literary texts of all sorts form subjectivity. She
sees in Benveniste's analysis a structure that can illumine this process.
Silverman suggests that a third category needs to be added to
Benveniste's "speaking subject" and "subject of speech." She would
add the category "spoken subject."[18] This refers to the subject constituted by identification with the subject of speech. This multipli-
cation of categories may seem irritatingly obscure and jargony, but
it proves very useful in sorting out what goes on in the process of

[16] Benveniste, "The Nature of Pronouns" and "Subjectivity in Language," in *Problems in General Linguistics*, 217–230.
[17] Benveniste, 226.
[18] Silverman, 43–53, 194–201, esp. p. 47.

reading a text and the way in which it forms subjectivity. In everyday conversation, such as Benveniste considered, the speaking subject, the subject of speech, and the spoken subject coincide, that is,
the speaking subject *is* the one who performs the act of identification
with the subject of speech. I am the one speaking; the pronoun "I"
refers back to me; and I identify myself with that pronoun and what
I predicate in relation to it. But in literary texts (poems, narratives,
films, etc.) that is not necessarily the case. Instead the three subjects
are generally distinguishable. Although the parallels are not exact, it
may help to think of the speaking subject as equivalent to the
author/implied author (as the producer of the speech), the subject
of speech as the narrator or central character, and the spoken subject as the reader who is invited to identify with the central character or narrating voice.

   The process by which this act of identification is produced is
referred to as "suture," the investment that an individual makes in
the subject position offered to him or her within a given discourse.[19]
The outcome of successful suture is that the reader/hearer/viewer
agrees to be "spoken" by the text, agrees to be represented by the
signifiers of the discourse. The consequence of suture is that the
reader gains access to a symbolic order, the symbolic order of the text,
and so becomes a subject in that discourse. The presence of the subject in the discourse is not direct, however, but always mediated by
that linguistic "substitute" or "stand in." This may be a pronoun
("I"), a personal name ("Carol"), a term of classification ("citizen"),
a fictional character ("Robinson Crusoe"), and so forth. The formation of subjectivity in a symbolic order depends upon the subject's willingness to become absent to itself by permitting a fictional
character, sometimes simply called "I," to stand in for it. In much
of Deuteronomy, for instance, the speaking subject is Moses (or the
implied author), the subject of speech is "you," and the spoken subject is the reader or hearer who agrees to be represented by the
pronoun "you." In order to have access to the world of meaning
structured in Deuteronomy and to have a place in it, the reader/hearer
has to become absent to himself/herself and allow that character
"you" to represent him or her.[20]

---

[19] S. Hall, 6.
[20] The process described here is somewhat oversimplified and suggests a once-
and-for-all process of identification. Although generally sympathetic to the psycho-

The structure by which the subject is formed through language is the same whether one is talking about everyday speech or literary texts; but the degree of identification is not the same. It is for this reason that the question of *Sitz im Leben* is important for the issue of the formation of subjectivity in the Hodayot. The Hodayot and other first person singular texts like them present some distinctive features. As literary texts the Hodayot are not simply everyday speech. The question is whether they are more like "Now I lay me down to sleep" or "Call me Ishmael." Consider for a moment a text like a traditional prayer ("Now I lay me down to sleep") or a creed ("I believe in God the Father Almighty") or a pledge ("I pledge allegiance to the flag"). Such first person texts are tremendously powerful agents for the formation of subjectivity because they combine aspects of everyday speech and literary speech. As in everyday speech, the speaking subject (the one who recites) and the spoken subject (the one who agrees to be represented) coincide. When I say, "Now I lay me down to sleep," the signifier "I" refers to me, not to the anonymous person who first wrote it. As with literary texts, however, the symbolic order constituted through "Now I lay me down to sleep" (the childlike ethos of its rhythms and rhymes, the simple piety, the orientation to death, the belief in a soul that is the essence of the self and that survives the body, etc.) comes already formed. In order to pray that prayer I have to become absent to myself (that is, to a self formed through other discourses and symbolic orders) and allow the signifier "I" and all that is predicated of it to stand in for me. Another way of putting it would be to say that such a speech act strategically obscures who the speaking subject is. It is precisely this ambiguity about *whose* words these are that makes such a first-person singular prayer, creed, or pledge so powerful an instrument in the formation of subjectivity.[21]

---

dynamic approach of Silverman and Hall, Holland et al., depend more on the Bakhtinian notion of the "authoring" of a self in a dialogic process. They make the following suggestion: "A better metaphor for us is not suture, which makes the person and the position seem to arrive preformed at the moment of suturing, but codevelopment—the linked development of people, cultural forms, and social positions in particular historical worlds" (33).

[21] One can—and often does—repeat such prayers, creeds, or pledges in a rote fashion. There is no magical process involved here. But for those for whom these texts are meaningful, the way the subject is located in identification with the "I" of the speech is fundamental to the effectiveness of such speech practices.

But now one must return to the question: Are the Hodayot more like "Now I lay me down to sleep" or "Call me Ishmael"? Do they summon one to identify *with* the "I" or *as* the "I" of the speech? In either case the Hodayot are important in the formation of subjectivity but they would do their work in different ways depending on how they were read. This question is an extremely difficult one to answer because we have almost no information about how the Hodayot were used. There have been various suggestions: that they were recited as part of the annual covenant ceremony, that they were the texts of communal daily prayers, that they were recited at meals, that they were read privately, or that there were multiple occasions for use. The suggestion that seems to me most plausible is that originally made by Bo Reike.[22] Reike drew attention to Philo's description of the banquets of the Therapeutae and Therapeutroides. At those banquets, when the exposition of scripture is concluded, the head of the community "rises and sings a hymn composed in honor of the Deity, either a new one of his own composition, or an old one by poets of an earlier age" (*Vit. Cont.* 80; trans. Winston). Following him, other members of the community would sing hymns as well. Reike suggested that the communal meals at Qumran provided a similar occasion for which the prayers of the Hodayot might have been written and recited.

If Reike is correct, then the Hodayot (at least those called the Hodayot of the community) would be like "Now I lay me down to sleep" in that a prayer from the collection could be selected as the individual's "own" prayer. Even if one assumes a form of use in which a designated reciter read the Hodayot at the covenant ceremony or for daily worship, it still seems that in hearing the words spoken each individual would have understood them as prototypical rather than as unique to the reciter. For the purposes of this analysis I am adopting Reike's suggestion as my working hypothesis.[23] Even if this reconstruction of the *Sitz im Leben* should turn out not to have been the case, the basic thrust of my argument would not be affected. However they were read or recited, repeated exposure

---

[22] Reike, "Remarques sur l'histoire de la form (Formgeschichte) des textes de Qumran."

[23] How the Hodayot of the persecuted leader fit Reike's suggestion is taken up in the next chapter.

to the Hodayot would have created what Geertz calls a template, "inducing in the worshiper a certain distinctive set of dispositions . . . which lend a chronic character to the flow of his activity and the quality of his experience."[24]

I do not want to lose sight, however, of Reike's suggestion that, on the analogy of what Philo reports of the Therapeutae, the Hodayot may not have been simply a textual corpus for reading and reciting, but perhaps a collection of models for oral performance. The repeated and even stereotypical set of topoi, motifs, concepts, and patterns of emotion that one finds in the Hodayot suggests that there was a communal understanding of the patterned way in which one should give thanks to God and describe one's experience and sense of identity. Having heard enough of these prayers, it would not be difficult to compose one that fit the model. Holland and her associates noted a similar phenomenon in their study of the genre of personal stories in Alcoholics Anonymous groups. Alcoholics Anonymous is a type of figured world, which "has constructed a particular interpretation of what it means to be an alcoholic, what typical alcoholics are like, and what kinds of incidents mark a typical alcoholic's life."[25] Since no one is born into the figured world of Alcoholics Anonymous, its cultural system and the AA identity must be learned. Although there are a variety of modes for such learning (for example, AA literature, relations with sponsors), one particularly important means of appropriating the identity is learning to tell one's "personal story." Although there is no explicit instruction, a new AA member learns by listening to others and then by beginning to articulate his own experience in the forms and categories he has heard. The telling of such stories is interactive in AA meetings, with older members challenging "inappropriate" narratives by new members and recalling their own past erroneous interpretations of events in their lives and by reinforcing what has been appropriately narrated. Gradually the new member comes to appropriate as his or her own the identity and figured world of AA. The structures and processes of AA meetings and an ancient Jewish sectarian community can scarcely be

---

[24] Geertz, *Interpretation of Cultures*, 95. One might compare Holm-Nielsen's discussion of the "I" of the Hodayot as a distributive "I" that represents the community as such and thereby also each individual member of it ("Ich" in den Hodajoth und die Qumrangemeinde," 222).

[25] Holland et al., 66.

directly compared, but the fundamental elements of identity formation are not all that different. Not only did the sectarian learn the
outlines of the typical sectarian identity from compositions like the
Hodayot, but through the disciplines of rebuke and examination
described in the Serek ha-Yahad he also learned which were considered inappropriate or erroneous articulations of his experience and
which were well received and rewarded by his fellows.

The effects on identity formation of such public performance should
not be underestimated. As Holland and colleagues note, "As a public event, one that is not only observable but material and co-par-
ticipatory, the telling encompasses body practices, including vocalization,
that realize structures of affect and disposition. Not only social the-
orists, from Durkheim and Mauss to Bourdieu, but any participant
in such performances would tell you that the fellow-feeling born in
these ceremonies is a powerful means of identification."[26] Although
one cannot know how Hodayot were used at Qumran, my working
hypothesis will be that they originated in just such events of oral
composition in communal settings and that a certain number of them
were written down and collected in the various versions of the
Hodayot found in Caves 1 and 4. The resulting collections were
probably used in a variety of ways, though I find no reason to think
that the written collections would have displaced oral practices. All
of this, however, must remain in the realm of reasoned speculation.

"I" AND "YOU" IN THE HODAYOT

I refer to the Hodayot as "prayer," using that term broadly to designate language addressed to God, not merely precative language.
In asking about the formation of subjectivity through the Hodayot,
it is crucial to take account of how that particular form of speech
is involved. Although the prayer of the Hodayot is uninterrupted
and continuous, it is not, as Fisch has properly observed about the
Psalms, a monologue.[27] Indeed, monologue is a category that has
been rather thoroughly eroded in recent discussions about language.
It is by now a commonplace to say that all our utterances are implic-

---

[26] Holland et al., 87.
[27] Fisch, 108.

itly addressed to an other. Even speech to oneself can be recognized as inherently dialogical, an "I" talking to its "me," as Kenneth Burke says, quoting Herbert Mead.[28] Even though all speech may have dialogical elements, there are obviously different degrees to which the character of the word as addressed may be marked in various genres. Prayer by its very nature is highly explicit in its orientation to an other. One of the principal effects of this self-conscious awareness of the other is that the speaker constitutes himself in the gaze of and at least in part from the perspective of this other. In addressing God the speaker becomes aware of how he must appear in the eyes of God, an awareness that is present in the words themselves and thus in the "verbal shape" the speaker assumes in the discourse.[29]

The relationship of speaker and addressee in prayer is in many ways a special case of dialogical speech. Although in general one's words and the verbal shape one gives oneself will change depending on whether one addresses someone of higher or lower status, an intimate or a stranger, the language of prayer implies a uniquely definitive relationship. The radically other quality of the addressee of prayer means that the speaker is constituted not as tenant or landlord, daughter-in-law or matriarch, but *as such*, as a person. Armed with the tools of a hermeneutics of suspicion, modern critics are inclined to dispute the universalizing pretense of the discourse of prayer. All kinds of social hierarchies and interests are smuggled into the language of prayer, critics claim; and indeed they are. The specific social interests and identities of the Qumran community saturate the language of the Hodayot. But the relationship between speaker and addressee in prayer tends to mask these social dimensions precisely because of the universal and absolute quality of the speech situation. Consequently, the language of prayer with its address to an absolute "you" is a very powerful instrument for the formation of subjectivity.

---

[28] Burke, *Philosophy of Literary Form*, 380.

[29] Cf. Voloshinov's comments (86): "Orientation of the word toward the addressee has an extremely high significance. In point of fact, a *word is a two-sided act* . . . As word it is precisely *the product of the reciprocal relationship between speaker and listener, addresser and addressee.* Each and every word expresses the "one" in relation to the "other." I give myself verbal shape from another's point of view, ultimately from the point of view of the community to which I belong. A word is a bridge thrown between myself and another. If one end of the bridge depends on me, then the other depends on my addressee. A word is territory shared by both addresser and addressee, by a speaker and his interlocutor" (emphasis in the original).

Prayer also differs from many ordinary forms of address in the degree to which the identity and character of the "I" and the "you" are the explicit topics of discourse. They are not, of course, equally represented or of the same significance in the discourse of prayer. At least in the biblical tradition, prayer begins with the address to and characterization of God. In prayers of praise, such as the Hodayot, explicit discourse about God often dominates. Since I am specifically concerned with the formation of sectarian subjectivity, it is not the construction of the image of God per se that interests me; rather it is in the ways in which the act of constructing that image simultaneously constructs the speaker. Equally important is paying attention to the precise ways in which the speaker inserts himself explicitly into the discourse of the prayer. One can see this, for instance, in the way in which the opening address of the Hodayot defines a subject position for the speaker.

As is well known, all the preserved introductory formulas of the Hodayot are variations of "I thank you, O Lord, that . . ." or "Blessed are you, O my God, because. . . ." Even though the compositions do not imitate the form of the classical thanksgiving psalm, the introductory formulas orient the reader to thanksgiving as the paradigmatic mode of experience. From the variety of relationships between worshiper and God in the repertoire of biblical tradition the Qumran community has selected one—benefaction—as its privileged expression. Although a variety of moods, attitudes, and expressions occur in the Hodayot, they are all subordinated to the fundamental relationship established in the opening words that cast the speaker in the role of recipient.[30] The divine gift is variously described: as deliverance from deadly peril, as a spirit of insight that transforms the speaker, as pardon for sin, as election to the lot of the righteous, and so forth. All that follows is an exploration of the significance of the fundamental characterization of the speaker as recipient of a divine gift. That is what constitutes him as subject.

---

[30] The examination by Schuller ("Petitionary Prayer," 38–42) of petitionary elements in the Hodayot only confirms the dominance of praise over petition. Both the frequency of praise in relation to petition and the nature of the things asked for contrast sharply with the repertoire one might find, for instance, in the biblical book of Psalms. Similarly, Knohl ("Between Voice and Silence," 29) observes that the doctrine of predestination at Qumran "did not allow for petitional prayer in the usual sense of the word." One might only pray for the very things for which the speaker elsewhere gives thanks.

This is not to say that no one in Israel felt thankful to God before the Qumran community. The point is rather about the *syntax* of religious speech. In the biblical tradition psalms of thanksgiving are linked with psalms of complaint as correlated forms of speech. The thanksgiving may even explicitly recall the previous appeal. "Yahweh my God, I cried out to you, and you healed me" (Ps 30:3). More broadly, Israel's praise frequently recalled past deliverance, the memory of which formed the basis for present appeals. The "conversation" with God involved both stances. At Qumran that link does not exist. It is not by mere chance that the Qumran community did not produce a collection of texts that began "Hear my cry, O Lord." To be sure, lament *motifs* are used in the Hodayot but they are contained within the frame of thanksgiving. Moreover, even in the recollection of distress, there is seldom a recollection of a cry for help—at most the speaker represents himself as having "held fast." Where thanksgiving and complaint exist as two parts of a single religious orientation, such as Jacobsen has illumined in his study of personal religion in Mesopotamia and Israel,[31] the thanksgiving has one meaning. Where the connection is broken and thanksgiving alone is present, it has a different meaning and different implications for the formation of subjectivity. The speaker in the biblical lament or thanksgiving is a moral agent in his own story: although he may be vulnerable, he cries out and is answered. That is not the case at Qumran. As will be seen more clearly in the analysis of the first hodayah discussed below, he is not an agent but an agency through whom God works.

Another aspect of the subject position of the speaker in the Hodayot bears comparison with the speaker in the Psalms, and not just in the psalms of thanksgiving. Like the speaker in the Psalms, the speaker in the Hodayot is a witness, one who testifies about what God has done. Both the Psalms and the Hodayot locate an important part of the speaker's subjectivity in this very act of declaring.[32] Because the subject's relation to his own experience is different in the Psalms and in the Hodayot, so the nature and significance of his testimony will be different. In the psalms of thanksgiving the psalmist characteristically glorifies God as one who "has not hidden his face from

---

[31] Jacobsen, *Treasures of Darkness*, 147–164.
[32] For the relationship of speaking and subjectivity in the biblical Psalms, see Fisch, 115–17, 134.

[the afflicted], but has heard, when he cried to him" (Ps 22:24b). Thus the psalmist becomes not only an agent in his own deliverance but through his testimony also becomes an agent in building up the larger community of worshipers (as in Ps 22:27–31). The sectarian's formative moment is not that of crying out and being heard but one of recognition of his place in an already scripted drama. Even when the Hodayot use the drama of danger and deliverance, so familiar from the Psalms, it is not the deliverance per se but the insight into the true meaning of his experience that is what the speaker has to tell. Nor does his praise *do* something in the same way as that of the psalmist. Rather it joins him with the angelic chorus of praise, beings who also "make known your glory in all your dominion, because you have shown them what [they had] not se[en . . .]" (1QH^a 5:17).

The identity that the Hodayot confers on its subject is that of one whose duty and destiny it is to praise God. Even more definitively than in the Psalms, the Hodayot locates the core of the individual's subjectivity in its voice. From the perspective of the Hodayot a sectarian without a voice to praise would be almost literally unthinkable. Not only is this sense of the purpose and destiny of the speaker a theme in the Hodayot; the very form of the Hodayot reinforces this centrality of the voice, for the Hodayot are virtually all in first-person singular speech.[33]

What one finds in the Hodayot, however, is not simply an unproblematic self-consciousness of oneself as a witness to God's glory and a voice of testimony. Every discourse that confers an identity must also persuade those whom it addresses of its truth. Dominant discourses of meaning in societies do this primarily through an implicit appeal to common sense: this is just "how things are." Since sectarian subjectivity is, by definition, a marginal phenomenon, the plausibility of its symbolic order and the identity it confers on the individual must be more directly and self-consciously established. The Hodayot approaches this issue by making subjectivity itself, especially as it is focused in the speaking voice, problematic.

---

[33] The fluctuation between I and we that intrigues Fisch in the biblical Psalms is extremely rare in the Hodayot. It occurs in 1QH^a 7:2–10. A first-person plural suffix occurs in 1QH^a 6:1, but in a broken context. The "self-glorification" hymn, best preserved in 4QH^a 7 ii 14–23 contains a section including second-person plural imperatives and first-person plural forms.

The Blinking I (1QH^a 7:15–24 and 5:1–6:7)

There are two ways that the self is constituted in the Hodayot: vis à vis the divine other and vis à vis the human other. These are like vertical and horizontal coordinates that locate the self within a space of meaning. In each case, however, that location is fraught with paradox. In this and the following two sections I wish to examine some of the Hodayot in which the central focus is on the relationship between the speaker and God. Then I will consider the relation with the human other.

The place to begin to examine the construction of the self in the Hodayot is with the issue of knowledge. As an explicit theme it is ubiquitous in the Hodayot, as a survey of such terms as דעת, בינה, שֵׂכֶל, מַחֲשָׁבָה, ר, will quickly indicate. What interests me here is not the issue of knowledge as a topic or content of the Hodayot; what I am trying to uncover is the way in which one who recites or hears these compositions comes to experience his sense of self as constituted by his relation to knowledge. How do the Hodayot provide an experience that persuades the reader that his identity is that of one who *knows*? How do they form the special quality of the voice that one encounters in the Hodayot? The composition contained in 1QH^a 7 provides an opportunity to see. The beginning of the hodayah is apparently contained in 1QH^a 7:11 and may be a hymn of the Maskil.[34] Although the beginning is rather badly broken, the speaker appears to confess his freely given love of God and devotion to God's mandates. A small *vacat* in line 15 introduces the body of the text. A rhetorical question in line 24 signals a transition in the poem.

1QH^a 7:15–24

(15) And I know, by means of the understanding that comes from you, that it is not through the power of flesh [that an individual may be righteous,
nor] does (16) the way of a person belong to himself,
nor is a man able to direct his steps.

---

[34] As discussed in the preceding chapter, knowledge is particularly associated with the Maskil. In this regard, however, he epitomizes the ideal of sectarian character in general.

יאל

And I know that the inclination of every spirit is in your hand,
    [and all] its [activity] (17) you established before you created it.
    How could anyone change your words?

You alone [created] (18) the righteous,
    and from the womb you prepared him for the time of favor,
        to be protected in your covenant and to walk in all (your ways),
        and to [. . .] over him (19) through your overflowing compassion,
        and to relieve all the distress of his soul, for eternal salvation
            and everlasting peace without lack
    and you made (20) his honor higher than that of flesh. *vacat*

But the wicked you created for the [time of] your wrath;
    and from the womb you dedicated them for the day of slaughter.
        (21) For they walk in the way that is not good,
        and they despise your [. . .] covenant,
        [and] their soul abhors your [. . .]
        and they do not take pleasure in anything (22) that you have
            commanded
        but they choose what you hate.

All your [. . .] you prepared in order to execute great judgments upon
        them
        (23) before all the eyes of your creatures.
    And it will be a sign and a por[tent] for everlasting [generations],
        so that all may know your glory and your great (24) strength.

(15) ואני ידעתי בבינתך
כיא לא ביד בשר [יצדק איש]
[ולא ל]אדם (16) דרכו
ולא יוכל אנוש להכין צעדו

ואדעה כי בידך יצר כול רוח
[וכול פעולת]ו (17) הכינותה בטרם בראתו
ואיכה יוכל כול להשנות את דבריכה

רק אתה [ברא]תה (18) צדיק
ומרחם הכינותו למועד רצון
להשמר בבריתך ולתהלך בכול[35]
ולה[. . .] עליו (19) בהמון רחמיך
ולפתוח כול צרת נפשו לישועת עולם ושלום עד ואין מחסור
ותרם (20) מבשר כבודו *vacat*

ורשעים בראתה ל[קץ] חרונכה
ומרחם הקדשתם ליום הרנה
(21) כי הלכו בדרך לא טוב

---

[35] Apparently the word דרכיך has been omitted by the scribe.

וימאסו בבריתכ[ה]
[. . .]ך תעבה נפשם
ולא רצו בכול אשר (22) ציותה
ויבחרו באשר שנאתה

כול[. . .]ך הכינותם לעשות בם שפטים גדולים
(23) לעיני כול מעשיך
ולהיות לאות ומו[פת לדורות] עולם
לדעת כול את כבודך ואת כוחך (24) הגדול

Most obviously, a speaker of a passage like this comes to experience himself as one who has knowledge by reciting it, by telling what he knows about God's plan for the world and by hearing himself tell it. That is one of the important ways in which the Hodayot formed the sense of self of the sectarian. Much more subtle business is going on here, however. One might notice that the passage begins with the phrase "I know," a phrase repeated in line 16, and again in lines 25, 26, and 28. Although the frequency of the phrase is greater here than in other Hodayot, the expressions "I know that . . ." or "these things I know . . ." occur throughout the compositions. But does the phrase really have to do with knowledge? It is often said that the references to knowing in Qumran literature do not refer to a theoretical knowledge; rather "they have more to do with personal contact and feeling, consideration and involvement."[36] Such expressions serve, not only in religious language, but also in ordinary conversation to establish the context within which persons relate to one another and understand their situations (as when Abram says to Sarai, "I know that you are a beautiful woman," Gen 12:11). Indeed, here in the Hodayot the expressions have something of the quality of a confessional statement rather than a cognitive one. To say "I know that . . . one's own conduct does not belong to a person . . ." is not so much a statement of knowledge as acknowledgement. Moreover the sentiment expressed in line 12 is a pious cliché (see Prov 16:9; Jer 10:23). Several things, however, disrupt the bland familiarity of both the throwaway phrase ידעתי ("I know") and of the pious sentiment it introduces.

An introductory phrase that is a habit of speech is rather like a dead metaphor. No one attends to its particular meaning until the metaphor or phrase is revived by disturbing the smooth way in which

---

[36] Reike, "Da'at and Gnosis," 255.

it fits into speech. Here the disrupting element is provided by the following parenthetical phrase בבינתך ("by the understanding that comes from you"). In such company ידעתי ("I know') loses its innocence. The trivial statement "Yes, I realize . . ." is now freighted with the presence of divine revelation. The disruption produced by בבינתך carries forward as well into the pious statement about the limits of human autonomy. That statement is, after all, what everyone knows. But now the speaker claims that his relationship to such acknowledgment is through a gift of divine insight. The effect of the disrupting presence of בבינתך ("by the understanding that comes from you") is to subject ordinary language to something like an x-ray. The sectarian and the nonsectarian may "know" the same thing, but the sectarian also sees and knows something that is hidden behind ordinary language.

What the sectarian knows that the ordinary person does not know is introduced in the companion sentence that begins in line 16 with ואדעה ("and I know"). This sentence serves as an interpretation of the ordinary language of the first sentence. Where the first sentence was articulated in what one might call unmarked language (the common, ordinary words everybody uses), the second one introduces terms and expressions distinctly marked with the inflection of the sectarian community (כול רוח, "every spirit," הכינותה בטרם בראתו, "you established before you created it"). This juxtaposition of ordinary language in one sentence and sectarian language in the next is a feature that occurs elsewhere in Qumran literature, most notably in the beginning of the Serek ha-Yahad (1QS 1:1–15; see chapter 4). Its effect is simultaneously to appropriate received religious language, to reinterpret its meaning, and implicitly to contest other understandings. The innocent "I realize . . ." is now paired with a more freighted "and I know . . ." that introduces the esoteric teaching about predestination that provides the true meaning of the common pious phrases. The knowledge presented here is profound, for the speaker understands that limits to human self-direction are based on the predetermination of the righteous and the wicked in the plan of God for the world. He presents himself as one able to encompass in his discourse the entire significance of human existence from creation to final end; and he is able to make distinctions and judgments about the fundamental patterns of human conduct and their meaning. The powerful knowledge of the speaker bursts through the ordinary language with which he began.

But there is something more. The initial confessional statement in lines 15–16 is not just ordinary language. An explicit scriptural allusion to Jer 10:23 is woven into it; and the significance of its presence must be considered. Compare the two texts:

Jer 10:23 (the words echoed in 1QH^a are underlined)

> ידעתי יהוה כי לא לאדם דרכו
> לא־לאיש הלך והכין את־צעדו

I know, O Lord, that the way of a person does not belong to himself, nor does it belong to a man, as he walks, to direct his steps.

1QH^a 7:15–16 (the words of Jeremiah are underlined)

> ואני ידעתי בבינתך כיא לא ביד בשר [יצדק איש
> ולא ל]אדם דרכו ולא יוכל אנוש להכין צעדו

And I know, by means of the understanding that comes from you, that it is not through the power of flesh [that an individual may be righteous, nor] does the way of a person belong to himself, nor is a man able to direct his steps.

It is not only ordinary language but scripture that is subjected to the x-ray of sectarian knowledge. The significance of Jermiah's confession is available to the speaker in a way that presumably was not known to Jeremiah himself (a relationship between the prophetic message and its inspired interpretation also apparent in the Qumran pesharim; see 1QpHab 7:1–5). More remains to be said, however, about the significance of this intertextual allusion for the formation of sectarian subjectivity.

As has long been recognized, the Hodayot are extremely rich in intertextual allusions to scripture. The variety of ways in which scripture is quoted, interpreted, invoked, echoed, and imitated is so great that it still exceeds every attempt to organize and classify it.[37] Given the enormous range of relationships with scripture, it would be absurd to suggest that a single type of use or significance occurs in every instance. Moreover, the Hodayot are not unique in the practice of intertextual allusions to scripture. The majority of Second Temple writings, especially poetry, reflect this feature. Nevertheless, the density of intertextual allusion in the Hodayot is remarkable. It can

---

[37] See the discussion in Holm-Nielsen, "The Use of the Old Testament in the Hodayot," *Hodayot*, 301–15; Kittel, "The Problems of Biblical Language," *The Hymns of Qumran*, 48–55; Fishbane, "Use, Authority and Interpretation of Mikra at Qumran."

hardly be accounted for simply as common convention. In this particular passage, at least, one particular function of intertextual allusion can be discerned.

Although it would be interesting to reflect on what the author of this composition thought he was doing when he incorporated the allusion to Jeremiah, I am more concerned to think about the reader or hearer's relation to its presence. Certainly this is speculation, but purposeful speculation. The authors of the Hodayot were obviously masters of scripture, intimate with its contents to an astonishing degree but the same cannot be said for all the persons within the community who read or heard these texts. Especially in the case of adult converts, those who entered the community would have come with varying degrees of knowledge of scripture. It would have been within the community and through its disciplines of study and worship that their knowledge of the text was perfected. If one looks back at the passage in question, it is worth noting that the verse from Jeremiah is not simply quoted. It is, one might say, secreted into the passage, broken up into several sections and interspersed with other phrases. The passage presents no puzzle to the one who misses the allusion; meaning is not denied to the one who fails to see it. But once the allusion is perceived, the passage takes on new resonances of meaning and significance. The moment of first perception is the moment of seeing something hidden. It is not only a moment of seeing the depth of the text but a moment of experiencing oneself as "knowing" in a way that was not previously available. This sort of intertextual allusion both trains the sectarian (one begins to listen differently, alert for the double resonance of phrases) and it rewards the increasingly proficient reader with the evidence that he is indeed one who knows.

Even in this brief passage, which is hardly remarkable within the corpus of the Hodayot, there are multiple ways in which the reader's subjectivity is formed around the recognition of himself as one who knows. The source of this identity is expressly stated, as the speaker acknowledges that the knowledge through which he speaks is not his own but God's. This gift of knowledge is in a very real sense what brings the speaker into being as a subject and forms the essence of who he is. Both the wicked and the righteous live out the fates predetermined for them by God in a drama staged for the glory of God. Neither has an autonomous will. But the righteous knows what the wicked does not, and through knowledge has a different quality of participation in his own existence. Although the Qumran sectarians would not have looked at it in quite this way, the gift of subjectivity that they acknowledge in the phrase בבינתך is inseparable from the experience generated through the recitation of the Hodayot. It is in the *act* of telling before God what God has caused him to know that the speaker receives and appropriates his identity.

A powerful sense of presence manifests itself in the voice that speaks 1QH^a 7:15–24, one that seems unshakable. It is precisely what gives substance and presence to that voice, however—the knowledge that it wields so skillfully—that also threatens to undermine it. The self is constituted in the Hodayot as a subject of knowledge, that is, as a center of consciousness formed by knowledge. However, the self of the Hodayot is not only a subject of knowledge but an object of knowledge as well. The voice that speaks also directs attention to its "own self," the "I" of the Hodayot. This self-confrontation may be articulated either in terms of the general human condition or in explicitly first-person terms. The similarity in the rhetoric of the third-person and first-person passages suggests that their significance is much the same. When the voice that speaks directs attention to itself, it is often a moment of judgment and horrified recoil. This self-confrontation produces a sort of bifurcation of subjectivity, which is enacted over and over again in numerous Hodayot. The self of the Hodayot is at once both the knower and the known, the observing and observed self. What goes on in this dynamic is crucial to the formation of the sectarian.[38]

One could, of course, observe that this dynamic is actually implicit in all acts of what one calls self-reflection. There has to be a certain self-alienation for a person to comment on his or her own feelings or perceptions. To speak of oneself in the past or future requires an imaginative separation of that past or future self from the one who now speaks. This sort of self-reflection is typical of the Psalms. In the Hodayot, however, that implicit self-alienation is made thematic and is enacted in the dramatic form of the composition. The bifurcation of the self as a subject of knowledge and an object of knowledge is cultivated as an experience that holds the clue to who one is. But it is not just the sectarian per se who is the focus of the crisis. The

---

[38] See the similar dynamics in the Maskil's hymn in 1QS10:1–11:22, discussed in chapter 4.

moment of crisis, in which the self is experienced as a subject of knowledge and an object of knowledge is often presented specifically as a crisis in knowledge or a crisis in speech.[39] The recognition of the observed self throws into question the knowledge and discourse that is constitutive of the observing self.[40] The work of the Hodayot is above all to validate the knowledge and discourse of the community in the face of, and as it will turn out, by means of the distinctive, paradoxical structure of the self.[41]

---

[39] See, e.g., the Hodayot that begin in 1QH^a 5:1, 9:1, 17:38, 20:4.

[40] The contrast with the Psalms can be seen here. Even in Psalms in which the speaker strongly judges his own actions and motives, the introspective self is essentially a unity of consciousness. In the Hodayot what is put into question is the capacity of the very voice that is speaking to make the judgments it is making.

[41] One has to be particularly careful not to read into the Hodayot other, later practices and patterns of subjectivity that have similar structures. The phenomenon of the divided self is attested in many societies. Most probably, it is a feature of the neurological structures of the brain, given meaning and significance in different ways by different cultures. In the Western tradition it has been particularly associated with Augustine. See, e.g., Bright, "Singing the Psalms: Augustine and Athanasius on the Integration of the Self."

Puritan disciplines of self-examination offer a number of interesting analogies to the phenomenon described in the Hodayot, but also fundamental differences. An excellent treatment of Puritan subjectivity can be found in Paden, "Theatres of Humility and Suspicion: Desert Saints and New England Puritans." Paden draws attention to the following analysis of the diaries of the Puritan Thomas Shepard by Michael McGiffert in *God's Plot: The Paradoxes of Puritan Piety*, 18–19. "Day after day these pages declared their author's existence both as the self that suffers and as the self that observes, weighs, and tries to understand. Shepard's piety is above all else percipient. Metaphors of light and enlightenment pervade the *Journal*. 'I saw' is his characteristic statement: 'I saw how I was without all sense as well as sign of God, estranged from the life of God . . .'; '. . . on Sabbath morning I saw the Lord frowning on me in several providences . . .'; 'I saw the Lord had let me see my unbelief and desire the removal of it.' Shepard sees, and is seen—a Chillingworth, as it were, and equally a Dimmesdale: there lies Shepard flattened out in wholly genuine anguish, but there, simultaneously, is that other Shepard, perpendicular, cognitively masterful, the seeing I, lifting his pen to make a diagnostic or prescriptive note in his *Journal*." Further on McGiffert observes how Shepard manages a "subtle psychological transaction whereby anxiety is transmuted into assurance which is transmuted into anxiety, in Sisyphean sequence" (25). Several features bear comparison with the Hodayot: the "percipient" language, the division of the "I" between the observing and the observed, and the purposefully sustained fluctuation of mood; but there are equally great differences. The Puritan self to a much greater degree than the Qumran self provides the actual locus of struggle between God and the forces opposing God (but see 1QS 3–4). In the Hodayot at least, the crisis of the self appears to be more specifically linked to a concern to validate the knowledge possessed by the community. More generally, the differences that Fisch (108–14) describes between the "lyrical subjectivity" of the Puritans and the Romantics and the subjectivity of the Psalms would also apply here. Despite the stereotypical form

The hodayah in 1QH^a 5:1–6:7 provides a good example of this dynamic. The composition has been reconstructed by Puech as a hodayah of the Maskil.[42] Knowledge of the mysteries of God is a prominent theme. Although the introduction is broken, there are evocations of the Maskil's teaching in the Two Spirits section of 1QS 3–4.

1QH^a 5:1–3

(1) [A melody. For the Ma]skil, that he may prostrate himself be[fore God . . .] works of God
(2) [. . .] and give understanding to the simple [. . .] forever
(3) [. . .kn]owledge and give humankind understanding about [. . .] flesh and the counsel of the spirits of [. . .]they conduct themselves

(1) [מזמור למש]כיל להתנפל לפנ[י אל . . .].[מעשי אל
(2) [. . .].[ולהבין פותאים].[. . .]שי עולם
(3) [. . .ד]עת ולהבין אנוש בשר וסוד רוחו[ת . . .]ש התהלכו

The Hodayot proper begins with a long section concerning the "mysteries of the plan" (רזי מחשבת) that God has established (5:6) and in which God has instructed the speaker (וברזי פלאך הודע[תני, 5:8).[43] Echoes of 1QS 3–4 are also present in the dualistic language.

1QH^a 5:9–13

(9) [. . .] You yourself have revealed the ways of [truth] and the works of evil, wisdom and folly [. . .] righteousness
(10) [. . .] their deeds, truth and insight, iniquity and folly. All have walked [. . .]
(11) [. . .] and eternal mercies for their seasons for peace or for destruction for all [. . .]
(12) their [judg]ments. Everlasting glory and [. . . and] eternal joy for a deed of [. . .] for a d[eed of]
(13) [ev]il.

(9) אתה גליתה דרכי [אמת] ומעשי רע חוכמה ואולת[. . .].[צדק
(10) [. . .].[מעשיהם אמת ובינה עולה ואולת כול התהלכ[ו.
(11) [. . .].[וחסדי עולם לכול קציהם לשלום ושחת כול מ[. . .]

---

of Shepard's experience, his language does evoke a "personal presence" that is alien to the language of the self at Qumran.

[42] Puech, "Un hymne essénien," 63.

[43] For this reading see Puech, "Un hymne essénien," 66. In Puech's numeration the phrase occurs in line 19.

[מש]פטיהם כבוד עולם ו[. . . וש]מחת עד למעשה[. . .]שים למ[עשה] (12)
ע[ר] (13)

Although there is <u>no explicit reference to two guiding spirits</u> in the
preserved sections of text, <u>it may be that "these"</u> in line 13 refers
to the two spirits.

1QH^a 5:13–19

(13) And these are the ones whom [you] pre[pared from ages] of old
to judge through them (14) all your creatures before you created
them—
together with the host of your spirits and the congregation of
[the heavenly beings
wi]th your holy firmament and [al]l its hosts,
together with the earth and (15) all that springs from it in the
seas and in the deeps—
[according to] all that was planned for them for all the everlasting
epochs (16) and the eternal visitation.

For you yourself prepared them from ages of old and the work of
[. . .] among them
so that (17) they might make known your glory in all your
dominion—
for you showed them what they had not s[een . . . wh]ich was
of old—
and in order to create (18) new things,
to destroy that which stood in ancient times,
and to r[aise] up that which exists for ever.

For [you] yourself es[tablished them . . .]
and you yourself exist (19) forever and ever. *vacat*
And in the mysteries of your knowledge [you] apportioned all these
things,
in order to make known your glory.

(13) ואלה אשר הכ[י]נותה מקדם [עולם
לשפוט בם (14) את כול מעשיך בטרם בראתם
עם צבא רוחיך ועדת [אלים]
[ע]ם רקיע קודשך ו[כו]ל צבאותיו (15)
עם הארץ וכול צאצאיה בימים ובתהומות
[כ]כול מחשבותם לכול קצי עולם (16) ופקודת עד

כי אתה הכינותמה מקדם עולם ומעשה [. . .]תה בם
בעבור (17) יספרו כבודך בכול ממשלתך
כי הראיתם את אשר לא ר[או . . . א]שר קדם
ולברוא (18) חדשות
להפר קימי קדם
ול[הק]ים נהיות עולם

כי א[ת]ה ה[כי]נ[וחם . . .[
vacat ואתה תהיה (19) לעולמי עד
וברזי שכלכה פלנ[תה] כול אלה
להודיע כבודך

The voice one encounters in such a passage is the voice of one who indeed knows deep mysteries and is able to describe them. The crisis comes as the knowing, observing self turns its gaze on itself. Even though the passage is couched in third-person forms of speech, there is no doubt that the speaker describes himself in these terms. What he perceives is hardly what one steeped in any of the discourses of Second Temple Judaism would recognize as a "self" at all.

1QH[a] 5:19–22

(19) [But how] is a spirit of flesh to discern (20) all these things
and to grasp the secret coun[sel of your] great [wonder]?
And what is one born of woman amid all your fearful works?

He is (21) a thing constructed of dust and kneaded with water.
[Sin]ful gui[lt] is his foundation,
ignominious shame, and a so[urce] of pollution,
and a spirit of error rules (22) him.

And if he acts wickedly, he will become [a sign] forever
and an emblem for generations, an eternal horror among flesh.

[ומה אף ה]וא רוח בשר להבין (20) בכול אלה (19)
ולהשכיל בסוד [פלאך ה]נדול
ומה ילוד אשה בכול מעשיך הנוראים

והוא (21) מבנה עפר ומנבל מים
אש[מת חט]אה סודו
ערות קלון ומקור נדה
ורוח נעוה משלה (22) בו

ואם ירשע והיה [לאות ל]עולם
ומופת דורות דראון עד בבשר

Here is a being without capacity for knowledge or moral judgment and action. Described in terms of dust and water, it lacks the animating breath of God that distinguishes a living being from inert stuff (see Gen 2:7). The "spirit" that does characterize it is either the wonderfully oxymoronic "spirit of flesh" or the "spirit of error" that indicates its inability to direct itself properly. No wonder that it is an object of loathing and horror to the voice that contemplates it.

A real difference exists between this characterization of the human

subject and the language of self-abasement found in the Psalms. For
the most part the language of the Psalms is the language of misery,
not self-loathing (see, e.g., Psalm 69). The low estimation of the
speaker is often the opinion of others rather than his own evaluation
(e.g., Psalm 22). Even when the speaker confesses guilt (e.g., Psalms
25, 32, 38, 51), there is no total self-repudiation.[44] Moreover, as
Jacobsen has shown, in this tradition the apparent self-humiliation
is inextricably linked with an implicit self-importance.[45]

By contrast, in the Hodayot the self enacts its own nothingness
in radical contrast to the being of God. To its pollution corresponds
the holiness of God; to its guilt, God's righteousness; to its inability
to will and to do, God's uniquely autonomous will and creative
power; to its lowliness among the works of God, God's own absolute
incomparability.[46] In considering similar texts from other traditions,
sociologist of religion Peter Berger referred to such expressions as
"masochistic theodicy," the cultivation of the nothingness of the self
in relation to the absolute being of God. I would prefer to refer to
this as the cultivation of the masochistic sublime. Speaking of the
uses of masochism in such articulations, Berger says, "it transforms
the self into nothingness, the other into absolute reality. . . . [The
other] is posited as total power, absolute meaning, that is, as a *realis-
simum* into which the tenuous realities of one's own subjectivity may
be absorbed."[47] These different languages of the self in the Psalms
and in the Hodayot are grounded in different models of the relationship with God. The parental model, which acording to Jacobsen
underlies the Psalms, is coordinated with the language of vulnerability and neediness. The model of God as absolute being that one
finds in the Hodayot generates and is generated by a language of
the self as nothingness.

---

[44] The closest one comes to such language of loathing is in a short passage in
Ps 14:1b, 3//53:2b, 4, though there the language is not referred directly to the
speaker. The only remotely comparable tradition of the loathsomeness of human
existence is to be found in three passages in Job (4:17–21; 15:14–16; 25:4–6). There
is no direct connection between these passages and the traditions in the Hodayot,
however. For discussion of the Joban material see Newsom, *The Book of Job*, 138–150.

[45] Jacobsen, 150.

[46] Kuhn, 27–29, calls these passages examples of *Niedrigkeitsdoxologie*. See also
Lichtenberger, 73–87.

[47] Berger, *Sacred Canopy*, 56.

The matter of the relationship between the observed and observing self is perplexing. Such a question would not occur to one to raise in connection with the Psalms. There the self may be suffering and guilty, but its speaking voice seems wholly unified with its experience. Indeed the quality of that voice is generated out of the suffering and guilt it experiences. In the Hodayot, however, the observed self does not appear as a being capable of the self-reflectiveness or the subtle consciousness that one encounters in the speaking voice of the prayer. Indeed it does not and cannot generate the voice that says "I know." The understanding, the בינה that constitutes that voice, is בינתך, "*your* understanding." Its understanding is a gift, not a given. The elusive quality of the consciousness constituted by that quality is apparent in the ambiguous relation of the pronominal suffix to the noun. Grammatically, it may be either an objective or subjective genitive. Perhaps it would be better to say that it is both. Although generally translated as a subjective genitive (your understanding = the understanding that comes from you), it also points to an objective relationship, since it is knowledge of God and God's activity as well as knowledge from God.

Where, then, is the self of the Hodayot? On the one hand, as one tries to trace out the self, observed and described, it vanishes into a human nullity. But if one tries to trace out the self that observes and speaks, it, too, elusively vanishes back into God. The subject constituted by the Hodayot is neither the one nor the other but is dynamically produced as the uneasy intersection of the two. It is an unstable construction that defies representation as a unitary consciousness. I certainly would not want to say that the authors of the Hodayot were proto-postmodern deconstructionists, but what is produced in the Hodayot is a type of what the postmodernists called a "decentered self." In a way that is far more radical than what one would find in the Psalms, the initial impression of the speaking subject as a coherent source of experience, meaning, and expression is progressively disrupted. Knowledge and discourse are finally validated, not by the reconstitution of a unified self but precisely by the sacrifice of such a self. One could trace this process in the lines following the section quoted above (1QH^a 5:22–6:7), but the dynamic is more clearly preserved in the hodayah contained in 1QH^a 9. This text also provides an opportunity to see how certain other aspects of sectarian subjectivity are developed.

LOCATING THE SOURCE OF THE SECTARIAN VOICE (1QHᵃ 9:1–39)

The beginning of the composition is unfortunately not preserved but probably occurred at the very bottom of col. 8 or the first lines of col. 9.[48] As the text becomes legible, the topic is praise of God. In an act of praise the speaker constructs the object of praise by the qualities selected for attention and by the traditions and style of language used. In the process the speaker also constructs a character for himself. The selection of language and traditions will reveal something of what sort of a person this is who speaks. The speaker will also construct his subject position by the stance taken with respect to the object of praise: whether the speaker shares or lacks the qualities of the one praised; what motivates the praise; whether the speaker's act of praise is effaced or made a focus of attention; how the act of praise affects the one who utters it; what meaning it has for the one who speaks; and so forth.

In the passage in question the qualities of God initially praised are various: power, counsel, jealousy (but also patient judgment), and righteousness. But in line 7 a long section begins (lines 7–20) in which the wisdom of God in creation is explored in detail.

1QHᵃ 9:7–20

(7) In your wisdom [you] es[tablished the generations of] eternity,
 and before you created them, you knew their deeds (8) for everlasting
  ages.
[For without you nothing] is done,
 and nothing is known without your will.
You yourself formed (9) every spirit,
 and [. . .] and the standard for all their deeds.

And you yourself stretched out the heavens (10) for your glory,
 all [. . .] you established according to your will,
 and strong winds according to their rules,
 before (11) they came to be ho[ly] messengers.
 [. . .] to the eternal spirits in their dominions:
 luminaries according to their mysteries,
 (12) stars according to thei[ir] paths,
 [and all the storm winds] according to their task,
 flashes and lightning according to their service,

---

[48] See the reconstruction of Puech, "Quelques aspects," 52.

and the treasuries (13) devised for th[eir] purposes
[. . .] according to their mysteries. *vacat*

You yourself created the earth through your strength,
(14) the seas and the deeps
[. . .] their [inhabi]tants you established through your wisdom,
and all that is in them (15) you set in order according to your will.

[. . .] for the human spirit that you fashioned in the world
for all the days of eternity (16) and everlasting generations
to [. . .] in their times.
You allotted their service throughout all their generations
and jud[gm]ent (17) in the times appointed for them according to the domi[nion]
[. . .] their [. . .] for every generation,
and a visitation for their recompense together with (18) all their afflictions [. . .]

And you allotted it to all their offspring
according to the number of the generations of eternity
(19) and for all the everlasting years.
[. . .] and in the wisdom of your knowledge
you established their destiny before (20) they existed.
According to [your] wi[ll] everything [comes] into being;
and without you nothing is done. *vacat*

(7) ובחכמתכ]ה[ה]כינותה דורות[עולם
ובטרם בראתם ידעתה}כול{ מעשיהם (8) לעולמי עד
]כי מבלעדיכה לא[א יעשה כול
ולא יודע בלוא רצונכה
אתה יצרתה (9) כול רוח
ו]. . .[ומשפט לכול מעשיהם   *vacat*

ואתה נטיתה שמים (10) לכבודכה
כול].. ה[כינותה לרצונכה
ורוחות עוז לחוקיהם
בטרם (11) היותם למלאכי ק]ודש[
]. . .[לרוחות עולם בממשלותם
מאורות לרזיהם
(12) כוכבים לנתיבות]ם[
]וכול רוחות סערה[למשאם
זקים וברקים לעבודתם
ואוצרות (13) מחשבת לחפצי]ה[ם
]. . .[לרזיהם   *vacat*

אתה בראתה ארץ בכוחכה
(14) ימים ותהומות
]. . . יו[שביהם הכינותה בחוכמתכה
וכול אשר בם (15) תכנתה לרצונכ]ה[

[...] לרוח אדם אשר יצרת בתבל
לכול ימי עולם (16) ודורות נצח
למ[...]ל בקציהם
פלנתה עבודתם בכול דוריהם
ומש[פ]ט (17) במועדייה[49] לממשל[ת]
[...]יהם [...] לדור ודור
ופקודת שלומם עם (18) עם[50] כול נגיעיהם [...]ה

ותפלנה לכול צאצאיהם
למספר דורות עולם
(19) ולכול שני נצח
[...]ה ובחכמת דעתכה
הכ[י]נותה תע[ו]דהם בטרם (20) היותם
ועל פי רצ[ו]נכה י[ה]יה כול
ומבלעדיך לא יעשה   *vacat*

The qualities of divine creativity are expressed in a way familiar from other Qumran texts. What is celebrated is the ability to intend, to plan, to effect (cf. 1QS 3:15–17). No activity stands outside the divine plan. Everything that happens is simply the making visible of the divine plan in which everything was already known. What marks the created world as the expression of the divine plan is its obedient and rule-ordered activity. The vocabulary of order is extensive: standard, rules, domains, paths, tasks, service, purposes, and mysteries (which are esoteric purposes). Creator and creation are symmetrically arranged. Autonomy marks the one; heteronomy the other.

Almost any text can be said to articulate a pattern of desire, but texts of praise especially so.[51] An object of praise is an object of desire. An act of praise, because it attempts some form of connection between the desiring subject and the object of its desire, is especially active at this kind of work. But just as some desires are stimulated through the text, others are prohibited and must be repressed. The composition in 1QH[a] 9 does not inspire in its readers the desire for autonomy: to intend, to plan, and to effect. That belongs to God. To desire that would be tantamount to blasphemy. The desire for autonomy is not allowed to emerge. Instead, the desire the text stimulates is the desire to discover oneself as ordered, ruled, and known from of old, a subject whose destiny was always intended. This recog-

---

[49] Restore מ.
[50] Delete one occurrence of עם as dittography.
[51] Booth, *The Company We Keep*, 201–24.

nition draws one close to the plan of God and thus to the object of all desire.

The passage would not be so persuasive if it merely stated its values. The reader is persuaded that he is already "that kind of desirer," to use Booth's phrase, because the voice that speaks enacts its subjectivity. The act of praise that runs from line 7 through line 20 is a beautifully ordered discourse. It is contained within an inclusio that praises God's primordial wisdom and foreknowledge in closely similar expressions (lines 7–9 and 18–20). In between it maps the cosmos: the heavens (lines 9–13), the earth and the seas (lines 13–15), and the human realm (lines 15–18). The syntax, even though difficult to decipher in places, clearly makes use of elaborate parallel structures, especially in lines 11–13. The vocabulary, as noted earlier, is replete with expressions for ordered obedience. Only one who has already been shaped by a desire to be "set in order according to your will" (line 15) can speak like this.

The character created by this voice, which can speak so clearly about the divine will and plan, about the mysteries of the heavens, the orderly structures of the cosmos, and even about events of future judgment, is quintessentially a character who has intimate understanding of the sorts of knowledge that are the provenance of God. In fact, just at the conclusion of this act of praise the speaker steps outside of the frame, so to speak, to comment on what makes possible his act of praise and what constitutes him as a subject of knowledge: "These things I know because of the insight that comes from you, for you have opened my ears to wondrous mysteries" (אלה ידעתי מבינתכה כיא גליתה אוזני לרזי פלא, line 21).

Yet immediately upon uttering these words, the subject that has spoken so sublimely seems plunged into crisis as it contemplates itself.

1QH^a 9:21–23

 (21) But I am a creature of clay and a thing kneaded with water,
  (22) a foundation of shame and a well of impurity,
  a furnace of iniquity, and an edifice of sin, a spirit of error,
  perverted, without (23) understanding, and terrified by judgments
  of righteousness.

(21) ואני יצר החמר ומגבל המים

(22) סוד הערוה ומקור הנדה

כור העוון ומבנה החטאה רוח התועה

ונעוה בלא (23) בינה ונבעתה במשפטי צדק

The language of self-loathing is unleashed as the self repudiates itself in disgust. Described in terms that are the inverse of the divine autonomous will, wisdom, and righteousness, it is a creature of inert clay and water, without understanding, both unclean and guilty. The result of this self recognition is to call into question the meaning and value of the author's speech.

1QH^a 9:23–25

(23) What could I say that is not already known?
  Or what could I declare that has not already been told?
Everything (24) is engraved before you in an inscription of record
  for all the everlasting times
    and the cycles of the number of the eternal years
      with all their appointed times.
(25) They are not hidden nor missing from your presence.

מה אדבר בלא נודע (23)
ואשמיעה בלא סופר
הכול (24) חקוק לפניכה בחרת זכרון
לכול קצי נצח
ותקופות מספר שני עולם
בכול מועדיהם
ולוא נסתרו ולא נעדרו מלפניכה (25)

This is a curious passage. Coming as it does, immediately after the annihilating self-evaluation, the first lines apparently denigrate the speech of the speaker. He can offer nothing new, nothing not already possessed. The nullity of the self is experienced even in the performance of praise, an act that had earlier seemed to place the speaker in a privileged, powerful position. Note, however, that the confession of personal lack merges almost imperceptibly into a confession of divine fullness. The resolution to the crisis of subjectivity and speech lies in this dynamic of the masochistic sublime. But the hodayah is not yet ready to move forward to resolution. The composition turns again to the inadequacies of speech. Just as his speech about God was felt to be inadequate, so he finds it impossible to speak in defense of himself in the presence of God.

1QH^a 9:25–27

(25) And how should a person explain his sin?
  And how should he defend his iniquities?
(26) And how should he reply to righteous judgment? *vacat*

To you, O you God of knowledge,
>belong all works of righteousness (27) and the counsel of truth.
But to mortal beings
>belong the service of iniquity and the works of deceit. *vacat*

(25) ומה יספר אנוש חטאתו
ומה יוכיח על עוונותיו
(26) ומה ישיב עול⁵² כול משפט הצדק   *vacat*
לכה אתה אל הדעות
כול מעשי הצדקה (27) וסוד האמת
ולבני האדם
עבודת העוון ומעשי הרמיה   *vacat*

The two elements of this double crisis are apparently related, since the hodayah suggests elsewhere that moral cleanness is necessary for one who would praise God (lines 32–33). Thus the recognition of the speaker's sinful condition renders his very act of praise deeply problematic. The resolution to this crisis of speech is achieved by pursuing the logic of null subjectivity to its conclusion. Even speech, traditionally that most intimate expression of self,[53] derives not from some autonomous self but from God.

1QH^a 9:27–31

(27) You created (28) breath for the tongue,
>and you know its words,
>and you establish the fruit of the lips before they exist.
You set the words to verse,
>(29) and the utterance of the breath of the lips by measure.
And you bring forth the lines according to their mysteries
>and the utterances of the breath according to their design,
>in order to make known (30) your glory
>and to recount your wonders
>>in all the deeds of your truth
>>and your righteous j[udgments]
>and to praise your name (31) with the mouth of all who know you.
According to their insight they bless you for ever and [ever.] *vacat*

(27) אתה בראתה (28) רוח בלשון
ותדע דבריה
ותכן פרי שפתים בטרם היותם

---

[52] Waw in עול is written above the line. The scribe appears also to have attempted to correct כול to על. Perhaps the text intended was ומה ישיב על משפט הצדק.

[53] See Fisch, 107–8.

ותשם דברים על קו
(29) ומבע רוח שפתים במדה
ותוצא קוים לרזיהם
ומבעי רוחות להשבונם
להודיע (30) כבודכה
ולספר נפלאותיכה
בכול מעשי אמחכה
ומ[שפטי צ]דקכה
ולהלל שמכה (31) בפה כול יודעיכה
לפי שכלם יברכוכה לעולמי [עד]   *vacat*

There is some question whether lines 28–29 use technical terminology for poetic speech, as my translation suggests.[54] Whether or not
they do, the important thing is that the speaker's speech is recognized as being ordered, ruled, subject to design, just like the phenomena of the cosmos described in the earlier part of the composition.
Only as the speaker rejects any claim of autonomous speech does
his discourse receive value. He has standing to speak, not because
he can demonstrate his righteousness but because of God's gift of
speech.

1QH[a] 9:31–34

(31) You, through your compassion (32) and your great kindness,
  have strengthened the human spirit in the face of affliction
[. . .] you have cleansed from great iniquity
  (33) in order to recount your wonders before all your creatures.
And [I will make known in the assembly of the sim]ple[55] the judgments
  of my affliction
(34) and to all humankind all your wonders
  by which you have shown yourself strong [through me. . . .]

(31) ואתה ברחמיכה (32) ונדול חסדיכה
חזקתה רוח אנוש לפני נגע
[. . .] טהרתה מרוב עוון
(33) לספר נפלאותיכה לנגד כול מעשיכה
ו[אנידה בקהל פ]תיים משפטי נניעי
(34) ולבני אנוש כול נפלאותיכה
אשר הנברתה [. . .]

---

[54] See the discussion of Bergmeier and Pabst, "Ein Lied von der Erschaffung der Sprach."

[55] Following the restoration suggested by García Martínez and Tigchelaar, 160.

The poem then concludes with the enactment of this newly empow-
ered speech in an address in the bold wisdom style: "Hear, O you
sages, and you who ponder knowledge," etc. (שמעו חכמים ושחי דעת,
1QHᵃ 9:34–35).

This composition is a tour de force for the construction of the
reader's subjectivity. It begins with a beautifully crafted act of praise
that implies a speaker of powerful knowledge. Yet at the same time
it discourages the desire for autonomy and offers as desirable an
existence that is measured, governed, and subjected by the divine
autonomy. The positive appeal of such a subjectivity is reinforced
by staging a crisis for the self and its speech. If its speech is grounded
in itself, then such speech is valueless, for the individual is utterly
vile. Only by recognizing that nothing comes from the self, that there
is no autonomous self, can one receive the speech that unites the
speaker with the object of its desire and so empowers it. What the
prayer enacts is an evacuation of the self and a reconstruction of it
as an effect of God. Discourse and the self are secured only through
the dynamic experience of negation.

CREATION THROUGH NEGATION (1QHᵃ 17:38–18:12)

A composition like that in 1QHᵃ 9 does not simply express a subjective experience that is somehow prior to language. Rather, it is
through the resources of language that such an experience of oneself is made possible. In rhetorical terms the crucial resource of language that generates the divided, unstable, and rather masochistic
subject of this hodayah is the negative. In that text the negative is
enacted as a drama, a crisis of contradiction as the self discovers
what it is not. The crisis of contradiction is resolved not by dis-
solving but by insisting on the contradiction: the simultaneous recognition of the nothingness of the self and the powerful voice of
knowledge with which it speaks. The negative does more than just
sketch a formal pattern of the subject as a site of contradiction, however. It is also the means for generating a convincing experience of
the power and presence of God.

The polarities created by the operations of the negative are a
source of creative transformation and energy, a sort of linguistic
engine. In the Hodayot the negative is not employed only in a drama
of self-crisis but also in the mode of ecstatic praise that simultaneously

generates self and God. The best example of the creative energy of the negative is the short hodayah in 1QH^a 17:38–18:12. A few lines are broken at the beginning, but continuous text begins with line 18:2. Stylistically, negative statements alternate with rhetorical questions, the implied answer to which is a negative term. The latter is an especially apt rhetorical device, since the negative answer exists in the place of absence—as the word not said, because it goes without saying.

1QH^a 18:2–5

(2) Without your will nothing can be.
　　No one can contemplate [your] wi[sdom]
　　(3) [and on] your [myst]eries no one can gaze.

And what, then, is a mortal being—
　　he is only earth, *vacat*
　　(4) shaped [from clay],
　　whose return is to dust—
　　that you have caused him to understand wonders such as these,
　　and that the secret counsel of [your] tr[uth] (5) you have made
　　　known to him? *vacat*

(2) ובלוא רצונכה לא יהיה
ולא יתבונן כול בחוכ[מתכה]
(3) [ובר]זיכה לא יביט כול

ומה אפהו אדם
ואדמה הוא　　　*vacat*
(4) [מחמר] קורץ
ולעפר תשובתו
כי תשכילנו בנפלאות כאלה
(5) ובסוד אמ[תכה] תודיענו　　　*vacat*

Through the language of paradox, it is the insistence on the negative that provides the validation of the subject. The more the negation of the self is insisted upon, the more the self is grasped as the site of divine activity:

1QH^a 18:5–7

(5) But as for me, dust and ashes,
　　what can I devise unless you desire it?
　　And what can I plan (6) without your will?
　　How can I be determined unless you cause me to stand firm?
　　And how can I have insight unless you have formed it (7) for me?

What can I say unless you open my mouth?
And how shall I answer unless you give me insight? *vacat*

ואני עפר ואפר (5)
מה אזום בלוא הפצתה
ומה אתחשב (6) באין רצונכה
מה אתחזק בלא העמדתני
ואיכה אכשיל [56] בלא יצרתה (7) לי
ומה אדבר בלא פתחתה פי
vacat ואיכה אשיב בלוא השכלתני

These operations on the subject not only validate it but provide convincing experience of the power of God. Since no speech, will, or action can be attributed to the speaker's own power, the fact that he does speak, will, and act is evidence of the effective power of God. The hodayah is not structured as a logical argument ("I experience God's power in my own being; therefore God is powerful in the cosmos"), but its persuasive effect does depend in large part on its ability to generate a direct experience, from which the confidence in God's power then flows.

1QH^a 18:8–12

(8) Behold, you are the prince of gods, the king of the glorious ones, lord of every spirit, and ruler of every creature.
(9) Apart from you nothing is done.
Nothing is known without your will.

There is none except for you.
(10) There is none beside you in strength,
There is none before your glory,
And for your strength there is no price.

Who (11) among all your wondrous great creatures
can summon the strength to stand before your glory?
(12) And what is one who returns to his dust
that he should summon [such stren]gth?
For your glory alone you have done all this.

הנה אתה שר אלים ומלך נכבדים (8)
ואדון לכול רוח ומושל בכל מעשה
ובמלעדיכה לא יעשה כול (9)
ולא יודע בלוא רצונכה

---

[56] The word אכשיל should be corrected to אשכיל.

ואין זולתך
(10) ואין עמכה בכוח
ואין לנגד כבודכה
ולגבורתכה אין מחיר

ומי (11) בכול מעשי פלאכה הגדולים
יעצור כוח להתיצב לפני כבודכה
(12) ומה אפהוא שב לעפרו
כי יעצור [כו]ח
רק לכבודכה עשיתה כול אלה

In a composition such as 1QH[a] 17:38–18:12 the negative is the essential rhetorical resource that generates and validates the self, its discourse, and God. But negation, as Kenneth Burke observed, comes in two forms, the "is not" and the "shall not," the ontological and the moral.[57] Conceptually, these may be distinguishable, but rhetorically they often transmute into one another. In 1QH[a] 17:38–18:12 the "is not" is the featured form of the negative. But, as is well known, much of the rhetoric of Qumran literature develops the energies of the moral negative, the polarities of righteousness and wickedness, truth and deception, and so forth. That language is also fundamental for the formation of the self in the Hodayot. It emerges most clearly in what one might call narratives of conflict.

GENERATING THE SELF IN SYMBOLIC NARRATIVES OF CONFLICT
(1QH[a] 10:20–30)

The fundamental feature of the self as it is produced in the Hodayot is that it is formed at the site of contradiction. In the Hodayot considered in the previous sections, that contradiction is between the nothingness of human nature and the powerful knowledge that comes from God. In the examples to be considered in this and the following sections, contradiction takes the form of conflict between opposing forces: God and the wicked. How the speaker is situated within that conflict is what confers identity.

In cols. 10–11 a number of relatively well-preserved Hodayot consist almost wholly of highly figurative accounts of distress and deliverance. These compositions are located immediately before the extended sequence of Hodayot that represent the persona of the per-

---

[57] Burke, "Postscripts on the Negative," *Language as Symbolic Action*, 469–79; "Third Analogy" and "Epilogue: Prologue in Heaven," *Rhetoric of Religion*, 17–23, 273–316.

secuted leader (found in cols. 12–16), where themes of conflict are also prominent. At least one of the Hodayot in cols. 10–11, the one in 10:1[?]–19, clearly presents the persona of the persecuted leader. Although my focus in this chapter is primarily on the community hymns, I do wish to consider the disputed compositions in 10:20–30, 11:1[?]–18, and 11:19–36 as well, since I think they address the problem of the formation of sectarian subjectivity, whether they are finally judged to be community Hodayot or ones of the persecuted leader.

The short hodayah in 1QH^a 10:20–30 is shaped by a traditional motif from the literature of personal psalmody, a narrative of attack and deliverance. Roughly speaking, the hodayah divides into two parts: first a summary and interpretation of the event, followed by the vivid description of the attack and its resolution. Norbert Lohfink gives a more detailed analysis of its structure. He discerns an intro-duction (lines 20–22) followed by two parallel strophes introduced by והמה ("and as for them," lines 22–23 and 23–25) in which the theological meaning of the situation is described. A longer strophe (lines 25–28), introduced by ואני ("and as for me"), recalls the speaker's words and feelings at the time of the crisis. The conclusion (lines 28–29) resolves the tension of the dramatic recollection in parallel statements introduced by ואני and והם, statements that have strong verbal links with the introduction. The whole of the hodayah is brought to an end with a modified citation from Ps 26.12 (lines 29–30).[58]

1QH^a 10:20–30

(20) I thank you, O Lord,
> that you have placed my soul in the bundle of life,
>> (21) and that you have protected me from all the snares of the pit;
> [for] ruthless people sought my life
>> when I clung (22) to your covenant.

As for them—
> they are a council of deception and a congregation of baseness.
> They do not know that my station comes from you
> (23) and that by your kindness you save my life;
> for from you come my steps.

---

[58] Lohfink, 49–51.

And as for them—
    on account of you they have menaced (24) my life,
    so that you may be glorified in the judgment of the wicked
    and manifest your strength through me before mortal (25) beings;
    for by your kindness do I stand.

And I said—
    Warriors have encamped against me,
    surrounding me with all (26) their weapons of war.
    Arrows for which there is no cure destroy,
    and the flame of the spear devours trees with fire.
    (27) Like the roar of mighty waters is the tumult of their shout,
    a pulverizing rain destroying a multitude.
    And when their waves mount up, deception and (28) nothingness
      burst forth toward the constellations.

But as for me—
    though my heart melted like water,
    my soul held fast to your covenant.

(29) And as for them—
    the net they spread against me seized their feet,
    and the snares they hid for my life—they themselves fell into
      them. *vacat*

But my feet stand upon level ground.
    (30) (Far away) from their assembly I will bless your name. *vacat*

(20) אודכה אדוני

כי שמחה נפשי בצרור החיים

(21) ותשוך בעדי מכול מוקשי שחת

כ[י] עריצים בקשו נפשי

בתומכי (22) בבריתכה

והמה סוד שוא ועדת בליעל

לא ידעו כיא מאתכה מעמדי

(23) ובחסדיכה תושיע נפשי

כיא מאתכה מצעדי

והמה מאתכה נרו (24) על נפשי

בעבור הכבדכה במשפט רשעים

והגבירכה בי נגד בני (25) אדם

כיא חסדכה עמדי

ואני אמרתי חנו עלי גבורים

סבבים בכל (26) כלי מלחמותם

ויפרו חצים לאין מרפא

ולהוב חנית באש אוכלת עצים

(27) וכהמון מים רבים שאון קולם

נפץ זרם להשחית רבים
למזורות יבקעו (28) אפעה ושוא בהתרומם נליהם

ואני במוס לבי כמים
ותחזק נפשי בבריתך

(29) והם רשת פרשו לי תלכוד רנלם
ופחים טמנו לנפשי נפלו בם *vacat*

ורנלי עמדה במישור
(30) מקהלם אברכה שמכה *vacat*

As in a biblical thanksgiving prayer the event this hodayah recalls
is one "recollected in tranquility." That is to say, the crisis it nar-
rates in such vividness is contained temporally through an act of recollection and textually through the calm certainties expressed at the
beginning and end of the prayer. As in the thanksgiving psalms, the
events narrated belong to the realm of symbolic expression and are
not literal descriptions. In contrast to the thanksgiving psalms, however, the narrative is not a symbolic representation of a genuinely
recollected anomic experience (illness, conflict, bad fortune) but a
representation of the speaker's situation within a quasi-mythic account
of the world. The function of the description in the hodayah is normative.[59] Situating the speaker within the account of contending
forces, the hodayah gives him a subject position within this symbolic
order. The threat and deliverance is not a moment of the past but
an integral part of the speaker's fundamental condition, one that the
hodayah enables to be experienced over and over again.

In several ways the pattern of similarities to and differences from
classical psalmody enables one to grasp how a traditional language
of the self is reinflected in this hodayah to produce a quite different
experience of self. Comparable to the Psalms that feature enemies,
the plot of the hodayah defines the identity of the speaker oppositionally
in relation to the "council of deception" and "congregation of base-
ness" who attack him. This oppositional structure is underscored

---

[59] This is not to deny the paradigmatic function of the biblical thanksgiving
psalms, which provided a normative structure for experiencing anomic events. To
the extent that such thanksgiving psalms eventually were separated from their original life settings and became part of the general language of piety, then they, too,
could be seen as providing a template for the meaning of one's life per se, not just
a particular experience within it.

linguistically by the prominence of the contrasting independent pronouns "they" and "I," which occur at structurally significant points. Despite the emphasis that the pronouns seem to place on the relationship of "they and I," this relation is more complex than that between the classical psalmist and his enemies. In the hodayah both parties, "they" and "I," are primarily related by the "you" who is God. In terms of the plot the fundamental opposition turns out not to be between the speaker and his enemies but between the enemies and God. The speaker notes that it is "on account of you they have menaced my life" and that the ultimate purpose of the attack is "so that you may be glorified . . . and manifest your strength through me." Already in the Psalms the psalmist may represent himself as pious and his enemies as impious, or even say that God's enemies are his enemies (Pss 139:19–24; 119:21–22). The opposition between the psalmist and his enemies, however, remains fundamentally a human conflict, in relation to which the psalmist actively seeks divine aid, giving as his reason the fact that he is on God's side and his enemies are not.

What happens in the Hodayot is what Kenneth Burke would call the perfecting of a motive. The impiety of the enemies is now adduced not merely as a characteristic but as the basis for their actions. One of the consequences of the transfer of the fundamental opposition from speaker versus enemies to God versus enemies is the increasing passivity in the representation of the speaker of the hodayah. The classical psalmist may be unable to deliver himself from his foes, but he does appear as an agent in his own drama, calling on God for help and often promising something of value, his praise, in return (e.g., Psalm 142). In the hodayah under consideration there is no recollection of a cry for help. The self constructed in this and similar Hodayot is not an agent but, one might almost say, a site of divine activity. It serves as a ground situated between God and the ruthless, an object to be attacked, an object to be defended. In formal terms the speaker's self is what allows for a sort of "communication" between the polar terms of the conflict. God does not so much act *for* the speaker (as in the Psalms) but rather *through* him (cf. 1QH^a 12:8, 23; 13:15). In essence the meaning of the speaker's life is rhetorical. He is a sign.

If the speaker is a sign, he is also a reader of signs and a reader of himself as a sign. It is this quality that lifts him above the status of passive object and gives him a means of participation in the drama. In contrast to the ruthless ones' inability to interpret ("they do not know . . ."), the speaker provides the correct but hidden meaning of the events. The speaker is made to be an observer of himself, and a significant portion of his identity is invested in this perceiving "I." In this hodayah, however, attention is not focused primarily on creating the self as an instrument of God's knowledge. Here the major work is to create the self as a register of the cosmic conflict that structures all of history and of the divine purpose that underlies it.

It would appear that all of that is accomplished in the first six lines of the hodayah. From the perspective of simple information, the second part is purely repetitious. But its dramatic form, presenting the speaker's sensations in the face of attack, points to its particular function. Subjectivity may be a condensed form of explanation, but for it to have persuasive effect it must be grasped not as explanation but as an experience of the most immediate sort. The second part of the hodayah makes use of a variety of poetic and imagistic devices to create an immediate experience of the subjectivity it cultivates.

The emotional structure of the passage is one of rising terror, crisis, and resolution, a structure clearly marked in the text by the repetition of independent pronouns ("And as for me, I said. . . . and as for me. . . . and as for them. . . ."). Such a pattern suggests that the moment of crisis will hold the key to the experience of the self that is to be grasped. The recitation begins with the speaker's recollection of an experience of terror and utter vulnerability. The governing image is one of war, which, according to Lohfink, is developed through a series of associatively linked images of weapons, fire, storm, even a storm of apparently cosmic dimensions.[60] All of this suggests the utter inability of the speaker to protect himself. The climactic moment is the speaker's confession of simultaneous terror and trust: "though my heart melted like water, my soul held fast to your covenant"; or one might translate the consonantal text in a way that emphasizes the passivity of the speaker even more: "though my heart melted like water, you strengthened my soul through your covenant"

---

[60] Lohfink, 51. There remains, however, considerable disagreement about the precise meaning of למזורות יבקעו (translated here as "burst forth toward the constellations").

(line 28). The terminology of the self is worth noting. Seven times the speaker uses a noun to refer to himself. In six of these cases it is נפש ("soul/life"). Here at the climactic moment of the narrative the speaker uses a double designation, paralleling נפש ("soul") with לב ("heart"). These two terms, like their rough English equivalents, do not, of course, refer to two different parts of the self, but they do mark the inner conflict for the subject who experiences himself as the scene of this cosmic confrontation. They are the inner emotional correlates of the external forces. The resolution of the crisis begins with the strengthened soul's overcoming of the melting heart, a resolution that is then depicted in the external frame. The violent attack is turned reflexively on its perpetrators, leaving the speaker standing securely "on level ground," an image that recalls the reference to divinely ordained steps and station in the first part of the prayer.

That double sensation of terror and trust is the key to the formation of subjectivity in this composition and is its paradigmatic moment. Because he shares a certain common ground with them, the speaker is vulnerable to the onslaught of the massed forces of the wicked. That vulnerability is real and must be experienced as such. Through the knowledge that the speaker has been granted of the cosmic drama and of his role as a sign in it, however, he understands that his fate is under the protection of God. Thus, the overcoming of terror by trust, the strengthening of his soul, is the inner, subjective correlate of the ultimate victory of God over the forces of wickedness. His own subjectivity, the emotional as well as the cognitive patterns that form his identity, becomes a warrant for the plausibility of the sectarian world.

One other aspect of the formation of subjectivity in this hodayah requires comment. It also involves contrast, specifically the contrast between the fundamentally collective representation of the enemies (סוד, עדה, line 24) and the solitariness of the speaker. The loneliness of the suffering or persecuted one is a motif familiar from Psalms,[61] although there the psalmist's hope is for restoration to a community.[62] In the hodayah it is different. Disagreement exists as to the

---

[61] E.g., Ps 102:7–0. See van der Toorn, *Sin and Sanction*, 89. Seidel, *Das Erlebnis der Einsamkeit*, 21–66.

[62] E.g., Ps 142:7. See Fisch, 113.

proper interpretation of the final line of the hodayah, in which Ps
26:12 is cited. Some wish to see in it a reference to the speaker's
own community,[63] but syntactic and orthographic difficulties make
that interpretation unlikely.[64] Logically, the suffix on מקהלם can only
refer back to the speaker's enemies. Whereas the psalmist says "in
the great congregation I will bless Yahweh," the speaker in the
hodayah says "away from their congregation I will bless your name."
The emphasis is on separation, not union. As Lohfink says, "Der
Beter bliebe ein einzelner, der gegen die offizielle Gemeinde- or
Kirkenrealität Israels steht."[65]

Lohfink's remark points first of all to the often noted function of
the Hodayot in cultivating the sense of estrangement from the dominant culture that is necessary for the formation of sectarian identity. What seems more striking, however, is that the narrative imagery
of the hodayah does not transfer the speaker from the hostile and
wicked congregation to the true fellowship of the sect. The imagery
depicts him only in relation to God, not in relation to a counter-
community. Attempts to argue on this ground that the composition
must therefore reflect the experiences of the Righteous Teacher before
the formation of the community are naively literalistic.[66] However
surprising it may seem, it is characteristic of the Hodayot that references to the sectarian community are quite rare. In fact, explicit
discussions of the sectarian community occur almost exclusively in
the Hodayot of the persecuted leader, which will be analyzed in the
following chapter. For the most part, the phenomenon of the community is always kept just beyond the horizon of perception in the
Hodayot of the ordinary sectarian. Even the reference to "covenant"
in 1QH[a] 10:20–30 is presented only in terms of the relation of the
speaker and God. Its manifestation in sectarian structures simply does

---

[63] So Holm-Nielsen, *Hodayot*, 44.

[64] One would expect *yod* to be written if מקהלם were to be understood as "the
assembled ones." Licht's suggestion (*Thanksgiving Scroll*, 63) that מתוך קהלם = מקהלם
is questionable on the grounds that there is no antecedent for the final *mem*, if it
is understood as referring to the speaker's community. It seems most probable that
here the prepositional *mem* has a severative force, "away from," and that the final
mem refers to the סוד and עדה of the speaker's enemies, as above. Similarly, Delcor,
Les Hymnes, 106; Dupont-Sommer, *Essene Writings*, 207; Vermes, *Complete Dead Sea
Scrolls*, 258; Knibb, 169–70.

[65] Lohfink, 55.

[66] Delcor, *Les Hymnes*, 106.

not enter into the representation of this hodayah. The experience that this and other compositions make available to the speaker is first of all a solitary and individual experience.

This is not to say that these Hodayot had no function in the building up of the community. They provided distributively for each member a similarly formed experience. In a later section I suggest various ways in which the Hodayot did prepare individuals for the communal life of the sect as it is represented in the Serek ha-Yahad. Perhaps it is not so unusual, however, that the Hodayot configure the individual's experience apart from the supportive structures and meaning provided by the community. One might compare the stories of "salvation" in evangelical churches or the stories told by members of Alcoholics Anonymous. Although recited in public gatherings and vital in terms of sustaining the community and its figured world, these narratives, too, tend to focus on the experience of the individual and to stop short of describing the role of the community itself. In those cases, as with the Hodayot, the first person accounts serve to create a standardized experience for all members of the community.

SELF AND OTHER (1QH^a 11:1–18)

The fundamental characteristic of Qumranic subjectivity is that it is produced at the point of contradiction or of contending forces in a moment of crisis and is often represented as a bifurcated or divided self. Although there is generally some resolution of the division, the dividedness is not decisively overcome. The structure of the self is, as the title of Huppenbauer's excellent book has it, *Der Mensch zwischen zwei Welten*. This symbolic structure is present both in 1QH^a 9, where it is represented in terms of a crisis in the knowing subject, and in 1QH^a 10:20–30, where it is a crisis in the emotional register. Despite the similarity in the formal structure of the self in these two compositions, there seems to be a significant difference between the representation of subjectivity. The speaker in the latter hodayah may experience conflicting emotions, but the narrating voice seems quite as stable and unified as the voice of a traditional thanksgiving psalm. The crisis, when it comes, is not one that involves a significant decentering of self. The difference, of course, is where the element of negativity is located. The condition for unifying the speaking self is the externalizing of the negative.[67] Insofar as the negative can be projected outward, the self is unified and its boundaries are defined with clarity. The very fact that the speaker is attacked by enemies of God gives him identity with God. But to the extent that the negative is represented as within oneself, then the defining boundaries tend to dissolve. Even in those compositions that are constructed as symbolic narratives of conflict, the self is seldom depicted as unambiguously unified. The reason for this is quite apparent. Since, according to the sectarian worldview, those whom God has chosen do not possess any intrinsic merit but owe any claim to righteousness purely to the generosity of God, there remains a tantalizing and disturbing degree of similarity between the righteous and the wicked, the saved and the damned. Two of the Hodayot from 1QH[a] 11 provide good examples of the way in which this ambiguity can be exploited in the representation of the self and its paradigmatic story of distress and deliverance.

The hodayah in 1QH[a] 11:1[?]–18 is an extremely difficult text, not because of poor transmission but simply because its intricate poetics make such extraordinary demands on the reader. The beginning of the composition is lost, and it is not evident whether it begins at the very top of col. 11 or whether it is a continuation of the composition that begins in 10:31–39. This hodayah has given rise to a variety of widely divergent interpretations of the birth imagery that dominates it. One line of interpretation sees it as an account of the birth of a messianic figure.[68] That is certainly wrong. The entire description is explicitly introduced as an extended simile. "I was in distress like a woman in labor giving birth to her first-born" (1QH[a] 11:7). To be sure, the metaphor of birth is commonplace for the in-breaking of eschatological events but here eschatological motifs are used in the service of the speaker's account of his own experience.[69]

---

[67] Not coincidentally, the decisive resolution of inner division by the removal of falsehood from the individual's flesh is the symbolic representation of the eschatologically transformed self in 1QS 4:18–23.

[68] The basic arguments for this interpretation were laid out by Chamberlain, "Another Qumran Thanksgiving Psalm"; Dupont-Sommer, "La mère du Messie et la mère l'aspic"; Delcor, "Un psaume messianique de Qumran."

[69] For various refutations of the messianic hypothesis see Mowinckel, "Some Remarks on Hodayot 39:5–20"; Silberman, "Language and Structure in the Hodayot (1QH 3)"; Hinson, "Hodayoth, III, 6–18: In What Sense Messianic?"; S. Brown, "Deliverance from the Crucible"; Holm-Nielsen, *Hodayot*, 61–64; Maier, 73.

Somewhat more plausible is the suggestion that the text describes the birthing of the community by its leader, generally understood to be the Teacher of Righteousness.[70] Other texts exist that refer to the leader's nurture of the community in metaphorical terms (e.g., 1QH^a 15:20–22). In those instances, however, the relationship between the leader and the community is significantly developed. Here the emphasis is not on the relationship between mother and child but on the dangers of the birth process. Betz's argument, like the messianic interpretation, goes astray in focusing on the particular image in isolation from its deployment in the hodayah as a whole. Although most fully developed, the image of the pregnant woman is grouped with two other images that also characterize the speaker's situation, a storm-tossed ship and a besieged city. What is common to all three images is the element of life-threatening danger.[71] The most convincing interpretation of the text is that which takes it as a highly developed metaphorical representation of the crisis and deliverance (pun intended) of the speaker. In this view it is similar to the hodayah in 10:20–30.[72]

In the hodayah, after an initial confession of thanks (fragmentarily preserved in lines 3–5), the speaker refers to the endangerment he experiences. In the elaboration of the birth imagery the first narrative movement is the story of the successful birthing (lines 7–10). A brief transitional passage follows (lines 10–12) before the account of the unsuccessful birthing of the other pregnant woman (lines 12–18).

1QH^a 11:1–18

(3) [. . .] You have caused my face to shine [. . .]
(4) [. . .] for yourself with eternal glory, together with all [. . .]
(5) [. . .] your mouth and you saved me from [. . .] and from [. . .]

---

[70] Betz, "Die Geburt der Gemeinde durch den Lehrer."

[71] See, e.g., Hinson, 201.

[72] Whether the text is to be grouped with the Hodayot of the persecuted leader is debated. Jeremias, 171, counts it as such; Becker, 54, considers it probable; and Kuhn, 21–26, rejects its inclusion. I find Kuhn's reasoning the most persuasive. Even if it could be shown that the sect understood this hodayah as referring to the persona of the Teacher of Righteousness, it would not greatly affect my interpretation. What is at issue in this composition is not a question of leadership functions per se but the identity formed by the community's sectarian worldview.

(6) *vacat* Now [my] soul [. . .] they regard me,
    and make [my] soul like a ship on the depths of the sea
    (7) and like a fortified city before [its enemy].
I was in distress like a woman giving birth to her firstborn,
    when her pangs have come upon her
    (8) and sharp pains are upon her womb opening,[73]
    causing spasms in the crucible of the pregnant woman.

As children come to the womb opening of death,
    (9) so she who is pregnant with a manchild suffers in her birth
        pangs.
For at the womb opening of death she delivers a male,
    and in the birth pangs[74] of Sheol there bursts forth (10) from the
        crucible of the pregnant woman
        a wonderful counselor with his might,
    and the manchild is delivered from the mouth of the womb by
        the one who is pregnant with him.

All wombs act suddenly,[75]
    (11) and there are sharp pains at the time of their births
    and shuddering for those pregnant with them.
And so at the time of his birth all these pangs come (12) upon the
    crucible of the pregnant one.
    And she who is pregnant with nothingness[76] is subject to painful
        labor,
    and the womb opening of the pit is subject to all the things (that
        cause) shuddering.

(13) And the foundations of the wall quake
    like a ship upon the surface of the waters,
    and the clouds thunder with tumultuous noise,
    and the dwellers in the dust are (14) like those who go down to
        the seas,
    terrified by the roar of the waters.

---

[73] The several occurrences of משברים and משברי מות contain a play on words involving *mashber* ('womb opening') and *mishbar* ('breakers'). See Isa 37.3; 2 Sam 22.5. The word play cannot be imitated in English.

[74] חבלי שאול is another play on words, relating חבל ("bonds") and חבל ("labor pains"). It is also possible that other nuances are echoed, for other synonyms also exist: חבל ("destruction") and חבל ("fetus").

[75] The plural verbs and pronouns in lines 10–11 have been a source of difficulty for translators and interpreters. The simplest solution is to read these lines as general statements, similar to the observation in line 8 that "children come to the womb opening of death."

[76] אפעה is parallel to שוא in 1QHᵃ 10:28 and may be related to אפע (Isa 42:14, parallel to אין). The word אפעה means 'serpent' in Isa 30:6; 50:5; Job 29:16. A learned play on words is likely.

And their sages are for them like sailors on the deeps,
> (15) when all their wisdom is reduced to confusion by the tumult
>> of the seas,

> when the deeps boil up over the sources of the waters,
> and the waves surge up on high,
> (16) and the breakers of the water with their noisy roar.

And as they seethe, Sh[eo]l [and Aba]d[don] open up;
> [al]l the arrows of the pit (17) together with their retinue
> make their sound heard at the abyss.

(18) Then the gates of [Sheol] open [for all] the works of nothingness.
> Then the doors of the pit close upon the one who is pregnant
>> with injustice,

> and the eternal bars upon all the spirits of nothingness. *vacat*

(3) [. . .] לי האירותה פנ[י.] [. . .]

(4) [. . .] לכה בכבוד עולם עם כול [. . .]

(5) [. . .] פיכה ותצילני מ[.]ם.[.]ומ [. . .]

(6) *vacat* יחשובוני [. . .] עתה נפש[י]

וישימו נפש[י] כאוניה ב[מ]צולות ים

(7) וכעיר מבצר מלפני [אויביה]

אהיה בצוקה כמו אשת לדה מבכריה

כיא נהפכו ציריה

(8) וחבל נמרץ על משבריה

להחיל בכור הריה

כיא באו בנים עד משברי מות

(9) והרית נבר הצרה בחבליה

כיא במשברי מות תמליט זכר

ובחבלי שאול יניח (10) מכור הריה

פלא יועץ עם נבורתו

ויפלט נבר ממשברים בהריתו

החישו כול (11) משברים

וחבלי מרי[ץ]77 במולדיהם

ופלצות להורותם

ובמולדיו יהפכו כול צירים (12) בכור הריה

והרית אפעה לחבל נמרץ

ומשברי שחת לכול מעשי פלצות

וירועו (13) אושי קיר

כאוניה על פני מים

ויהמו שחקים בקול המון

ויושבי עפר (14) כיורדי ימים

נבעתים מהמון מים

---

77 The text is obscure. A commonly accepted emendation is to read חבל נמרץ instead of חבלי מרץ.

וחכמיהם למו כמלחים במצולות
כי תתבלע (15) כול הכמתם בהמות ימים
ברתוח תהומות על נבוכי מים
ויתגרשו לרום גלים
(16) ומשברי מים בהמון קולם
ובהתרגשם יפתחו ש[או]ל [וא][בד][ון]
[כו]ל חצי שחת (17) עם מצעדם
לתהום ישמיעו קולם
ויפתחו שערי [שאול לכול] מעשי אפעה
(18) ויסגרו דלתי שחת בעד הרית עול
ובריחי עולם בעד כול רוחי אפעה *vacat*

As with the text in col. 10, the body of this composition begins by exploring the experience of hostility from enemies. A series of images— ship at sea, besieged city, woman in labor—are used to describe the situation. The sequence of images suggests that the common element is one of imminent danger from forces over which one has no control.[78] In that regard the passage is similar to the presentation of the self in 1QH^a 10:20–30. With the introduction of the image of the pregnant woman, however, the hodayah comes upon its dominant symbol, one that becomes the focus for the rest of the prayer. Traditionally, Israelite poets invoked the simile of a woman in labor to describe the physical anguish and fear that overcomes persons about to be attacked in war (e.g., Isa 13:7–8a; Ps 48:5–7; Jer 6:23–24; 49:24; Isa 21:3).[79] There is no parallel in the Hebrew Bible, however, for the elaboration of the metaphor as it is carried out here, especially in its exploitation not only of the physical pain connected with labor but also of the results of labor, the birth of a child.

If the composition merely made use of the "plot" of labor and delivery, then it would be very similar to the dramatic structure of the hodayah in 10:20–30. But that is not all that is going on here. What is most striking about the composition is the double structure of plot and symbolic characters. There is not one pregnant woman here but two. The speaker has, one might almost say, an "evil twin"

---

[78] The only image that might initially suggest a different nuance is כעיר מבצר ('like a fortified city'); but Holm-Nielsen (*Hodayot*, 53) observes correctly that "the words need not indicate strength, but merely a town with a surrounding wall, which could be besieged in war, cf. 1 Sam 6.18, in contrast to the unfortified village. According to Jastrow, it can simply mean 'besieged town' in Rabbinic usage. In any case it is obvious that the expression does not indicate strength, if it is correct to read the following מלפנ[י אויב], as is mostly done."

[79] See the analysis of the image in Darr, "Like Woman, Like Warrior."

whose parallel but contrasting fate is narrated in the second half of the composition. Such a doubling and inversion of the symbol chosen to represent the speaker's own subjectivity suggests that issues of identity rather more complex than those encountered in 1QHᵃ 10:20–30 are being explored here.

Doubling, as the trope that dominates the symbolic structure of this hodayah, is even present on the linguistic level in the use of puns. Although word play is present in other Qumran literature, it is not generally characteristic of the Hodayot. Here, however, double meanings abound. The expressions משברים and משברי מות contain a play on words involving *mashber* ("womb opening") and *mishbar* ("breakers"). A similar ambiguity is exploited in the phrase חבלי שאול, where *ḥēbel* ("labor pains") is brought together with *ḥebel* ("bonds"). Even the term for womb is not the ordinary one but the expression כור ("crucible"), which is employed in constructions that pun on בכור ("firstborn"). Finally, the fetus of the second pregnant woman is called אפעה, a word that is probably a play on אפעה ("serpent") and אפעה/אפע ("nothingness").

The emphasis on doubling in the representation of symbolic characters and narrative structure and in the manipulation of language suggests that one consider more closely the strategic significance of the central image of the pregnant woman. A pregnant woman is, after all, an ambiguously dual being, one body with two lives. A woman pregnant with a גבר ("a manchild") represents this duality even more, since she combines the two sexes in one body. A woman pregnant with אפעה ("viper" or "nothing") is a monstrous combination of the human and the nonhuman and/or being and nonbeing. It remains to be seen, of course, the extent to which the speaker's identity is invested not only in the image of the woman but also that of the גבר ("manchild") with whom she is pregnant. As will be discussed below, the גבר plays a crucial role in the symbolic dynamics by which the underlying problem of subjectivity is resolved in this hodayah.

As in so many of the Hodayot, meaning is constructed along two axes. There is the linear, syntagmatic movement forward of the phrases and sentences themselves; there is the vertical, paradigmatic, retarding movement of a dense intertextuality. Within the four lines of text that narrate the plot of the birth, there are no fewer than nine specific biblical allusions (Jer 13:21; 4:31; 1 Sam 4:19; Mic 2:10; Isa 37:3; 2 Sam 22:5 [twice]; Isa 66:7; 2 Sam 22:6; Isa 9:5).

I mean it more than half facetiously when I say that the narrating
voice speaks a pregnant language. The reader or hearer formed by
the poetics of the Hodayot will attend not only to the manifest, surface meaning but simultaneously to the inner meaning that is being
constructed through the juxtaposition of biblical allusions.[80] The intertextuality and the punning word plays work together to create the
sense of a double structured language.

Consider the line of the passage that begins "I was in distress like
a woman giving birth to her firstborn, when her pangs have come
upon her and sharp pains are upon her womb opening, causing spasms in the crucible of the pregnant woman" (אהיה בצוקה כמו
אשת לדה מבכריה כיא נהפכו צידיה וחבל נמרץ על משבריה להחיל בכור
הריה). The phrase כמו אשת לדה ("like a woman giving birth") is from
Jer 13:21, and the term מבכריה ("her firstborn") apparently from Jer
4:31.[81] Both biblical passages occur in the context of judgment against
a sinful Jerusalem and describe the anguish and even death that she
faces. The succeeding allusion has overtones that are even more
grim, for כיא נהפכו צידיה ("when her pangs have come upon her")
is an allusion to 1 Sam 4:19, where Eli's daughter-in-law dies giving
birth to the inauspiciously named Ichabod when she hears about the
capture of the ark. There, too, the larger context is one of judgment on a failed priestly house. In keeping with the pattern, the
phrase וחבל נמרץ ("and sharp pains") is taken from a passage of
judgment in Mic 2:10. While the manifest content of the speaker's
words have established that his situation is one of acute distress, each
of his phrases is drawn from a context in which the distress is directly
related to sinful failure. It is important to stress that the speaker neither explicitly claims nor repudiates these overtones of guilt. They
merely hang in the air like a whisper of anxiety not even consciously
acknowledged.

To this point at least, although intertextual allusions have been
thick, there has been no reason to assume a double meaning for
any of the words. That changes, however, with the unusual form
משבריה. What is odd is that the context requires the word *mashber*,
"birth canal" or "womb opening"; and yet that word is always used

---

[80] See the discussion of 1QH[a] 7 above.

[81] Baumgarten and Mansoor ("Studies in the New *Hodayot*," 189, n. 8) suggest
that the scribe has reversed the *resh* and *yod* of מבכירה, the form found in Jer 4:31.
For other suggestions see the discussion of Holm-Nielsen, *Hodayot*, 53.

in the singular (2 Kgs 19:3//Isa 37:3; Hos 13:13). How a reader
actually pronounced the word is unclear, for the plural form that is
written certainly suggests the similar sounding *mishberim* ("breakers"),
which always occurs in the plural (2 Sam 22:5; Jon 2:4; Pss 42:8;
88:8; 93:4). The unusual form requires that the speaker either violate context or grammatical form. A contradiction is forced upon
the reader at the linguistic level. At the level of meaning the double voicing of the word requires him to acknowledge the moment
of birth as the moment of danger. A further pun underscores the
point. It has been inconclusively debated whether כור ("crucible")
was or was not a slang term for "womb" in Hebrew or Aramaic
usage of the author's day.[82] In either case, its metaphorical use here
is clear and evocative, as most translators recognize.

The next pair of phrases initially appears simply to draw out the
image of danger, in which the image of the womb opening (and
perhaps the birth waters that flow through it) is overlaid with the
image of the waters of death: "as children come to the womb opening of death, and she who is pregnant with a manchild suffers in
her birth pangs" (כיא באו בנים עד משברי מות והרית גבר הצרה בחבליה).
Here again, the language is pregnant with hidden meaning that only
becomes evident if one attends to the intertextual allusions. The first
half of the line is actually formed from a juxtaposition of two biblical phrases: כי באו בנים עד־משבר וכח אין ללדה ("for children come
to the womb opening, but there is no strength for birthing," 2 Kgs
19:3//Isa 37:3) and כי אפפני משברי־מות ("for the breakers of death
have encompassed me," 2 Sam 22:5). The splicing produced by the
hodayah does indeed effectively gloss "womb opening" as the place
of the "breakers of death." But something else occurs as well, something that is evident only to one who attends to the pattern of intertextual reference. Whereas the previous descriptions of the speaker's
distress had been taken from words of judgment upon a sinful people, both of these phrases come from a different context. They are
both attributed to faithful Israelite kings who were delivered from
distress by God. The first phrase comes from the words of lament
with which Hezekiah prefaces his pious request that Yahweh turn

---

[82] Baumgarten and Mansoor (190) cite the Aramaic כורא in *b. Shabb.* 140b, which,
according to Jastrow's *Dictionary*, is a euphemism for the female pudenda. Silberman
(101–103) rebuts the analysis of the Aramaic word and its relevance for 1QHᵃ 11.

away the Rab-shakeh from the gates of Jerusalem. The second phrase comes from the thanksgiving song of David that he sang "on the day when Yahweh delivered him from the hand of all his enemies, and from the hand of Saul" (2 Sam 22:1). What is particularly interesting is that the surface context of the hodayah and the subtext of the biblical allusions are not "in sync." Whereas the syntagmatic movement of the surface context still describes distress, the paradigmatic index of the intertextual allusion speaks of impending deliverance. Only in the next line, which describes the successful birth, do surface content and intertextual allusion converge. Danger and promise coexist in the tension between the syntagmatic and paradigmatic dimensions of the text, as they do for the pregnant woman. The final synchronization of these two levels of language resolves the tension, as the successful birth does for the woman in labor.

The final section of this part of the hodayah reads: "for at the womb opening of death she delivers a male, and in the birth pangs of Sheol there bursts forth from the crucible of the pregnant woman a wonderful counselor with his might" (כיא במשברי מות תמליט זכר ובחבלי שאול יניח מכור הריה פלא יועץ עם גבורתו). Here, the phrases from David's psalm of thanksgiving that recollected his distress, משברי מות ("breakers of death") and חבלי שאול ("bonds of Sheol," 2 Sam 22:5, 6), are paired with phrases that evoke divinely ordained, redemptive births. The phrase תמליט זכר ("she delivers a male") is the phrase used of Zion in Isa 66:7 to describe God's faithfulness in restoring Jerusalem: "Before she was in labor she gave birth; before her pain came upon her she delivered a son" (trans. NRSV). Similarly, פלא יועץ ("wonderful counselor") comes from Isa 9:5, where it describes the birth of the king who brings redemption.

The occurrence of this latter phrase has caused much speculation about the possible "messianic" meaning of the hodayah, speculation that has been soundly refuted. The significance of the phrase cannot be determined by taking it out of context but only by realizing that here it is part of an elaborately developed conceit for describing the distress and deliverance of the speaker along much the same lines as that of 1QH^a 10:20–30. Only in this case, given the nature of the metaphor, deliverance is the successful delivery of a baby. It is thus no accident that the child is given a name redolent of overtones of redemption and divine election. Any question about its further significance, however, must be asked not in isolation but rather in terms of the symbolic economy of the whole composition. Before

that can be made clear, it is necessary to examine the rest of the
hodayah.

The material that follows, from the end of 11:10 to the beginning
of 11:12, is difficult because of the plural forms. As I understand
the text, there are four short hemistichs in an a-b-b-a grammatical
pattern (verbal clause/nominal clause/nominal clause/verbal clause).
In terms of content the three hemistichs with plural forms are general statements about the nature of pregnancy and delivery: the
moment of crisis comes suddenly when its time arrives, and with it
all the pains associated with labor. It should be clear why the metaphor
of pregnancy is so appealing to the author of the hodayah. It has
a predestinarian, eschatological structure, with a "judgment" of life
or death at its final moment. The final hemistich of this series returns
from the general to the particular ("and so at the time of his birth
all these pangs come upon the crucible of the pregnant one"). But
who is the referent of its masculine singular pronoun and who is
the pregnant woman? At this point in the composition it would seem
obvious that the pronoun and noun would point back to the figures
already mentioned, though it also seems a bit redundant, since their
crisis has been successfully resolved. That initial clarity of reference
is quickly put into question, however.[83] Immediately following this
line the speaker introduces a new character, the הרית אפעה (the
woman "pregnant with nothingness") whose own moment of crisis
occupies the remainder of the hodayah. Do the phrases ובמולדיו
("and at the time of his birth") and כור הריה ("crucible of the pregnant one") then point forward to this woman and her monstrous
fetus? The description of her labor echoes two of the terms from
the immediately preceeding lines (חבלי מרץ/חבל נמרץ, "sharp pains"
and פלצות/מעשי פלצות, "shuddering"), further associating the new
figure with that description. I am perhaps belaboring what may seem
a small point, but the ambiguity produced by this juxtaposition is a
strategic one. The reader's first impulse is certainly to identify with
ובמולדיו and כור הריה as the symbolic terms representing his subjectivity in this text. But then he must draw back. Has he just committed the error of identifying with the figure that is in fact his polar
opposite? The service this ambiguity performs is to draw attention

---

[83] S. Brown (249) addresses the problem of the referent without, however, considering the ambiguity to be strategic.

to the play of same and opposite in the symbolic structure of the composition and implicitly to the problem of identity that the composition addresses.

The whole symbolic economy of this composition is organized around the comparison and contrast of the two female figures. They are, in their pregnant state, quite alike. Specifically, both are subject to the pains and dangers of labor, described in similar terms. But for one, the outcome is the birth of extraordinary new life, while for the other the outcome is death.[84] Who or what the second woman represents is never made explicit. What we do know is that she shares a similarity of condition with the speaker but experiences a diametrically opposite fate. That pattern, however, provides an adequate clue to the meaning of the figure.

One of the ambiguities that the sectarian speaker of the Hodayot has to confront is why his fate is different from that of other human beings. He can make no claim to possessing intrinsic special value, for he is essentially the same as others. He is only a creature of clay and water, impure and guilty. Sheol has every right to him. In the representation of the two pregnant women, the composition acknowledges that common identity and all the claims of death upon it. But if that common (and terrifying) aspect of oneself is acknowledged, what accounts for the diametrically opposite fates? On the symbolic plane it is nothing visible but rather that which is hidden in each woman. What is hidden in one is the viper/nothingness, and in the other the manchild, the wonderful counselor. Symbolically, the manchild is to the pregnant woman as the בינה ("insight"), the תורה ("teaching"), the סוד אמת ("secret of truth"), the רוח ("spirit"), and

---

[84] The use of paired, positive and negative female figures is a frequent device used by male writers to structure their symbolic worlds. Usually they are presented as paired protecting and threatening figures, such as the wife and the seductress. See Newsom, "Woman and the Discourse of Patriarchal Wisdom." The reason for this symbolic use is insightfully discussed by Moi (*Sexual/Textual Politics: Feminist Literary Theory*, 150), who suggests that because women occupy a marginal position in the symbolic order they come symbolically to represent its limit or border. They can take on the properties alternatively of the protecting, shielding qualities of the border or of the chaotic realm that lies on the outside of the border. Pregnancy, not only as the radically female role but also as the liminal state between being/non-being of the fetus, is an especially powerful symbol. What is distinctive about the Hodayot is the use of the pregnant woman as a direct metaphor for the figure of the speaker. Perhaps the appeal of such a symbol is also related to the strategic position on the margin of symbolic orders occupied by sectarian movements.

the דעת ("knowledge") are to the speaker in other compositions (see, e.g., 1QHᵃ 6:8; 13:9–11; 20:11–13). It is the divinely given insight that accounts for the crucial difference between the self and the other. Here, too, the aspect of divine knowledge is the characteristic emphasized in the identification of the manchild and the wonderful counselor. Not only does יועץ ("counselor") have overtones of effective understanding,[85] but so does the complementary phrase עם נבורתו ("with his might"). As Wernberg-Møller has shown, נבורה often has the nuance of powerful knowledge rather than physical might.[86] The speaker's subjectivity in this hodayah is represented by both the pregnant woman and the child to whom she gives birth. The same double structured identity, formed at the intersection of human vulnerability and powerful divine knowledge that one encounters in 1QHᵃ 9 is also developed here. In this complex hodayah, however, it is also connected with the attempt to distinguish the speaker's identity from that of his other, his enemy.

The resolution of the narrative is similar to that of 1QH 10:20–30, in which the evil that the opponents attempted recoils upon themselves, though here it is somewhat more complex in its workings. The prayer opened with the speaker describing his attack by others in terms of a ship at sea, a besieged city, and a pregnant woman. Having been "delivered" by negotiating the dual death/life values available in the images of childbirth, and having cast his opponents in the role of a monstrously pregnant woman, he then describes her death in childbirth through the echoing images of trembling city walls and a storm at sea. The symbolic negativity of the vulnerability and deathwardness that menaced the speaker at the beginning of the composition has been cast out and placed on the other. The subliminal overtones of guilt registered in the intertextual allusions are explicitly attached to the other, who is said to be "pregnant with iniquity." What is interesting about this composition is that it shows how the imagery of a bifurcated experience of self can be manipulated in such a way as to discharge at least temporarily the disturbing threat to the self that such a subjectivity entails. The way this is done, of course, is by projecting that inner division outward through the image of a symbolic other. This is not to say that the

---

[85] Mowinckel, "Zwei Qumran-Miszellen," 297–98.
[86] Wernberg-Møller, *Manual of Discipline*, 74.

Hodayot definitively resolve a divided subjectivity through the symbolic magic of their imagery and use of language. If anything, they do the opposite, calling into being and enhancing the sense of a self constructed at the intersection of human nothingness and divine intentionality. But the tension inherent in such a structure of the self is periodically discharged through symbolic structures that allow one to grasp proleptically the eschatological resolution of life and death, good and evil, the saved and the damned.

"I am a Camera": Perspective and Identity (1QH^a 11:19–36)

The problem of anxiety about the essential similarity between "the saved and the damned" and the problems it poses for sectarian subjectivity recur in the hodayah that immediately follows. The text and translation given below follow the strophic analysis of Bonnie Kittel.[87]

1QH^a 11:19–36

Introduction
(19) I thank you, O Lord,
that you have redeemed my life from the Pit
    and from Sheol-Abaddon (20) you have lifted me up to an
      eternal height,
    so that I walk around on a limitless plain.
    And I know that there is hope for the one whom (21) you have
      formed from the dust for the eternal council.

Strophe A
A perverted spirit you have purified from great sin,
    that it might take its place with (22) the host of the holy ones
    and enter into community with the congregation of the children
      of heaven.
And you cast an eternal destiny for the man with the spirits (23) of
      knowledge,
    that he might praise your name in a common rejoicing
    and recount your wonders before all your creatures.

---

[87] Kittel, 56–80. Her analysis is also followed by Lohfink, *Lobgesänge der Armen*, 92–98.

Strophe B

But I, a creature (24) of clay—
    what am I? A thing kneaded with water.
    And how should I be reckoned?
    What strength have I?
For I stand in the realm of wickedness
    (25) and with the vile is my lot.
    The soul of the poor one dwells in great turmoil
    and overwhelming destruction dogs my steps.

Strophe C

(26) As all the traps of the pit open
    and all the snares of wickedness spread wide,
    and the net of the detestable is over the surface of the waters—
(27) As all the arrows of the pit fly without turning back,
    and they let fly without hope—
As the line is cast for judgment,
    and the lot of wrath is (28) upon the abandoned,
    and an outpouring of fury is upon the hypocrites,
    and the time of wrath (comes) for all worthlessness,
    and the cords of death encompass without escape—

Strophe D

(29) And the torrents of Belial surge over all the high banks
    like a consuming fire on all their shores,[88]
    destroying every tree, green (30) and dry from their channels.
And it sweeps on in tongues of flame until there is none left of all
    who drank from them.
    It consumes the foundations of clay (31) and the expanse of the
    dry land.
    The bases of the mountains turn to flame,
    and (their) flinty roots to torrents of pitch.
And it consumes as far as the (32) great deep.
    And the torrents of Belial split open to Abaddon,
    and the creatures [?] of the deep roar with the tumult of churning
    mud.
And the land (33) screams on account of the destruction that has come
    upon the world.
    And all its creatures shout,
    and all who are upon it go mad
    (34) and stagger at the great destruction.

---

[88] The meanings of אנף and שואב are uncertain, although אנף is probably to be
related to M. Heb. and J. Aram אנף, which can refer to a "wing," "shoulder," or
"band." My translation of שואב follows the suggestion of Knibb (178) and the parallelism of the lines.

Strophe E

For God thunders with his roaring power

and his holy habitation roars (35) with his glorious truth.

And the host of heaven give voice

[and] the eternal foundations reel and shake.

And the battle of the warriors (36) of heaven pours forth upon the world,

and there is no turn[ing back un]til the consummation.

It is determined forever; and there is nothing like it. *vacat*

Introduction

אודכה אדוני (19)

כי פדיתה נפשי משחת

ומשאול אבדון (20) העליתני לרום עולם

ואתהלכה במישור לאין חקר

ואדעה כיא יש מקוה לאשר (21) יצרתה מעפר לסוד עולם

Strophe A

ורוח נעוה טהרתה מפשע רב

להתיצב במעמד עם (22) צבא קודשים

ולבוא ביחד עם עדת בני שמים

ותפל לאיש גורל עולם עם רוחות (23) דעת

להלל שמכה ביחד רנה

ולספר נפלאותיכה לנגד כול מעשיכה

Strophe B

ואני יצר (24) החמר

מה אני מגבל במים

ולמי נחשבתי

ומה כוח לי

כיא התיצבתי בגבול רשעה

(25) ועם חלכאים בגורל

ותגור נפש אביון עם מהומות רבה

והוות מדהבה עם מצעדי

Strophe C

בהפתח כל פחי שחת (26)

ויפרשו כול מצודות רשעה

ומכמרת חלכאים על פני מים

בהתעופף כול חצי שחת לאין השב (27)

וייורו לאין תקוה

בנפול קו על משפט

וגורל אף (28) על נעזבים

ומתך חמה על נעלמים

וקץ חרון לכול בליעל

וחבלי מות אפפו לאין פלט

Strophe D

(29) וילכו נחלי בליעל על כול אנפי רום

כאש אוכלת בכול שנאביהם

להתם כול עץ לח (30) ויבש מפלניהם

ותשוט בשביבי להוב עד אפס כול שותיהם

באושי חמר תאוכל (31) וברקוע יבשה

יסודי הרים לשרפה

ושורשי חלמיש לנחלי זפת

ותאוכל עד תהום (32) רבה

ויבקעו לאבדון נחלי בליעל

ויהמו מחשבי תהום בהמון נורשי רפש

וארץ (33) תצרח על ההווה הנהיה בתבל

וכול מחשביה ירועו

(34) ויתהוללו כול אשר עליה

ויתמוגגו בהווה גד[ו]לה

Strophe E

כיא ירעם אל בהמון כוחו

ויהם זבול קודשו באמת (35) כבודו

וצבא השמים יתנו בקולם

[ו]יתמוגגו ויראדו אושי עולם

ומלחמת גבורי (36) שמים תשוט בתבל

ולא תש[ו]ב ע[ד] כלה

ונחרצה לעד ואפס כמוה *vacat*

Significant verbal links between the conclusion of the preceding hodayah and the beginning of this one point to the symbolic nexus on which this anxiety is focused—the claim of Sheol. Where the woman pregnant with a viper/nothingness was consigned to the Pit and Sheol at the conclusion of the earlier text, this prayer opens with thanks that "you have redeemed my life from the Pit, and that from Sheol-Abaddon you have brought me up to an eternal height" (lines 19–20). Various polar terms are used to mark the transformation of the speaker's situation: low/high; dust/eternal council; perverted spirit/holy ones; and so forth (lines 19–23). The prayer would initially appear to build on the externalizing of the negative in the previous composition in order to consolidate a sense of the distinction between self and other, good and evil, saved and damned, and in so doing reinforce a relatively unified subjectivity. Instead, the crisis emerges again, signaled by the language of self-confrontation that underscores the susceptibility of the speaker to the dust of death. This conflict in the speaker's experience of self, which occurs in the first few lines of the hodayah, establishes the problematic that motivates the rest of the composition. In this hodayah, however, there is no plot of personal attack and deliverance such as shaped 1QH^a 10:20–30, nor is there a symbolic separation between self and other, life and death, as was enacted in the birthing images of the immediately preceding composition. Indeed, although it is difficult to say just where, one rather loses track of the individual whose plight is the focal point of the first part of the hodayah, as the imagery of eschatological battle takes over. Even at the end, as Kittel notes, "the poet's personal problem is not referred to again."[89] Nevertheless, she insists that "an answer to his problem is given, when the poem is contemplated in its entirety."[90] Kittel sees the resolution in the way in which the concluding strophe incorporates most of the key words from the preceding strophes, an observation to which Lohfink adds, by noting that the concluding images of the heavenly host and eternal foundations correspond to the opening images of the host of holy ones and the eternal lot.[91] As helpful as these observations are, they only begin to uncover the ways in which the recitation of this hodayah both engenders and then resolves the problem of identity.

One of the puzzling literary features of this composition is its abrupt transitions and lack of thematic integration, despite an apparently sophisticated formal structure. As Kittel says, "this poem seems to be composed of chunks."[92] Much of the difficulty in understanding how the composition works may stem from our own lack of a governing metaphor to guide our reading. In his analysis Lohfink supplies that needed metaphor, when he suggests that we understand what takes place in the aesthetic of this hodayah by reference to the techniques of modern filmmaking. His remarks are worth quoting in full:

> Man begreift ihn am besten, wenn man einen Vergleich aus der heutigen Filmtechnik heranzieht. Dort kann es, gerade an Filmanfängen, vorkommen, dass zunächst eine Totalaufnahme gebracht wird, etwa eine Stadtlandschaft, von einem Hubschrauber aus aufgenommen. Dann folgt ein Schnitt, und man befindet sich in einer Strasse, wo ein bestimmtes Haus und dort ein Fenster in den Blick kommt. Dann folgt wieder ein Schnitt, und man erlebt in Nahaufnahme eine Szene innerhalb des Zimmers. Schließlich vielleicht nochmals ein Schnitt, und man

---

[89] Kittel, 73.
[90] Kittel, 73.
[91] Lohfink, 95.
[92] Kittel, 76.

hat nur noch ein einzelnes Gesicht aus der Szene in Grossaufnahme
und erlebt an diesem Gesicht nun gewissermassen das ganze.[93]

The analogy to distance shots, close-ups, cuts—and I would add,
dissolves and tracking shots—not only discloses how the aesthetic of
this intensely visual and auditory composition works but also provides an insight into the underlying technique by which the reader's
subjectivity is formed: the manipulation of perspective. Following the
sequence of the shifting scenes of the composition will reveal how
this takes place.

The hodayah opens with a series of locative images. Where the
speaker is placed and the perspective from which he recounts his
experience thus comes immediately into view. Height and unimpeded
expanse characterize his placement (an eternal height, a limitless
plain), contrasting with the low and constricted places from which
he has been raised up (the Pit, Sheol-Abaddon), places which, by
being mentioned, are also included in the horizon of perception. In
Strophe A, too, the question of placement is explicitly addressed, as
the speaker refers, now in general, rather than specifically personal
terms, to being stationed (להתיצב במעמד) with the host of the holy
ones. This heavenly perspective is closely associated with the knowledge of God's wonderful deeds, which those belonging to the eternal lot recount as they stand before (לנגד) all God's creatures. It is,
as Lohfink suggests, a thoroughly panoramic opening scene.

In the first abrupt "scenic cut" the perspective contracts radically,
as the speaker's gaze is turned self-reflexively upon his own being.
In film-making terms the technique is a shot/reverse shot. That is,
the field *from* which the first scene is perceived becomes the object
of perception in the second shot. With the language of self-loathing
familiar from other Hodayot, the speaker characterizes himself in
terms of earthly elements, clay and water, and as a being weak and
without esteem. As the perspective widens out from its focus on the
speaker's self, terms of placement again appear. Only now the speaker
stands not with the holy ones in an eternal lot but stands in the
territory of wickedness (התיצבתי בגבול רשעה) in the lot of the vile
(ועם חלכאים בגורל).[94] In contrast to the unbounded space (מישער לאין)

---

[93] Lohfink, 96. His observations could also be fruitfully applied to certain prophetic
poetry, especially Jeremiah.
[94] The perfect verb התיצבתי does not refer to some past condition but to the
speaker's present human situation. See Kuhn, 62.

חקר) of the first scene, space here is described in terms of boundaries (נבול). Even at the level of syntax the speaker is figured as
confined and hedged in. Kittel analyzes the bicolon in line 25 (ותגור
נפש אביון עם מהומות רבה והוות מדהבה עם מצעדי) as an instance of
"reversal of object," an a-b-c, c-b-a pattern. The primary terms in
the bicolon are inverted to form a chiastic parallelism, while the
preposition עם occupies the same position. "The bicolon is thus a
set of interlocking statements: the poet stands in the midst of disaster and disaster encompasses the poet."[95] The perspective of the narration is now not only earthly rather than heavenly but focused on
the speaker's immediate and vulnerable situation rather than on a
panoramic view.

The next scenic transition would be better described in cinematic
terms as a dissolve rather than a cut. The speaker's self-reflections
about being subject to tumults and disasters are overlaid with a vivid
description of those dangers. It is as though the camera moves again
from focusing on the speaker to focusing through his eyes. What he
describes is the beginning of eschatological events; but following his
confession of distress, one hears them initially with reference to the
speaker's own vulnerability.

The syntax of Strophe C has a climactic structure. The erupting
violence is described in three infinitive clauses, each resumed by a
waw-consecutive imperfect verb in what is sometimes called a "when . . .
then" sequence. Given the vivid immediacy of the description, I have
preferred to translate "as."[96] The first two infinitives introduce the
activities of the forces of the Pit; the third announces the falling of
the line of judgment upon evil in a series of five images. Its syntactical completion, however, is not an account of divine action but
the bursting forth of the rivers of Belial. It is as though divine
judgment itself is what provokes the fiercest outpouring of the power
of evil.

Although the syntactic patterns link וילכו נחלי בליעל to the end
of Strophe C, in her division of strophes Kittel presents the phrase
as the beginning of Strophe D. Her reasons are cogent. As she says,
"with Strophe D it is almost as if a new poem has begun."[97] Not

---

[95] Kittel, 69.
[96] The issue of whether the description is future-oriented is beside the point; what
is described here is not a matter of linear temporality.
[97] Kittel, 71.

only is the vocabulary completely different, as Kittel notes, but one
might also add that a very different sort of description—much more
visual and much more auditory—begins with the introduction of torrents of Belial. Moreover, this section has a tight narrative unity, as
the successive aspects of the destruction of the cosmos are described.
The transition between Strophes C and D is thus complex and skillful. To return again to the cinematic analogy, one might compare
this technique to the tracking shot. Linking two scenes, it nevertheless accomplishes a shift of perspective. At least in some instances,
it may be used precisely to shift the viewer's point of identification.[98]
Because the process happens smoothly, the shift may be accomplished
without conscious recognition. That, I think, is what lies behind the
sense some commentators have of losing track of the speaker in this
hodayah. The continuity of the narrative of the eschatological events
is such that one hardly notices the shift in perspective. One is still
invested in the terror of being overcome by the tumults and disasters now unleashed. But the perspective from which the description
takes place is in fact no longer the worm's eye view of Strophe B
but the bird's eye view of the opening perspective. Though the torrents of Belial consume the ground, they do not consume the ground
on which the speaker stands and from which he sees.

The speaker's perspective can be assessed by noting the way in
which the description of the torrents of Belial and their effects are
narrated. Even though the events recounted reduce the world to
chaos, the events are described in a highly organized, structured
sequence. First the fiery torrents of Belial destroy the watery areas
with their vegetation and animals. Then they destroy dry land and
mountains. Next the great deep and the underworld are breached.
Having described the destruction by the torrents of Belial through
images of dissolution, the second part of the destruction is represented by a linked series of sound images. First, the inhabitants of
the deep roar. Their sound is followed by the screaming of the creatures of the earth. Then, in a scene shift that could be described as
an auditory dissolve, the screaming of the creatures of the earth is
overlaid by battle shouts, as God and the host of heaven engage in
the war of the end of the world.[99] By the final strophe one cannot

---

[98] Silverman, 211.
[99] The trope of the auditory dissolve is not a novelty here. At least two other

help but register the change in perspective that had in fact begun some lines before. The "camera" again has the panoramic perspective with which it began. Although the "personal problems of the psalmist" may not be explicitly referred to in the way that they are at the end of the hodayah in 1QH^a 10:20–30, the resolution of the crisis of the self is fully evident in the quality of the voice that speaks the concluding words. The words are brief, calm, and sure: "It is determined forever; and there is nothing like it" (line 36).

The narrator of the hodayah is the powerful voice of knowledge generated by the purposes of God. Through the mysteries of God he has been "stationed with the host of the holy ones . . . in order to recite your wonderful acts before all your creatures" (lines 22–24). Indeed this hodayah is precisely such a recitation. But the price of such knowledge is self-knowledge, the recognition of the guilt that attaches to the self. In reciting the wonderful acts of God, the speaker must tell of himself and in so doing encounter his own bifurcated identity as one who belongs to an "eternal lot with the spirits of knowledge" and also the "lot of the vile." Although the speaker must enter into the perspective of that wretched self in the course of the narration, the governing perspective remains that of the one whom God has redeemed and lifted up. Indeed, it is by persisting in the narration that he secures his identity.

Discourse and Counter-Discourse: Forming the Self Through a Language of Knowledge and Humility (1QH^a 4:17–25)

The individual who understands himself to be formed by the intersection of divine intention and human nothingness in the context of a cosmic drama of contending forces has a self that is inescapably structured by the tension of its polarities. The particular form of his moral consciousness will also be constituted by that irresolvable contradiction. One of the effects of such a structure of the self is that it finds expression in introspection. If one is to use that term to characterize the Hodayot, one has to distinguish it from the rather different

---

examples can be mentioned from prophetic poetry. In Jer 4:34 the auditory image of the woman in labor is overlaid by the sound of daughter Zion being murdered. In Isa 42:13–14 the battle cry of the divine warrior is overlaid by the cry of a woman giving birth.

forms of introspective subjectivity that emerge in late Greco-Roman antiquity, in which the examination of the concrete details of one's activities provided what Foucault called a "technology of the self."[100] The language of the self in the Hodayot is quite indifferent to quotidian realities. Like the language of the Psalms, it is schematized. By the term introspection I am pointing to a formal structure that allows the self (however its contents are defined) to become an object of reflection to the self. In the Hodayot there is a characteristic movement in which the divinely given insight (which is constitutive of the sectarian's subjectivity) is used reflexively to give knowledge of the self. That movement or gesture is what creates a space of introspection. For the Qumran sectarian the practice of reciting and/or hearing the Hodayot would have been a part of the "technology" by which the introspective self was appropriated and cultivated.

The moral problem of the self that is illumined by the particular introspective practice of the Hodayot is fairly easy to identify. The gift of insight has filled the speaker not only with the desire to praise God but also with the desire to be conformed to the divine will to do "everything that you love and despise everything that [you] hate, [and do] what is good in your eyes" (1QH^a 4:24). That same insight has caused him to know that as a human being he is not capable of doing what he most desires ("As for me, a source of bitter mourning was opened to me [. . .] trouble was not hidden from my eyes when I understood the dispositions of human beings and the return of humanity [to the dust . . .] to sin, and to the grief of guilt," (1QH^a 19:19–21). The moral pain of such a self-understanding is the unclosable gap between knowing and doing. As with the crisis in knowledge that was addressed in 1QH^a 9, this contradiction can only be resolved, paradoxically, by intensifying the polarities. Everything must be seen as coming from God; nothing from the human individual.

Obviously, humility is a vital personal virtue in such a moral discourse. Humility is initially produced by the divinely given insight that illumines the nature of the speaker, but it is also to be cultivated, along with the thankfulness to which it is closely related, as the appropriate response to what God has done. It is through the introspective practice of self-examination and critique provided by the Hodayot that the speaker commends himself to God's mercy,

---

[100] Foucault, "Technologies of the Self," 16–49.

for it is only through God's continuing graciousness that the speaker can be given the ability to do what is good in God's eyes.

The moral language of the Hodayot and the way in which it cultivates a profound humility can be seen in a composition such as 1QH[a] 4:17–25, despite the frustration of many broken lines.

1QH[a] 4:17–25

(17) [I thank yo]u, on account of the spirits which you have granted me,
    that I may find the speech to recite your righteous acts,
        the longsuffering (18) [. . .] and the deeds of your strong right
        hand.
    [and to confess][101] my previous sins,
    and to [prostrate] myself,
    and to beg for mercy concerning (19) [. . .].. of my deeds and
        the perversity of my heart.
For I have wallowed in impurity,
    and from the fellowship I [. . .],
    and I have not joined myself to (20) [. . .].
For to you yourself belongs righteousness
    and to your name belongs blessing for eve[r.]
[Act according to] your righteousness
    and ransom (21) [your servant;]
    [but let] the wicked be utterly consumed.

As for me, I understand that
    (for) the one whom you have chosen [you perfect] his way
    and through insight (22) [. . .you draw] him back from sinning
        against you.
    And in order [to restore] to him his humility
        through your disciplines and through [. . .] his heart. *vacat*
(23) [. . .] your servant from sinning against you
    and from stumbling in all the words of your good favor.
Strengthen [. . .] against spirits (24) [. . .]
    [that he may c]onduct himself according to everything that you
    love
    and despise everything that [you] hate,
    [and do] what is good in your eyes.
(25) [. . .] in my members; for your servant is a spirit of fle[sh]. *vacat*

(17) [אוד]ך מרוחות אשר נתתה בי
אמצאה מענה לשון לספר צדקותיך

---

[101] The restoration is uncertain. García Martínez and Tigchelaar (1:148), for example, suggest סל]יח[ות, "[the pardon]ing of my former offenses."

ואדוך אפים (18) [. . .]ך ומעשי ימין עוזך

[ולהוד]ות על פשעי ראשונים

ולה[תנפ]ל ולהתחנן על (19) [. . .] מעשי ונעויית לבי

כי בנדה התגוללתי

ומסוד [. . .]תי

ולא נלאיתי (20) [. . .]

כי לך אתה הצדקה

ולשמך הברכה לעול[ם]

[עשה כ]צד[קתך]

ופדה (21) [את עבדך]

[וי]תמו רשעים

ואני הבינותי כי את אשר בחרתה [תתם] דרכו

ובשכל (22) [. . . תמ]שכהו מחטוא לך

ול[הש]יב לו ענותו

ביסוריך ובנס[. . .]ה לבו *vacat*

(23) [. . .] עבדך מחטוא לך

ומכשול בכול דברי רצונך

חזק מ[. . .]ד על רוחות (24)[. . .]

[לה]תהלך בכול אשר אהבתה

למאוס בכול אשר שנא[תה]

[ולעשות] הטוב בעיניך

(25) [. . .]לחם בתכמי

כי רוח בש[ר] [עבדך] *vacat*

Even in its damaged condition the structure of this brief hodayah is fairly clear. After initial words of gratitude,[102] the speaker summarizes in parallel infinitive clauses the content of his prayer: words of praise and words of confession, self-abasement, and supplication. The focus of the prayer is already indicated through the fact that only one verb of praise is balanced by three related to the speaker's need for God's mercy. The next section of the composition is also structured in parallel fashion through two כי clauses, the first and longer of which describes the speaker's sinful behavior, the second of which characterizes God. Next comes the request for redemption, which is followed by a reflection on the speaker's understanding of how God's

---

[102] Thanking God for the gift of plural spirits is unusual. Elsewhere, however, God is thanked for giving the speaker insight (1QH[a] 6:8), "your holy spirit" (1QH[a] 4:26), a "spirit of knowledge" (1QH[a] 6:25), "the spirit of your compassion" (1QH[a] 8:17), etc. Presumably, all of these are intended by the plural here. The gift of these spirits enables the speaker to find the knowledge and the voice with which to respond (both implied in the phrase מענה לשון, "the answer of the tongue," i.e., speech).

redemption takes place. There is probably a further request for divine aid, assuming that one should supplement an imperative verb before עבדך in line 23 and should read חזק before the other lacuna. The results of this divine aid in reforming the conduct of the speaker are described in three parallel infinitive phrases in line 24. The last line apparently contains a concluding characterization of the speaker that motivates the appeal.

As is typical of the Hodayot, there is a relentless consistency in the way in which all moral initiative is attributed to God and utter moral incapacity is attributed to the speaker. Although this is most explicit in the contrasting כי clauses, it is also implied in the passivity of the speaker as the object of God's "ransoming." The very possibility of a moral life depends upon God's action in choosing one. Even then, the phraseology of the hodayah suggests that the inclination of the person is to sin, and that he is only prevented from his natural tendency by God's initiative. Even after the second request, which envisions the speaker's being able to live a life of proper conduct, the conclusion returns to the theme of the fundamental moral incapacity of the speaker in the expression "spirit of flesh."

It takes practice to talk like that. The whole inherited moral vocabulary with which the author of the hodayah works—the vocabulary of obedience, sin, conducting one's life, doing what is good, and so forth—was crafted in a very different discursive context with a very different assumption about human moral agency.[103] And yet the speaker manages to use this inherited vocabulary in a way that seems both coherent and persuasive, even while denying that fundamental assumption. He puts the inherited words together into a new kind of talk that ultimately changes their meaning and significance—and that changes the nature of the person who speaks them. What takes place in the Hodayot is a rather significant challenge to and reformation of the dominant moral language of Second Temple Judaism. It is easier to sense the difference than to specify precisely how it is managed. At least some of the mechanisms can be noticed, however.

As discussed above, a basic context for the language and a basic disposition for the one who speaks it is established by the uniform

---

[103] Whether one looks at the Psalms, the deuteronomistic tradition, the wisdom writings, or at prophetic admonitions, the fundamental though often unspoken assumption is of individual moral agency.

practice of beginning each composition with words of blessing or
thanks. As a verbal gesture, it is analogous to assuming a physical
posture of humility. Establishing such a context already begins to
naturalize the language of the Hodayot that minimizes human agency.

Another part of this literary framing is the cultivation of the contrast
between God and human beings as the context within which reflection
on sin and obedience takes place. It is certainly possible within
Israelite traditions of prayer to speak of one's uprightness and moral
conduct. Those occasions are often (though by no means exclusively)
in contexts in which one's own conduct is compared with that of
one's enemies. It becomes much more difficult to speak of—or believe
in—one's moral achievements if one is alternating between language
characterizing God and language characterizing self; and that is precisely where the Hodayot locate reflections on moral character.

These literary constraints on language are important, but by themselves might simply lead one to abandon traditional moral language
as impossible or incoherent. That is not, of course, what the Hodayot
do. Rather they insist on the essential importance of that moral language even as they deny moral agency. To do that requires not just
an affective appeal to humility but a well articulated logical argument. This is what gives the Hodayot their often noted didactic quality. The whole possibility of a moral life depends on understanding
the mysteries of the plan of God. The logic of that predestined drama
offers internally consistent explanations for the coherency of moral
law without autonomous moral agents. Although the hodayah quoted
here only hints at that explanation, it is more explicit in others, such
as 1QH^a 7:11–31, quoted earlier in this chapter. To put it in Kenneth
Burke's terms, the "scope" or "circumference" within which the moral
life is discussed is infinitely larger in the Hodayot than in traditional
contexts.[104]

It would seem that the denial of moral agency would be such a
sharp departure from inherited assumptions that it would be a difficult
value to grasp. However, it is never presented as a denial of a traditional assumption in the Hodayot. Instead, it appears to be the
logical conclusion of a belief in divine sovereignty. Again, Burke's
terminology is apt, as he describes such a rhetorical movement as

---

[104] Burke, *Grammar of Motives*, 77–85.

"perfecting."[105] If one "perfects" the notion of divine sovereignty, one ends up with a denial of other, independent wills. Consequently, that of which the Hodayot attempts to persuade its readers is not something strange but only the profound consequence of something true.

This tendency to "perfect" a notion is not unrelated to the tendency, discussed above, for Qumran discourse to proceed by citing a piece of received tradition and then pairing it with a restatement in sectarian terminology. The sectarian reinterpretation typically either sets the cliche in a wider cosmic scope or in much more absolute terms (e.g., 1QH^a 7:15–17). Such a habit of speech, framed as statement and (reinterpretive) restatement, provides a mode by which the inherited moral vocabulary may be reaccented and made to refer to contexts and concepts that were not present in its traditional uses.

In addition, a word may be reaccented by making it keep company with other words that lend their own meanings to it or by using it in statements or constructions that require it to take on new connotations. One of the best attested examples of this is the reaccentuation of the word צדקה in Qumran diction. In addition to its traditional meanings it takes on the overtone of "graciousness."[106] Although there are other passages in which this enrichment of meaning is even clearer, it occurs distinctly enough in 1QH^a 4. Here, for instance, it is parallel in the introductory words of the hodayah to "long-suffering" as well as "the deeds of your strong right hand." The company it keeps gives it both the nuance of "victories," a traditional meaning, and "acts of grace," not a traditional one. Similarly, it is God's צדקה to which the speaker makes appeal to be ransomed. Since he clearly cannot *deserve* to be ransomed, it is to God's צדקה as compassionate, merciful graciousness that he appeals. The element of "distributive justice"[107] is not absent, since the wicked are also to be condemned; but that is clearly not the basis on which the speaker appeals for his own deliverance. The effect of such a reaccentuation of the word צדקה is not just to alter the conception of God but also to alter the meaning of what it means for an individual to be צדיק. As Sanders correctly stresses, it still means "perfection

[105] Burke, *Language as Symbolic Action*, 16–20.
[106] Sanders, *Paul and Palestinian Judaism*, 306–12.
[107] Sanders, *Paul and Palestinian Judaism*, 310.

of way";[108] but now that perfection of way is dependent upon the
graciousness of God.

One final element of the moral discourse of this hodayah requires
further comment. Even though there is little overt reference to the
community and its significance in the Hodayot, the moral language
that it speaks is linked in various ways with the community and,
indeed, is not understandable apart from it. When the speaker of
this hodayah comes to explain how it is that the righteousness/grace
of God enables one who is not a moral agent nevertheless to live a
life of perfection of way, he names two things that are both said to
keep one "from sinning against [God]"—insight (שכל) and "your disciplines" (יסוריך). These are not casually chosen words but words
with a specific context and resonance in Qumran speech. The context within which they should be heard has already been established
earlier in the hodayah. The terms by which the speaker confessed
his sin all echo the language of the Serek ha-Yahad. "Perversity" is
the criterion by which one is demoted within the hierarchy of the
community (1QS 5:24); "wallowing in impurity" (cf. 1QS 4:22)
describes the condition that characterizes even sectarians before the
eschatological purification; סוד in this context is most likely an allusion to the fellowship of the community,[109] even though the broken
context does not allow one to complete the phrase; and "joining
oneself to" (cf. 1QS 5:6) is the phrase that describes entry into the
sectarian community. Thus when the speaker of the hodayah refers
to "insight" and "disciplines," it is specifically their meanings within
the communal life of the sect that are in view. Although שכל is a
quality that is given by God, it is examined and evaluated through
the practices of the community (1QS 5:21, 23, 24; 6:14, 19; 9:13,
15). Its nonabstract, moral quality is also indicated by the fact that
in the Serek ha-Yahad it is paired with "deeds" as the criteria for
the periodic evaluation. Even more explicitly "disciplines" is a term
that points to the praxis of the community as the means by which
the contradiction of a moral life without an autonomous moral agent
is resolved. Of the one who balks at entering the community because
of "the stubbornness of his heart" the Serek ha-Yahad says that "his
soul has spurned the disciplines involved in the knowledge of the

---

108 Sanders, *Paul and Palestinian Judaism*, 311.
109 Holm-Nielsen, *Hodayot*, 248, nn. 12, 13.

precepts of righteousness" (1QS 3:1). It is the community, with its disciplines and its ability to "purify the knowledge" (1:13) of its members, that mediates between the righteousness of God and the "spirit of flesh" that characterizes its members. It is in short not possible to live a moral life, "to do what is good" in God's eyes, apart from the community and its disciplines.

The point of this discussion has not been to describe the *beliefs* of the Qumran community about the moral life but to draw attention to the distinctiveness of the way in which the Hodayot talk about it. The Hodayot offer the reader a language that is both familiar and transformed, a language in which surfaces are illumined by glimpses of depths of meaning. It is a language both of logic and affect. Even though it bestows an identity as one of the elect, one who learns to speak this language will be deeply marked by a character of humility. By the same token one who has been formed in humility will find this language not only natural but inevitable.

There is nothing polemical about 1QH^a 4:17–25 or others that resemble it (cf. e.g., 1QH^a 19:15–27). It does not appear to be engaged in contesting with the enemies of the sect as some of the other Hodayot do. Rather it appears simply to be concerned with nurturing a disposition of humility and a desire to do the will of God. But every act of formation is also an act of estrangement. Every act of discourse is also an act of counter-discourse. In many respects the texts that are dedicated "simply" to teaching a language with which to talk about the common moral concerns of late Second Temple Judaism may be the most effective polemical texts. Once a person is steeped in the language of the Hodayot, then other languages are disclosed to be "unspeakable." They appear faulty and defective or shallow and superficial. The characters who speak them may claim piety, but since their words are so clearly not words of piety, they can only be deluded or hypocrites. This alienation from other moral languages reassures the sectarian of the truth of his own knowledge and further secures his identity.

Even a modern reader can perform an experiment that will reveal how this works. One has only to immerse oneself in several of the Hodayot like the one quoted above, reading them with all the sympathetic imagination possible, and then turn to a comparable text from another roughly contemporary source, for instance, Psalm 119, Ben Sira, or the Psalms of Solomon.

Consider the following excerpts from Psalm 119.

Vv. 65–70

> You have dealt well with your servant, O Lord, according to your work.
> Teach me good judgment and knowledge, for I believe in your commandments.
> Before I was humbled I went astray, but now I keep your word.
> You are good and do good; teach me your statutes.
> The arrogant smear me with lies, but with my whole heart I keep your precepts.
> Their hearts are fat and gross, but I delight in your law.
> It is good for me that I was humbled, so that I might learn your statutes.
> The law of your mouth is better to me than thousands of gold and silver pieces.

vv. 97–102

> Oh, how I love your law! It is my meditation all day long.
> Your commandment makes me wiser than my enemies, for it is always with me.
> I have more understanding than all my teachers, for your decrees are my meditation.
> I understand more than the aged, for I keep your precepts.
> I hold back my feet from every evil way, in order to keep your word.
> I do not turn away from your ordinances, for you have taught me.

vv. 121–128

> I have done what is just and right; do not leave me to my oppressors.
> Guarantee your servant's well-being; do not let the godless oppress me.
> My eyes fail from watching for your salvation, and for the fulfillment of your righteous promise.
> Deal with your servant according to your steadfast love, and teach me your statutes.
> I am your servant; give me understanding, so that I may know your decrees.
> It is time for the Lord to act, for your law has been broken.
> Truly I love your commandments more than gold, more than fine gold.
> Truly I direct my steps by all your precepts; I hate every false way (trans. NRSV).

What a different quality of self speaks in these lines. It foregrounds itself in the language, saying "I do this" or "I do that." The very number of verbs of which "I" is the subject is striking. Thought the speaker claims to have been humbled, he does not speak about this in any detail. Although he may say "my flesh trembles for fear of you, and I am afraid of your judgments," the speaker of this psalm seems to have no vocabulary with which to speak of his sins and his failings. When he does turn his gaze inward, it becomes a brash self-recommendation as he unashamedly names his moral accomplishments.

His stance before God is also noteworthy. In contrast to the grateful humility of address to God that begins each Qumran Hodayot, the speaker of Psalm 119 begins with a focus on human beings. "Happy are those whose way is blameless, who walk in the law of the Lord. Happy are those who keep his decrees, who seek him with their whole heart, who also do no wrong, but walk in his ways" (vv. 1–3). From the perspective of the Hodayot this language fails to attribute to God what comes from God but rather speaks as if it were in the power of each person simply to do what is right. Both the speaker of Psalm 119 and 1QH^a 4 use imperative verbs to seek God's aid, but the tone and effect are strikingly different. The speaker of Psalm 119 importunes God with repeated demands, often offering as motivation his own moral achievements. The speaker in the Hodayot makes his plea only after careful preparation of thanksgiving and confession, and motivates his plea by his own moral incapacity.

The speaker of Psalm 119 also makes much of wanting to be taught precepts, decrees, commandments, and statutes. But from the perspective of the Hodayot, there is a flatness to this language, a lack of scope, that betrays his inability to understand. Only insight into divine mysteries can disclose the true meaning of divine commands. There is no depth or resonance, no perspective of the plan of God in his speech. Both speech and speaker appear to be flawed.

Ben Sira fares even worse. After immersion in the language and sentiments of the Hodayot, a passage like Sir. 15:11–16 sounds obtuse and shallow.

> Say not, "It was God's doing that I fell away" for what he hates, he does not do.
> Say not, "It was he who set me astray"; for he has no need of the wicked. Abominable wickedness the Lord hates; he does not let it befall those who fear him.
> It was he, from the first, when he created humankind, who made them subject to their own free choice.
> If you choose, you can keep his commandment; understanding is the doing of his will.

> There are poured out before you fire and water; to whichever you
> choose you can stretch forth your hands (trans. Skehan).

Where Ben Sira says that "he placed them in the hand of their free
will (יצר), the speaker of 1QH^a 7:16 says that "the inclination (יצר)
of every spirit is in your hand." The hodayah's assertion stakes out
the moral high ground of humility, a quality much valued in Second
Temple piety. Although there is little likelihood that Ben Sira's teachings were a polemical response to any Qumran teachings (the generally accepted dates of the compositions would make that impossible),
he does appear to be caricaturing a comparable predestinarian ethic
by claiming that it is the equivalent of blasphemously blaming God
for sin. Indeed his use of the expression מבראשית ("from 'in the
beginning'") suggests that he is engaging on its own grounds a predestinarian discourse rather like that developed at Qumran, one that
seeks explanations in distant origins through an interpretation of normative biblical texts. But such rhetorical tactics would not be persuasive to one who was formed by the piety of Qumran. Instead
Ben Sira would likely appear to be appallingly superficial and arrogant. Where Ben Sira says, "If you choose" (תחפץ), the hodayah says
that it is God's choosing (בחרתה) that first makes obedience possible.
By contrast with the hodayah's subtle analysis of how the moral life
is possible, Ben Sira's advice appears the equivalent of "Just do it"
or "Just say no." Indeed, there is a clear distinction between an indi-
vidualistic orientation in Ben Sira (one that resonates in the modern-
day slogans) and a communal orientation in the moral language of
the hodayah, with its insistence on the disciplines God has provided
through the Yahad.

Not only Ben Sira's language but also the persona that his language creates for him would have seemed flawed to the Qumran
community. One might object that it is not apt to compare the persona created in a wisdom teaching with that created in a prayer
text. But the point I would make is that the Qumran community
placed its reflections on the conditions for the moral life significantly
in prayer texts because the stance of prayer prevented just the sort
of arrogant and self-complacent persona that a wisdom style might
encourage.

I have set up these comparisons between the hodayah and Psalm
119 and Ben Sira 15 as a heuristic exercise for the modern reader.
I am not claiming that this is in fact how a Qumran sectarian read

either one of these particular texts. Especially in the case of Psalm 119, which was probably considered to be inspired scripture by the sect, it is doubtful that a sectarian could have read it simply as an utterance or model of one type of piety. Special reading conventions governed the reading of scripture, as we know from the pesharim and from the ways in which scripture was cited and interpreted in the Hodayot and in other Qumran texts. Indeed, anyone who has taught the Bible in a modern college or seminary knows the extent to which special reading conventions continue to govern the way in which readers prevent the Bible from saying anything that they consider to be offensive to their piety. My point is not about how Qumran sectarians read scripture but rather about how they would have been likely to hear other languages of piety in the living religious culture around them. As this experiment makes evident, becoming steeped in a particular way of talking does indeed estrange one from other ways of approaching the same ground. It makes one hear what one never heard before in the language of others; and it gives one the tools with which to identify its flaws and inadequacies.

SELF AND COMMUNITY IN THE HODAYOT

Curiously, relatively little is said about the relationship between the individual and the community in the Hodayot, especially in the so-called Hodayot of the community.[110] There are a few references to the "covenant" to which the speaker holds fast, but not much reference to the community formed by this covenant. This reticence is perhaps due to the genre of the Hodayot and their relation to the traditions of personal psalmody. Even as compared with the Psalms, however, reference to the congregation within which the speaker stands is elusive in the Hodayot. References to community tend to be community with the angels rather than to the sect itself. That is not to say that the Hodayot are irrelevant for an understanding of the social structures of the sect. Quite the contrary. There is no subjectivity outside of a social context, since subjectivity is formed through social discourse. Moreover, the particular forms of subjectivity

---

[110] The problems of community formation are more explicitly addressed in the Hodayot of the persecuted leader.

available will be correlated with particular forms of social organization.[111] Even if all we had recovered from the Dead Sea caves were the so-called community hymns of the Hodayot, it would probably have been possible to deduce that they were produced by a highly structured society with a strong disciplinary emphasis. The extent to which personal autonomy is minimized, even undermined, in the Hodayot would imply that the authority for organizing and guiding the conduct of the self was largely vested in some form of communal structures and institutions.

If that is the case, however, one might wonder why so much energy is devoted to the development of such an extensive literature of first-person singular prayer as the Hodayot. In fact, it is not odd at all, if one again recalls the musings of Michel Foucault, cited above in connection with the Serek ha-Yahad concerning "how . . . certain kinds of interdictions required the price of certain kinds of knowledge about oneself" and what one "must know about oneself in order to be willing to renounce anything."[112]

As discussed in the chapter concerning the Serek ha-Yahad, we do know a great deal about the Qumran community's "interdictions." The person who entered the covenant of the community agreed to renounce much. He swore to submit to the authority of the community in matters of halakah. His relations with persons outside the group were severely restricted. His own property was put at the disposal of the community. He was required to undergo periodic examinations of his conduct and opinions, examinations that determined his status within the community. His activities throughout the day were closely ordered. Even the activities of eating and drinking were made the subject of discipline. Speech and behavior, including gestures, garments, and even bodily functions were subject to regulation. Infractions of rules resulted in varying degrees of penalty.

What the Hodayot do is to engender the knowledge about himself that a sectarian needed for the *askesis* of the community to seem meaningful, even self-evidently correct and appropriate. It is worthwhile to recall some of the representations of the self in the Hodayot and the way in which they would have served to ground the social practices of the community. In the drama of persecution and deliv-

---

[111] See the discussion of R. Brown, 28–63.
[112] Foucault, "Technologies of the Self," 17.

erance enacted in several of the Hodayot the sectarian's knowledge of himself as an object of hatred and violent attack by the forces of wickedness not only provides a measure of relief from the ambiguities of a bifurcated self but also naturalizes the requirements of strict separation from those outside the sect. In a very direct way sentiments of affinity and estrangement are cultivated, providing an emotive basis for the practices of separation that constructed boundaries for the sectarian community.[113] From time to time scholars have questioned whether the Qumran community was quite as "hermetically sealed" as some of its rhetoric would lead one to believe. It is difficult to say, since we lack basic information about the actual daily life of the community. What one can learn from the Hodayot is not whether members of the community did or did not have contact with outsiders but rather with what kind of sentiments they were encouraged to perceive those within and without the community. The schooling of the sentiments of affinity and estrangement is much more intensely cultivated through the Hodayot of the persecuted leader and will be taken up in more detail in the next chapter.

Less often remarked but extremely important is the formation of the self as a speaking subject, as examined in the first part of this chapter. The persona of the Hodayot is one who gives an account of himself. Reflective and self-reflective, the voice of these compositions is formed by the knowledge it has received from God. The cultivation of individuals whose sense of self was deeply connected with the act of speech was important because of the centrality of discourse in the life of the community. Not fortuitously, the community often designates itself as עצת היחד. It is fundamentally a group of persons seeking to be conformed to the "righteous counsel" of God (1QS 1:13) through a form of life that has at its center the act of taking counsel together. The extended account of the "session of the Many" in 1QS 6 gives a sense of the high value placed on the ability to engage in the discipline of giving counsel. Periodically, too, members had to respond to questioning concerning their "insight" or "spirit" and "deeds," an examination that was apparently conducted in a public fashion. To be able to give an account of oneself was an essential requirement for life in the community. What one sees in the Hodayot is a model of the sentiments, values, insights,

---

[113] Lincoln, 8–11.

and diction expected of members. Indeed, as suggested above, the
Hodayot themselves may be the fruit of an exercise of self-presentation in which all members participated.[114] Certainly the act of reading or listening to them would have accustomed the members of the
community to a sense of self that is articulated in self-presentation.
The knowledge of self generated through the Hodayot is grounded
in a radical contrast between the self and God. As illustrated by the
hodayah in 1QH^a 9, the speaker knows himself as a wholly het-
eronomous being. Predestined for his fate, he is in a sense simply
an effect of God, not so much a protagonist in a cosmic drama as
a sign of divine activity. The sectarian's knowledge of his own nonau-
tonomous status prepares him in general for a communal rather than
an individual orientation. The sectarian's recognition of his role is
made possible because he is graced with insight into the primordial
divine plan. He also comes to know himself as one who deeply
desires the righteousness of God and the ordered beauty of the divine
plan. But as one who is governed by "a spirit of error" and who
does not intrinsically possess the resources to achieve this reformation of the self, he also desires the community's disciplines of obedience that will bring him into right order. Thus the Hodayot form
a subject who does not encounter the regulation of time, conduct,
speech, and so forth in the community as a restriction on self but
as the fundamental conditions for the experience of his true self.

The desire to be conformed to the will of God is not unproblematic. Several of the Hodayot examined above enact a crisis of
the self in which the enlightened, knowing aspect of the subject confronts its persistently recalcitrant sinfulness and uncleanness. This
personal account of self-confrontation and self-discovery has its counterpart in the practices of the community. Mutual reproof apparently constituted a significant element in the social regulation of the
community. Although mentioned only briefly in the Serek ha-Yahad,
public reproof seems to have been a feature of the annual review.[115]
But private reproof and reproof before witnesses are also assumed
to have been established and regulated forms of conduct among the
membership, and were necessary preliminaries to bringing a more

---

[111] Reike, "Remarques," 43.
[115] Knibb, 114.

formal charge before the assembly.[116] Such a practice may obviously be a source of dissension as well as of social control, as the regulation of reproof in the Serek ha-Yahad suggests. The receptiveness of members to accepting rebuke (at least in principle) is enhanced because they have rehearsed their own persistent incapacity for obedience in the Hodayot. In this way the Hodayot provide the kind of knowledge about oneself that Foucault suggests is the price of certain kinds of discipline.

There is one aspect of community discipline that has not yet appeared to be addressed by the Hodayot, namely, the thoroughly hierarchical structure of the community. In general ways, of course, the Hodayot prepare a subject amenable to a hierarchical social life. Both the desire for order and the recognition of the individual's innate sinfulness are important elements that can support a hierarchical order. Taken by themselves, however, the Hodayot would seem to be just as suitable to an egalitarian social order. After all, except for the Hodayot of the leader, they provide a *common* experience for members. Moreover, they overturn established hierarchies of the cosmos, such as one finds in Psalm 148 and the Song of the Three Youths, by claiming fellowship with the angels in a community of praise. There is, however, one hodayah that undertakes explicitly to justify the hierarchical order of the community.

KNOWLEDGE, THE SELF, AND HIERARCHY (1QH^a 6:8–22)

The speaker of the hodayah in 1QH^a 6:8–22 is evidently a leader within the community. This composition is generally not associated with the so-called Hodayot of the Righteous Teacher, however, because it lacks the motifs of persecution and revelatory disclosure that are associated with that group of prayers. The role that the speaker attributes to himself in this composition is one that the Serek ha-Yahad assigns to the Maskil, the task of establishing the hierarchical order of the community (1QS 9:14–16; cf. the similar task of "the Paqid at the head of the Many" in 1QS 6:14, who is sometimes identified with the Maskil and sometimes with the Mebaqqer).

---

[116] See 1QS 5:24–6:1 and 4Q477 Rebukes Reported by the Overseer. Hempel, "Who Rebukes in 4Q477?"; Reed, "Genre, Setting and Title of 4Q477."

Even though this hodayah is not introduced with the phrase למשכיל,
as are certain of the other Hodayot (1QH^a 5:1; 7:11; 20:4; 25:10),
the persona of the speaker is almost certainly the Maskil. A feature
that characterizes at least two of these compositions is the connections between their language and that of the Serek ha-Yahad. The
hodayah of the Maskil in 1QH^a 5 has verbal links with the Two
Spirits section of 1QS 3–4. The hodayah of the Maskil in 1QH^a 20
has strong similarities with the liturgical calendar and hymn of 1QS
10–11. Similarly, the hodayah in 1QH^a 6:8–22 reflects several aspects
of the vocabulary of the Serek ha-Yahad, including the technical terminology of sectarian procedure.[117]

Two particularly interesting features appear in this composition.
The first is its attempt to connect the rhetoric of the formation of
the self as it is developed in the Hodayot with the rhetoric of community formation as it occurs in the Serek ha-Yahad. These are not
incommensurate discourses, since they are both languages of the sect,
but they are distinctive and were largely cultivated in different settings within the life of the community. Since the language of community formation is the "alien" discourse in this genre, what the
speaker must do is to commend or naturalize it within the horizon
of the diction of the Hodayot. Thus it will be important to trace
how these two languages are related to one another in the composition of this piece.

The second, closely related feature is the strongly self-justifying
tone of the composition. Although addressed to God, as are all the
Hodayot, one has the distinct impression that the speaker is implicitly addressing the members of the sect through his prayer. The quality of self-justification invites one to speculate about the rhetorical
situation that may have produced this hodayah. One can easily imagine how the Maskil's authority for examining members and assign-

---

[117] Compare לפי רוחות [תפ]ילם בין טוב לרשע in 1QH^a 6:11–12 with וינחילן לבני
איש לדעת טוב [ורע לה]פיל גורלות לכול חי לפי רוחו in 1QS 4:26; cf. also 1QS 2:20;
9:14. Compare וכן הונשתי ביחד כול אנשי סודי לפי [ש]כלו אנישנו in 1QH^a 6:18–19
with ואיש כבוד כפיו לקרבו ולפי שכלו להגישו in 1QS 9:15–16. The use of יחד in the
hodayah I take to be the same technical use as in 1QS. Compare לבינתך וכן תנישני
in 1QH^a 6:13 with ברחמיו תנישני in 1QS 11:13. The use of קרב in 1QH^a 6:14 corresponds to the use in 1QS 6:16, 19, 22; 9:15; etc. There are other less striking
similarities between the diction of this hodayah and the Serek ha-Yahad (e.g., 1QH^a
6:10–11 and 1QS 1:3) that add to the overall sense of close connection between
the two texts.

ing hierarchical status could have been a source of resentment and dissension, and this hodayah in 1QH^a may well have been a Maskil's reply to his critics. If so, it provided a clever rhetorical strategy. Hodayot, as first-person singular prayers, are intensely personal forms of speech. By presenting his case in this form, what the Maskil puts at issue is not a particular decision or a community practice but himself. The language of the formation of the self in the Hodayot, however, always involves some form of self-effacement, so that the effective power of the speaker is seen to be derived from God. Thus, by adhering to the language of self-presentation in the Hodayot, the Maskil links his own bona fides to that of God and so provides a powerful justification for his decisions. He acts through the knowledge that has been given to him by God. Even if the hodayah under consideration was composed for such a specific purpose, its presence in the scroll indicates that it became a part of the repertoire of Hodayot available in the community. In that capacity its rhetorical function would have been less directly addressed to a crisis of dissension, but it would have still served to underwrite the institutional authority of the Maskil and his decisions.

The language and rhetoric of the composition can best be studied by attending first to its strophic organization. Introductory phrases, syntactical and content parallelism, independent pronouns, and various introductory particles articulate the structure fairly well.

1QH^a 6:8–22[118]

Strophe A
(8) [Blessed are you,] O Lord,
    who places insight in the heart of your servant
    (9) [so that] he may underst[and all] these things,
    and have in[sight . . .,]
    and have self-control with respect to evil deeds,
    and bless (10) rightly all who choose your will,
    [and choose all t]hat you love,
    and abhor all that (11) [you hate].

---

[118] The text was reconstructed by Emile Puech ("Quelques aspects," 44–45, 52–55) from Sukenik col. 14:8–22 + fr. 15b ii + 44 + a previously unedited fragment. Although I tend to follow the somewhat more conservative readings of García Martínez and Tigchelaar, in certain instances I prefer the readings of Puech. Where they differ significantly, the other reading is noted.

Strophe B

And you have given your servant insight [. . . spi]rits of humankind.
  For according to the spirits [you] cast the lot for them between
    (12) good and evil,
  [and you] arrange [. . . to gui]de them (in) their activity.

Strophe C

And as for me, I know because of the insight that comes from you
  (13) that through your goodwill toward a p[er]son you mul[tiply
    his portion] in your holy spirit.
  And thus you draw me closer to your understanding.
  And as (14) I approach, I become zealous toward all who commit
    guilty deeds and (toward) people of deceit.
  For all who are near to you do not disobey your command,
    (15) and all who know you do not pervert your words.
  For you are righteous
    and all your chosen ones are true.
  All iniquity (16) [and wick]edness you will destroy forever,
    and your righteousness will be revealed to the eyes of all your
      creatures. *vacat*

Strophe D

(17) [And as for]me, I have knowledge by means of your abundant
    goodness
  and by means of the oath I pledged upon my life, not to sin against
    you
    (18) [and] not to do anything evil in your eyes.

Strophe E

And thus I advance in the community all the men of my fellowship.
  According to (19) his [un]derstanding I bring him forward,
    and according to the amount of his portion I love him.
  But I will not pardon an evil one,
    and a sh[a]meful bribe I will not acknowledge.
  (20) [And] I will no[t] exchange your truth for wealth
    or (exchange) for a bribe any of your judgments.
  Rather, according as ..[. . . a per]son, (21) [I will lo]ve him,
    and according as you repel him, thus I will abhor him. *vacat*
  And I will not bring into the fellowship of [your] tr[uth]
    [any] who turn away (22) [from] your [co]venant. *vacat*

Strophe A

(8) [ברוך אתה] אדוני
הנותן בלב עבד[ך] בינה
(9) [לה]שכי[ל בכו]ל אלה
ולהת[בונן...].
ולהתאפק על עלילות רשע

ולברך (10) [ב]צדק כול בוחרי רצונך

[ולבחור את כול א]שר אהבתה

ולתעב את כול אשר (11) [שנאתה]

Strophe B

ותשכל עבדך [. . . רו]חות אנוש

כי לפי רוחות [תפ]ילם בין (12) טוב לרשע

[ות]כן [. . . לנ]חותם[119] פעולתם

Strophe C

ואני ידעתי מבינתך

(13) כי ברצונכה בא[נו]ש הרבי[תה נחלתו]120 ברוח קודשך

וכן תגישני לבינתך

ולפי (14) קורבי קנאתי על כול פועלי רשע ואנשי רמיה

כי כול קרוביך לא ימרו פיך

(15) וכול יודעיך לא ישנו דבריך

כי אתה צדיק

ואמת כול בחיריך

וכול עולה (16) [ור]שע תשמיד לעד

ונגלתה צדקתך לעיני כול מעשיך *vacat*

Strophe D

(17) [וא]ני ידעתי ברוב טובך

ובשבועה הקימותי על נפשי לבלתי חטוא לך

(18) [ול]בלתי עשות מכול הרע בעיניך

Strophe E

וכן הונשתי[121] ביחד כול אנשי סודי

לפי (19) [ש]כלו אנישנו

וכרוב נחלתו אהבנו

ולא אשא פני רע

ושחד ב[ו]שה[122] לא אכיר

(20)[ו]ל[א] אמיר בהון אמתך

ובשוחד כול משפטיך

כי אם לפי. . . אי[ש] (21) [אוה]בנו

---

[119] In place of Puech's reading לנ]חותם "to gui]de them" García Martínez and Tigchelaar read להוד]עתם, "to sho]w them."

[120] In place of Puech's reading הרבי[תה נחלתו] García Martínez and Tigchelaar read תנב]רתה נורלו עם].

[121] The text reads the hophal, הונשתי ("And thus I was advanced in the community of the men of my fellowship"). Although not impossible, such a reading makes it difficult to construe the following sentence and to identify the antecedent for the object suffixes in the phrases לפי שכלו אנישנו וכרוב נחלתו אהבנה. The text reads more easily if one emends the hophal הונשתי to the hiphil הגשתי.

[122] Where Puech reads ושחד ב[ו]שה, García Martínez and Tigchelaar read וש[וחד רשע].

וכרדקך אותו כן אתעבנו *vacat*
ולא אביא בסוד א[מתך]
[כול] שבי [מב]ריתך[123](22) *vacat*

The text is divided into two main parts by a *vacat* in the second half of line 16. This spatial division corresponds to a change in the content. In the first part of the text the speaker describes the gift of divine insight that he has received and the consequences of that gift for him. The second half of the text is explicitly concerned with the hierarchical structure of the community and the speaker's role in establishing and maintaining it. A small *vacat* separates the concluding line, and a long one after it indicates the conclusion of the text.

Statements about the gift of knowledge to the speaker form the basic skeletal structure of the text. In the form printed above, these statements are flush with the margin. These elements include (1) the participle הנותן that follows the formulaic introduction in line 8, (2) the waw-consecutive verb ותשכל in line 11 that introduces the specific knowledge God has entrusted to the speaker, (3) the often used phrase ואני ידעתי בבינתך in line 12, and (4) another instance of ואני ידעתי in line 17. All of the remaining material is subordinated to these statements of knowledge, both logically and in terms of the syntactical markers. With these preliminary observations about structure it is possible to see how the interweaving of language of self and community takes place and how this interweaving is related to the rhetorical purposes of the composition.

The speaker's emphasis at the beginning of the prayer on God-given knowledge as the basis of the self and of any capacity it has for moral judgment is wholly in keeping with the presentation of the self in other Hodayot. The sentiments and the expression of them embody the humility proper to members of the sect. In the second strophe something more distinctive emerges. Although the line is unfortunately broken, it appears that the knowledge that God gives to the speaker is specifically knowledge about human spirits, that is, the knowledge that the Maskil is entrusted to teach in the Two Spirits Treatise of the Serek ha-Yahad. The specifically dualistic understanding of the division of humankind is referred to, and perhaps also predestinarian ideas. In this respect the passage resembles

---

[123] Where Puech reads א[מתך [מב]ריתך כול] שבי, García Martínez and Tigchelaar read א[שר לא הח[שבו [בבר]יתך, "th[ose who are not inclu]ded [in] your [coven]ant."

the hodayah in col. 5, which Puech identifies as a hodayah of the Maskil, and which also contains echoes of 1QS 3–4.

It is with the third strophe, however, that language from the organization of the community first begins to be employed in a subtle way. The strophe opens with a phrase about knowledge common in the diction of the Hodayot, "And I know by means of the insight that comes from you" (ואני ידעתי בבינתך). The observation that it introduces, about God's increasing the portion of those he favors, is also found in another hodayah, 1QH[a] 18:28. At this point the speaker makes a clever move. In applying the general statement to himself, he says, "and thus you draw me closer to your understanding; and as I approach. . . ." The verbs used here to refer to the relation of the speaker to God are terms drawn from the organization of the hierarchy of the community. Specifically, they occur together in the instructions to the Maskil in 1QS 9:15–16 ("He [the Maskil] shall admit him [the prospective member] according to the cleanness of his hands and cause him to approach according to his insight. And likewise his love and his hatred" [trans. Knibb]). Here, however, the institutional overtones of these words are not yet brought into focus; instead, the words are adapted to the discursive practices of the Hodayot and used to talk about the relationship of the individual to God. Although the connection is not made explicit, setting the discourse of the piety of the Hodayot alongside the language of the instructions to the Maskil does give the words a double voicing. They vouch for the piety of the Maskil, in that he situates his instructions within the horizons of the Hodayot's language of personal piety; but they also validate his role in that the words implicitly analogize God to the office of the Maskil (an analogy that will be developed in the opposite direction later in the hodayah).

One should note the consequence that the speaker draws from the fact of his having "approached" God: he does not tolerate evildoers. This statement is immediately followed by justifying statements (introduced by כי) that one who has drawn near to and knows God does not rebel against or alter God's words. That is to say, God's judgment is his judgment (and vice versa). Essentially the same message is repeated in the final כי clause. If I am correct in seeing in this hodayah the defense of a Maskil against criticism, it would appear that demotion or expulsion of community members was the issue that provoked dissension. It is important to note, however, that to this point nothing whatsoever has been said about actual institutional

practices. The speaker has merely established his character before
God and before his human audience in accordance with the prayer
practices of the Hodayot.

In the second part of the prayer, however, the speaker does become explicit about the reason for which it has been important to
establish his character. The introduction to the strophe that begins
in line 17 begins, familiarly enough with the formula, "And I know"
(ואני ידעתי). The verb, however, appears to have no object, but is
used absolutely (cf. 1QH^a 19:14). The emphasis lies on the means
by which knowledge is obtained. Notably, the goodness of God is
paired with the first reference to the institutional structures of the
sect: the oath. ("And as for me, I have knowledge by means of your
abundant goodness and by means of the oath I pledged upon my
life, not to sin against you and not to do anything evil in your eyes.")
Exactly how the oath is related to knowledge is not entirely clear.
The content of the oath as it is represented here serves, however,
to underscore the bona fides of the speaker.

A textual problem complicates the translation of the following sentence. The text reads וכן הונשתי, which would require the translation, "*And thus I was advanced* in the community of all the men of
my council." That is to say, the speaker's own advancement according to merit would vouch for his decision-making according to the
same principles. The transition between this line and the following
one would be quite abrupt, however. It is sometimes suggested that
the verb be emended to a hiphil form rather than a hophal. "And
thus I advance in the community all the men of my council. . . ."
(וכן הנשתי).[124] In either case it is clear that the speaker is explicitly
justifying his practices in terminology parallel to that of the instructions in 1QS 9:15–16.

The language of self-justification that follows, concerning not taking a bribe or showing favoritism, is significant, since the same language is used to affirm the integrity of God in 1QH^a 7:27–28. The
contrastive כי אם ("rather"; Waltke-O'Connor 39.3.5d) introduces the
concluding lines that again align the judgment of God with the decision of the Maskil.

As an occasional piece designed to counter a crisis of dissension

---

[124] So Delcor, *Les Hymnes*, 264; Dupont-Sommer, *Essene Writings*, 244; Vermes,
Complete Dead Sea Scrolls, 248.

or as a general defense of a sectarian institution, this hodayah is an accomplished piece of rhetoric. But it also shows how the dominant symbolic representations of the self in the Hodayot are corrected and complemented by the language of the Serek ha-Yahad. As the analysis of the other compositions has shown, the Hodayot tend to represent the self through images of conflict and contradiction. Enemy and "wicked other" language contrasts with the vulnerable self but the self can also be represented both as elevated companion of heavenly beings and as vile, unclean wretch. Almost invariably, the Hodayot operate with polar terms and virtually unmediated extremes. Such is the language of the individual in the Hodayot. The Serek ha-Yahad also knows the language of binary opposition (both in terms of insiders and outsiders and in terms of the internalized dualism of the two spirits that struggle within the heart of every member). Its task, however, as a document for community formation, is to find a mediating language, for it must provide for the making of insiders out of outsiders and for the shaping of individuals into a Yahad. In one sense the community is the sum of its parts. Although based on a fundamental distinction between the righteous and the wicked, the community incorporates elements of sinfulness as well as of obedience, and elements of error as well as of insight, because these elements are present in the individuals who are its members. But the community is not simply the individual writ large. It is precisely in its organization that it differs from the individual. Because it is structured as a hierarchy of knowledge, it is capable of nurturing the gift of knowledge in individual members and providing the disciplines that make obedience to the will of God possible. Here, however, I am interested in seeing how the language of community formation characteristic of the Serek ha-Yahad is introduced into the rather different language of the Hodayot.

The crucial passage for the introduction of this mediating language occurs in Strophes B and C. In Strophe B the speaker makes generic statements about humankind that establish a binary division ("for according to the spirits [you] cast the lot for them between good and evil," lines 11–12). The binary division is then complicated by the assertion of a fluidity of divine spirit within the ranks of the good ("through your goodwill toward a p[er]son you mul[tiply his portion] in your holy spirit," line 13). Such language is unusual, although not unparalleled in the Hodayot, where the language of opposition or of paradox usually prevails. The notion of gradation is, however, always implicit in the potentialities of binary classification. Presence/Absence can be transmuted into More/Less. Indeed, the genius of a binary distinction is that like the children's toy Silly Putty, it can be made either to stretch or to snap, according to the needs of the one manipulating it. That is, it can be made to provide the basis for an absolute distinction or a relative one.

Although the notion of gradation is introduced by a figure of quantity, the favored image in this hodayah, parallel to and perhaps borrowed from the Serek ha-Yahad, is not quantity, but proximity. Implicitly, the image is one of God at the center, with elect individuals stationed at varying distances from the center, according to the degree of divine goodwill/holy spirit that each possesses. This is no "great chain of being," however, for the consequence of being drawn closer to the center is that one begins to make the binary judgment between guilty and righteous, deceit and truth, that is characteristic of God's judgment, too.

The problem of nurturing community solidarity and discipline is thus an important part of the work that Hodayot do. This task, however, is primarily addressed by the Hodayot of the leader, which are considered more fully in the following chapter.

CHAPTER SIX

THE HODAYOT OF THE LEADER AND THE NEEDS OF SECTARIAN COMMUNITY

THE "I" OF THE LEADER: TEACHER OF RIGHTEOUSNESS OR MEBAQQER?

One of the perennial questions about the Hodayot concerns the nature of the "I" who speaks in them and whether some of them at least should be related to the figure known as the Teacher of Righteousness. That is an extremely difficult question, and the claims that have been made seem often to say as much about the presuppositions of the scholar in question as about the Hodayot. Although early on in the discussion the question was often framed in terms of authorship, the futility of trying to marshal evidence to show that a particular individual did or did not compose a text has generally been recognized. Whoever wrote them, the more significant question is whether or not the Hodayot, or at least some of them, represent the persona of the Teacher of Righteousness. Without doubt there are certain Hodayot in which the "I" is distinguishable from the community and presents itself as having special responsibilities or leadership functions vis-à-vis other members of the community. Sometimes the speaker is represented as engaged with enemies of the community or in conflict with members of the community or in a protective and nurturing relationship with them. As scholars distinguished these compositions as a distinctive subset of the Hodayot, attempts were made to identify a profile of other features that seemed to characterize them (e.g., motifs of the speaker as a conduit of revelation; reports of distress; particular vocabulary or syntax).[1] But it should be stressed that these further criteria cannot function independently. The only reliable criterion for distinguishing a separate group of Hodayot is whether or not the speaker represents himself

---

[1] See, e.g., Jeremias, 168–77; Becker, 50–56; Kuhn, 21–26; Douglas, "Power and Praise in the Hodayot."

as distinct from the community in the capacity of leader. Among
those who distinguish hymns of the Teacher from Community hymns,
the compositions most often identified as hymns of the leader are:
1QH^a 10:3–19; 12:5–13:4; 13:5–19; 13:20–15:5; 15:6–25; 16:4–17:37.
Scholars disagree about several others because the secondary criteria used to identify them differ.

This much seems generally persuasive. But what about the other
widespread assumption that these compositions are to be understood
as representing the persona of the Teacher of Righteousness? That
is a much trickier question than I think it is generally taken to be.
I wish to subject it to some scrutiny and to set alongside it a modified
form of an old alternative suggestion, that the "I" in this group of
compositions represents the persona of the current leader of the community, perhaps the Mebaqqer rather than the historical Teacher.
Another way to put this suggestion is to say that these Hodayot
articulate a leadership myth that was appropriated by the current
leader in much the same fashion that the ordinary member identified
with the "I" of the so-called Hodayot of the community. Ultimately,
I do not think the evidence exists either to disprove the hypothesis about the Teacher of Righteousness or to prove the alternative.
It is important, however, to loosen the grip that this hypothesis about
the Teacher of Righteousness has had on our scholarly imaginations.

One of the effects of the dominance of the hypothesis about the
Teacher of Righteousness and the Hodayot has been the tendency
to direct scholarly inquiry in historical directions. One asks about
the life of the Teacher, or about his experiences and thoughts, or
about his teachings, or about how the community perceived him.[2]
Even in revisionist work the question tends to be traditio-historical,
investigating the relation between traditions about the Teacher in
the Hodayot and other documents. What tends to get left to one
side is how these Hodayot functioned over time, as they were continually read or recited, to shape the ethos of the community and
to address perennial questions of sectarian life. These kinds of questions are certainly not incompatible with the hypothesis that the
Hodayot of the leader represent the persona of the Teacher; and in
an earlier article I attempted to ask just those questions on the
assumption that the community understood these Hodayot to refer

---

[2] This approach has been revived recently by Wise, *The First Messiah*.

to the life of the Teacher of Righteousness.[3] But the more I have pursued the issues of the formation of character and community throughout the sectarian literature of Qumran the less comfortable I have become with that assumption. For reasons that I will detail below I have come to adopt as a working hypothesis the assumption that these Hodayot articulate the leadership myth of the existing community. I realize that this position is not provable either, and at appropriate places I will indicate how the alternative hypothesis about the Teacher of Righteousness would affect the arguments I make. But first I want to examine the arguments for and against these alternative interpretations of the persona of the Hodayot of the leader.

The classic form of the argument identifying the Teacher of Righteousness as the author of a distinctive subset of the Hodayot was made by Gert Jeremias. After having discussed alternative proposals by Bardtke and Licht, Jeremias says:

> Was sich an positiven Argumenten dafür beibringen lässt, dass der Lehrer der Verfasser unserer Psalmen ist. Zunächst und vor allem dies: Die Pescharim liessen uns den Lehrer als denjenigen erscheinen, der von Gott gelehrt (pHab 2,7ff.; 7,4f.) der Gemeinde die allein gültige Toraauslegung brachte, der das begründete, was das Sein der Gemeinde ausmachte. Daneben findet sich nun in den Hodajot (der wohl ältesten Qumranschrift) ein Ich, das mit dem gleichen Anspruch, es bringe allein die wahrhaft gültige Lehre, auftritt. Es is völlig undenkbar, dass es in der Gemeinde von Qumran in kürzester Zeit zwei Männer gegeben hat, die beide mit dem revolutionären Anspruch vor die Gemeinde traten, mit ihrer Lehre das Heil zu bewirken und dass beide Männer von der Gemeinde akzeptiert wurden. Es kann nur ein und derselbe Mann sein, der aus den Schriften der Gemeinde als sie prägend hervortritt. Neben diese mehr allgemeine Erwägung tritt nun aber auch manche äussere Übereinstimmung: Von dem Lehrer sagte der pHab, dass er von Gott gelehrt sei—eben dieses sagt mehrfach auch der Beter der Hodajot. So wie Gott dem Lehrer der Gerechtigkeit die göttlichen Geheimnisse kundtat (pHab 7,5), so weiss der Beter der Hodajot zu sagen, dass Gott ihn in dem Wahrheitsgeheimnis unterrichtet habe. Von dem Lehrer, hiess es, dass er Streit in seiner Gemeinde erlebte,—eben dieses berichtet auch der Beter der Hodajot. Der Lehrer wurde von dem Frevelpriester verfolgt—der Beter der Hodajot weiss von Gegnern, die ihn veranlassen wollen, seine Lehre gegen Schmeichelei

---

[3] Newsom, "Kenneth Burke Meets the Teacher of Righteousness."

zu vertauschen, wobei in beiden Texten die unterschiedliche Befolgung
des Kalenders der äussere Anlass zum Streit ist. Der pHab berichtete,
dass der Lehrer im Exil lebte—der Beter sagt von sich, dass er aus
seinem Land vertrieben worden sei wie ein Vogel aus seinem Nest.
Den Lehrer nannte der 4QpPs37 den Gründer der Gemeinde—der
Beter behauptet von sich, erst die Gemeinde ermöglicht zu haben.
Dies alles führt zwingend zu dem Ergebnis, dass hier die gleiche Person
gemeint ist.[4]

Jeremias's argument contains several points, some of them assumed,
some of them explicitly argued. For him the identity of the speaker
in these Hodayot is established above all by the correspondence
between the self-representation of the speaker in these Hodayot and
what is said about the Teacher of Righteousness in the pesharim.
Although this is not an implausible conclusion, it is far from definitive.
Not only the similarities but also the differences have to be accounted
for. On the assumption that the figure represented by these Hodayot
is a historical individual, one cannot help but be troubled by the
fact that the speaker is never clearly identified either by superscrip-
tions or in the body of the compositions. The term "teacher" (מורה)
does not occur in the Hodayot, nor do they refer to the other rather
specifically identified opponents of the teacher, the Wicked Priest
from the pesharim or the Man of the Lie from the pesharim and
the Damascus Document. In defense of the hypothesis one might
argue that the difference in genre accounts for the generality of language in the Hodayot and the greater specificity in the other compositions. But the fact remains that the similarities that Jeremias and
others have pointed to are similarities of *theme* (conduit of divine mysteries; care for the community; betrayal by the community; conflict
with opponents; etc.). The question that has to be pressed is whether
this similarity of theme is sufficient to require an identification of
the speaker with the historical figure of the Teacher of Righteousness.

Jeremias believes that it is, because he makes an assumption that
seems to him so obvious that he does not even argue for it explicitly. What Jeremias assumes is that the language of the Hodayot is
essentially referential. Even though couched in highly colored, symbolic expressions, he assumes that it points to the particular historical experiences of a particular historical individual.[5] The extent to

---

[4] Jeremias, 176–77.
[5] Jeremias is fairly cautious about trying to deduce actual historical information

which Jeremias simply takes this as a given is reflected in the innocence with which he argues that there could hardly have been two
such individuals in the history of the community as are represented
in these Hodayot. The possibility that he never examines, even in
his arguments against Bardtke and Licht, is whether these Hodayot
may be defining a *role* and its *mythos* rather than a concrete historical individual and his experiences. I will explore this hypothesis further below. But first there is one more issue about the relationship
between the Hodayot and the pesharim to discuss.

Philip Davies has argued for greater skepticism in evaluating the
relationship between the pesharim and the Hodayot. They cannot,
he insists, be used as independent and mutually confirming sources.
Davies's primary interest is in forcing a reconsideration of the usefulness of the pesharim for historical reconstruction, not in a re-
evaluation of the theories about the Hodayot; but his observations
are also pertinent to this issue. Davies sees the relationship between
the Hodayot and the Habakkuk Pesher in particular as a traditio-
historical and literary relationship, in which the Habakkuk Pesher
uses the Hodayot as a source of information or at least as a source
of terminology with which to describe the life of the Teacher of
Righteousness. In particular, Davies tries to show how certain general terms in the Hodayot become more concretized in the pesharim.
"How is it that plurals in 1QH^a ('teachers of lies. . . . seers of falsehood') have become singulars in 1QpHab (the 'Man of the Lie')?
This is, as we shall see, a more general phenomenon, whereby rather
vaguer plural terms in the Hymns become soubriquets for discrete
individuals, or for identifiable parties, in the *pesharim*."[6] Not all of
the evidence that he presents is equally persuasive, but in certain
cases at least, the literary relationship he describes appears to be
well founded. What, then, does this suggest about the Hodayot and
the Teacher of Righteousness? Davies himself remains agnostic about
the question of the Teacher of Righteousness as the author of any
of the Hodayot, but he concludes that the use of the Hodayot as a
source for details about the life of the Teacher in the pesharim

---

about the Teacher from the Hodayot because of the vagueness of the language in
which they are cast. But he does not doubt that the compositions allude to concrete experiences, even if we cannot reconstruct them now.

[6] Davies, *Behind the Essenes*, 97.

implies that these Hodayot at least were being *read* within the community as autobiographical compositions. That, it seems to me, is a more plausible interpretation of the data than the one Jeremias provided. But it, too, may claim more than is necessary. If, as I suggested, the Hodayot of the leader were used to articulate a leadership myth parallel to the mythos of the ordinary member developed in the Hodayot of the community, then these compositions would be a natural source for language and motifs for the authors of the pesharim to draw on as they attempted to relate biblical texts to the life of the Teacher of Righteousness. The traditional language with which the current leaders of the community described their role vis-à-vis outsiders and insiders might naturally be assumed to pertain as well to one who was remembered as a distinctively important leader of the past. But such use would not necessarily imply that the Hodayot of the leader were understood to refer exclusively to the Teacher of Righteousness. The model I have suggested would, however, be consistent with the absence in the Hodayot of specific expressions and terms that pertain to the representation of the Teacher in other texts.

To make a case for the hypothesis that the Hodayot of the leader articulate a leadership myth requires the exploration of three issues: whether the language is consistent with "generic" situations rather than specific incidents; whether the representation of the leader is consistent with what we otherwise know of institutional leaders in the Qumran community; and how the collection of Hodayot as a whole is to be understood.

With respect to the first issue, it is extremely difficult, and perhaps impossible with the evidence available to us, to devise a set of criteria that could reliably determine whether language in the Hodayot refers in symbolic terms to specific or generic situations. Scholarship on the canonical Psalms has come increasingly to view the language of distress and conflict there as highly formulaic. It has a normative quality. Descriptions of distress, conflict, vindication, and so forth, serve as patterns for experience that direct both affects and actions. This function of language is generally granted as also characterizing the Hodayot of the community. But why is there hesitation about assuming that the same function governs the Hodayot of the leader? The question is seldom addressed explicitly, but it appears that scholars have felt uncomfortable with that suggestion because they believe that acute conflict with other Jewish groups, episodes of possible schism, and a type of charismatic leadership that could speak of "those who have joined themselves to my witness" or "those who are in covenant with me" only characterized the life of the community during its formative stages. Therefore the representations of conflict and dissension, as well as the language of personal relations between leader and community, could only correspond with the realities of the community's life during a particular formative period. That is a plausible interpretation but it begs some important questions about the relation of language to reality within the context of a sectarian community.

Especially when conflict is at issue, one should be extremely careful in assuming a correlation between language and reality. The great danger to a sectarian community is not opposition but indifference from the outside world and wavering commitment within. These are chronic problems; indeed, problems that increase as time elapses since the period of foundation. Various strategies may emerge to meet these problems, but the discourse of the community about itself and the world is crucial. Mary Douglas and Aaron Wildavsky comment on voluntary, sectarian societies:

> For this kind of organization to persist, each sectarian needs the others' concurrence in an image of threatening evil on a cosmic scale: for this, the idea of global, irreversible damage serves well. They also need a model of the godly or good society, the sect itself, to counterpoise against ungodliness or worldliness outside and to justify their own control of their own group. They need the idea of conspiracy to accuse disloyal members of plotting with outsiders; the large-scale evilness of the conspiracy is necessary to justify expulsion.... The sect needs enemies. It encourages thinking in either/or terms because of the political focus on that dividing line between saints and sinners.[7]

What Douglas and Wildavsky suggest is that this sort of representation of the sect and the world tends to get constructed independently of actual "realities." It is not the concrete history of the formation of the sect but rather the structural needs of sectarian existence that nurture such a symbolic construction, one which the sectarians do take as descriptive of reality in a profound way.

From this perspective the question of the relationship between the Hodayot of the leader and actual conditions looks different, and it

---

[7] Douglas and Wildavsky, *Risk and Culture*, 123–24.

is possible to envision how, even in the calmest periods of the Qumran community's existence, the current leader of the sect might represent himself as engaged in sharp conflict against rival figures who would be intent on seducing the flock or represent himself as the object of betrayal from within. Such representations would simply be part of the mythos that identifies the leader's crucial role in negotiating the chronic tensions of sectarian existence.

This much of the argument seems quite plausible as an alternative to the hypothesis that these Hodayot represent the Teacher of Righteousness. In recent years scholars have become much more aware of the naiveté of assuming that language is transparent to reality and more aware of the extent to which language is constitutive of what we take to be "the way things are." But a more serious objection to the hypothesis that these Hodayot are a mythos of leadership arises when one compares the representation of leadership in the Hodayot with the representation of leadership in other Qumran literature. Jeremias himself objected to Licht's suggestion that the Hodayot be associated with the Mebaqqer or the Maskil by saying that the Mebaqqer had chiefly organizational functions and that the Maskil was a shadowy figure without individual personality.[8] He sums up his rejection of the association of the speaker of these Hodayot with an institutional leader in these terms: "Der Beter der Hodajot unserer Gruppe will mehr sein als nur der Leiter der Gemeinde: Er is mit göttlichem Wissen betraut, er ist von Gott als Heilbringer eingesetzt."[9]

Before responding to Jeremias's objections, I think it is important to present them in an even stronger fashion. The representation of leadership in the Hodayot is markedly different from the representation of leadership in the Serek ha-Yahad or the Damascus Document.[10] In the Hodayot the leader is represented in a highly personal way.

---

[8] Jeremias, 175. Licht, *The Thanksgiving Scroll*, 22–26.
[9] Jeremias, 176.
[10] The relationship between the Qumran community and the community described in the Damascus Document is one of the most vexed issues in Qumran studies. Although the communities are related in some fashion, the nature of that relationship remains unclear. Both the Damascus Document and the Serek ha-Yahad are generically similar as rules for their communities. While their organizational terminology differs in some respects, both documents refer to the offices of Paqid, Maskil, and Mebaqqer in similar fashion. See the discussion of Metso, "Qumran Community Structure."

The language, to be sure, is stereotyped and traditional language, borrowed in part from the Psalms, but it presents the speaker as a figure of emotion, an object of personal hatred and personal loyalty. This personal element is highlighted in expressions such as "those yoked to my witness" or "those in covenant with me." The speaker does not appear as integrated into a hierarchically organized community but stands apart from the community as a solitary leader. In sharp contrast the descriptions of community life in the Serek ha-Yahad, although partial and obscure in many respects, represent leadership in distinctly non-personal terms. It is difficult in the Serek ha-Yahad even to discern an overall leader. The Mebaqqer appears to have a special role in presiding at the assembly of the Many (1QS 6:12) and, if he is the same figure as the "officer at the head of the Many" (1QS 6:13–15), also has a special role in the investigation, instruction, and admission of new members. But the account coordinates the description of his responsibilities with the authority of the assembly itself, so that no picture of a strong leader of intense personal authority emerges. The overlap of functions with respect to the instruction and advancement of members between the Mebaqqer, the Paqid, and the Maskil (see 1QS 9:12–21) has made it difficult to determine if these are separate offices or alternative titles for the same one.[11] Even in the Damascus Document, where the responsibilities and authority of the Mebaqqer are more fully discussed, the very fact that his responsibilities are the subject of discussion in a Rule suggests the extent to which it is an institutionalized rather than a personal form of authority. The distance between the representation of leadership in the Serek ha-Yahad and the Damascus Document on the one hand and in the Hodayot on the other seems great indeed.

   I have made this argument as strong as I can because I think it is weighty but I also think that it is seriously flawed. The mistake it makes is in comparing isolated elements from various texts (in this case the representation of leadership) with each other. What has to be reckoned with in making a comparison is that one is dealing with two vastly different discourses in the Hodayot on the one hand and

---

[11] Most conclude that the Mebaqqer and the Paqid are the same but are to be distinguished from the Maskil. See Metso, "Qumran Community Structure," 439–440 for a review of various positions.

in the Rules on the other. Each discourse has a very different rhetorical genius, very different capacities and limitations, and very different intentionalities in rendering the world. They are different ways of talking, and even if they are talking about "the same thing," it will appear different in the two discourses.

But what is at issue here is whether or not the two discourses *are* in fact talking about the same thing (i.e., the leadership role within the community) or about different things (i.e., a unique historical leader on the one hand and an institutional leader on the other). Thus one seems to be at something of a dead end. What may help shed some light on the issue is to reflect on how the two discourses treat what *is* the same thing, namely, the representation of the ordinary sectarian and his experience. Here, too, an enormous difference exists between the two ways of talking. In the Hodayot the institutional community is scarcely in view as the compositions represent the individual's mythos. The decisive relationships are those between God and the self on the one hand, and the drama of self-confrontation on the other, as the individual negotiates a subjectivity formed by divine spirit and human nothingness. The language of knowledge is a language of inspiration (the gift of a spirit) and revelatory disclosure (making known wondrous mysteries). If I am correct in attributing the hodayah in 1QH^a 10:20–30 and 11:1–18 to the ordinary sectarian rather than the leader, then he, too, is represented as a solitary individual besieged by enemies and saved by God for the purposes of God's manifestation of glory. Certainly 1QH^a 11:19–36, which is generally regarded as a hodayah of the community, represents the individual as redeemed from guilt and the eschatological judgment not by entry into the sect but by being placed with a heavenly community of rejoicing. The language throughout is highly personal and highly emotional. A heightened, dramatic, highly figured quality characterizes the experience. In sharp contrast, the individual projected by the discourse of the Rules is thoroughly integrated into the institutional structures of the community. His identity is fixed by rank and by practices of hierarchical etiquette and obedience. Speech, which is a divine gift in the Hodayot, is here constrained and closely regulated. The emotionality that is integral to the Hodayot finds no place in the Serek ha-Yahad or is present only in terms of the negative emotions that require control. Life is a matter of highly organized, daily disciplines. The point is simply this: there is also a great gulf between the representation of the ordinary community member in the Hodayot and the Rules. Yet no one suggests, I think, that these are not "the same" members. Rather, it is a matter of two very different discourses with very different ways of representing what it means to be a sectarian.

Correspondingly, I am suggesting that the Hodayot of the leader can be seen as an analogous representation of the leader's role in the characteristic language and symbolic forms of the Hodayot. The personal nature of authority, the solitariness, the heightened representation of conflict and bringing of salvation are not simple referential claims but rather the way one talks in this kind of discourse. In fact, if one examines the major themes and symbolic representations of the Hodayot of the leader, what appears is a virtual inventory of the major responsibilities attributed to the Mebaqqer in the Serek ha-Yahad and in the Damascus Document. Of the Hodayot upon which there is the most agreement that they represent the persona of the leader, two articulate the sharp boundary between outsiders and insiders (1QH^a 10:3–19; 12:5–13:4); two deal with internal disaffection (1QH^a 13:20–15:5; 16:4–17:41); one speaks of the upbuilding of the community by the leader (1QH^a 15:6–25); and one represents him as vindicated and purified by God and relates this experience to the availability of the covenant for those who seek it (1QH^a 13:5–19). This last composition, which in my opinion has rather tenuous grounds for being associated with the leader, is linguistically closely linked to the composition that immediately follows, one of the Hodayot in which the issue is disaffection from the leader.

In the Serek ha-Yahad and the Damascus Document the Mebaqqer is also a "gate" and "boundary" figure who regulates relationships between the inside and the outside. He is the one who examines and ranks prospective members of the community and who receives their possessions when they enter (1QS 6:20; CD 13:11–12; cf. the Paqid in 1QS 6:14–15); and in the Damascus Document it is explicitly said that "No member of the camp shall have authority to admit a man to the congregation against the decision of the Guardian of the camp" (CD 13:12–13; trans. Vermes). He is also the one who oversees the relationships between members and nonmembers. "No member of the Covenant of God shall give or receive anything from the sons of the Pit except for payment. No man shall form any association for buying and selling without informing the Guardian of the camp. . . ." (CD 13:14–16; trans. Vermes). The Mebaqqer also has responsibility for the nurture of the community, for instruction in the "mighty deeds" of God and "all the happenings of eternity" (CD 13:8). Indeed, his care for the community is expressed—even in the Damascus Document—in rather personal terms, one of which is the same as that used of the leader in the Hodayot: he loves his community "as a father loves his children" (CD 13:9; cf. 1QH^a 15:20–21), he carries them "like a shepherd his sheep," and "shall loosen all fetters that bind them that in his Congregation there may be none that are oppressed or broken" (CD 13:9–10; trans. Vermes). These are highly evocative images, which are also part of the traditional repertoire of images for God's saving care. As the mirror image of his responsibilities for the upbuilding of the community, the Mebaqqer is the central figure who must deal with disputes and dissension. He is the one who records capital offenses witnessed by only one member (CD 9:18–19), and who must decide on the appropriate punishment for a member who backslides. The rule for the Mebaqqer of all the camps, which appears to be parallel to that of the Mebaqqer in the local camps, says that any suit or judgment is to be brought before him (CD 14:11–12).

It takes no great leap of the imagination to see how these relationships and responsibilities could be figured by the type of discourse one finds in the Hodayot, with its personalizing, dramatizing, and confessional forms of speaking. Boundary functions are figured as conflicts with rival interpreters and as the protection of the community from those who would seduce them. Instruction is figured as disclosure of mysteries and counsel. Upbuilding and nurture are personalized. So, too, are backsliding and disaffection, which are represented as personal rejection of the leader. This hypothesis by no means excludes the possibility that these little dramas of sectarian life build on actual instances of conflict and protection. But in their repetition over decades of use they would have come to form the dramatized expression of the habitual functions of leadership within the sectarian community.

This comparison between the representation of the responsibilities and persona of the Mebaqqer in the Damascus Document and in the Hodayot is offered for heuristic purposes only, since uncertainties remain about the leadership structure at Qumran and its relation to the leadership structure reflected in the Damascus Document. A few scholars have even suggested that the Mebaqqer, Paqid, and

Maskil are all simply alternate terms for the same office,[12] though the majority consider the office of the Maskil to be distinct from that of the Mebaqqer. Within the Hodayot the four psalms associated with the Maskil (1QH^a 5:1; 7:11; 20:4; 25:10) have certain similarities in language and theme with those portions of the Serek ha-Yahad introduced by the heading *lmskyl* (cf. 1QH^a 5:13–19 and 1QS 3:13–4:26; 1QH^a 20:4–9 and 1QS 9:26–10:8). But they seem quite different in tone and self-representation from the psalms of the persecuted leader. Thus I am reluctant to merge the categories of the Hodayot of the Maskil and those of the persecuted leader, unless Puech is correct that these headings do not introduce particular compositions but serve to subdivide the collection into five sections. If this is the case, then perhaps the issue deserves reconsideration.[13]

As I indicated above, I do not think that a definitive case can be made either for the hypothesis that the Hodayot of the leader be associated with the Teacher of Righteousness or for the hypothesis that they be associated with an institutional role held by successive leaders. Although I have tried to show that some of the arguments by which the case for the Teacher of Righteousness was made depended on a naive view of language and the relation of alternative discourses within a single community, the hypothesis remains one plausible interpretation of the evidence. What finally tips my own inclination in the direction of the alternative hypothesis is the question of how to make sense of the Hodayot as a whole. The Hodayot clearly contain compositions representing the persona of the ordinary member and compositions explicitly associated with the Maskil. Given that, it seems to me more economical to assume that the subset of compositions under consideration here also pertains to a community leader rather than to assume that these, anomalously, pertain to a historical personage. It should also be borne in mind that these Hodayot are not simply compositions about a leader, whether historical or contemporary. They are themselves *acts* of leadership, verbal attempts to articulate a community through the self-presentation of the persona of the leader. In the following sections I do not attempt to examine all of the psalms of the leader but select four

---

[12] Trebolle Barrera, "The Essenes of Qumran," *People of the Dead Sea Scrolls*, 57. Vermes, *Dead Sea Scrolls in English*, 18–25.

[13] Puech, "Quelque aspects," 52–53.

that illumine various ways in which the self-representation of the
leader serves to shape the community and to negotiate certain problems in sectarian life.

MAPPING: THE LEADER AT THE CENTER (1QH^a 10:3–19)

Whether or not the Hodayot of the leader were originally composed
as responses to particular situations, they address chronic issues in
sectarian life. One of these is the need to define clear boundaries
for the community. As the comments from Douglas and Wildavsky
quoted above suggest, identity for the sect is formed oppositionally.
The Hodayot create a symbolic world in which the leader's function is central to the process of defining those boundaries. The leader
is presented as the point of definition that divides good from bad,
inside from outside. Obviously, such a role enhances the leader's
importance for the life of the community. In the hodayah to be considered first, the symbolic economy not only underscores the leader's
significance but also pre-emptively discourages internal resistance to
the leader's role.

1QH^a 10:3–19

According to the calculations of Emile Puech,[14] the preceding hodayah
concludes in the line that corresponds to line 1 or 2 in the text of
García Martínez and Tigchelaar. One should thus restore the introductory phrase of the the the new hodayah (אודך אדוני כי ...) at the
beginning of line 2 or 3. Since the lines of the column contain an
average of ten words and (judging from the well-preserved composition
in the lower half of the column) poetic lines contain an average of
four or five words, one can estimate that approximately five to eight
poetic lines are missing before the nearly continuous text begins with
ומשמיעי שמחה לאבל ינ[ון] in line 5. From that point on it is fairly
easy to analyze the hodayah in strophes introduced by imperfect
verbs plus *waw*. What I would consider the introductory section of
the composition takes as its theme God's gift of support to the speaker
in the face of opposition. This introductory section concludes with

¹⁴ Puech, "Quelques aspects," 52.

the tricolon of second-person singular verbs (ותתן/ותסמוך/ותעמד). The main body of the text, which explores the speaker's relationship to two contrasting groups, is articulated by introductory verbs that refer to the speaker's situation (ואהיה/ואני הייתי) and the actions of the opponents (ויהפוכו).

> (3) [I thank you, O Lord, that . . .]
>   [. . .] all the works of iniquity
>   (4) [. . . and] you place [. . .] righteousness in all [. . .]
>   (5) [. . .] crushes[. . .]
>   and announcing joy to sor[rowful] mourning
>   (6) [. . . pe]ace to all the rumored destructions
>   [. . .] strong [. . .] for the weakness of my heart
>   and forces of [strength] (7) in the face of [afflic]tion.
>
> And you have given the answer of the tongue to my uncir[cumcised] lips,
>   and you supported my soul with strength of loins (8) and powerful might.
> You have maintained my steps in the realm of wickedness.
>
> And I have been a snare to sinners
>   but healing to all (9) who repent of sin,
>   discernment to the simple,
>   and a resolute purpose for all whose hearts are troubled.
>
> And you made me an (object of) reproach (10) and derision to the treacherous,
>   but a counsel of truth and understanding to those whose way is upright. *vacat*
>
> And I have been, on account of the iniquity of the wicked,
>   (11) a slander on the lips of the ruthless.
>   The scornful gnash their teeth.
>
> And I myself have become a mocking song for sinners,
>   (12) and against me the assembly of the wicked rages.
>   And they roar like the stormy seas
>   when their waves crash,
>   heaving up slime (13) and mud.
>
> But you made me a banner for the elect of righteousness,
>   and an interpreter of knowledge by means of wondrous mysteries,
>   *vacat* in order to test (14) [persons] of truth
>   and to try those who love discipline.
>
> And I have been a man of contention to the interpreters of error,
>   but a [man of] (15) [pe]ace to all who see what is so.

And I have been a spirit of jealousy to all who seek sm[ooth things,]
(16) [and all] the deceitful ones roar against me
like the sound of the mighty roaring waters.
Base schemes are [all] (17) their [tho]ughts.

And they cast into the pit the life of the man
in whose mouth you established teaching,
and (18) in whose heart you set understanding,
in order to open a source of knowledge for all who understand.
But they falsified them,[15] by means of uncircumcised lips (19) and
an alien tongue
for a people without understanding,
so that they might be cast down in their error.

(3) [. . .] כי אדוני [אודך]
[. . .] עולה[.] מעשי כול [. . .]
(4) [. . .] בכל[.] צדק חי [. . .]חשם[ו]
(5) [. . .]מכ[.] מחץ[. . .]
ינ[ו]ן לאבל שמחה ומשמיעי
(6) [. . .]ה[ו]עמש הוות לכול ש[. . .]
[. . .]לבבי למוס חזקים[.]
[נ]ע[ני] לפני (7) [כוח] ומאמצי

שפתי [רו]ל[ע] לשון מענה ותתן
כוח ואמוץ (8) מותנים בחזוק נפשי ותסמוך
רשעה בנבול פעמי ותעמד

לפושעים פה ואהיה
פשע שבי (9) לכול ומרפא
לפתיים ערמה
לב נמהרי לכול סמוך ויצר

לבוגדים וקלס (10) חרפה ותשימני
דרך לישרי ובינה אמת סוד   *vacat*

רשעים עון על ואהיה
עריצים בשפת דבה (11)
שנים יחרוקו לצים

לפושעים נגינה הייתי ואני
תתרגש רשעים קהלת ועלי (12)
ימים כנחשולי ויהמו
עליהם בהרגש
ינרושו וטיט (13) רפש

וחשימני נס לבחירי צדק
vacat ומליץ דעת ברזי פלא
לבהון (14) [אנשי] אמת
ולנסות אוהבי מוסר

ואהיה איש ריב למליצי תעות
ו[איש] (15) [של]ום לכול הוזי נכוחות

ואהיה לרוח קנאה לנגד כל דורשי חל[קות]
(16) [וכול] אנשי רמיה עלי יהמו
כקול המון מים רבים
ומזמות בליעל [כול] (17) מ[ח]שבותם

ויהפוכו לשוחה חיי גבר
אשר הכינותה בפי ותלמד{נ}ו[^16]
בינה (18) שמחה בלבבו
לפתוח מקור דעת לכול מבינים
וימירום בערול שפה (19) ולשון אחרת
לעם לא בינות
להלבט במשנתם *vacat*

As a first-person singular prayer of thanksgiving, the leader's hodayah, like those of the individual, is above all an instrument for conferring identity on the speaker. This function is particularly clear in the framework of verbs that shape the main part of the composition, verbs that alternate between "I have become . . ." and "you [God] have made me. . . ." The speaker's identity and character are defined not only through the content of the statements that he predicates about himself but also through the style of self-presentation. A leader's identity has significance beyond his personal self-understanding, of course. Who he is and is perceived to be has implications for the identity of the community and its members. Furthermore, in a voluntary society the self-presentation of a leader can be an important instrument for nurturing community solidarity. His self-presentation can be understood as an appeal, designed to evoke a certain kind of response. The genre of the prayer of thanksgiving, adapted in the Hodayot, is particularly well suited for such a task. Even though nominally addressed to God, it was traditionally intended to be overheard by the community and served a function of building up the

---

[^16] The text is disturbed here. The scribal correction, inserting *nun* after *dalet* in ותלמדו has only made matters worse. The simplest solution is to ignore the scribal correction and to redivide the words, taking *waw* as a conjunction introducing בינה. Thus read אשר הכינותה בפיו תלמד ובינה שמחה בלבבו.

congregation through a personal account that motivated confidence in God. Here, although confidence in God is certainly part of its work, the emphasis has shifted to strengthening the congregation through creating confidence in the leader who speaks. Although these functions will work somewhat differently, depending on whether the hodayah was understood to present the persona of the historical leader of the past or the present leader of the community, the basic rhetorical strategy is essentially the same.

The hodayah under discussion here not only confers an identity on the speaker but also provides a schematized map of the social world. A strong binary pattern prevails, seen most clearly in the paired epithets for the outsiders and insiders. The outsiders are "sinners," the insiders "those who turn from sin"; the outsiders are the "treacherous," the insiders are those "whose way is upright"; the outsiders are "interpreters of error," the insiders are those "who see what is so." The symbolic economy of the poem is not simply a binary one, however. The communities identified by these epithets do not interact directly but rather receive definition as opposites through their relation to a central figure, that of the speaker. The poetic trope through which the assertions are made is rooted in the Psalms. There the psalmist may say "I have become *x* to *y*." See, for example, Ps 69:9 ("I have become a stranger to my brothers, and a foreigner to my mother's sons"; cf. Pss 31:12; 71:7; 109:25). In the Psalms, however, even when such statements are developed in parallel bicola, the parallelism is always synonymous. The psalmic pattern is never developed in antithetical fashion, as it is in this hodayah: "I have become *x* to *y*, but *x'* to *y'*." The difference is significant, for the antithetical binary pattern creates a figure of totality that can be graphically represented in this manner:

The formal pattern, coupled with the broadly definitive religious categories in which it is articulated, emphasizes the centrality of the speaker—the leader of the community—as the one who articulates the structure of world and meaning. He is the mediating figure through whom definition takes place. In addition to the "horizontal"

pattern that the speaker forms in relating antithetical groups to one another through himself, he is also at the center of a "vertical" pattern. Although the statements of the hodayah define groups in relation to the speaker, the epithets by which the groups are identified are not those that characterize the relation of those persons to the speaker (e.g., enemies, haters, foes versus friends, neighbors, kin) but rather epithets that characterize their relationship to God ("sinners," "those who repent of sin," etc.). Their relationship to God, however, is made visible and identifiable through their relationship to the speaker. Again, one could represent this pattern graphically as follows:

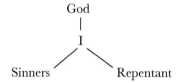

In this hodayah the character of the leader is defined by a technique analogous to taking bearings from different locations and noting where they intersect. Every line that is traced runs through the figure of the speaker, thus securing for him a position both central and powerful.

Despite the initial appearance of a balanced, antithetical structure in the symbolic representation of the composition, a clearly marked asymmetricality exists in the way the speaker is related to the two groups who are identified in this hodayah. The outsiders, the sinners, are represented in terms of the attitudes *they* take toward the speaker and the actions prompted by those attitudes: reproach, derision, slander, jealousy; gnashing of teeth, singing of mocking songs, raging, roaring, contending, casting into the pit. In sharp contrast nothing is said of the attitudes assumed by the speaker's community or any actions they might take toward him. They are not said to love or be loyal to him or to support and sustain him. They are represented purely as beneficiaries of the speaker's activity. He provides them with healing, discernment, resolute purpose, counsel, a banner, knowledge, and peace.

The appearance of a marked asymmetry in a text that is so obviously shaped by a binary pattern draws attention to itself. But what is the significance of this particular asymmetry? I think it is this: The text both hides and acknowledges the central importance of the community's response to the leader. By presenting the leader in "objective" terms, it hides the role that community acceptance plays. Yet at the same time, by presenting the leader in terms of the benefits he confers on the community, it constitutes an appeal for their positive response, offering them grounds for loyalty to his leadership. This is not to suggest that there is any trace of pleading on the part of the speaker. His insistence that his role as mediator of knowledge is to test and try the community underscores a strong authority, even as his characterization of his community as "persons of truth" and "those who love knowledge" attributes to them a character that will respond wholeheartedly to what he offers. There is, in fact, a kind of symbolic preemptive strike that discourages anything except a supportive attitude toward the leader, since opposition will, by definition, make one an outsider and a sinner.

The relation of the leader to the outsiders is developed in a striking way, as can be seen if one looks at the dynamics of passivity/activity in the hodayah. In the entire composition, the leader is not the subject of any finite verbs except the verb "to be." Activities of the speaker are, of course, implied in the nouns that characterize his relationship toward the community. But the choice to represent these as nouns rather than as verbs underscores that the primary perception of the speaker is in terms of who he is or what he represents rather than what he does. The only subjects of active verbs are God and the opponents. Even God's activities are of a behind-the-scenes type. In the main part of the hodayah they are restricted to "placing" and "establishing" the speaker. The sinners on the other hand are characterized by loud, noisy, and ultimately self-destructive actions. The speaker's initial image of himself as a "snare" is apt. He is God's bait and noose, whose very being is sufficient to provoke the sinners to the actions that will both expose what they are and lead to their downfall.

The representation of the leader as passive rather than aggressive toward the sinners is characteristic of other Hodayot and seems to be a firm part of the model of leadership created in them. The roots of this image are to be found in the Bible. Psalms of lament are one of the most obvious sources, for there the speaker's victimization is part of his appeal to God. But only in Jeremiah and in the characterization of the servant in Isaiah 53 is passive endurance of the aggression of others linked to ultimate vindication of the speaker and of God's purposes. Moreover, the self-image of the speaker as a hidden trap for the wicked is closely connected with the predestinarian theology of the sect. The dynamics of the conflict are fixed in the structures of reality. The role of the sectarians, leader and member alike, is not one of aggression against evildoers but one of knowledge and endurance. While the speaker's role is distinctive, he models the proper stance for all sectarians. Although one cannot move naively from symbolic representation to social reality, the pattern of passivity articulated here fits well with other statements in Qumran literature (e.g., 1QS 9:21–23) and with what we know of the Essenes from other sources. Unlike the way the Pharisees are depicted as acting in Josephus, in the Gospels, and in Rabbinic sources, the Essenes do not seem to have cultivated public confrontation as a mode of establishing themselves in public opinion.[17] A hodayah like the one under consideration here both makes sense of that mode of behavior for sectarians and reinforces their tendency to behave in such a way. We do not know whether or not, despite the tendency of the Qumran community not to seek out confrontation, they were in fact the object of hostility, as the hodayah suggests. But perhaps one should not take the language of the hodayah so literally and referentially. The whole mythos of the community, with its understanding of a dualistic confrontation between righteousness and wickedness means that, as the representative of God's truth, the leader *must* arouse the hostility of the wicked. Actual hostile words and actions are not required to make the hodayah plausible to the sectarian community. The very existence of alternative discourses can be construed as rejection of or hostility toward the community's leader and teacher. Whether or not the outsiders obliged the sectarians by behaving in the way they were supposed to—at least after the confrontation between the Wicked Priest and the Teacher of Righteousness—compositions such as this one reinforced

---

[17] This would be the case even if MMT is understood as a direct communication with opponents. What I am concerned about here is habitual or characteristic modes of interaction. Some Essenes may have had certain public roles, for example the prophetic pronouncement Josephus attributes to the Essenes Judas, Menahem, and Simon (*Ant.* 13.311–13; *J.W.* 1.78–80; *Ant.* 15.372–79; and *Ant.* 17:345–48; *J.W.* 2.113). Knohl's speculation (*The Messiah before Jesus*, 58–62) that Menachem the Essene is the Menachem to whom the Jerusalem Talmud (*y Hag.* 2:2[77b]) attributes a confrontation with the Pharasaic sages that results in his excommunication only underscores the point. Menachem does not confront his rivals until in his opinion the day of vengeance has arrived.

the normative view of the world embedded in the sectarian mythos.

How does the hodayah construct the image of the enemies? Does the composition refer, even in highly symbolic terms, to an actual group, or is the whole image simply the product of the need to construct a definitional other: the sect's own image turned upside down? These are extremely difficult questions and cannot be answered with certainty. One feature that stands out in the depiction of the enemies' antagonism is the predominance of oral and auditory images. There are references to tongue, lips, teeth. Verbal acts are abundant in the way hostility is represented: reproach, derision, slander, mocking songs, raging and roaring, and so forth. The background to much of this imagery is the preoccupation with reputation in an honor-based culture, as one sees in the way in which similar imagery is used in the Psalms. Here that imagery has been taken up and used in a somewhat different way. The parallelism between "reproach and derision" and "counsel of truth and understanding" indicates that the conflict is located in the lively arena of the cultural counter-discourse about torah, where different groups vied for influence in the competition to define the will of God.

The opponents represented in the hodayah are often identified as the Pharisees, primarily on the basis of the possible pun involved in the epithet דורשי חלקות, "seekers of smooth things," a phrase taken from Isa 30:9–10. The expression could be understood here as a deformation of דורשי הלכות, "seekers of halakot." The verb דרש certainly has overtones in this context of the act of interpretation. Although "halakah" is not a term that the Qumran community used in its own speech, it could be a mocking reference to the technical terminology of its rivals. Although this identification is tempting, I am inclined to be somewhat cautious about taking the schematized language of the hodayah as a literal representation of a Pharisaic/Essene rivalry. For one thing, it is not at all clear that the term הלכה was even in use at this time as a designation for "a legal opinion or ruling about proper Jewish conduct."[18] Moreover, the differences in social organization, social interaction, and membership that characterizes the Pharisees and Essenes (see chap. 2) suggest that they were probably not often in direct conflict. The priests in Jerusalem formed the more "natural" object of opposition for the Qumran commu-

---

[18] Meier, 150–55.

nity. This is not to say that the Pharisees were not also at times the object of the community's polemic. But to begin with a phrase like "seekers of smooth things" and deduce from it the identity of the sect's main rival is potentially misleading. Qumran's need for enemies is also internally generated by the dynamics of their existence as a sect, and their construction of those enemies in the symbolic language of the Hodayot is largely made in their own image, an "evil twin." As schematic language, it can be made applicable to many different concrete others but is not wholly generated by the actual features of other groups.

The symbolic patterns I have described so far, in which the leader mediates vertically between God and the sinners/repentant ones, and horizontally between insiders and outsiders, do not exhaust the relationships modeled in this composition. There is actually a certain slippage in the formal patterns of the hodayah. For the most part the sinners are represented as the binary opposite of the speaker's community, with the speaker as the mediating term that defines them. But because the sinners are depicted as engaged in hostility toward the speaker, they also occupy a symbolic position as his enemies. The use of parallel terms (although not in parallel poetic constructions) also facilitates this oppositional pairing of the speaker and the sinners. He is an "interpreter of knowledge"; they are "interpreters of error." He thanks God for giving "the answer of the tongue to [his] uncircumcised lips," while the sinners falsify divine teaching "by means of uncircumcised lips and an alien tongue." The sinners are thus not merely those outsiders who are the negative counterpart of the community formed by his leadership; they are also his rivals. They are the alternative discourses that threaten the plausibility of the sectarian symbolic world. In that regard they are dangerous and must be disqualified. In the hodayah that will be discussed next the depiction of rivalry is much more explicit. Here it is subtle and does not fully emerge until the end of the composition (lines 14–19).

The rivalry between the speaker and the sinners is brought to a focus in the concluding strophe of the composition (lines 17–19). There the sinners' opposition moves from verbal raging to an act of violence; but the main concern of the concluding strophe is not on the speaker's fate but on contrasting the relation between the speaker and truth on the one hand and the relation between the sinners and truth on the other. It is through this contrast that the speaker will be vindicated and his rivals disqualified. Despite the textual and

grammatical difficulties of the passage, its structure can be clarified
by attending to the parallelism. The most overt parallels are between
מבינים (line 18), a term for the speaker's community, and לא עם בינות
(line 19), a term I take to refer to those influenced by the sinners.
Correspondingly, the terms בערול שפה ולשון אחרת (lines 18–19) contrast the sinners negatively with the speaker in their relation to knowledge. The speaker's task is to "open a source" or provide knowledge
for his community, whereas the sinners' action is in changing or fal-
sifying knowledge. Thus one final map is sketched in this hodayah,
one that could be represented as follows:

Speaker as interpreter (מליץ דעת)	↔	Rivals as false interpreters (מליצי תעות)
Speaker's teaching/understanding (תלמד/בינה)	↔	Rivals' falsification (וימירם)
Speaker's community (מבינים)	↔	Rivals' community (עם לא בינה)

Here again in an indirect way the speaker appeals to the community for its loyalty. Those who rage against him are also purveyors
of what is dangerous, even deadly (להלבט במשנתם, "cast down in
their error"), in contrast to the "source of knowledge" that the speaker
offers. What is hinted at here but not fully developed is an ideological map of truth, a topic that is explored more fully in the
hodayah to be considered next.

What, then, does this hodayah accomplish in terms of the mythos
of leadership? Above all, it establishes the leader as quite literally
definitive, the central point of reference for all understanding. The
leader's self-presentation in terms of his benefits to the community
is an implicit appeal for community loyalty. It does so without entering into the often murky territory of the failure of community solidarity, a topic that other Hodayot do address (see 1QH[a] 13:20–15:5,
discussed below). In his role as recipient of the slanders and hostility of sinners the speaker not only satisfies the sect's need for enemies but models the type of character and behavior that the sect
tried to cultivate in its members, one that was implied in the theology of the community. Indeed, his own account of himself also
makes plausible the relation between his leadership and the sect's
theology, justifying a way of conduct that does not initiate conflict

with sinners but concentrates on the cultivation of a closed community of truth.

The Map of Truth (1QH^a 12:5–13:4)

This lengthy composition is closely related to the one previously discussed. Not only is it related in its projection of antithetical rival discourses, but there are also striking similarities of diction (compare ומירום [10:14] with ה[ן]תעום [12:7]; compare מליצי רמיה [ה]תעום [12:7]; with בערול שפה ולשון אחרת לעם לא בינות להלבט במשגתם [10:18–19] with להמיר תורתכה... בחלקות לעמכה [12:7]; and וילבטו בלא בינה [12:10–11] and ומזמת בליעל [כ]ול [12:16]; compare [ב]ל[ן]ע[ן]ג שפה ולשון אחרת and כל מחשבת מ[ח]שבתם [10:16–17] with זממו עלי בליעל [12:10] and בליעל [12:12–13] and זמות בליעל יחשובו [12:13–14]. The hodayah in col. 12–13 might well be understood as taking up the undeveloped possibilities of the concluding strophe of 1QH^a 10:3–19, where the speaker and his opponents were imaged as rival teachers of contrasting communities. In its development of this pattern, however, the hodayah under consideration here undertakes a rather more ambitious agenda. It sketches out a map of an ideology of truth and the kind of identities implied by such an ideology.

Every developed ideology aspires to be a conceptually closed system. From within the perspective of a well-functioning ideology, some things seem obvious and self-evident because of the organizing power of the ideology. Other things cannot be seen at all—are literally unimaginable—because they are closed out by that ideology. Since no ideology is fully adequate to the complexities of actual social and historical conditions, it inevitably encounters contradictions that threaten to expose the ideology as a construct, and indeed, as one lacking plausibility. The task for ideology is to resolve such contradictions in a way that reaffirms the ideological perspective and prevents an unmediated glimpse of the historical and social contradictions that the ideology is an attempt to efface or to master.[19]

In describing the belief system characteristic of Qumran thought as an "ideology of truth" I am referring to its privileging of knowledge of God's will as the key to reality and to the pervasively binary

---

[19] Jameson, *Political Unconscious*, 47–49.

way of representing this knowledge and its opposite. Although a
variety of particular words may be used to refer to these notions,
perhaps the most explicit pairing is אמת and עול, roughly "truth"
and "perversity." Certainly other ways of organizing the world exist,
as well as other ways of constructing a discourse of knowledge, rather
than through such a binary scheme. Like all ideological constructions, Qumran's ideology of truth is historically conditioned. Such a
conceptualization would be unthinkable in Israel before the Second
Temple period. The conditions necessary for its emergence have
been sketched in chapter 2: the problem of community identity and
boundaries in the reconstructed institutions of Second Temple Judea,
the creation of rival definitions of Israel that posited an internally
divided people, and the emergence of torah as a central object of
cultural competition, one that came to be increasingly conducted in
terms of rival claims to knowledge of torah. Behind all of this activity lurked the massive threat to the plausibility of Israel's whole self-
understanding brought about by the historical impact of the centuries-
long rule of great international empires over the previously independent
small nations and states. An ideology of truth was one strategy for
finding a resolution in the sphere of the imagination for such an
intractable social contradiction and its repercussions. In chapter 3
above I attempted to read beneath the ideological concepts to uncover
the "political unconscious" of the Two Spirits Treatise. Here, however,
it is not the socio-historical subtext I wish to examine but the contradiction expressed at the level of ideology itself, as well as its role
in the construction of a distinctive form of sectarian identity.

1QH^a 12:5–13:4

The hodayah is divided into sections by the use of introductory independent pronouns. The pronouns הם/המה and אתה introduce the
strophes in the first part of the hodayah; the pronoun אני introduces
most of the strophes in the second part. In general this division corresponds to a focus on the nature of the speaker's rivals in the first
part and his confession and self-presentation in the second. Beyond
these features the hodayah does not appear to be highly structured
at the poetic level.

> (12:5) *vacat* I thank you, O Lord,
>   that you have illumined my face by your covenant
>   and [. . .] (6) I seek you.
>   As sure as dawn you appear to me as pe[rfect l]ight

But they [. . .] your people [. . .]
>   (7) They used slippery [wo]rds on them.
>   Deceitful interpreters [l]ed them astray,
>   and they came to grief without understanding.
>   Truly, (8) their deeds [partake] of madness,
>   for I am rejected by them.
>   They have no regard for me when you show your strength through me,
>   for they chase me away from my land (9) like a bird from (its) nest.
>   All my friends and my relatives are driven away from me,
>   and they regard me as a broken pot.

And they, the (10) lying interpreters and the deceitful seers
>   have concocted base schemes against me,
>   to exchange your law, which you impressed upon my heart,
>   for seductive words (11) for your people.
>   They withhold the drink of knowledge from the thirsty
>   and for their thirst they give them sour wine to drink,
>   so that they may gaze upon (12) their error,
>   acting like fools on their feast days,
>   getting snared in their nets.

But you, O God, despise every (13) base plan,
>   and it is your counsel that will stand,
>   and the plan of your mind that will be established forever.

But they, the hypocrites, (14) concoct base schemes
>   and seek you with a divided heart.
>   And so they are not steadfast in your truth.
>   A root that grows poison and wormwood is in their thoughts,
>   (15) and in the stubbornness of their heart they explore,
>   and they seek you among idols.
>   The stumbling block of their sin they have placed before themselves,
>   and they enter (16) to seek you from the mouth of the lying prophets
>   who are themselves seduced by error.

And they [with] m[oc]king lips and an alien tongue speak to your people,
>   (17) deceitfully turning all their deeds to madness.
>   For they have not chosen the way of your [heart],
>   and they do not listen to your word,
>   for they say (18) of the vision of knowledge, "It is not certain";
>   and of the way of your heart, "It isn't that."

But you, O God, will answer them,
>   judging them (19) in your strength [according to] their idols
>   and the magnitude of their sins,

so that they will be seized in their own machinations,
    those who are estranged from your covenant.
(20) You will cut off in ju[dgm]ent all the people of deceit,
    and the seer of error will be found no longer.
For there is no folly in all your works,
    and there is no (21) deception [in] the plan of your mind.
Those who are dear to you will stand before you forever,
    and those who walk in the way of your heart (22) will be
    established everlastingly.

[And as for] me, when I cling to you, I gather strength
    and rise up against those who despise me.
My hand is against all who have contempt for me,
    for (23) they have no regard for [me al]though you show your
    strength through me.[20]
And you have appeared to me in your strength as perfect light.
    You have not covered in shame the faces of (24) all who are
    examin[ed] by me,
    who have met together for your covenant.
Those who walk in the way of your heart listen to me,
    and they marshal themselves before you (25) in the fellowship
    of the holy ones.
You bring their cause to victory
    and truth according to justice.
You will not let them be led astray by the hand of the vile
    ones, (26) as they planned to do to them.
    But you will put a dread of them upon your people,
        and (bring) destruction to all the peoples of the lands
        to cut off in judgment all (27) who transgress your command.

And through me you have caused light to shine upon the faces of the
    many,
    and you have increased (them) until they are without number.
For you have made me understand (28) your wonderful mysteries,
    and in your wonderful secret counsel you have shown yourself
    strong to me.
You have done wonders before the many for the sake of your
    glory
    and in order to make known (29) your mighty deeds to all
    the living.

What being of flesh is like this?
    What creature of clay is able to do wondrous great deeds?
    It (exists) in sin (30) from the womb,
    and until grey hair (it exists) in faithless guilt.

---

[20] For the restoration and interpretation of the line, see Holm-Nielsen, *Hodayot*, 83–84.

I know that righteousness does not belong to humankind,
  nor perfection (31) of way to a mortal.
To El Elyon belong all the works of righteousness.
  The way of humanity is not established except by the spirit
    God has fashioned for it,
      (32) in order to perfect a way for mortal beings,
      so that all his creatures may know his mighty strength
      and his abundant compassion toward all the children (33)
        of his good will.

And as for me, trembling and quaking seized me,
      and all my bones were shattered.
  My heart melted like wax before the fire.
    And my knees gave way (34) like water hurling down a slope.
  For I am mindful of my guilty acts together with the unfaithfulness
    of my ancestors,
    when the ungodly rose against your covenant,
    (35) and the vile ones against your word.
  And I said, "In my sin I have been abandoned, far from your
  covenant."
    But when I remembered the strength of your hand
    together with (36) your overflowing compassion,
  I gathered strength and I arose
    and my spirit held fast to (its) place in the face of affliction.
  For [I] supported myself upon (37) your kindness
    and upon your overflowing compassion,
  because you pardon sin,
    and the cl[eansing] of a person from guilt (comes) through
      your righteousness.
  (38) But it was not for humankind [. . .] you have acted
    For you yourself created the righteous and the wicked [. . .]
  (39) I held fast to your covenant until [. . .]
    (40) [. . .] your [. . .]
  For you are truth and righteous are all [your deeds. . .]
    [day] (13:1) to day with the [. . .]
  [. . . the greatness] (2) of your forgiveness
    and the abundance [of your compassion . . .]
  (3) And when I knew these things [I] was comforted
    [. . .]
  (4) according to your good will
    and in your ha[nd] is the judgment of them all. *vacat*

אודכה אדוני *vacat* (12:5)
כיא האירותה פני לבריתכה
ומ[. . . (6) . . .] אדורשכה
וכשחר נכון לאור[תו]ם הופעתה לי

והמה עמכה [. . .]

(7) [. . . דב]רים החליקו למו
ומליצי רמיה [ה]תעום
וילכטו בלא בינה
כיא [עשו] (8) בהולל מעשיהם
כי נמאסי[^21] למו
ולא יחשבוני בהגבירכה בי
כיא ידיחני מארצי (9) כצפור מקנה
וכול רעי ומודעי נדחו ממני
ויחשבוני לכלי אובד

והמה מליצי (10) כזב וחוזי רמיה
זממו עלי בליעל
להמיר תורתכה אשר שננתה בלבבי
בחלקות (11) לעמכה
ויעצורו משקה דעת מצמאים
ולצמאם ישקום חומץ
למע[^22] הבט אל (12) תעותם
ולהתהולל במועדיהם
להתפש במצודותם

כי אתה אל תנאץ כל מחשבת (13) בליעל
ועצתכה היא תקום
ומחשבת לבכה תכון לנצח

והמה נעלמים זמות בליעל (14) יחשובו
וידרשוכה בלב ולב
ולא נכונו באמתכה
שורש פורה רוש ולענה במחשבותם
(15) ועם שרירות לבם יתורו
וידרשוכה בגלולים
ומכשול עוונם שמו לנגד פניהם
ויבאו (16) לדורשכה מפי נביאי כזב
מפותי תעות

והם [ב]ל[וע]נ שפה ולשון אחרת ידברו לעמך
(17) להולל ברמיה כול מעשיהם
כי לא בחרו בדרך [לב]כה
ולא האזינו לדברכה
כי אמרו (18) לחזון דעת לא נכון
ולדרך לבכה לא היאה

כי אתה אל תענה להם
לשופטם (19) בגבורתכ[ה] כ[נ]לוליהם וכרוב פשעיהם
למען יתפשו במחשבותם

---

[^21] Read נמאסתי instead of נמאסי or נמאסו.

[^22] Read למען instead of למע.

אשר נזורו מבריתכה

(20) ותכרת במ[שפ]ט כול אנשי מרמה

וחוזי תעות לא ימצאו עוד

כי אין הולל בכול מעשיך

ולא (21) רמיה [ב]מזמת לבכה

ואשר כנפשכה יעמודו לפניכה לעד

והולכי בדרך לבכה (22) יכונו לנצח

[וא]ני בתומכי בכה אתעודדה

ואקומה על מנאצי

וידי על כול בוזי

כיא (23) לא יהשבונ[י] ע[ד] הגבירכה בי

ותופע לי בכוחכה לאורתום

ולא טחתה בבושת פני (24) כול הנדרש[ים] לי

הנועדים יחד לבריתכה

וישומעוני ההולים בדרך לבכה

ויערוכו לכה (25) בסוד קדושים

ותוצא לנצח משפטם

ולמישרים אמת

ולא תתעם ביד הלכאים (26) כזומם למו

ותתן מוראם על עמכה

ומפץ לכול עמי הארצות

להכרית במשפט כול (27) עוברי פיכה

ובי האירותה פני רבים

ותגבר עד לאין מספר

כי הודעתני ברזי (28) פלאכה

ובסוד פלאכה הגברתה עמדי

והפלא לנגד רבים בעבור כבודכה

ולהודיע (29) לכול החיים גבורותיכה

מי בשר כזאת

ומה יצר חמר להגדיל פלאות

והוא בעוון (30) מרחם

ועד שבה באשמת מעל

ואני ידעתי כי לוא לאנוש צדקה

ולוא לבן אדם תום (31) דרך

לאל עליון כול מעשי צדקה

ודרך אנוש לוא תכון כי אם ברוח יצר אל לו

(32) להתם דרך לבני אדם

למען ידעו כול מעשיו בכוח גבורתו

ורוב רחמיו על כול בני (33) רצונו

ואני רעד ורתת אחזוני

וכול גרמי ירועו

וימס לבבי כדונג מפני אש

וילכו ברכי (34) כמים מונרים במורד

כי זכרתי אשמותי עם מעל אבותי

בקום רשעים על בריתך

(35) והלכאים על דברכה

ואני אמרתי בפשעי נעזבתי מבריתכה

ובזוכרי כוח ידכה

עם (36) המון רחמיכה

התעודדתי ואקומה

ורוחי החזיקה במעמד לפני נגע

כי נשען[תה]י (37) בהסדיכה

והמען רחמיכה

כי תכפר עוון

ולטה[ר] אנוש מאשמה בצדקתכה

(38) ולא לאדם [...] עשיתה

כי אתה בראתה צדיק ורשא [...]

(39) [...] אתחזקה בבריתכה עד [...]

(40) [...]יכה

כי אמת אתה וצדק כול [מעשיכה...]

[יום] (13:1) ליום עם הד[...]

[רוב] (2) סליחותיכה

והמון [רחמיכה...]

(3) ובדעתי אלה נחמ[תי ...]

(4) על פי רצונכה

ובי[ד]כה משפט כולם *vacat*

Despite its similarities with 1QH^a 10:3–19, the different focus of this hodayah is signaled by the motive for thanks. In 1QH^a 10:3–19 thanks was given for strength and support before enemies; here it is for illumination. Thus the issue of truth is identified at the beginning of the hodayah as the central problem to be addressed. The symbolic drama is also differently structured than in 1QH^a 10:3–19. Here the conflict is not represented as the rivals' direct hostility toward the speaker. Instead two other relationships preoccupy the text: the relationship between "them" and "your people" (i.e., God's people, Israel), and the relationship between "your people" and the speaker. The problem that is framed in the first strophe is a classic one for sectarian communities: how to account for rejection by the larger society. Although the rejection of the speaker by "your people" is described in terms of persecution, the images are drawn from the stereotypical language of the Psalms and probably should not be taken literally. What motivates the hodayah may be public indifference as easily as persecution. Indifference, too, is rejection, but not as internally useful as persecution. In either case the fundamental contradiction remains: despite the fact that the sect possesses the truth about the will of God, they remain a minority even within God's own people.

The attitude of the Qumran community to the larger society is one of ambivalence and complexity and is treated differently in different texts. On the one hand, the sect depended in part on the larger society for recruits but it also had to depict itself as radically separate (see, e.g., 1QS 5:1–3). How the larger society is represented will depend in large part on the particular rhetorical needs of the situation at hand. The sharp boundary division between insiders and outsiders in 1QHᵃ 10:3–19, considered above, served to give definition to the leader and boundaries for the community. Here a more complex relationship is outlined as the hodayah attempts to deal with a different issue, the ideological contradiction of rejected truth. By naming the larger society as "your people," the speaker gives them a positive value but one that also intensifies the contradiction. How is it that *God's* people reject God's truth? Their rejection is presented as a kind of irrationality (בהולל, 12:8). But that in itself is insufficient; such irrationality must be motivated. A villain is needed—a seducer. This is the role supplied by "them," figures who represent the rivals of the speaker in the competition to persuade "your people." In an insightful pun on the word "rivals" Kenneth Burke noted that in French the word *rivales* refers to the opposite banks of a river.[23] So here, "they" are the mirror image of the speaker, the image of perverted teaching that seduces and destroys where it should correct and save. The rivals are depicted as actually motivated by the pleasure they receive from watching the confusion and destruction of "your people."

In the scheme of the hodayah the rivals occupy a logically necessary place in resolving the contradiction faced by the sectarian status of the Qumran community. That does not mean that the sect did not in fact have rivals, such as the priests in Jerusalem and the Pharisees, but only that one should be cautious in moving too quickly from the symbolic figures of the Hodayot to actual social entities. What one encounters in this hodayah is the acute hypostatization of the various rival discourses that competed with the Qumran community for influence in Second Temple Judaism.

Although much of the hodayah is concerned with just these three

---

[23] Burke, *Grammar of Motives*, 34. Burke attributes the observation to the poet Coleridge.

human actors ("I," "your people," and "them"), there is a fourth role that is introduced to complete the symmetrical pattern: the speaker's community. They are identified as "all who are examined by me," "who have met together for your covenant," who "listen to me," "who marshal themselves together before you" (12:24–25) and, in the technical terminology for the sect, as "the many" (12:27). Just as the speaker and "they" were depicted as mirror images of each other, so "the many" are the mirror image of "your people." Unlike "your people" they are responsive to the speaker. Even though the motif is not developed extensively in the hodayah, the speaker's community is also the object of seduction by "them," a seduction that fails because of God's mercy: "You will not let them be led astray by the hand of the vile ones, as they planned to do to them" (12:25–26).

The little drama described in this hodayah is one that in romance novels one would recognize as seduction and betrayal versus redemption through true love. As a formal pattern, the design of four actors paired in opposite but mirroring relationships is a frequently used device for mapping the closure of an ideological system. Fredric Jameson has adapted Greimas's semiotic square as a heuristic device for mapping such systems of ideological closure.[24] In this case I find it helpful for disclosing the dynamics that underlie the construction of the hodayah. The square is generated by the identification of an opposition. This is not necessarily a logical contradiction but "an antinomy for the mind, a dilemma, an aporia, which itself expresses— in the form of an ideological closure—a concrete social contradiction.[25] The antinomy or conceptual scandal in this case may be identified as truth and its rejection. The square is developed by identifying the simple opposite of the two main terms:

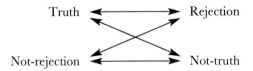

[24] Jameson, *Political Unconscious*, 166–169, 254–257. See also Jameson's foreword to Greimas, *On Meaning: Selected Writings in Semiotic Theory.*
[25] Jameson, *Political Unconscious*, 254.

The formal pattern can be filled out with the characters of the
hodayah: "I," "your people," "they," "the many."

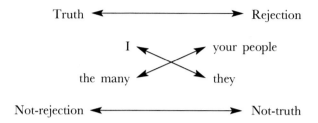

The square is not just a static map of contradiction, however. It also
sketches the range of logical options for resolving the contradiction.
These possibilities are disclosed as one attempts to mediate between
the various pairs of terms. Only one combination will prove gener-
ative, but that one will resolve the contradiction. Starting with the
pair at the top of the schema, "I" and "your people," the contradiction might be resolved if the speaker could persuade all of Israel
of the truth he speaks, but within the ideological framework of the
hodayah that possibility is given up. No hope is held out here for
an ultimate persuasion of Israel at large ("I am rejected by them.
They have no regard for me when you show your strength through
me," 12:8). The reason that "your people" continue to reject truth
is explained by the same logic that discloses why it is not possible
for "your people" to reject the not-truth of the speaker's rivals, "they."
The reason is that the relation between "they" and "your people"
is perceived as one of deceitful seduction ("And they, the lying interpreters and deceitful seers . . . [have prepared] seductive words for
your people," 12:10–11). The consequence of this failure to resist
seduction by the speaker's rivals is the ultimate destruction of "your
people" ("You will put a dread of them [the many] upon your people . . . to cut off in judgment all who transgress your command,"
12:26–27). Moving to the third set of oppositions, it is not possible
that the position of untruth represented by the speaker's rivals will
persuade "the many," for they are under divine protection ("You
will not let them be led astray by the hand of the vile ones," 12:25–26).
The only viable relationship is that between "I" and "the many,"
which is described in terms of divinely inspired teaching ("And
through me you have caused light to shine upon the faces of the
many," 12:27). The consequence of this teaching and reception of
truth is eschatological salvation ("Those who walk in the way of your

heart listen to me, and they marshal themselves before you in the fellowship of the holy ones. You bring their case to victory and truth according to justice," 12:24–25). In this way the threatening contradiction of the rejection of truth by the majority of God's people is successfully resolved.

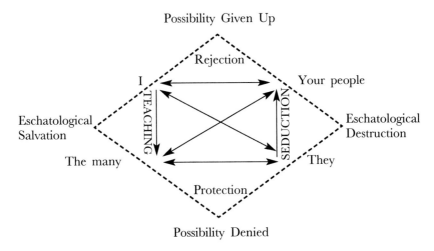

By resolving the contradiction in this fashion, rejection by the larger society can now be seen—not as a threat to the sect's ideology of truth—but as an essential part of the pattern of meaning. The escape from contradiction provided by such a text is only temporary, however. The map of truth sketched by this hodayah marks the relationship between the leader and the community as the crucial link. That relationship, far from being the untroubled relationship of perfect receptivity that is depicted here, was also subject to considerable strains, as the hodayah to be considered next makes clear.

Before turning to that composition, however, there is one other issue to be examined, the contrasting characters of "I" and "they." The largest part of the hodayah is given over to characterizing "them" and to revealing the character of the speaker. Why is this so important? I suggest that it is connected with Qumran's ideology of truth. Consider how differently knowledge is represented in this hodayah and, for instance, in the book of Ezra-Nehemiah. There, as noted in the discussion in chapter 2, the opposite of knowledge is ignorance, a representation that undergirds the mission of public teaching and the creation of a community of persuasion. At Qumran the opposite of knowledge is not ignorance but falsity or perversion, a very different pairing. This is what I have been referring to here as the characteristic of an ideology of truth. Some important things are implied by this ideology. The speaker's rivals cannot be seen merely as wrong or mistaken. They must be liars and deceivers. Lying is a logically interesting phenomenon, because one of the preconditions of lying is knowing the truth. Thus the speaker's rivals are necessarily posited as having some sort of access to the truth, though the hodayah does not explain exactly how this occurs. But consistently, the language that describes the rivals attributes knowledge of the truth to them: they lie and deceive, they "*withhold* the drink of knowledge," and they "*exchange your law* for seductive words for your people" (12:10–11). Their flaw is not in their knowledge but in their will. For the ideology of truth, knowledge and moral character are intrinsically related.

How does someone committed to such an ideology of truth imagine the mind and moral character of a liar? The hodayah examines this question by describing how "they" seek God. In formal terms what characterizes the liar is the capacity to sustain doubleness within himself. The liar seeks God, as the hodayah so evocatively puts it, בלב ולב, "with a divided heart" (12:14). He is, as we might say less elegantly, able to compartmentalize. Or again, the hodayah represents him as engaging in a kind of self-interference, by himself placing a stumbling block in his own path. Closely related is the image of self-contradictory actions, "seeking God . . . among idols" (12:15). There is even the image of a doubled doubleness in which the liar uses a spiritual authority who also engages in such self-interference: seeking God through lying prophets who are themselves seduced by error (12:15–16). Even to a modern reader there is something quite ghastly about this representation of self-perverting knowledge, all the more so because such persons do possess the power that knowledge gives.[26] They exercise their power cunningly, carrying their doubleness into the social realm, as people "who hide themselves" (12:13, i.e., "hypocrites," niphal participle of עלם).

The hodayah does not describe the origin of such a character and

---

[26] Certain representations of the demonic in Jewish and Christian tradition draw on this same dynamic, representing the devil as a fallen angel and as the great liar.

makes no attempt to associate it with the metaphysical speculations on human nature that one finds in the Two Spirits section of the Serek ha-Yahad. Rather, it invokes the moral language of the Deuteronomistic prophetic tradition: stubbornness of heart.[27] Although other terminology is used in the wisdom tradition, the same character type is recognizable there, too, as the autonomous self who refuses instruction and is immune to correction. It is closely related to the type of fool the wisdom tradition terms the נבל.[28] Just how dangerous such a character was perceived to be at Qumran is disclosed in the strenuous efforts taken to exclude such persons from the community. The double-minded person who "walks in the stubbornness of his own heart" is excluded by a curse in the covenant liturgy of the Serek ha-Yahad (1QS 2:11–14; see discussion in chapter 4).

In a certain sense a formal resemblance exists between the character of the liar and the character of the person of truth in that both are formed as divided selves, possessing a doubled consciousness. But the structure and function of that sense of inner division is quite different. The liar knows the truth of God but asserts his own autonomy over against it ("For they say of the vision of knowledge, 'It is not certain'; and of the way of your heart, 'It isn't that'"; 12:17–18). For the person of truth, however, the divine knowledge is the instrument through which he looks at his being of flesh and confronts his guilty self. Far from being stubborn of heart, the person of truth enacts a self-sacrifice, negating all of his human being before the being of God. (See chapter 5 for a discussion of the dynamics of this divided consciousness in the Hodayot of the community).

The speaker of this hodayah gives a particularly bravura performance of such self-negation. He begins his self-presentation with a general comparison between the worthlessness of every being of flesh as compared with the righteousness of El Elyon (12:29–33). He acknowledges that "the way of humanity is not established except by the spirit God has fashioned for it" (12:31), and then demonstrates through his own confession how this works. First the speaker describes his physical devastation as he becomes aware not only of his own guilt but of guilt going back for generations (12:33–35). This

---

[27] The particular term used here, שרירות, occurs in Deut 29:18; Ps 81:13; and otherwise, only in the Deuteronomistic prose of Jeremiah.
[28] Crenshaw, *Old Testament Wisdom*, 46; Fox, 38–43.

act of self-confrontation through the knowledge of God's truth is the very antithesis of the self-interference practiced by the liars. The line that follows, however, is somewhat ambiguous. It could be read "And I said, 'In my sin I have been abandoned, far from your covenant," or "And I said in my sin, 'I have been abandoned, far from your covenant.'" Read in the first way, the statement is simply one of humility, a recognition of the speaker's unworthiness. Read in the second way, even the sense of abjection to which his self-examination has led can be an occasion for sin, since it causes the speaker to doubt God's intention to be merciful. But the speaker gives up even this temptation to establish his own identity as an abandoned and abject being by focusing not on himself but on God, recalling God's power and compassion. Through that reorientation he is indeed "established by the spirit God has fashioned" for him (12:31), as he describes his renewed strength and the ability of his spirit to hold fast in the face of affliction (12:36). His purified understanding now comforts him (13:3) and he concludes with an affirmation of divine sovereignty.

The hodayah found in 1QH^a 12:5–13:4 not only defines leadership within the community but serves as an act of leadership. It defuses the threat to the plausibility of the sect's discourse caused by others' rejection, showing how their rejection is a necessary part of the pattern of truth. It also discloses the contrasting character between liars and persons of truth and allows the membership of the sect to see for themselves that their leader is beyond doubt a man of truth.

Addressing Disaffection: Rhetorical Strategies in the Hodayot and in the Serek ha-Yahad (1QS 7:15–25 and 1QH^a 13:20–15:5)

The Hodayot of the leader are variously concerned with the problems of the formation and leadership of a sectarian community. Locating the community in a moral world of significant choices and defining the boundaries that articulate sectarian identity are an important part of their work. But there are also inner-community problems of a predictable sort to be addressed, including disaffection and conflict with established leadership. These are chronic problems that the sociology of sectarianism teaches one to expect. Whether or not these Hodayot were written in response to specific, acute situations,

their topics would have remained pertinent throughout the life of
the sect.

The genre of the Hodayot, and in particular its relation to the
tradition of biblical thanksgiving psalms, endows it with rhetorical
possibilities and limitations for the task of addressing disaffection and
dissension. Like the thanksgiving psalms, which were addressed to
God but clearly intended to be heard also by members of the psalmist's
community, the Hodayot of the leader assume a dual audience. Thus
the leader speaks, though only indirectly, to his community. Moreover,
the tradition of prayer that influences the Hodayot is one in which
the speaker's subjectivity is elaborately displayed: accounts of experiences, social humiliations or triumphs, emotions, hopes, fears, and
even physical sensations are all marshaled as part of the discourse
of the self at prayer. In the biblical psalms such self-presentation
may have functioned to attract the attention of the deity, to reha-
bilitate the speaker in the view of his fellows, and to witness to the
power of the deity. But what, one needs to ask here, would be the
uses of such a discourse of the self for negotiating issues of disaffection
within a sectarian community? The genre of prayer, with its address
to God, rules out a direct appeal to the human audience to behave
in a certain way or to adopt a certain stance. The speaker must
persuade through indirection. Various kinds of conduct, attitudes,
and persons may be praised and blamed in the course of a hodayah,
but these specific arguments are all embedded in an appeal that consists finally in an extended act of self-presentation. It is the speaker
himself that the audience will accept or reject. These Hodayot thus
project a personal and charismatic form of leadership in which the
leader's authority is grounded in the personal attachment of his followers, who trust his claims to have received divine revelation.
Virtually nothing is said about concrete social organization. The
whole focus is on the presentation of the leader's subjectivity.

What should one make of the fact that the model of leadership
and social organization implied in the Hodayot is radically different
from that described in the Serek ha-Yahad, with its emphasis on
bureaucratic and impersonal forms of leadership in a hierarchically
structured community? Although personalities always matter to some
extent, the organization described in the Serek ha-Yahad seems
designed to limit their influence. One way of resolving these apparently discrepant depictions of social organization and leadership is
to assume that they belong to two different periods of the sect's his-

tory. Such a suggestion fits well with the hypothesis that these Hodayot are the compositions of the Teacher of Righteousness or at least are written as though they were his words. It would also correspond with a recognized pattern of the evolution of some sectarian organizations, a kind of Weberian replacement of charismatic personal leadership with a hierarchical and formalized mode of organization and leadership, reflected now in the Serek ha-Yahad.

Such a scenario is possible but certainly not necessary. Many organizations contain both rule-oriented hierarchical structures and personal forms of leadership that are articulated through different discourses and in different settings.[29] In particular, one should resist the temptation to move too quickly from these Qumran texts to sociological description. Texts do not transparently render social reality. As rhetorical acts, however, they are, *part of* the social life of the communities in which they were used. Since there is every reason to believe that both the Hodayot and the Serek ha-Yahad were simultaneously active parts of the sect's discourse about itself for most of the period of its existence, it is important to consider how they may have functioned in providing complementary ways of representing the society and its leadership.

This is one of the contexts in which it does make a difference whether the Hodayot of the leader were understood as referring primarily to the Teacher of Righteousness or not. If they were, then the charismatic form of leadership that is embodied in them would have been limited by the fact that the Teacher was a figure of history, not present reality. However much the Hodayot gave a sense

---

[29] The comments of Douglas and Wildavsky are instructive: "We have noticed that some religious sects are conspicuously more short lived and prone to fission than others and that the best survivors tend to have adopted hierarchical forms of organization. . . . How did the Shakers survive? Our first explanation is that they held property in common and our second is that they created their own form of hierarchy. Holding property in common in itself is not enough. There is also the will to make compartments and regulations which obscure most political issues and lighten the burdens of deciding on issues too hot to avoid. Some of the communities which broke up never managed to turn the personal authority of their founders into institutional forms. Others gave over their life decisions to committees" (113–14; I have reversed the order of the quotations). That last remark suggests that the advantages of bureaucratic organization are not without their costs, one of which is precisely the depersonalizing of the ethos of the community. In times of stress, what will there be to remain loyal *to*? I suggest that the Qumran community owed its remarkable longevity in part to its success in combining institutional authority with elements of personal attachment.

of the immediacy to the persona of the Teacher, and however much
he embodied the ideal of the movement and formed a focus of loyalty, the sectarians' experience of him would not be continuous with
their experience of the sect's institutional leaders. The highly personal appeal of the Teacher might even have functioned to inhibit
such a mode of leadership by others. The two modes of leadership
would have been compartmentalized. On the other hand, if the
Hodayot of the leader were spoken by the institutional leaders as
their own prayers and as rendering their own subjectivities, then the
complementary rhetorics of the Hodayot and the Serek ha-Yahad
would have been coordinated in a very different way. They would
still have been compartmentalized by the different *Sitzen im Leben*.
But both models of leadership would have been part of the repertoire of the sect's actual leaders.[30]

It remains difficult to know which reconstruction is more accurate, though for reasons given at the beginning of this chapter, I
favor the latter scenario. In both cases, however, the complemen-
tarity of the two discourses of leadership suggests that the Qumran
community found a way to combine institutional authority with elements of personal attachment as it struggled to negotiate the chronic
problems of its own marginality in Jewish society and the disaffection
of some of its members.

To appreciate the way in which the institutionalized, bureaucratic
ethos of the Serek ha-Yahad and the personal ethos of the Hodayot
could work to complement each other, it is useful to compare the
way each treats the problem of disaffection among community members. The two texts to be compared are 1QS 7:15–25 and 1QHᵃ
13:20–15:5.

The relevant portion of the Serek ha-Yahad reads as follows:

> (15) The man who goes about slandering his neighbor (16) shall be
> excluded from the purity of the many for one year and fined. But a
> man who goes about slandering the community shall be sent away
> from them and (17) shall never return.
>
> The man who makes complaints about the authority of the com-
> munity shall be sent away and shall not return. But if it is against his
> neighbor that he makes complaints (18) without cause, he shall be
> fined for six months.

---

[30] Note, by analogy, the inclusion of the personal hymn of the Maskil at the end
of the Serek ha-Yahad.

The man whose spirit so deviates from the fundamental principles of the community that he betrays the truth (19) and walks in the stubbornness of his heart, if he returns, he shall be fined for two years. In the first year he shall not touch the purity of the many, (20) and in the second he shall not touch the drink of the many, and he shall sit behind all the men of the community. When he has completed (21) two years, the many shall be asked about his affairs. If they allow him to draw near, he shall be registered in his rank, and afterwards he may be asked about judgment. (22) But no man who has been in the council of the community for ten full years (23) and whose spirit turns back so that he betrays the community, and who leaves (24) the many to walk in the stubbornness of his heart, shall ever return to the council of the community. Anyone from the men of the commun[ity who has any]thing to do (25) with him in regard to his purity or his wealth whi[ch . . .] the many, his sentence shall be the same: he shall be sent [away] (trans. Knibb, 124).

Both the hodayah, which will be considered below, and the set of regulations just quoted are about the same sort of problem. But the language each uses could not be more different. That is not a trivial matter. Each form of language offers its users a different symbolic structure, a different vocabulary of motives, a different type of community, a different sort of self. Consequently, the situation they serve to focus, the problem of disaffection, has a very different meaning in each of these available languages. In the Serek ha-Yahad the language is that of rule and breach, punishment and restoration. It is an utterly impersonal language. The characters are "the man who," "his neighbor," "the community," "they." There is no place here for the expression of emotion. Outrage, pain, doubt, disappointment, inner conflict—all such matters are simply unsayable in the language of rules and laws. One is inclined to think that they are unsayable because the central character in this language is not a person but an institution—the Yahad. That would not be quite correct, although it leads in the right direction. In other contexts one can speak as though a collective entity had personal qualities, even emotions. But the language of rules and penalties is a language in which one not only refrains from speaking of institutions as though they were persons but in which one speaks of persons as though they were components of an institutional system. The formalism of such language is not merely a matter of style. It also shapes the realities of which it speaks.

The affective dimension of existence is not the only thing obscured in the symbolic world of legal regulations. We are so accustomed to

the language of legal authority that it is easy to overlook the con-
structive force of such language. The passage cited above lists a series
of grave challenges to the authority of the community, an inventory
of destabilizing behaviors. There is no reason to think that the leg-
islation had a purely hypothetical character. And yet, an impression
of instability and precariousness is not at all what one derives from
that passage. Just the opposite is the case. But how is it that the
text manages to speak of all these counter-institutional threats and
leaves one persuaded of the institution's authority and stability? In
part, it is the way in which the parties to the conflict are presented.
The transgressor is a single individual ("a person who does such-
and-such"), whereas the punishing agent is the collectivity. The
prospect of large-scale defection or challenges to authority, a situation that would put in question the very efficacy of law, is simply
not contemplated. Transgression is always limited and punishable.
This projection of relative power is also implied in the way in which
defection is treated. The text does not deal with defection per se. It
does not hold up for our inspection a case in which someone is
beyond the power of the community. Instead it contemplates cases
of *expulsion* of disaffected members (7:15–18, 24–25) and cases in
which a *defector seeks* readmission (7:18–24). In the case of the one
who has been a member for less than two years, it grants readmission on stringent terms. For the one who has been a member for
more than ten years, it denies readmission. What the reader of the
text sees is the power of the community in dealing with deviants
and supplicants.

There are other ways, too, in which the authority of the community is constructed in the language of rules. The world placed
before the reader of these rules (and indeed of most legal texts) is
an ahistorical, apolitical world in the sense that the conflicts, com-
promises, changes, and necessities that produced its particular fab-
ric of rights and obligations are repressed. Its contingent character
is completely obscured. All that appears is the assertion of norms,
the catalogues of possible infractions, and the mechanisms for restoring equilibrium. In the case of the Serek ha-Yahad this quality of
absoluteness even extends to the authoritative voice of the text.
Traditionally, Israelite law drew authority from the identification of
the speaking voice as that of God or a mediator such as Moses. But
if one asks who authorizes the rules in the Serek ha-Yahad, there
is no personal voice to which they may be attributed. Rather, their

authority is projected precisely by the lack of any such voice. This is simply "the way things are," "how one does things." It is the authority of utter matter-of-factness.

In sum, the regulations at the end of col. 7 of the Serek ha-Yahad give instructions for dealing with various expressions of serious disaffection from members of the community. But they do much more than that. The resources of the legal language itself, the limits it sets to what can be said, and the selection of examples all work together to create a text that persuades its reader to a belief in the authority, legitimacy, and effectiveness of the community. To the disgruntled it serves as a word of warning; to the one who doubts the stability of the community it speaks a word of confidence; and to the members who must from time to time take disciplinary measures it reassures them of the rightness and efficacy of their actions. Though one may not be accustomed to thinking of such legal language as rhetorical, it is every bit as much a rhetorical act as the highly charged words of the Hodayot.

But how differently the Hodayot deal with the same sort of problems with which 1QS 7 deals. The confessional "I"-style of the Hodayot organizes its rhetorical world around the experiences of a single person. The rhetorical ground is not that of institutional but of personal relations. Disaffection is not a breach of obligations but a matter of betrayal. Correspondingly, it is not the dispassionate language of institutional procedure that one finds, but the language of the emotions. The immediate resolution provided by the regulations is missing here. Far more important than the possible action that could be taken against the transgressors is the process of giving a character to each of the parties. The betrayers are portrayed as monstrous villains. The one betrayed, far from being depicted as able to discipline or expel his opponents, is rather shown as one who suffers deeply from their attacks. His vulnerability is very much a part of the rhetorical strategy. The audience, too, is persuaded to a different stance. Rather than confident assurance, it is urged to solidarity.

The rhetorical strategy followed in this composition can be better appreciated if one takes a closer look at the prayer itself. Although the text does not have a strongly marked formal structure, there is a fairly regular alternation of topics. For convenience's sake I have termed these alternating sections "strophes," although they vary greatly by length. After an introduction blessing God for not abandoning the speaker (13:20–22), the prayer may be outlined as follows:

A^1. Antagonism of the speaker's associates (13:22–25)

B^1. Divine assistance (13:25–26)

A^2. Antagonism of the speaker's associates; effect on the speaker (13:26–32)

B^2. Divine assistance (13:32–33)

A^3. Antagonism of the speaker's associates; effect on the speaker (13:33–14:3)

B^3. Divine assistance (14:3–19)

A^4. Defection of "those who had attached themselves to my witness"; effect on the speaker (14:19–24)

B^4. Divine assistance (14:24–?)

A^5. Antagonism of speaker's associates (?); effect on speaker (15:1–5)

1QH^a 13:20–15:5

Introduction
(13:20) Blessed are you, O Lord,
for you have not abandoned the orphan,
    and you have not despised the poor one,
for your strength is [without lim]it
    and your glory (21) without measure.
Wonderful warriors are your servants,
    and a humble people (has a place) in the sweepings of [your] feet.
[. . .] with those who are eager (22) for righteousness,
    to lift up from the mire the community of all the poor (who are objects) of (your) kindness.

Strophe A^1
And as for me, I have become [. . .]
    a cause of controversy (23) and quarrels with my neighbors,
    and an object of jealousy and anger to those who enter into covenant with me,
    an object both of grumbling and murmuring to all who are associated with me.
Ev[en those who] eat my bread (24) have raised the heel against me.
    All who are associated with me in fellowship speak ill of me with evil lips,
And the people of my [congrega]tion are refractory (25) murmurers all around.
    Concerning the secret you have hidden in me they go about as slanderers to the children of destruction.

Strophe B¹
But in order to magnify my [wa]y,
      and on account of (26) their guilt,
you have hidden the spring of understanding
      and the foundation of truth.

Strophe A²
And as for them, they plot the destruction they have in mind with
      [b]ase [schemes].
      They put out (27) a lying tongue like the venom of serpents
          that shoots forth time and time again.
And like creatures that slither in the dust they spew [their] venom,
      [the poison] of vipers (28) for which there is no charm.
It has become an incurable pain and a malignant affliction in the
      bowels of your servant,
      causing [the soul] to stumble and bringing an end (29) to
      strength,
      so that he could not stand firm.
And they overtook me in distress without a refuge,
      and no [. . .]
And they make a noise (30) on a zither, complaining against me,
      and on stringed instruments in unison they murmur noisily.
Amid ruin and desolation turmoil has seized me,
      and pains like the distress (31) of a woman in labor.
My mind is in tumult within me;
      I am clothed in darkness,
      and my tongue cleaves to the roof of my mouth.
For they surround me with their heart's destructiveness,
      and their purpose (32) reveals itself to me for bitterness.
The light of my face had darkened into gloom,
      and my brilliance has been changed into blackness. *vacat*

Strophe B²
But you, O my God, (33) you have opened a broad space in my heart.

Strophe A³
Yet they have continued to make it tight with distress,
      and they hedge me in with deep darkness.
I consume the bread of sighs,
      (34) and my drink is endless tears.
For my eyes are darkened with frustration,
      and my soul by the bitterness of the day.
Sighs and grief (35) surround me,
      and shame is upon (my) face.
My bread is changed into conflict
      and my drink into an accuser.

[They] have entered [my] very bones,
(36) making the spirit stumble and bringing an end to strength,
according to the mysteries of sin,
which alter the creatures of God through their guilt.
For [I] have been bound with cords (37) that cannot be sundered,
and chains that cannot be broken,
and a stro[ng] wall [. . .]
and bars of iron and doors [of bronze that cannot (38) be opened.]
My prison is reckoned with the deep, (a place) without [refuge]
[. . .]
(39) [Torrents of Be]lial encompass my soul [. . .] without [es]ca[pe . . .]

[Approximately three column lines of text missing]

(14:2) [. . .] my heart with contume[ly . . .]
and destruction without limit, and annihilation without mea[sure . . .]

Strophe B³
[But you, O my God,] (4) you opened my ears [for the correc]tion
of those who reprove in righteousness
together with [. . .]
[. . .] (5) from the assembly of fraud and from the fellowship of violence.
You brought me into the council of [. . .]
[. . .] guilt
(6) I know that there is hope for those who repent of transgression,
and for those who abandon sin [. . .]
[. . .] to walk (7) in the way of your heart without iniquity.
And I am reassured concerning the tumult of the people
and concerning the roar of k[ing]doms when they gather together.
[. . .] whom (8) you raise up
as survivors among your people
and a remnant among your inheritance.
And you refine them in order to purify (them) from guilt. *vacat*
For all (9) their works are in your truth,
and in your kindness you judge them with overflowing compassion
and abundant forgiveness,
teaching them according to your command (10) and establishing
them in your counsel,
according to the rectitude of your truth.
For your glory and for your own sake [you] have acted
[to magni[fy the law and [. . .]
[. . .] (11) the people of your counsel in the midst of humankind
that they may recite for everlasting generations your wonderful
deeds,

and [medi]tate on [your] mighty acts (12) without ceasing.
All the nations will acknowledge your truth and all the peoples your
glory,
for you have brought [. . .] your secrets (13) to all the people
of your counsel.
And in a common lot with the angels of the presence,
without intermediary among the h[oly ones . . .]
[. . .] (14) its fruit for [. . .]
and they return at your glorious command.
And they are your princes in the lo[t . . .]
[. . .] (15) a sprout like the fl[ower of the field] forever,
causing a shoot to grow into the branches of an eternal planting.
And it cast shade over all the w[orld,]
[and] its [top] (reached) (16) to the clou[ds,]
[and] its roots as far as the deep.
All the rivers of Eden [watered] its [foli]age,
and it will exist [for days without] (17) limit.
And it [. . .] over the world without end,
and as far as Sheol (went) [its roots.]
[And] the spring of light became an (18) eternal source without lack.
In its bright flames all the child[ren of iniquity] will burn,
[and it will become] a fire that burns up all (19) guilty people
until they are utterly destroyed.

Strophe A⁴
But they, who had attached themselves to my witness, have let themselves be persuaded by [lying] in[terpreters],
[. . .] in the service of righteousness.
(20) You, O God, had commanded them to seek profit away from
their ways,
in the way of ho[liness, by walking] in it;
where the uncircumcised and unclean and violent (21) do not
cross over it.
But they wander constantly from the way of your heart
and in [great] calamity [. . .] they faint.
And Belial holds counsel (22) with their heart,
[and on acc]ount of a scheme of wickedness they wallow in guilt.
And I [am] like a sailor on a ship in raging (23) seas.
Their waves and all their breakers have roared against me.
A whirling wind (blew) [and there was neither] stillness to restore the
soul,
nor (24) a path to direct the way upon the surface of the water.
The deep roared until I groaned,
and [my] so[ul reached] the gates of death.

Strophe B⁴

But I became (25) like one who enters into a fortified city
and finds refuge in a high wall until deliverance (comes).
I le[an] on your truth, O my God,
for you (26) lay the foundation upon rock
and the crossbeam according to the plumbline of justice and the
level of t[ruth],
in order [to tr]y the tested stones of a strong building that will
not be shaken.
All who enter it will not stagger,
for no stranger will enter (it).
Its [gat]es are shielding doors that allow no (28) entry
and strong bars which cannot be shattered.
No troop with its weapons of war can enter,
with the end of all the sw[ords] (29) of the wars of wickedness.
And then the sword of God will come quickly at the time of judgment.
All the children of His t[ru]th will rouse themselves to put an
[end to] (30) wickedness,
and all the children of guilt will be no more.
The warrior will stretch his bow,
and he will open the citadels of the heaven[s] (31) upon an endless
plain,
and (he will open) the eternal gates to bring forth the weapons
of war.
They will be migh[ty] from one end (of the earth) to [the other].
(32) [. . .] and no escape for a guilty creature.
To utter destruction they will trample (them) down,
without re[mnant or] hope in the multitude of [. . .]
(33) And there will be no refuge for all the champions of war. *vacat*
For to El Elyon [. . .]
(34) And those who lie in the dust raise up a standard,
and the worms of the dead lift up a banner
to [. . .] . . . (35) in the wars against the insolent.
And when the scourging flood passes by, it will not enter the fortified
place [. . .]
(36) [. . .] for plaster and as crossbeams not [. . .]
(37) [. . .]
(38) [. . .] truth [. . .]

[Approximately three column lines of text missing]

Strophe A⁵

(15:1) *vacat* As for me, I am speechless [. . .]
(2) [. . . (my) ar]m is broken from its joint,
and my foot sinks into the mud.
My eyes have sealed shut from seeing (3) evil,
my ears from hearing of bloodshed.

My mind is appalled by the plan of wickedness,

> for Belial is (present) when their (4) destructive inclination shows itself.

All the foundations of my frame shake,

> and my bones are scattered.

My bowels heave like a ship in a raging (5) wind,

> and my heart is in turmoil to the point of destruction.

A whirling wind engulfs me because of the devastation caused by their sin. *vacat*

Introduction

(13:20) ברוך אתה אדוני

כי לא עזבתה יתום

ולא בזיתה רש

כי נבזרתכה [לאין חק]ר

וכבודכה (21) לאין מדה

ונבורי פלא משרתיכה

ועם ענוים בטאטאי רנלי[כה]

[...] עם נמהרי (22) צדק

להעלות משאון יחד כול אביוני חסד

Strophe A¹

ואני הייתי על ע[...].[דני

לריב (23) ומדנים לרעי

קנאה ואף לבאי בריתי

ורנן ותלונה לכול נועדי

נ[ם או]כלי לחמי (24) עלי הנדילו עקב

וילזו עלי בשפת עול כול נצמדי סודי

ואנשי [עד]תי סוררים (25) ומלינים סביב

וברז חבתה בי ילכו רכיל לבני הוות

Strophe B¹

ובעבור הנדל [דר]כי[31]

ולמען (26) אשמחם

סתרת מעין בינה

וסוד אמת

Strophe A²

והמה הוות לבם יחשובו ב[זמות ב]ליעל[32]

פתחו (27) לשון שקר כחמת תנינים פורחת לקצים

וכזוחלי עפר יורו לחמת[ם][33]

---

[31] Reading with Puech, *La croyance*, 349.

[32] García Martínez and Tigchelaar read וא[נ]שי ב[ל]יעל.

[33] Following Licht, who suggests an allusion to Ps 58:5, Puech, *La croyance*, 349, restores [ראש] להתי. García Martínez and Tigchelaar read להתו[ף מבלנות].

[ורוש] פתנים (28) לאין חבר

ותהי לכאיב אנוש

וננע נמאר בתחכמי עבדכה

להכשיל [נפש] ולהתם (29) כוח

לבלתי החזק מעמד

וישינוני במצרים לאין מנוס

ולא [. . .]³⁴

ויהמו (30) בכנור ריבי

ובנגינות יחד תלונתם

עם שאה ומשואה זלעופות אחזוני

וחבלים כצירי (31) יולדה

ויהם עלי לבי קדרות לבשתי

ולשוני לחך תדבק

כי³⁵ סבבוני בהוות לבם

ויצרם (32) הופיע לי מרורים

ויחשך מאור פני לאפלה

והודי נהפך למשחור *vacat*

Strophe B²

ואת אלי (33) מרחב פתחתה בלבבי

Strophe A³

ויוספוה לצוקה

וישוכו בעדי בצלמות

ואוכלה בלחם אנחה

(34) ושקוי בדמעות אין כלה

כי עששו מכעס עיני

ונפשי במרורי יום

אנחה וינון (35) יסובבוני

ובושת על פנים

ויהפך לי לחמי לריב

ושקוי לבעל מדנים

ויבוא[ו] בעצמ[י]

(36) להכשיל רוח ולכלות כוח

כרזי פשע משנים מעשי אל באשמתם

כי נאסר[תי] בעבותים (37) לאין נתק

וזקים ללוא ישברו

וחומת עו[ז . . .]

ובריחי ברזל ודלתי[ן] נחושת ואין (38) פתוח[

[ו]כלאי עם תהום נחשב לאין [מנוס . . .]

---

³⁴ The remaining traces are difficult. Puech, *La croyance*, 350, on the basis of fg. 29 1, suggests the reading ולא בהבדל ממשפחות. The meaning, however, is obscure.

³⁵ Following the reading of Puech, "Quelques aspects," 46, on the basis of fg. 29 3.

(39) [נחלי ב]ל[ן]על אפפו נפשי

ל[...] לאין [פ]ל[ט ...]³⁶

[...] (14:2) לבי בנאצות [...]³⁷

(3) והוות לאין חקר וכלה לאין מד[ה...]³⁸

Strophe B³

[ואתא אלי] (4) נליתה אוזני [למו]סר מוכיחי צדק

עם [...]

[...] (5) מעדת שוא ומסוד חמס

ותביאני בעצת [...]

[...] אשמה

(6) ואדעה כי יש מקוה לשבי פשע

ועוזבי חטאה בה[...]

[...] להתהלך (7) בדרך לבכה לאין עול

ואנחמה על המון עם

ועל שאון מ[מ]לכות בהאספם

[...]עתי אשר³⁹ (8) תרים

למצער מחיה בעמכה ושארית בנחלתכה

ותזקקם להטהר מאמתכה *vacat*

כיא כול⁴⁰ (9) מעשיהם באמתכה

ובחסדיך תשפטם בהמון רחמים ורוב סליחה

וכפיכה להורותם (10) וכיושיר אמתכה להכינם בעצתכה

לכבודכה ולמענכה עשי[תה]

לו[נד]ל תורה ו[...].[...]ל[...]

[...] (11) אנשי עצתכה בתוך בני אדם

לספר לדורות עולם נפלאותיכה

ובנבורות[י]כה יש[והו]⁴¹ (12) לאין השבת

וידעו כול נוים אמתכה וכול לאומים כבודכה

כי הביאותה [...].[סו]דכה⁴² (13) לכול אנשי עצתכה

ובגורל יחד עם מלאכי פנים

ואין מליץ בנים לק[דושים]

[...] (14) פריו כיא [...].[...]ל[...]

והם ישובו בפי כבודכה

---

³⁶ Puech, *La croyance*, 351, following Licht.

³⁷ According to the reconstructions of Puech and Stegemann about three column lines are lost at the top of col. 14. The line numeration here, following that of Sukenik, does not reflect this missing material. See Puech, *La croyance*, 351.

³⁸ Following Puech, *La croyance*, 351.

³⁹ The suggestion of Dupont-Sommer and Licht to read [כי י]דעתי אשר is, as Puech (*La croyance*, 351) points out, grammatically uncharacteristic of the Qumran texts. His own suggestion, however, הו[ן]פעתי אשר, also seems awkward.

⁴⁰ So Sukenik, followed by García Martínez and Tigchelaar. Puech suggests כול [תח]ט, "[tu vas con]domner toutes."

⁴¹ Probably an error for ישוחחו.

⁴² So Puech, *La croyance*, 352.

ויהיו שריכה בנור[ל . . .]

[. . .] (15) פרח כצי[ץ] השדה ע[ד] עולם

לנדל נצר לעופי מטעת עולם

ויצל צל על כול ת[בל]

[וצמרת]ו (16) עד שחקי[ם ו]שרשיו עד תהום

וכול נהרות עדן [הנחלחלת ד]ל[ין]ותהיה⁴³

והיה ל[י]מים לאי[ן]⁴⁴ (17) חקר

וי[. . .] על תבל לאין אפס

ועד שאול [שורשיה]

[ות]היה מעין אור למקו[ר] (18) עולם לאין הסר⁴⁵

בשביבי נונהו יבערו כול בנ[י עולה]

[והיה] לאש בוערת בכול אנשי (19) אשמה עד כלה

Strophe A⁴

והמה נצמדי תעודתי פותו במל[יצי שקר]

[. . .] בעבודת צדק

(20) ואתה אל צויתם להועיל מדרכיהם

בדרך קו[דש להתהלך] בה

וערל וטמא ופרי[ץ] (21) בל יעוברנה

ויתמוטטו מדרך לבכה

ובהווה [נדולה . . .] יכמוא

ויעץ בליעל (22) עם לבבם

[ומפ]ני מחשבת רשעה יתנוללו באשמה

[והי]תי כמלח באוניה בזעף (23) ימים

נליהם וכול משבריהם עלי המו

רוח עועיים [לאי]ן דממה להשיב נפש

ואי[ן] (24) נתיבת לישר דרך על פני מים

ויהם תהום לאנחתי

ונ[פשי תניע] עד שערי מות

Strophe B⁴

ואהיה (25) כבא בעיר מצור

ונעוז בחומה נשגבה עד פלט

ואש[ען] באמתכה אלי

כי אתה (26) תשים סוד על סלע

וכפיס על קו משפט ומשקלת א[מת]

ל[נ]טות אבני בחן לבנות (27) עוז ללוא תתזעזע

וכול באיה בל ימוטו

כי לא יבוא זר

---

⁴³ Schuller ("Hodayot," 139) notes that the trace of the head of *lamed* in the second position eliminates restorations such as תנדלנה or חשקינה. Following a suggestion of Stegemann, she reads a form of the root לחלל, attested in Mishnaic Hebrew.

⁴⁴ The restoration is confirmed by 4QHᵇ fr. 8:5,]עלימים ל[אין. Whether one should interpret the noun as "days" or "seas" remains uncertain.

⁴⁵ Read instead הסר.

[שע]ריה דלתי מגן לאין (28) מבוא
ובריחי עוז ללוא ישברו
בל יבוא נדוד בכלי מלחמתו
עם תום כול ה[ן רבות] (29) מלחמות רשעה
ואז תחיש חרב אל בקץ משפט
וכול בני א[ם]תו יעורו להכר[ית] (30) רשעה[46]
וכול בני אשמה לא יהיו עוד
וידרוך גבור קשתו
ויפתח מצורי השמ[י]ם[47] (31) למרחב אין קץ
ושערי עולם להוציא כלי מלחמות
ויעצו[מ]ו מקצה עד [קצה]
(32) [. . .] ואין פלט
ליצר אשמה לכלה ירמוסו
ואין שאר[ית ואין] תקוה ברוב [. . .]
(33) ולכול גבורי מלחמות אין מנוס   vacat
כי לאל עליון [. . .]
(34) ושוכבי עפר הרימו תרן
ותולעת מתים נשאו נס
לה[. .]. [. . .] (35) במלחמות זדים
בעבור[48] שוט שוטף בל יבוא במבצר [. . .]
(36) [. . .] להפל ככפיס לא
(37) . . . [. . .]
(38) אמת [. . .] . . . [49]

Strophe A[5]

(15:1) [. . .]   vacat   אני נאלמתי [. . .]
(2) [. . .]ע[זרו] נשברת מקניה
ותטבע בבבי[50] רגלי
(3) שעו עיני מראות רע
אוזני משמוע דמים
הׁשם לבבי ממחשבת רוע
כי בליעל עם הופע יצר (4) הוותם
וירועו כול אושי מבניתי
ועצמי יתפרדו
ותכמי עלו באוניה בזעף (5) חרישית
ויהם לבי לכלה
ורוח עועיים תבליעני מהוות פשעם   vacat

---

[46] García Martínez and Tigchelaar read להתם [בני] רשעה.

[47] So Puech, *La croyance*, 354.

[48] See Puech, *La croyance*, 355, for discussion of the reading.

[49] According to the reconstructions of Puech and Stegemann, approximately three column lines of text are missing at the top of column 15. These are not reflected in the line numeration here, which follows that of Sukenik. See Puech, *La croyance*, 355.

[50] One occurrence of ב should be deleted.

The most noticeable thing about the structure of the text is that it ends, not with a celebration of divine assistance (as would seem most fitting for a prayer of thanks) but with a description of the speaker's distress. This alone should alert one that something else is going on here besides simple thanks to God. But one needs to follow the sequence of the prayer as it unfolds in order to assess its rhetorical strategies. Although the introductory lines do not contain the pronoun "I," there is no doubt that the speaker is claiming for himself a traditional identity within a well-known moral language. He himself is to be seen as the "orphan" and the "poor one."

By the second century BCE these were terms that not only drew on the ancient paternalistic ethos of the Near East but also on a specifically religious reinterpretation of those terms as labels of rectitude and piety.[51]

Following this initial claim, the first movement of the text (A^1 and B^1) begins to sketch the conflict. Here, again, the speaker draws on traditional imagery from the psalms of complaint. He is, for example, "a cause of controversy and quarrels with my neighbors, and an object of jealousy and anger to those who enter into covenant with me" (13:22–23; cf. Pss 31:12; 38:12; 55:13–15; 69:9–13). In traditional psalmic language such statements are not merely descriptive but function as implicit claims that the speaker's antagonists are the ones in the wrong. Only toward the end of this section is the specific, sectarian context of the antagonism indicated: "with the secret you have hidden in me they go about as slanderers to the children of destruction" (13:25). Betrayal of esoteric knowledge to those outside the restricted group is hardly the type of misfortune addressed by the traditional psalms of complaint and thanksgiving. In actual fact, to whom such knowledge belonged and the morality of separating from a (possibly autocratic) leader or community may have been deeply ambiguous issues. The speaker here uses traditional language to colonize the new moral territory of sectarian ethics. Since the betrayers are unlikely to have been part of the audience that overhears this prayer of thanksgiving to God, the clarification is evidently intended for those who have not defected but whose loyalty needs to be reinforced. "Spin control," it would appear, has always been with us. The statement of divine assistance, though brief,

---

[51] Lohfink, 101.

is to the point (B¹, 13:25–26). The speaker is vindicated, his opponents are judged, and their efforts are claimed to have been unavailing.

The text, however, does not appear to be as concerned with the topic of divine assistance as with the vivid characterization of the conflict, to which it quickly turns again (A², 13:26–32). Indeed, the second statement of divine assistance in 13:32–33 does not bring the prayer to a moment of rest but merely serves as a transition to a renewed description of the conflict and its effects on the speaker (A³, 13:33–14:3). The verbal quality of the conflict is aptly captured in the image of snakes with their darting tongues and poisonous venom, and again with the noisy songs of complaint to which the speaker is subjected by his opponents. Even more than the highly colored description of the faithless ones, the lengthy descriptions of the emotional state of the speaker form the central focus of this part of the prayer.

The adaptation of the personal language of the complaint psalm to the sectarian communal context is evident in the following section, which describes the divine assistance (B³, 14:3–19). Although the speaker's suffering has been described in wholly personal terms, the relief is described in terms of God's provision of a community of repentance. The way in which the topic of the community is introduced is somewhat surprising. "[But you, O my God,] you opened my ears [to the correc]tion of those who reprove in righteousness" (14:3–4). Although several lines are unfortunately broken, there are other references to the moral discipline of the life of the covenanted community. "I know that there is hope for those who repent of transgression and for those who abandon sin" (14:6); "you refine them in order to purify (them) from guilt" (14:8); "in your kindness you judge them with overflowing compassion and abundant forgiveness" (14:9). Although cast in positive terms, the aspects of community life to which these expressions broadly refer had the potential for being occasions for disgruntlement and social friction. We know from the Serek ha-Yahad that members were encouraged to reprove one another concerning their faults and lapses, and a record of reproof is preserved in 4Q477 Rebukes Reported by the Overseer. Indeed, the Serek ha-Yahad is aware of the potential for social friction and regulates the ways in which reproof was to be conducted (1QS 5:24–6:1). The conduct of members was regularly reviewed, and offenses against the community's understanding of torah could result in a reduction of status (1QS 5:20–25). Although

I would not care to go too far in specifying the situation to which this hodayah is a response; in general terms at least, the system of moral examination, mutual critique, and status hierarchy would have provided the environment in which "refractory murmurers" (1QH[a] 13:24–25) could be expected to have been a recurrent problem. By developing the theme of the community as the source of hope and reassurance to the suffering speaker, the prayer makes an appeal for the value of the practices of the community, even those that may not have been pleasant. But the appeal is bolstered by the further description of the benefits of membership in this elect group—universal acclaim, communion with the angels, a metaphorical account of the community as the world tree, and as a "spring of light" in which all the guilty will be burned up (14:12–19).

A recapitulation of the scenario of conflict and relief occurs in A[4] and B[4] (14:19–38). Again the fault is identified as defection ("They, who had attached themselves to my witness, have let themselves be persuaded by [lying] in[terpreters]" 14:19) and as departure from "the way of ho[liness]" (14:20–21). The speaker's distress is presented under the image of a sailor caught in a raging storm (14:22–24), while the image of deliverance is that of a secure and fortified city (14:24–29). As before, the image culminates in a description of eschatological judgment, this time in a military idiom (14:29–38). Although the connection is not made explicitly in the text, Delcor is probably correct that the image of the fortified city is intended to suggest the covenanted community.[52] If so, it is curious that the community, which has in fact proven to be a place of instability, is described as sure and reliable. And the leader, who, on the evidence of this prayer, is a figure to be reckoned with, presents himself as deeply vulnerable, rescued from death and dissolution by the strength he receives from this community of God's truth. Indeed, the very image of the fortified city is one used to refer to the leader's own protection of the community in another text (1QH[a] 15:6–25). But perhaps this reversal is not so curious after all. Precisely in situations where the resolve of a group is in doubt, there may be an advantage in putting before them images of their proper role and crediting them with fulfilling their function, even if their performance has been a bit shaky.

---

[52] Delcor, *Les hymnes de Qumran*, 180.

It is now more explicable why the prayer ends as it does. The last lines of column 14 and the first lines of column 15 are unfortunately missing. Presumably they contained another description of faithless defection, for the last lines of the prayer are yet one more account of the speaker's suffering. Unlike the previous accounts, however, there is no following word of divine aid. We leave the speaker with his frame shaking, bowels heaving, and heart fluttering. Such an ending would be odd even in a psalm of complaint (see only Psalm 88), not to mention one that begins "Blessed are you, O Lord, for you have not abandoned the orphan." To conclude with the speaker's distress is to leave an empty space at the margin of the text. Four times the audience has been told that God has aided the speaker. In the last two cases the aid has been elaborately described as the faithful life of the community itself. By leaving what I have described as the empty space, the text encourages the audience to support the speaker by being the type of community he has described.

As I have attempted to demonstrate in this chapter, the Hodayot of the leader need to be examined not simply as expressive acts of prayer but as rhetorical acts. In various ways they exert leadership for a sectarian community and its chronic needs. Whether the compositions were understood to represent the persona of the historical Righteous Teacher or of the leader who recited them, they serve above all to construct a figure who is a compelling object of loyalty. *Who* he is in relation to God, the community, and their opponents is at the heart of these self-presentations. Through this means they help negotiate problems of sectarian fractiousness, provide the community with an acceptable understanding of acts of disaffection that might otherwise undermine confidence, and encourage sentiments of affinity with the leadership of the community. These compositions build up the community in other ways, as well, articulating important aspects of its figured world. Through their symbolic structures they map reality for the community, drawing with sharp lines the boundaries between the sect and the world outside and interpreting the contrasting character of the leader of the sect and his rivals. They give positive meaning to the rejection of (or indifference to) the sect by other Jews and provide an interpretive narrative context in which the truth possessed by the sect is validated. Finally, the leader offers himself as a model for the formation of sectarian character. His presentation of himself—his experiences, actions, and sentiments—models the character implied by the teachings of the sect. Even though, as leader, his role differs from that of the ordinary sectarian, he also presents himself as someone whose recognition of himself in the eyes of God is the same as that of every sectarian. Whoever wrote them, whoever recited them, in whatever social contexts they were heard—these compositions offer glimpses of the ways in which the discourse of leadership functioned in the life of the Yahad.

CONCLUSIONS

The notion that cultures are symbolically constructed through endless exchanges of social discourse is by now widely accepted. What is of more interest is the examination of the specific structures of discourse that constitute a particular "figured world." In this volume I have attempted to take soundings that indicate some of the ways in which the Qumran community was discursively formed. These few studies map only a small part of the complex terrain of the figured world of Qumran, but they do serve to suggest certain ways in which the sect constructed distinctive forms of self and community.

Although my primary interest in this book is in the internal discourse of the Qumran community, the discourse of a particular group always exists in relation to larger cultural conversations. While one might choose any number of topics to chart the discursive jostlings of different social groups in Second Temple Judaism, the conversation concerning torah is uniquely significant. Many scholars, including Baumgarten, Klawans, and Schiffman, have analyzed the distinctiveness of Qumran halakic concepts. But what various groups did socially with their knowledge of torah has been less studied. In my exploration of this issue I have attempted to make more visible the uses of such knowledge in terms of their value as social capital. The significance of different ways of knowing, of the different objects of knowledge, and of different transactions in knowledge among the various groups and authors of Second Temple Judaism should be evident even from this brief study, though it warrants a more detailed investigation than I have been able to provide here.

The major focus of my inquiry, however, has been on the way in which the figured world of the Qumran community is constructed and represented in two of the most significant of its documents: the Serek ha-Yahad and the Hodayot. What is perhaps most striking about these documents is the extent to which discourse about the self serves as a privileged mechanism for the construction of that figured world. This focus is most explicit in the Hodayot. Despite the many uncertainties concerning their composition and use in the life of the sectarian community, the Hodayot of the community clearly serve as templates for the distinctive experience of the self cultivated in the sect. Both by hearing others describe themselves in these poetic prayers and by the practice of articulating one's own experience in terms of the shaped story of the self in the Hodayot, the sectarian is drawn into a radical reinterpretation of his identity. To say that it is a reinterpretation is perhaps to stress the cognitive dimension too much. Speaking of himself with words like these, the sectarian acquires an immediate experience of himself different from that which he previously had.

Although I have analyzed only a portion of these compositions, together with their narrative structures and tropes, several distinctive features that shape the sectarian self-understanding are evident. Perhaps the most significant figure in those Hodayot that construct the speaker's self in relation to God is the vertiginous reversal of perspective in which the sectarian first speaks with the powerful voice of insight that he possesses as a gift from God and then uses that insight to view his own human nothingness. This characteristic movement creates a critical experience of the speaker's subjectivity as neither stable nor unified but as generated at the highly charged intersection of the observed and observing self. Various rhetorical tropes negate all moral value of the human nature of the speaker per se and lead him to grasp himself as something like an effect of God. This pattern, which is both an emotional and a conceptual one, I have termed the masochistic sublime.

The structure of the self in relation to God is the primary discourse of self-formation in the Hodayot, since they are all couched as prayers of gratitude addressed to God. But the formulaic narratives of the self also make considerable use of the relation between self and human other. Although the emphases vary, these are characteristically highly emotional accounts of endangerment and deliverance. They build on motifs and language of biblical complaint and thanksgiving psalms, and yet the self they construct is distinctively different. His endangerment is grasped not merely as an individual crisis but an aspect of a comprehensive cosmic conflict. Moreover, he lacks the quality of agency that characterizes the self at prayer in the biblical Psalms. What gives the speaker a kind of active participation in the preordained drama is not moral agency but rather his understanding of the significance of the events and his ability to articulate them. This knowledge is what constitutes his relationship to the events of his experience and indeed his identity. In some Hodayot the speaker is the site of conflict between the wicked and God. In others the speaker explores the terrifying paradox of his being—a part of sinful humanity and yet one of the redeemed elect. But in every case the drama of endangerment and deliverance becomes the normative story of the sectarian's life. As the Hodayot create a vivid and immediate experience for the sectarian, so the figured world of sectarian reality is naturalized for him.

Even though the Hodayot of the community rarely make reference to the structures of the community that are so much to the fore in the Serek ha-Yahad, the Hodayot do important work to provide the sectarian with what Foucault referred to as the kind of knowledge about himself that he would need in order to renounce his autonomy and submit willingly to the disciplines of the community. The Hodayot assist the sectarian in learning dispositions of humility and a willingness to submit to the reordering of his self according to the will of God as expressed in the sect and its leadership.

Although it seems likely to me that the work of the Hodayot of the community in shaping the docile subjects a disciplinary institutions needs was more intuitive than self-consciously strategic, a more intentional social function may characterize the Hodayot of the leader, especially if, as I suggest, they were compositions employed by current leaders of the sect, not understood as compositions by the historical Teacher of Righteousness. In many respects the Hodayot of the leader model the same characteristics of self-understanding and experience that are normative in the Hodayot of the community. Given the status of the leader, these aspects of the Hodayot would encourage emulation of the desired traits. Thus they serve as a kind of teaching by example. But in other ways the Hodayot of the leader address recurrent issues in the maintenance of sectarian community as they underscore the crucial role of the leader. In the symbolic world constructed in these Hodayot the leader defines the boundaries of the sect and is the conduit for many of the spiritual benefits that members of the sect receive. He interprets to the sect the mystery of their rejection by others and exposes the diabolical nature of his rivals and their competing discourse. And he deals with problems of disaffection within the membership of the sect, even as his self-presentation of his own character serves as an appeal for the loyalty of those who remain. Whether these Hodayot were composed initially in response to specific crises is impossible to tell, but their repeated use would have served as a kind of preventive maintenance, as sectarians became familiar with the classic forms of threat and response in the life of the community. Indeed, the evocation of certain forms of crisis, specifically the threat from external enemies and internal traitors, may well have had more to do with the construction of the necessary symbolic world of the sect than to specific historical realities.

Although the cultivation of normative forms of the self is most explicit in the Hodayot, concern for the formation of the self is also a major feature of the Serek ha-Yahad. It is important to remember that the focus on the self in these documents is not a concern for self-culture in the same way in which it emerges in certain aspects of Hellenistic moral philosophy. As I have argued, the preoccupation with the self in the Serek ha-Yahad is much better understood in relation to the nature of the sect as a disciplinary institution. In order to fulfill its purpose of cultivating a community of perfection in torah, the sect required disciplined and coordinated individuals. Part of this coordination involved the physical and temporal organization of the very bodies of the sectarians. Separated from "men of perdition," they arranged themselves in their ceremonies and council meetings according to a hierarchy of spirit and deeds of torah. More important, however, in the creation of the sectarian self was the relationship between knowledge and disciplinary power. Throughout the Serek ha-Yahad the sectarian is offered knowledge of the self that encourages his submission to the disciplines of the sect. In the introductory section of the document he is identified in terms of the motivations that have brought him to the sect. The recounting of the covenant ceremony, though it deals with many themes in sectarian life, seems to have been particularly shaped to focus on negative and positive character types. The desired dispositions were reinforced by the templates of self-identity in the Hodayot, with their cultivation of radical humility and the vulnerable and miserable image of the self without the gifts of divine salvation.

Nowhere, of course, is cultivation of knowledge of the self more explicit than in the Two Spirits Treatise. As a theoretical reflection on the nature and construction of the self, it is a document of great sophistication and subtlety. Here the self is a symbolic space, which mirrors in its structure and dynamics the very cosmic processes of the plan of God. Although the document does not explicitly relate its theoretical construction of the self to the disciplines of the community, its lists of good and bad character traits include many of the features that those disciplines were designed to enhance and diminish. The complexity of the language of the self in Qumran discourse is manifest in what I would call the conscious and the unconscious work done by the Two Spirits Treatise. Its conscious work, as I have described it, borrowing from Foucault, is to articulate what one needs to know about oneself in order to submit to the disciplinary power of the community. But the homology it establishes between the structures of the self and those of the cosmic process also allows it to do unconscious work. By making use of various apocalyptic tropes that also structure texts that deal with the theological contradiction between Gentile political dominance and the sovereignty of Israel's God, the Two Spirits Treatise provides a symbolic mechanism for overcoming a historically intractable issue.

Much of the rest of the Serek ha-Yahad, while not specifically focused on the formation of the self, nevertheless discloses how central this work was to the function of the sect. The processes of admission and yearly examination are classic examples of the way in which knowledge of self and disciplinary power are mutually created. Similarly, the preoccupation of the penal code with the regulation of the self—body, speech, and social interaction—underscores Foucault's observations on the disciplinary institution's concern with both the great and the minute dimensions of the self. The goal of the sect's efforts was the attainment of the community perfect in torah, described in the latter part of the Serek ha-Yahad. Fittingly, the document concludes with an account of the Maskil, the figure who more than any other represented the ideal selfhood of the community.

This discursive world of Qumran was one of immense richness and complexity, and my studies have touched on only a few of its dimensions. The particular construction of knowledge that was characteristic of the sect meant that for it to pursue its purpose of creating a community perfect in torah it would have to know many things: not only what God had revealed concerning torah itself, but also the plan of God expressed in cosmology, history, and eschatology. Of central importance, however, was knowledge of human nature itself, both in its structural aspects and as it was disclosed in the self-knowledge that came to individuals through life in the sect. By attending to the distinctive form of subjectivity cultivated at Qumran one is able to understand better one of the primary mechanisms by which it constructed its figured world.

BIBLIOGRAPHY

Abegg, Martin G., Jr. with James E. Bowley and Edward M. Cook, in consulta-
tion with Emanuel Tov. *The Dead Sea Scrolls Concordance. Volume One: The Non-
Biblical Texts from Qumran [Part One]*. Leiden and Boston: Brill, 2003.
Albani, Matthias. "Die lunaren Zyklen im 364-Tage-Festkalender von 4QMischmerot/
4QS^c." *Mitteilungen und Beiträge* 4 (1992): 3–47.
Albani, Matthias, and Uwe Glessmer. "Un instrument de mesures astronomiques à
Qumrân." *RB* 104 (1997): 88–115.
Alexander, Philip S. "The Redaction History of Serekh Ha-Yahad: A Proposal."
RevQ 17 (1996): 437–56.
——. "Rules." In *Encyclopedia of the Dead Sea Scrolls*, edited by Lawrence H. Schiffman
and James C. VanderKam, 799–803. New York: Oxford University Press, 2000.
Alexander, Philip S., and Geza Vermes. *Qumran Cave 4: XIX Serekh Ha-Yahad and
Two Related Texts*. DJD XXVI. Oxford: Clarendon Press, 1998.
Althusser, Louis. *Lenin and Philosophy*. Translated by Ben Brewster. New York: New
Left Books, 1971.
Ammerman, Nancy. *Bible Believers: Fundamentalists in the Modern World*. New Brunswick,
NJ, and London: Rutgers University Press, 1987.
Anderson, Gary. "The Status of the Torah before Sinai." *DSD* 1 (1994): 1–30.
Audet, Jean-Paul. "Literary and Doctrinal Relationships of the 'Manual of Discipline'."
In *The Didache in Modern Research*, edited by Jonathan A. Draper, 129–47. AGJU
37. Leiden: Brill, 1996.
Aune, David, and J. McCarthy, eds. *The Whole and Divided Self: The Bible and Theological
Anthropology*. New York: Crossroad, 1997.
Bakhtin, Mikhail M. *The Dialogic Imagination*. Translated by Caryl Emerson and
Michael Holquist. Vol. 1, University of Texas Press Slavic Series. Austin, TX:
University of Texas Press, 1981.
——. *Rabelais and His World*. Translated by Helene Iswolsky. Cambridge, MA: MIT
Press, 1968.
Bardtke, Hans. "Considérations sur les cantiques de Qumrân." *RB* 63 (1956): 220–33.
Barr, James. *Biblical Words for Time*. 2nd ed. Napierville, IL: Allenson, 1969.
Baumgärtel, F. "Zur Liturgie in der 'Sektenrolle' vom Toten Meer." *ZAW* 65 (1953):
264–65.
Baumgarten, Albert I. *The Flourishing of Jewish Sects in the Maccabean Era: An Interpretation*.
JSJSup 55. Leiden: Brill, 1997.
——. "Pharisees." In *Encyclopedia of the Dead Sea Scrolls*, edited by Lawrence H.
Schiffman and James C. VanderKam, 657–63. New York: Oxford University
Press, 2000.
——. "The Torah as a Public Document in Judaism." *SR* 14 (1985): 17–24.
Baumgarten, Albert I., Jan Assman, and Guy Stroumsa, eds. *Self, Soul and Body in
Religious Experience*. Studies in the History of Religions 79. Leiden: Brill, 1998.
Baumgarten, Joseph M., and Menachem Mansoor. "Studies in the New *Hodayot*
(Thanksgiving Hymns) II." *JBL* 74 (1955): 188–92.
Becker, Jürgen. *Das Heil Gottes: Heils- und Sündenbegriffe in den Qumrantexten und im Neuen
Testament*. SUNT 3. Göttingen: Vandenhoeck & Ruprecht, 1964.
Benveniste, Emile. *Problems in General Linguistics*. Translated by Mary Elizabeth Meek.
Miami Linguistics Series 8. Coral Gables, FL: University of Miami, 1971.
Berger, Peter. *The Sacred Canopy: Elements of a Sociological Theory of Religion*. Garden
City, NY: Doubleday, 1967.

Bergmeier, R., and H. Pabst. "Ein Lied von der Erschaffung der Sprach: Sinn und Aufbau von 1Q Hodayot I, 27–31." *RevQ* 5 (1965): 309–16.

Betz, Otto. "Die Geburt der Gemeinde durch den Lehrer." *NTS* 3 (1956/57): 314–16.

Bickerman, Elias. *From Ezra to the Last of the Maccabees: Foundations of Post-Biblical Judaism.* New York: Schocken Books, 1962.

———. *The Jews in the Greek Age.* Cambridge, MA: Harvard University Press, 1988.

Blenkinsopp, Joseph. "The Sage, the Scribe, and Scribalism in the Chronicler's Work." In *The Sage in Israel and the Ancient Near East,* edited by John G. Gammie and Leo G. Perdue, 307–15. Winona Lake, IN: Eisenbrauns, 1990.

———. "Temple and Society in Achemenid Judah." In *Second Temple Studies,* edited by Philip R. Davies, et al., 22–53. JSOTSup 175. Sheffield: JSOT Press, 1991.

———. *Wisdom and Law in the Old Testament: The Ordering of Life in Israel and Early Judaism.* Rev. ed. New York: Oxford University Press, 1995.

Bluedorn, Alan C. *The Human Organization of Time: Temporal Realities and Experience.* Stanford, CA: Stanford University Press, 2002.

Booth, Wayne. *The Company We Keep: An Ethics of Fiction.* Berkeley, CA: University of California Press, 1988.

Bourdieu, Pierre. *Language and Symbolic Power.* Translated by Gino Raymond and Matthew Adamson. Cambridge, MA: Harvard University Press, 1991.

———. *The Logic of Practice.* Translated by Richard Nice. Stanford, CA: Stanford University Press, 1990.

Bright, Pamela. "Singing the Psalms: Augustine and Athanasius on the Integration of the Self." In *The Whole and Divided Self,* edited by David Aune and John McCarthy, 115–29. New York: Crossroad, 1997.

Brin, Gershon. *The Concept of Time in the Bible and the Dead Sea Scrolls.* STDJ 39. Leiden: Brill, 2001.

———. "Regarding the Connection between the *Temple Scroll* and the Book of *Jubilees.*" *JBL* 112 (1993): 108–9.

Brooke, George J. "Torah in the Qumran Scrolls." In *Bibel in jüdischer und christlicher Tradition: Festschrift für Johann Maier zum 60. Geburtstag,* edited by Helmut Merklein, Karlheinz Müller and Günter Stemberger, 97–120. Frankfurt: Anton Hain, 1993.

Brown, Richard Harvey. *Society as Text: Essays on Rhetoric, Reason, and Reality.* Chicago: University of Chicago Press, 1987.

Brown, S. "Deliverance from the Crucible: Some Further Reflexions on 1QH III.1–18." *NTS* 14 (1967/68): 247–59.

Burke, Kenneth. *A Grammar of Motives.* Berkeley, CA: University of California Press, 1969.

———. *Language as Symbolic Action: Essays on Life, Literature, and Method.* Berkeley, CA: University of California Press, 1966.

———. *The Philosophy of Literary Form.* 3rd ed. Berkeley, CA: University of California Press, 1973.

———. *A Rhetoric of Motives.* Berkeley, CA: University of California Press, 1969.

———. *The Rhetoric of Religion: Studies in Logology.* Berkeley, CA: University of California Press, 1970.

Burkes, Shannon. *Death in Qoheleth and Egyptian Biographies of the Late Period.* SBLDS 170. Atlanta: Society of Biblical Literature, 1999.

———. "Wisdom and Apocalypticism in the Wisdom of Solomon." *HTR* 95 (2002): 21–44.

Byrskog, Samuel. *Jesus the Only Teacher: Didactic Authority and Transmission in Ancient Israel, Ancient Judaism, and the Matthean Community.* ConBNT 24. Stockholm: Almqvist & Wiksell International, 1994.

Camponovo, Odo. *Königtum, Königsherrschaft und Reich Gottes in den Frühjüdischen Schriften.* OBO 58. Freiburg: Universitätsverlag, 1984.

Carmignac, Jean. "Conjecture sur la première ligne de la Règle de la Communauté." *RevQ* 2 (1959–60): 85–87.

Carmignac, Jean, and Pierre Guilbert. *Les textes de Qumran traduits et annotés*. Paris: Letouzey et Ané, 1961.

Carrithers, Michael, Steven Collins, and Steven Lukes, eds. *The Category of the Person: Anthropology, Philosophy, History*. Cambridge: Cambridge University Press, 1985.

Carson, D.A., Peter T. O'Brien, and Mark A. Seifrid, eds. *Justification and Variegated Nomism*. Grand Rapids, MI: Baker Academic, 2001.

Chamberlain, J.V. "Another Qumran Thanksgiving Psalm." *JNES* 14 (1955): 32–39.

Charlesworth, James, et al. *Rule of the Community and Related Documents*. Vol. 1, The Princeton Theological Seminary Dead Sea Scrolls Project 1. Tübingen and Louisville, KY: J.C.B. Mohr (Paul Siebeck) and Westminster John Knox Press, 1994.

Chazon, Esther. "Liturgical Communion with the Angels at Qumran." In *Sapiential, Liturgical and Poetical Texts from Qumran: Proceedings of the Third Meeting of the International Organization for Qumran Studies Oslo 1998*, edited by Daniel K. Falk, F. García Martínez and Eileen M. Schuller, 95–105. STDJ 34. Leiden: Brill, 2000.

Christiansen, Ellen Juhl. *The Covenant in Judaism and Paul: A Study of Ritual Boundaries as Identity Markers*. AGJU 27. Leiden: Brill, 1995.

Cohen, Shaye J.D. "The Significance of Yavneh: Pharisees, Rabbis and the End of Jewish Sectarianism." *HUCA* 55 (1984): 27–54.

Collins, John J. *The Apocalyptic Imagination: An Introduction to Jewish Apocalyptic Literature*. 2nd ed. Grand Rapids, MI: Eerdmans, 1998.

———. *Daniel: A Commentary on the Book of Daniel*, Hermeneia. Minneapolis: Fortress Press, 1993.

———. "Forms of Community in the Dead Sea Scrolls." In *Emanuel: Studies in Hebrew Bible, Septuagint, and Dead Sea Scrolls in Honor of Emanuel Tov*, edited by Shalom M. Paul, Robert A. Kraft, Lawrence H. Schiffman and Weston W. Fields, 97–111. VTSup 94. Leiden: Brill, 2003.

———. "The Origin of the Qumran Community: A Review of the Evidence." In *To Touch the Text: Biblical and Related Studies in Honor of Joseph A. Fitzmyer, S.J.*, edited by M.P. Horgan and P.J. Kobelski, 159–78. New York: Crossroad, 1989.

Conway, Colleen M. "Toward a Well-Formed Subject: The Function of Purity Language in the Serek Ha-Yahad." *JSP* 21 (2000): 103–20.

Crenshaw, James L. *Education in Ancient Israel: Across the Deadening Silence*. New York: Doubleday, 1998.

———. *Old Testament Wisdom: An Introduction*. Rev. & enl. ed. Louisville, KY: Westminster John Knox Press, 1998.

Culler, Jonathan. *The Pursuit of Signs: Semiotics, Literature, Deconstruction*. Ithaca, NY: Cornell University Press, 1981.

Darr, Kathe Pfisterer. "Like Woman, Like Warrior: Destruction and Deliverance in Isaiah 42:10–17." *CBQ* 49 (1987): 560–71.

Davies, Philip R. *Behind the Essenes: History and Ideology in the Dead Sea Scrolls*. BJS 94. Atlanta: Scholars Press, 1987.

———. "Calendrical Change and Qumran Origins: An Assessment of VanderKam's Theory." *CBQ* 45 (1983): 80–89.

———. "Reading Daniel Sociologically." In *The Book of Daniel in the Light of New Findings*, edited by A.S. van der Woude, 345–61. BETL 106. Leuven: Leuven University Press, 1993.

———. "The Scribal School of Daniel." In *The Book of Daniel: Composition and Reception*, 2 vols. Edited by John J. Collins and Peter W. Flint, 1:247–65. VTSup 83. Leiden: Brill, 2001.

———. *Scribes and Schools: The Canonization of the Hebrew Scriptures*. Louisville, KY: Westminster John Knox Press, 1998.

Delcor, Mathias. *Les hymnes de Qumran (Hodayot): Texte hébreu, introduction, traduction, commentaire*. Paris: Letouzey et Ané, 1962.

————. "Un psaume messianique de Qumran." In *Mélanges bibliques rèdigès en l'honneur de Andre Robert*, 334–40. Paris: Bloud & Gay, 1956.

Dimant, Devorah. "Qumran Sectarian Literature." In *Jewish Writings of the Second Temple Period. Apocrypha, Pseudepigrapha, Qumran Sectarian Writings, Philo*, edited by Michael Stone, 483–550. CRINT sec. 2; vol. 2. Assen, Philadelphia: van Gorcum, Fortress, 1984.

Dohmen, C. "Zur Gründung der Gemeinde von Qumran (1QS VIII–IX)." *RevQ* 11 (1982): 81–96.

Doran, Robert. "The High Cost of a Good Education." In *Hellenism in the Land of Israel*, edited by John J. Collins and Gregory E. Sterling, 94–115. Notre Dame, IN: University of Notre Dame Press, 2001.

Douglas, Mary, and Aaron Wildavsky. *Risk and Culture: An Essay on the Selection of Technical and Environmental Dangers*. Berkeley, CA: University of California Press, 1982.

Douglas, Michael. "Power and Praise in the Hodayot: A Literary Critical Study of 1QH 9:1–18:14." Dissertation, University of Chicago, 1998.

Duhaime, Jean. "L'instruction sur les deux esprits et les interpolations dualistes à Qumrân (1QS III, 13–IV, 26)." *RB* 84 (1977): 566–94.

————. "Relative Deprivation in New Religious Movements and the Qumran Community." *RevQ* 16 (1993): 265–76.

Dupont-Sommer, André. *The Essene Writings from Qumran*. Translated by Geza Vermes. Gloucester, MA: Peter Smith, 1973.

————. "La mère du Messie et la mère l'aspic dans un hymne de Qoumrân." *RHR* 147 (1955): 174–88.

————. *Nouveaux aperçus sur les manuscrits de la mer Morte*. L'orient Ancien Illustré 5. Paris: Maisonneuve, 1953.

————. *Observations sur le Manuel de Discipline découvert près de la mer Morte*. Paris: Maisonneuve, 1951.

Eshel, Esther. "4Q477: The Rebukes by the Overseer." *JJS* 45 (1994): 111–22.

Falk, Daniel K. *Daily, Sabbath, and Festival Prayers in the Dead Sea Scrolls*. STDJ 27. Leiden: Brill, 1989.

————. "Qumran Prayer Texts and the Temple." In *Sapiential, Liturgical, and Poetical Texts from Qumran*, edited by Daniel K. Falk, Florentino García Martínez and Eileen M. Schuller, 106–26. STDJ 34. Leiden: Brill, 2000.

Fisch, Harold. *Poetry with a Purpose: Biblical Poetics and Interpretation*. Bloomington, IN: Indiana University Press, 1988.

Fishbane, Michael. *Biblical Interpretation in Ancient Israel*. New York: Oxford University Press, 1984.

————. "Use, Authority and Interpretation of Mikra at Qumran." In *Mikra: Text, Translation, Reading and Interpretation of the Hebrew Bible in Ancient Judaism and Early Christianity*, edited by Jan Muldar. CRINT sec. 2; vol. 1. Philadelphia: Fortress, 1988.

Fitzgerald, Aloysius. "*MTNDBYM* in 1QS." *CBQ* 36 (1974): 495–502.

Forkman, Göran. *The Limits of the Religious Community. Expulsion from the Religious Community within the Qumran Sect, within Rabbinic Judaism, and within Primitive Christianity*. ConBNT 5. Lund: CWK Gleerup, 1972.

Foucault, Michel. *The Care of the Self*. Vol. 3 of *The History of Sexuality*. New York: Random House, 1988.

————. *Discipline and Punish: The Birth of the Prison*. Translated by Alan Sheridan. New York: Random House, 1995.

————. "Technologies of the Self." In *Technologies of the Self: A Seminar with Michel Foucault*, edited by Luther H. Martin, Huck Gutman and Patrick H. Hutton, 16–63. London: Tavistock, 1988.

————. *The Use of Pleasure* Vol. 2 of *The History of Sexuality*. New York: Random House, 1990.

Fox, Michael V. *Proverbs 1–9*. AB 18A. New York: Doubleday, 2000.

Fraade, Steven. "The Early Rabbinic Sage." In *The Sage in Israel and the Ancient Near East*, edited by John G. Gammie and Leo G. Perdue, 417–36. Winona Lake, IN: Eisenbrauns, 1990.

Frei, Peter, and Klaus Koch. *Reichsidee und Reichsorganisation in Persereich*. OBO 55. Göttingen: Vandenhoeck & Ruprecht, 1984.

Fröhlich, Ida. "Daniel 2 and Deutero-Isaiah." In *The Book of Daniel in the Light of New Findings*, edited by A.S. van der Woude, 266–70. BETL 106. Leuven: Leuven University Press, 1993.

García Martínez, Florentino. "Calendarios en Qumran (I)." *EstB* 54 (1996): 327–48.

García Martínez, Florentino, and Eibert J.C. Tigchelaar. *The Dead Sea Scrolls Study Edition*. 2 vols. Leiden: Brill, 1997.

García Martínez, Florentino, and Julio Trebolle Barrera. *The People of the Dead Sea Scrolls: Their Writings, Beliefs and Practices*. Translated by Wilfred G.E. Watson. Leiden: Brill, 1995.

García Martínez, Florentino, and A.S. van der Woude. "A Groningen Hypothesis of Qumran Origins and Early History." *RevQ* 14 (1990): 521–44.

Gärtner, Bertil E. *The Temple and the Community in Qumran and the New Testament: A Comparative Study in the Temple Symbolism of the Qumran Texts and the New Testament*. Cambridge: Cambridge University Press, 1965.

Geertz, Clifford. *The Interpretation of Cultures*. New York: Basic Books, 1973.

———. *Local Knowledge: Further Essays in Interpretive Anthropology*. New York: Basic Books, 1983.

Glessmer, Uwe. "Calendars in the Qumran Scrolls." In *The Dead Sea Scrolls after Fifty Years: A Comprehensive Assessment*, edited by Peter W. Flint and James C. VanderKam, 213–78. Leiden: Brill, 1999.

Goodman, Martin D. "Texts, Scribes and Power in Roman Judaea." In *Literacy and Power in the Ancient World*, edited by Alan K. Bowman and Greg Woolf, 99–108. Cambridge: Cambridge University Press, 1994.

Goodman, Nelson. *Ways of Worldmaking*. Indianapolis, IN: Hackett, 1978.

Grabbe, Lester L. "The Social Setting of Early Jewish Apocalypticism." *JSOT* 4 (1989): 27–47.

Grossman, Maxine. "Priesthood as Authority: Interpretive Competition in First-Century Judaism and Christianity." In *The Dead Sea Scrolls as Background to Postbiblical Judaism and Early Christianity: Papers from an International Conference at St. Andrews in 2001*, edited by James R. Davila, 117–31. STDJ 46. Leiden: Brill, 2002.

Guilbert, Pierre. "Le plan de la 'Règle de la Communauté'." *RevQ* 3 (1959): 323–44.

Gunn, Giles. *The Culture of Criticism and the Criticism of Culture*. New York: Oxford University Press, 1987.

Hall, Edward T. *The Dance of Life: The Other Dimensions of Time*. Garden City, NY: Anchor Press/Doubleday, 1983.

Hall, Stuart. "Introduction: Who Needs 'Identity'?" In *Questions of Cultural Identity*, edited by Stuart Hall and Paul du Gay, 1–17. London: Sage Publications, 1996.

Harrington, Daniel J., S.J. *Wisdom Texts from Qumran*. London: Routledge, 1996.

Hempel, Charlotte. "Who Rebukes in 4Q477?" *RevQ* 16 (1995): 127–28.

Hengel, Martin. *The Zealots: Investigations into the Jewish Freedom Movement in the Period from Herod I until 70 A.D.* Translated by David Smith. Edinburgh: T. & T. Clark, 1989.

Hinson, Glenn. "Hodayoth, III, 6–18: In What Sense Messianic?" *RevQ* 2 (1960): 183–204.

Hoffman, Heinrich. *Das Gesetz in der frühjüdischen Apokalyptik*. SUNT 23. Göttingen: Vandenhoeck & Ruprecht, 1999.

Hoglund, Kenneth G. *Achaeminid Imperial Administration in Syria-Palestine and the Missions of Ezra and Nehemiah*. SBLDS 125. Atlanta: Scholars Press, 1989.

Holland, Dorothy, William Lachicotte, Jr., Debra Skinner, and Carole Cain. *Identity and Agency in Cultural Worlds*. Cambridge, MA: Harvard University Press, 1998.

Holm-Nielsen, Svend. *Hodayot: Psalms from Qumran*. ATDan 2. Aarhus: Universitetsforlaget, 1960.

———. "'Ich' in den Hodajoth und die Qumrangemeinde." In *Qumran Probleme: Vorträge des Leipziger Symposions über Qumran-Probleme vom 9. bis 14. Oktober 1961*, edited by Hans Bardtke, 217–29. Berlin: Akademie-Verlag, 1963.

Horsley, Richard and Patrick Tiller. "Ben Sira and the Sociology of the Second Temple." Paper presented to the Sociology of the Second Temple Group, SBL Annual Meeting. San Francisco, 1992.

Hunzinger, Claus-Hunno. "Beobachtungen zur Entwicklung der Disziplinarordnung der Gemeinde von Qumrân." In *Qumran-Probleme: Vorträge des Leipziger Symposions über Qumran-Probleme vom 9. bis 14. Oktober 1961*, edited by Hans Bardtke, 231–47. Berlin: Akademie-Verlag, 1963.

Huppenbauer, Hans Walter. *Der Mensch zwischen zwei Welten: Der Dualismus der Texte von Qumran (Höhle I) und der Damaskusfragmente: Ein Beitrag zur Geschichte des Evangeliums*. ATANT 34. Zürich: Zwingli Verlag, 1959.

Jacobsen, Thorkild. *Treasures of Darkness: A History of Mesopotamian Religion*. New Haven, CT: Yale University Press, 1983.

Jaffee, Martin S. *Torah in the Mouth: Writing and Oral Tradition in Palestinian Judaism 200 BCE–400 CE*. New York: Oxford University Press, 2001.

Jameson, Fredric. "Foreword." In *On Meaning: Selected Writings in Semiotic Theory*, Algirdas Julien Greimas, vi–xxii. Theory and History of Literature 38. Minneapolis: University of Minnesota Press, 1987.

———. *The Political Unconscious: Narrative as a Socially Symbolic Act*. Ithaca, NY: Cornell University Press, 1981.

———. "The Symbolic Inference; or, Kenneth Burke and Ideological Analysis." In *The Ideologies of Theory: Essays 1971–1986*, 137–52. Theory and History of Literature 48. Minneapolis: University of Minnesota Press, 1988.

Japhet, Sara. *I & II Chronicles*, Old Testament Library. Louisville, KY: Westminster/John Knox Press, 1993.

Jaubert, Annie. "Le calendrier des Jubilées et de la secte de Qumrân: ses origines bibliques." *VT* 3 (1953): 250–64.

Jeremias, Gert. *Der Lehrer der Gerechtigkeit*. SUNT 2. Göttingen: Vandenhoeck & Ruprecht, 1963.

Kamlah, Erhard. *Die Form der katalogischen Paränese im Neuen Testament*, WUNT 7. Tübingen: Mohr, 1964.

Kippenberg, Hans G. "Name and Person in Ancient Judaism and Christianity." In *Concepts of Person in Religion and Thought*, edited by Hans G. Kippenberg, Yme B. Kuiper and Andy F. Sanders, 103–24. Berlin: de Gruyter, 1990.

Kittel, Bonnie. *The Hymns of Qumran: Translation and Commentary*. SBLDS 50. Missoula, MT: Scholars Press, 1981.

Klawans, Jonathan. *Impurity and Sin in Ancient Judaism*. New York: Oxford University Press, 2000.

Klinghardt, Matthias. "The Manual of Discipline in the Light of Statutes of Hellenistic Associations." In *Methods of Investigation of the Dead Sea Scrolls and the Khirbet Qumran Site: Present Realities and Future Possibilities*, edited by Michael Wise, Norman Golb, John J. Collins and Dennis G. Pardee, 251–67. New York: New York Academy of Sciences, 1994.

Klinzing, Georg. *Die Umdeutung des Kultus in der Qumrangemeinde und im Neuen Testament*. SUNT 7. Göttingen: Vandenhoeck und Ruprecht, 1971.

Knibb, Michael A. *The Qumran Community*. Cambridge Commentaries on Writings of the Jewish and Christian World 200 BC to AD 200. Cambridge: Cambridge University Press, 1987.

Knohl, Israel. "Between Voice and Silence: The Relationship between Prayer and Temple Cult." *JBL* 115 (1996): 17–30.

——. *The Messiah before Jesus: The Suffering Servant of the Dead Sea Scrolls*. Translated by David Maisel. Berkeley, CA: University of California Press, 2000.

Knoppers, Gary N. "An Achaemenid Imperial Authorization of Torah in Yehud?" In *Persia and Torah: The Theory of Imperial Authorization of the Pentateuch*, edited by James W. Watts, 115–34. SBLSymS 17. Atlanta: Society of Biblical Literature, 2001.

——. "Hierodules, Priests, or Janitors? The Levites in Chronicles and the History of the Israelite Priesthood." *JBL* 118 (1999): 49–72.

——. "Jehoshaphat's Judiciary and 'the Scroll of YHWH's Torah'." *JBL* 113 (1994): 59–80.

Kronholm, Tryggve. "'Et." In *Theological Dictionary of the Old Testament*, edited by G. Johannes Botterweck, Helmer Ringgren and Heinz-Josef Fabry, 434–51. Grand Rapids, MI: Eerdmans, 2001.

Kugel, James L. "On Hidden Hatred and Open Reproach: Early Exegesis of Leviticus 19:17." *HTR* 80 (1987): 43–61.

——. *Traditions of the Bible: A Guide to the Bible as It Was at the Start of the Common Era*. Cambridge, MA: Harvard University Press, 1998.

Kuhn, Heinz-Wolfgang. *Enderwartung und gegenwärtiges Heil*. SUNT 3. Göttingen: Vandenhoeck & Ruprecht, 1966.

Kvanvig, Helge S. *Roots of Apocalyptic: The Mesopotamian Background of the Enoch Figure and of the Son of Man*. WMANT 61. Neukirchen-Vluyn: Neukirchener Verlag, 1988.

Lakoff, George, and Mark Johnson. *Metaphors We Live By*. Chicago: University of Chicago Press, 1980.

Laubscher, F. du T. "Notes on the Literary Structure of 1QS 2:11–18 and Its Biblical Parallel in Deut. 29." *JNSL* 8 (1980): 49–55.

Leaney, A.R.C. *The Rule of Qumran and Its Meaning*, New Testament Library. Philadelphia: Westminster Press, 1966.

Lentricchia, Frank. *Criticism and Social Change*. Chicago: University of Chicago Press, 1984.

Levenson, Jon. "Psalm 119 and the Modes of Revelation in Second Temple Judaism." In *Ancient Israelite Religion: Essays in Honor of Frank Moore Cross*, edited by Patrick D. Miller, Paul. D. Hanson and S. Dean McBride, 559–74. Philadelphia: Fortress Press, 1987.

Levine, Lee I. *The Ancient Synagogue: The First Thousand Years*. New Haven and London: Yale University Press, 2000.

Levine, Robert. *A Geography of Time: The Temporal Misadventures of a Social Psychologist, or How Every Culture Keeps Time Just a Little Bit Differently*. New York: Basic Books, 1997.

Licht, Jacob. *The Thanksgiving Scroll: A Scroll from the Wilderness of Judaea* [Hebrew]. Jerusalem: The Bialik Institute, 1957.

Lichtenberger, Hermann. *Studien zum Menschenbild in Texten der Qumrangemeinde*. SUNT 15. Göttingen: Vandenhoeck & Ruprecht, 1980.

Lichtheim, Miriam. *Ancient Egyptian Literature: A Book of Readings*. 3 vols. Berkeley, CA: University of California Press, 1973–80.

Lincoln, Bruce. *Discourse and the Construction of Society: Comparative Studies of Myth, Ritual, and Classification*. New York: Oxford University Press, 1989.

Lohfink, Norbert. *Lobgesänge der Armen*, SBS 143. Stuttgart: Katholisches Bibelwerk, 1990.

Maier, Johann. *Die Texte vom Toten Meer*. 2 vols. München: E. Reinhardt, 1960.

McBride, S. Dean. "Polity of the Covenant People: The Book of Deuteronomy." *Interpretation* 41 (1987): 229–44.

McGiffert, Michael. *God's Plot: the Paradoxes of Puritan Piety; Being the Autobiography & Journal of Thomas Shepard./ Edited with an Introd. By Michael McGiffert.* Amherst, MA: University of Massachusetts Press, 1972.

McKnight, Scot. *A Light among the Gentiles: Jewish Missionary Activity in the Second Temple Period.* Minneapolis: Fortress, 1991.

Meier, John P. "Is There *Halaka* (the Noun) at Qumran?" *JBL* 122 (2003): 150–55.

Metso, Sarianna. "Qumran Community Structure and Terminology as Theological Statement." *RevQ* 20 (2002): 429–44.

——. "In Search of the *Sitz Im Leben* of the Community Rule." In *The Provo International Conference on the Dead Sea Scrolls: Technological Innovations, New Texts, and Reformulated Issues,* edited by Donald W. Parry and Eugene Ulrich, 306–15. STDJ 30. Leiden: Brill, 1998.

——. *The Textual Development of the Qumran Community Rule,* STDJ 21. Leiden: Brill, 1997.

Milgrom, Jacob. *Leviticus 1–16.* AB 3. New York: Doubleday, 1991.

Milik, Józef. T. *Ten Years of Discovery in the Wilderness of Judea.* Napierville, IL: Allenson, 1959.

Moi, Toril. *Sexual/ Textual Politics: Feminist Literary Theory.* London: Methuen, 1985.

Mowinckel, Sigmund. "Mitteilungen zwei Qumran-Miszellen." *ZAW* 73 (1961): 297–99.

——. "Some Remarks on Hodayot 39:5–20." *JBL* 75 (1956): 265–76.

Murphy-O'Connor, Jerome. "The Damascus Document Revisited." *RB* 92 (1985): 223–46.

——. "The Essenes and Their History." *RB* 81 (1974): 215–44.

——. "La genèse litttéraire de la Règle de la Communauté." *RB* 76 (1969): 528–49.

Najman, Hindy. "Interpretation as Primordial Writing: Jubilees and Its Authority Conferring Strategies." *JSJ* 30 (1999): 379–410.

——. *Seconding Sinai: The Development of Mosaic Discourse in Second Temple Judaism.* SJSSup 77. Leiden; Boston: Brill, 2003.

Neusner, Jacob. *Judaism: The Evidence of the Mishnah.* 2nd ed. BJS 129. Atlanta: Scholars Press, 1988.

Newsom, Carol. "Apocalyptic and the Discourse of a Sectarian Community." *JNES* 49 (1990): 135–44.

——. "Apocalyptic Subjects: The Social Construction of the Self at Qumran." *JSP* 12 (2001): 3–25.

——. *The Book of Job: A Contest of Moral Imaginations.* New York: Oxford University Press, 2003.

——. "The Case of the Blinking I: Discourse of the Self at Qumran." In *Semeia 57: Discursive Formations, Ascetic Piety and the Interpretation of Early Christian Literature,* Part I, edited by Vincent Wimbush (1992): 13–23.

——. "Kenneth Burke Meets the Teacher of Righteousness." In *Of Scribes and Scrolls: Studies on the Hebrew Bible, Intertestamental Judaism, and Christian Origins,* edited by Harold W. Attridge, John J. Collins and Thomas H. Tobin, S.J., 121–31. Lanham, MD: University Press of America, 1990.

——. "Knowing as Doing: The Social Symbolics of Knowledge at Qumran." In *Semeia 59: Ideological Criticism of Biblical Texts,* edited by David Jobling and Tina Pippin (1993): 139–53.

——. "The Sage in the Literature of Qumran: The Functions of the *Maskil.*" In *The Sage in Israel and the Ancient Near East,* edited by John G. Gammie and Leo G. Perdue, 373–82. Winona Lake, IN: Eisenbrauns, 1990.

——. "Woman and the Discourse of Patriarchal Wisdom: A Study of Proverbs 1–9." In *Gender and Difference in Ancient Israel,* edited by Peggy Day, 142–60. Philadelphia: Fortress, 1989.

Niditch, Susan. *Oral Word and Written Word: Ancient Israelite Literature.* Louisville: Westminster John Knox Press, 1996.

Nitzan, Bilhah. *Qumran Prayer and Religious Poetry*. STDJ 12. Leiden: Brill, 1994.

Oakeshott, Michael. *The Voice of Poetry in the Conversation of Mankind*. London: Bowes and Bowes, 1959.

Olyan, Saul. "Ben Sira's Relationship to the Priesthood." *HTR* 80 (1980): 261–86.

Orton, David E. *The Understanding Scribe: Matthew and the Apocalyptic Ideal*. JSNTSup 25. Sheffield: JSOT Press, 1989.

Osten-Saken, Peter von der. *Die Apokalyptik in ihrem Verhaltnis zu Prophetie und Weisheit*. Theologische Existenz Heute 157. Munich: Kaiser, 1969.

———. *Gott und Belial; Traditionsgeschichtliche Untersuchungen zum Dualismus in den Texten aus Qumran*. SUNT 6. Göttingen: Vandenhoeck & Ruprecht, 1969.

Paden, William. "Theatres of Humility and Suspicion: Desert Saints and New England Puritans." In *Technologies of the Self: A Seminar with Michel Foucault*, edited by Luther H. Martin, Huck Gutman and Patrick H. Hutton. London: Tavistock, 1988.

Pouilly, Jean. *La Règle de la Communauté: son evolution littéraire*. CahRB 17. Paris: J. Gabalda, 1976.

Puech, Émile. *La croyance des Esséniens en la vie future: immortalité, résurrection, vie éternelle*. 2 vols. Ébib 2. Paris: J. Gabalda, 1993.

———. "Hodayot." In *Encyclopedia of the Dead Sea Scrolls*, edited by L.H. Schiffman and J.C. VanderKam, 365–69. New York: Oxford University Press, 2000.

———. "Un hymne Essénien en partie retrouvé et les Béatitudes." *RevQ* 49–52 (1988): 59–88.

———. "Quelques aspects de la restauration du rouleau des hymnes (1QH)." *JJS* 39 (1988): 38–55.

Qimron, Elisha. *The Hebrew of the Dead Sea Scrolls*. HSS 29. Atlanta: Scholars Press, 1986.

Rabin, Chaim. *The Zadokite Documents*. Oxford: Clarendon, 1954.

Ransom, John S. *Foucault's Discipline: The Politics of Subjectivity*. Durham, NC: Duke University Press, 1997.

Redditt, Paul L. *Daniel*. Sheffield: Sheffield Academic Press, 1999.

Reed, Stephen A. "Genre, Setting and Title of 4Q477." *JJS* 46 (1995): 147–48.

Reese, Günter. *Die Geschichte Israels in der Auffassung des frühen Judentums: Eine Untersuchung der Tiervision und der Zehnwochenapokalypse des Äthiopischen Henochbuches, der Geschichtsdarstellung der Assumptio Mosis dnd der des 4Esrabuches*. BBB 123. Berlin: Philo, 1999.

Reike, Bo. "Daat and Gnosis in Intertestamental Literature." In *Neotestamentica et Semitica*, edited by E.E. Ellis and M. Wilcox, 245–55. Edinburgh, 1969.

———. "Remarques sur l'histoire de la form (Formgeschichte) des textes de Qumran." In *Les manuscrits de la mer Morte: Colloque de Strasbourg 25–27 Mai 1955*, edited by Jean Daniélou, 38–44. Paris: Paris University Press, 1957.

Roop, Eugene F. "A Form Critical Study of the Society Rule (1QS) at Qumran." Dissertation, University of Michigan, 1972.

Runesson, Anders. *The Origins of the Synagogue: A Socio-Historical Study*. ConBNT 37. Stockholm: Almqvist & Wiksell International, 2001.

Safrai, Shemuel. "Education and the Study of the Torah." In *The Jewish People in the First Century: Historical Geography, Political History, Social, Cultural and Religious Life and Institutions*, edited by S. Safrai and M. Stern, 945–70. CRINT sec. 1; vol. 1. Philadelphia: Fortress, 1976.

Saldarini, Anthony J. *Pharisees, Scribes and Sadducees in Palestinian Society*. Wilmington, DE: Michael Glazier, 1988.

Sanders, E.P. *Jesus and Judaism*. Philadelphia: Fortress, 1985.

———. *Judaism: Practice and Belief 63 BCE–66 CE*. London: SCM Press, 1992.

———. *Paul and Palestinian Judaism: A Comparison of Patterns of Religion*. Philadelphia: Fortress, 1977.

Schams, Christine. *Jewish Scribes in the Second-Temple Period*. JSOTSup 291. Sheffield: Sheffield Academic Press, 1998.

Schiffman, Lawrence H. *The Halakhah at Qumran.* SJLA 16. Leiden: Brill, 1975.
———. *Sectarian Law in the Dead Sea Scrolls.* BJS 33. Chico, CA: Scholars Press, 1983.
Schuller, Eileen M. "Hodayot." In *Qumran Cave 4 XX: Poetical and Liturgical Texts, Part 2,* Esther Chazon, et al., 69–232. DJD XXIX. Oxford: Clarendon Press, 1999.
———. "Petitionary Prayer and the Religion of Qumran." In *Religion in the Dead Sea Scrolls,* edited by John J. Collins and Robert A. Kugler, 29–45. Grand Rapids, MI: Eerdmans, 2000.
———. "Some Contributions of the Cave Four Manuscripts (4Q427–432) to the Study of the Hodayot." *DSD* 8 (2001): 273–87.
Schwartz, Daniel R. "Law and Truth: On Qumran-Sadducean and Rabbinic Views of Law." In *Dead Sea Scrolls: Forty Years of Research,* edited by Devorah Dimant and Uriel Rappaport, 229–40. STDJ 10. Leiden: Brill, 1992.
———. "'Scribes and Pharisees, Hypocrites': Who Are the 'Scribes' in the New Testament?" In *Studies in the Jewish Background of Christianity,* 89–101. WUNT 60. Tübingen: J.C.B. Mohr (Paul Siebeck), 1992.
Seidel, Hans. *Das Erlebnis der Einsamkeit im Alten Testament.* Teologische Arbeiten 29. Berlin: Evangelische Verlagsanstalt, 1969.
Silberman, Lou H. "Language and Structure in the Hodayot (1QH 3)." *JBL* 75 (1956): 96–106.
Silverman, Kaja. *The Subject of Semiotics.* New York: Oxford University Press, 1983.
Ska, John Louis. "'Persian Imperial Authorisation:' Some Question Marks." In *Persia and Torah,* edited by James W. Watts, 161–82. SBLSymS 17. Atlanta: Society of Biblical Literature, 2001.
Skehan, Patrick W., and Alexander A. Di Lella. *The Wisdom of Ben Sira.* AB 39. New York: Doubleday, 1987.
Smiles, Vincent. "The Concept of 'Zeal' in Second-Temple Judaism and Paul's Critique of It in Romans 10:2." *CBQ* 64 (2002): 282–300.
Smith, Jonathan Z. *To Take Place: Toward Theory in Ritual.* Chicago: University of Chicago Press, 1987.
Stadelmann, Helge. *Ben Sira als Schriftgelehrter.* WUNT 6. Tübingen: J.C.B. Mohr (Paul Siebeck), 1980.
Stegemann, Hartmut. *Die Entstehung der Qumrangemeinde.* Bonn: Rheinische Friedrich-Wilhelms-Universität, 1971.
———. *The Library of Qumran, on the Essenes, Qumran, John the Baptist, and Jesus.* Grand Rapids, MI and Leiden: Eerdmans and Brill, 1998.
———. "The Material Reconstruction of 1QHodayot." In *The Dead Sea Scrolls Fifty Years after Their Discovery 1947–1997: Proceedings of the Jerusalem Congress, July 20–25, 1997,* edited by L.H. Schiffman, E. Tov and J.C. VanderKam, 272–84. Jerusalem: Israel Exploration Society and Shrine of the Book, 2000.
Sutcliffe, E.F. "The First Fifteen Members of the Qumran Community." *JJS* 4 (1959): 134–38.
Talmon, Shemaryahu. "The Calendar Reckoning of the Sect from the Judaean Desert." In *Aspects of the Dead Sea Scrolls,* edited by Chaim Rabin and Yigael Yadin, 162–99. Jerusalem: Magnes, 1958; 2nd ed. 1965.
Terdiman, Richard. *Discourse/Counter Discourse: The Theory and Practice of Symbolic Resistance in Nineteenth-Century France.* Ithaca, NY: Cornell University Press, 1985.
Tigchelaar, Eibert J.C. "In Search of the Scribe of 1QS." In *Emanuel: Studies in Hebrew Bible, Septuagint and Dead Sea Scrolls in Honor of Emanuel Tov,* edited by Shalom M. Paul, Robert A. Kraft, Lawrence H. Schiffman and Weston W. Fields. VTSup 94. Leiden: Brill, 2002.
———. *To Increase Learning for the Understanding Ones: Reading and Reconstructing the Fragmentary Early Jewish Sapiential Text 4QInstruction.* STDJ 44. Leiden: Brill, 2001.
Tiller, Patrick A. *A Commentary on the Animal Apocalypse of 1 Enoch.* SBLEJL 4. Atlanta: Scholars Press, 1993.

Toorn, Karel van der. *Sin and Sanction in Israel and Mesopotamia: A Comparative Study.* SSN 22. Assen/Maastricht: Van Gorcum, 1985.

Trebolle Barrera, Julio. "The Essenes of Qumran: Between Submission to the Law and Apocalyptic Flight." In F. García Martínez and J. Trebolle Barrera, *The People of the Dead Sea Scrolls: Their Writings, Beliefs and Practices*, 49–76. Translated by Wilfred G.E. Watson. Leiden: Brill, 1995.

VanderKam, James C. "2 Maccabees 6,7a and Calendrical Change in Jerusalem." *JSJ* 12 (1981): 52–74.

———. *Calendars in the Dead Sea Scrolls: Measuring Time.* London: Routledge, 1998.

———. *Enoch and the Growth of an Apocalyptic Tradition.* CBQMS 16. Washington: Catholic Biblical Association, 1984.

———. "The Origins and Purposes of the Book of Jubilees." In *Studies in the Book of Jubilees*, edited by Matthias Albani, Jörg Frey and Armin Lange, 3–24. TSAJ 65. Tübingen: J.C.B. Mohr (Paul Siebeck), 1997.

———. "The Origin, Character, and Early History of the 364–Day Solar Calendar: A Reassessment of Jaubert's Hypothesis." *CBQ* 41 (1979): 390–411.

———. "The Prophetic-Sapiential Origins of Apocalyptic Thought." In *A Word in Season: Essays in Honour of William McKane*, edited by James D. Martin and Phillip R. Davies, 163–76. JSOTSup 42. Sheffield: JSOT Press, 1986.

———. "The Temple Scroll and the Book of Jubilees." In *Temple Scroll Studies*, edited by George J. Brooke, 211–36. JSPSup 7. Sheffield: JSOT Press, 1989.

Vermes, Geza. *The Complete Dead Sea Scrolls in English.* New York: Penguin Press, 1997.

———. *The Dead Sea Scrolls in English.* Baltimore: Penguin, 1962.

Voloshinov, V.N. *Marxism and the Philosophy of Language.* Translated by L. Matejka and I.R. Titunik. New York: Seminar Press, 1973.

Waltke, Bruce K. and Michael O'Connor, *An Introduction to Biblical Hebrew Syntax.* Winona Lake, IN: Eisenbrauns, 1990.

Watts, James W. *Reading Law: The Rhetorical Shaping of the Pentateuch.* The Biblical Seminar 59. Sheffield: Sheffield Academic Press, 1999.

Weinfeld, Moshe. *Deuteronomy and the Deuteronomic School.* Oxford: Clarendon Press, 1972.

———. *The Organizational Pattern and the Penal Code of the Qumran Sect.* NTOA 2. Göttingen: Vandenhoeck & Ruprecht, 1986.

Weise, Manfred. *Kultzeiten und kultischer Bundesschluss in der "Ordensregel" vom Toten Meer.* StPB 3. Leiden: Brill, 1961.

Wernberg-Møller, P. *The Manual of Discipline.* STDJ 1. Leiden: Brill, 1957.

———. "Some Reflections on the Biblical Material in the Manual of Discipline." *ST* 9 (1956): 40–66.

White, James Boyd. *When Words Lose Their Meaning: Constitutions and Reconstitutions of Language, Character, and Community.* Chicago: University of Chicago Press, 1984.

Wibbig, S. *Die Tugend- und Lasterkataloge in Neuen Testament und ihre Traditionsgeschichte unter besonderer Berücksichtigung der Qumran-Texte.* BZNW 25. Berlin: Albert Töpelmann, 1959.

Williamson, H.G.M. *Ezra-Nehemiah.* WBC 16. Waco, TX: Word Books, 1985.

Wilson, Robert. "From Prophecy to Apocalyptic: Reflections on the Shape of Israelite Religion." In *Semeia 21: Anthropological Perspectives on Old Testament Prophecy*, edited by T.W. Overholt R.C. Culley (1981): 79–95.

Winston, David. *Philo of Alexandria: The Contemplative Life, the Giants, and Selections.* New York: Paulist Press, 1981.

Wintermute, O.S. "Jubilees: A New Translation and Introduction." In *The Old Testament Pseudepigrapha*, edited by James H. Charlesworth, 35–142. Garden City, NY: Doubleday, 1985.

Wise, Michael. *The First Messiah: Investigating the Savior before Jesus.* San Francisco: HarperSanFrancisco, 1999.

Wise, Michael, Martin Abegg, Jr., and Edward Cook. *The Dead Sea Scrolls: A New Translation.* San Francisco: HarperSanFrancisco, 1996.

Wright, Benjamin G III. "Putting the Puzzle Together: Some Suggestions Concerning the Social Location of the Wisdom of Ben Sira." In *SBL 1996 Seminar Papers*, 133–49. Atlanta: Scholars Press, 1996.

Wright, John W. Review of Christine Schams, *Jewish Scribes in the Second-Temple Period*. *JBL* 120 (2001): 553–54.

Yadin, Yigael. *The Scroll of the War of the Sons of Light against the Sons of Darkness*. Translated by Chaim and Batya Rabin. London: Oxford University Press, 1962.

Zerubavel, Eviatar. *Time Maps: Collective Memory and the Social Shape of the Past*. Chicago: University of Chicago Press, 2003.

SUBJECT INDEX

MODERN AUTHOR INDEX

PASSAGE INDEX

DEAD SEA SCROLLS AND THE DAMASCUS DOCUMENT

APOCRYPHA

ERRATA

Chap. 4

P. 168, n. 141: The last Hebrew word in line 7, reading right to left, should be
‫נהיה‬.

Chap. 6

P. 318, line 8: The first Hebrew word, reading right to left, should be ‫והמון‬.